TO

JANINE

Hoover Institution Publications 129

The Politics of Congo-Brazzaville

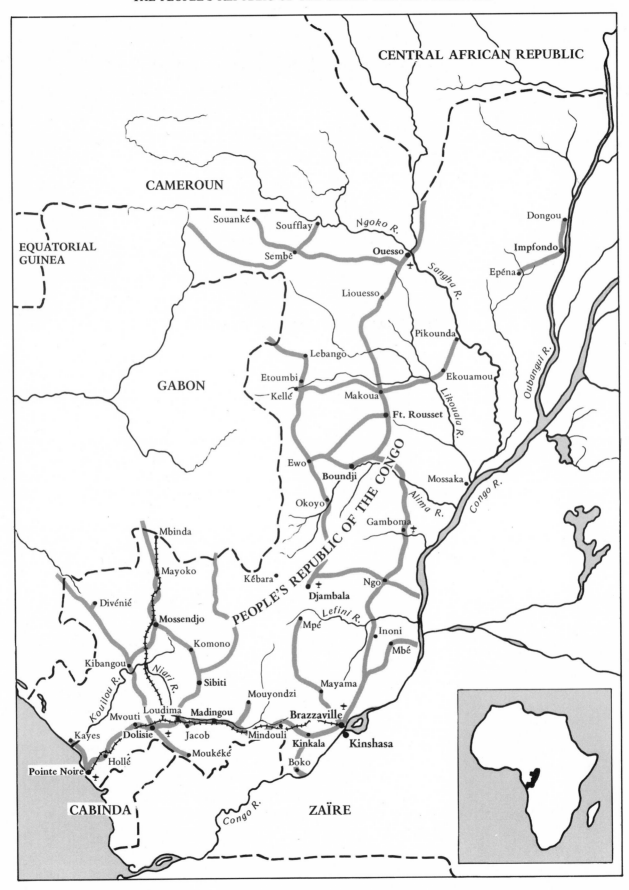

THE POLITICS OF CONGO-BRAZZAVILLE

by

RENE GAUZE

Translation, editing, and Supplement

by

Virginia Thompson and Richard Adloff

Hoover Institution Press
Stanford University
Stanford, California

The Hoover Institution on War, Revolution and Peace, founded at
Stanford University in 1919 by the late President Herbert Hoover,
is a center for advanced study and research on public and international affairs in the twentieth century. The views expressed
in its publications are entirely those of the authors and do not
necessarily reflect the views of the staff, officers, or Board of
Overseers of the Hoover Institution.

Hoover Institution Publication 129
International Standard Book Number 0-8179-1291-6
Library of Congress Card Number 73-75886
© 1973 by the Board of Trustees of the
    Leland Stanford Junior University
Printed in the United States of America

Service Information Congo

Fulbert Youlou

ABOUT THE AUTHORS

<u>René Gauze</u> was appointed Chef de Sûreté for southern Laos in 1945;
in 1950 he was transferred to a similar post in Oubangui-Chari,
where he remained until 1958.   He was then appointed Chef de Sûreté
for Moyen-Congo and subsequently became political adviser to
Stéphane Tchichelle when the latter became the Congo Republic's
Minister of Foreign Affairs.   In 1962 he was named head of the police
service in French Polynesia.   He has written two books on Oubangui-
Chari and has received many honors from France, Laos and the Congo,
most notably the Legion of Honor and the Academic Palms.

*   *   *   *   *   *   *

<u>Virginia Thompson</u> is a Research Associate at the Hoover Institution.
She received her Ph. D. at Columbia University and was a lecturer in
political science at the University of California, Berkeley from 1961 to
1972.   <u>Richard Adloff</u> is a Research Associate at the Hoover Institution.
The authors have jointly published seven titles, including <u>French West
Africa</u> and <u>The Emerging States of French Equatorial Africa</u>.

CONTENTS

TABLES

EDITORS' PREFACE

From 1950 to mid-1961, René Gauze was in charge of the French security
police (Sûreté) in two territories of the Federation of French Equatorial
Africa, first in Oubangui-Chari (1950-58) and then in Moyen-Congo. His assignment in those countries coincided with the critical years of transition
from a semicolonial status to autonomy and finally to independence. Mr.
Gauze twice accompanied Congo-Brazzaville's delegation to the United Nations
General Assembly in New York, and through the years of his service his position gave him access to information available only to the highest ranking
French officials. His own training, experience, and competence provided the
insight that enabled him to interpret authoritatively the data he acquired
and the events he witnessed.

This manuscript was written during the years when Mr. Gauze was stationed in Equatorial Africa, and was completed in 1963 when he was serving
in French Polynesia. Certain of Mr. Gauze's judgments of the Congo's politicians are controversial, and to some readers they may seem prejudiced and
unfair to the Africans. In this regard, it should be borne in mind that his
daily contacts with the Congolese leaders inevitably bred frustrations as
well as friendships. Moreover, his African career spanned the period between a relatively authoritarian colonial administration and the first years
of national sovereignty. Not surprisingly, Mr. Gauze's views were largely
determined by his era, his training, and his status as a French official responsible for protecting the administration against what he regarded as subversive activity. Seen in this context, his observations have value as a
historical document as well as an eyewitness account.

René Gauze's detailed political history of Moyen-Congo, a small but
strategically located country little known to the English-reading public,
covers the period after World War II through 1960-63, the first years of independence when Moyen-Congo had become the Congo Republic. Unfortunately, because Mr. Gauze left Brazzaville in June 1961 his first-hand observations
cease with that date; however, his analysis of the years preceding the overthrow of the republic's first president, Fulbert Youlou, throws light not
only on the causes of Youlou's downfall but also on the country's current
evolution. His account provides a background for analyzing the conflicts
between tribal leaders who headed political parties, and for the politico-
religious activities of the messianic sects. His appraisal of the role
played by the bureaucracy, and his depiction of the apathy and misery of the
underemployed Congolese peasantry and the frustration of the unemployed
urban proletariat, go far to explain why the Youlou government failed to win
popular support and how the exasperation in labor and youth organizations
led to the coup d'état of August 1963.

The history of Congo-Brazzaville's early years as an autonomous republic
and then as a sovereign state is very largely the story of Fulbert Youlou.

This is the story not of a statesman but of an exceptionally talented tribal leader. Youlou has been generally regarded simply as a bizarre anomaly among the francophone African heads of state, a man whose pretentious attempts to solve vast international problems and whose fondness for pastel-colored cassocks designed by Dior made him ludicrous in the eyes of many of his contemporaries, both African and Western. It is not surprising that these aspects of his personality have been stressed by his Congolese opponents and successors. Mr. Gauze's unique contribution is to give the first sympathetic portrait of the man. Youlou is here portrayed as a man catapulted into political prominence by personal ambition and by the special circumstances of his country and his era, a man who, having briefly acquired power by his native shrewdness and diplomatic activity, initially used his position and talents to calm racial strife and to unite political opponents inside his government.

Youlou's few accomplishments have been denigrated or forgotten largely because they were undone by the later policies that brought about his spectacular downfall. Nothing in the training, experience, or temperament of this priest-turned-politician had prepared him for the roles he tried to play in his own country and on the world stage. He received his formal education in a theological seminary; he grew up under an authoritarian colonial regime; he had never seen anything of the world until he became prime minister of Moyen-Congo's government council. As a priest he had refused to accept the discipline imposed by his ecclesiastical superiors, but later he became an autocrat. He preached national unity, but by displaying favoritism to his fellow Lari tribesmen he disrupted whatever superficial harmony he managed to achieve. He exhorted his compatriots to show civic spirit, to practice austerity, and to produce more, but he was the first to indulge in sumptuary expenditures when he felt they would enhance his personal popularity, authority, and prestige. He tried vainly to satisfy the insatiable demands of an overprivileged minority of politicians and civil servants and ignored the real needs of a miserable population. And although to a limited degree he was conscious of the limitations of his entourage and aware of his country's economic stagnation, he had no remedy to offer except a single industrial project—the Kouilou dam—which he was never able to realize.

As if the inconsistencies and shortcomings of Youlou's policy were not enough to ensure his government's failure, he compounded his distraction from the Congo's basic problems by his gratuitous involvement in foreign affairs. In this sphere he briefly pursued chimeras, such as an equatorial union and an independent Greater Bakongo republic, only to drop them when he encountered heavy opposition or when it appeared that they would interfere with more immediately realizable goals.

Mr. Gauze's account of Youlou's activities abroad draws attention to a neglected aspect of the African leader's character—his belief that he had a mission to fulfill as a world peacemaker. This conviction, probably a legacy from his priestly past, gave Youlou the self-assurance to champion such unpopular causes as the Katanga secession and to try to effect a reconciliation between the moderate and revolutionary African leaders, negotiate with the Portuguese government, and propose to Khrushchev that Brazzaville was the ideal site for a summit conference to settle the problem of Berlin. In these moves, considerations of prestige and self-interest obviously entered into his calculations, but there was also an element of ideology and generosity in his nature that partly explains his impulsiveness and extravagance. Similarly,

Youlou's support for Moïse Tshombe, leader of the Katanga secession, cannot be wholly attributed to his hope of getting financial backing for his Kouilou project, for it was also an expression of loyalty to a man he considered to be his friend. And his harsh measures against the radical youth and labor leaders were not taken solely because they had dared to oppose him but also because Youlou had an obsessive fear of communism.

In the last analysis, however, this complex political priest simply lacked the vision to grasp the long-term implications of his actions, and in seeking immediate success and prestige he frittered away all possibility of attaining the national unity and prosperity that were his ultimate aims. Thus under Youlou's leadership tribal divisions deepened and the parlous economic situation that antedated his accession to power only grew worse. This opened the way for the successive political upheavals that culminated in a military dictatorship.

In the decade that followed Youlou's overthrow, the Congo's political and economic orientation was profoundly modified, but its basic dependence on foreign aid and its susceptibility to alien influences remained and in fact increased with the advent of independence in 1960. Since then, the Congolese elite has been ideologically radicalized, the domestic economy progressively nationalized, and close relations with France and certain neighboring nations gradually weakened. At the same time, the country's economy has continued to depend on foreigners, its financial position has further deteriorated, and its government has become increasingly unstable. As Mr. Gauze's history of the early evolution of the Congo clearly shows, the potential for all these developments existed under the colonial administration and during Youlou's regime because they were inherent in the geographical, economic, and ethnic conditions of the country.

———————————

The original manuscript from which the major part of this book has been translated comprised 739 pages. In this translation, all the sections not dealing directly with Congo-Brazzaville have been eliminated. In so drastically compressing Mr. Gauze's work, the translator-editors may have inadvertently traduced the author's views, and for any such lapses they assume full responsibility.

A brief historical introduction has been provided as background for Mr. Gauze's account, and to give continuity and current information about the Congo's evolution, a final section on more recent developments has been added. Finally, with the aim of lightening the text, biographical data concerning most of the individuals mentioned in these pages have been concentrated in an appendix.

V. T.
R. A.

August 1973

xiii

INTRODUCTION

French Exploration and Occupation

In 1849 Libreville was founded on the coast of Gabon as a naval base for French ships attempting to suppress the slave trade and as a refuge for the first slaves that had been freed. It was from Libreville in 1875 that the Italian-born French naval officer Savorgnan de Brazza began the first of his explorations of the interior of central Africa. Five years later he succeeded in reaching the Congo River and in September 1880 made a treaty with "King" Makoko,[1] who thereby placed himself and his Batéké tribe under French protection and ceded to France the site of what became the town of Brazzaville. The possession of this region enabled France to frustrate the attempt made by another famous explorer, H. M. Stanley, to extend the domain of his sponsor, King Léopold of the Belgians, to the right bank of the Congo River. On Brazza's third expedition, in 1883, he joined forces with his lieutenant, Albert Dolisie, who had been making treaties with tribes of the lower Oubangui, and together they went on to explore the country as far as the west coast.[2] There Brazza made a similar protectorate treaty with the "king" of Loango, who ceded outright to France the area known as Pointe Indienne.

By that time the conflicting claims of the western European countries which had competitive bases in central Africa required some overall settlement. Their representatives met late in 1884, and early the following year signed the Act of Berlin. By its terms, France was not given direct access to the mouth of the Congo River but retained possession of the Niari basin and the lands explored by Brazza, and in return for certain concessions it agreed to internationalize its domain in the Congo. This Act was supplemented by a series of bilateral treaties which demarcated the frontiers of the possessions of the signatory nations as well as their zones of influence. A treaty with Portugal in 1885 established the boundary between the French Congo and Cabinda, and two others with the Congo Free State recognized the Oubangui-Congo rivers as the frontier between the French and Belgian territories.

After the abolition of the slave trade and the opening of the Suez Canal, the central African coast lost much of its importance to the imperial powers, so they moved into the hinterland to confirm their respective zones of influence by effective occupancy. The area carved out by France was placed under a governor in 1908 and was organized as the Federation of French Equatorial Africa (FEA) in 1910. It comprised the colonies of Moyen-Congo, Oubangui-Chari, Gabon, and Tchad. Theoretically, each of them retained economic and administrative autonomy, but the government-general installed at Brazzaville gradually centralized power in its hands. Because of FEA's remoteness from France, its lack of easily exploitable resources except timber, and its unhealthy climate, inadequate means of communication, and shortage of manpower, it was one of the most politically backward and economically under-developed parts of the French empire until World War II.

World War II and the French Reforms

This bleak picture changed almost overnight when FEA, under the leader-ship of Félix Eboué, the French Negro governor of Tchad, opted to join Free France in August 1940. For the next five years, FEA contributed to the Allied war effort manpower for the conquest of the Fezzan and North Africa as well as certain strategic raw materials, but its main importance was as a base and a point of transit. The port of Pointe Noire fueled the Allies' ships, the Congo-Ocean railroad worked to capacity to provision their troops and ship out FEA's produce, and Tchad's air fields were used by their planes flying between West Africa and the Middle East. FEA emerged from the war with its economy strengthened, its means of communication improved, and its reputation greatly enhanced.

Eboué was also responsible for long-term political and social reforms in the Federation. He strengthened indigenous African institutions by upgrading the chieftaincy and Notables and by checking detribalization. Customary courts under African judges were created to apply traditional laws modified by Western concepts of justice, mission schools were granted subsidies, and youth and cultural organizations were encouraged. Eboué also laid the ground-work for transforming the agricultural laborers on European plantations into a genuine peasantry. Considering that he headed the Federation for only three years, his accomplishments were impressive. The policies he initiated greatly influenced the delegates to the Free French conference held at Brazzaville in 1944, whose recommendations of political, economic, and cultural reforms marked a turning point in the history of French Black Africa. At the time of Eboué's death in May 1944, Brazzaville possessed a lycée, a military school, a powerful radio broadcasting station, labor and housing bureaus, and two African communes in its districts of Bacongo and Poto-Poto.

Population and Economic Resources

Of the four FEA territories, Moyen-Congo was often described as the one best equipped by man and least favored by nature. This was because its north-ern region, sometimes called the cuvette or central Africa's "green hell," was covered by dense forests and inundated for much of the year. It was drained by the Congo River and its many tributaries, which flowed into Stanley Pool. This pseudo lake of 450 square kilometers separated the capital cities of Brazzaville and Léopoldville, situated, respectively, on its northern and southern banks. The southern half of Moyen-Congo was better suited to human habitation than was the northern basin, but it had only one truly fertile region, the Niari valley. Although about one-fourth of the territory's total population lived in its four main southern towns, they lacked a productive supporting hinterland.

Moyen-Congo's population, which in 1957 totaled some 770,000 (see table 1), had nearly doubled since 1921, but it was unevenly distributed over an area of 342,000 square kilometers. About three-fourths of the population was rural; two-thirds lived in the south between Brazzaville and Pointe Noire, and one-third in the north on 60 percent of the total surface. The great majority of northerners resided in small villages scattered throughout the forest

TABLE 1

POPULATION OF CONGO (BRAZZAVILLE),
JANUARY 1, 1957[a]

District	Population aged over 15 years		Population aged 15 and younger		Total	Non-indigenous
	Male	Female	Male	Female		
Djoué...........	39,284	31,415	26,302	25,313	122,314	5,898
(Brazzaville)..	(31,500)	(23,621)	(19,441)	(18,903)	(93,465)	–
Kouilou.........	23,801	22,225	15,921	15,074	77,021	2,987
(Pointe Noire).	(11,410)	(9,463)	(6,951)	(6,837)	(34,661)	–
Pool............	26,086	52,791	28,130	26,977	133,984	196
Niari..........	36,773	53,930	25,519	22,635	138,857	716
Niari-Bouenza...	14,465	20,178	18,233	17,884	70,760	276
Alima-Léfini....	16,805	24,928	19,311	17,775	78,819	74
Likouala-Mossaka	23,618	36,795	18,530	16,199	95,142	128
Sangha..........	8,950	10,624	4,801	4,203	28,578	92
Likouala........	6,259	9,233	4,630	4,558	24,680	53
Total.........	196,041	262,119	161,377	150,618	770,155	10,422

Source: Based on Wagret, J.-D., Histoire et Sociologie Politiques de la République du Congo (Brazzaville), Paris, 1963, p. 123.

[a]Between 1946 and 1954, the Congo's population increased as follows (in round figures): 1946—626,000; 1948—646,000; 1950—675,000; 1952—683,000; 1954—733,200.

region, whereas the southerners were increasingly urbanized. As the federal capital of FEA, Brazzaville had the largest population of any Congolese town, comprising 31,000 African men and 23,000 women. The disproportionately large male element was due to the immigration of young men from rural areas; by contrast, in the surrounding countryside women outnumbered men by two to one.

The greatest economic asset of Moyen-Congo was its location bordering on the Congo River, which formed its frontier with the Belgian Congo, and on the Atlantic Ocean, where its coastline was 150 kilometers long. This location and the development of its means of communication enabled the territory to live almost wholly by its transit trade. Brazzaville expanded largely because it was situated at the southern extremity of the longest navigable stretch of the combined Oubangui and Congo rivers, and was linked by a 517-kilometer railroad and parallel road to the port and territorial capital of Pointe Noire.[3]

Despite its geographical advantages, Moyen-Congo was for many years a classical example of the économie de traite. That is to say, it received certain manufactured goods from France in exchange for such uncultivated commodities as ivory, gold, natural rubber, and rare woods. Congolese production and trade were dominated by the Compagnie du Haut-Ogooué and the Compagnie du Kouilou-Niari, which in the 1890s had been granted concessions covering, respectively, 107,000 square kilometers and 25,000 square kilometers. They also enjoyed fiscal advantages and had virtually unlimited control over the inhabitants of those vast areas. Moyen-Congo's economy did not fundamentally change until the concessionary period ended in 1930, and four years later the opening to service of the Congo-Ocean railroad profoundly modified the population pattern and means of communication in the area between Brazzaville and Pointe Noire. Yet neither these improvements nor those effected during World War II brought prosperity to Moyen-Congo.

In relation to its size and even to its population, Moyen-Congo's production was mediocre. Its exports were so small in volume and value and its revenues so meager that its budgets had the largest operating deficits of any territory of the Federation. Consequently, Moyen-Congo depended on the subsidies and loans granted by France and, to a much lesser degree, on Gabon's surplus revenues. As of 1958, Moyen-Congo had no known natural resources that were even potentially large revenue earners. To be sure, the Mayombé forest contained some valuable wood species and the Niari valley produced considerable tonnages of sugar cane, but neither would have achieved their current export levels had it not been for their proximity to the Congo-Ocean railroad. Of Moyen-Congo's so-called road network totaling nearly 9,000 kilometers, only 269 kilometers could be described as improved dirt roads, and the northern region was isolated for lack of the means of surface transportation. The territory was better provided with waterways, but the Congo artery was not navigable downstream from Brazzaville, and few of the Oubangui's main tributaries—the Likouala, Alima, and Sangha—could be used except by small boats and for only short distances.

The great equatorial forest blanketed much of Moyen-Congo, and about one-third of the territory's surface was covered by poor, sandy soil that gave only scanty harvests. Because of the diversity of its crops—manioc, rice, bananas, citrus fruits, tobacco, sugar cane, fiber plants, cocoa, coffee, peanuts, and oil palms—Moyen-Congo sometimes gave the impression of agricultural abundance. However, not even its oleaginous products, which

were its main agricultural export, were grown on a large scale, and many of
the others were produced in only insignificant quantities. For its disproportionately large urban population, foodstuffs had to be imported. These
could have been grown locally if the number of farmers—never large—had not
been steadily depleted by the exodus of young men to the towns. Even the
population's basic food, manioc, was not grown in sufficient quantity to
meet the territory's needs, and it was in vain that the administration had
encouraged the cultivation of rice and corn as substitutes.

Of the three regions selected in 1946 by the authors of Moyen-Congo's
Ten-Year Development Plan, only that of the Niari valley was a success,
largely because of the practice of scientific mixed farming by its French
settlers. More encouraging for the future was the implantation of some African cooperative societies, called paysannats, which succeeded in stabilizing their members on the land and increasing their production by improved
farming techniques. Animal husbandry and fishing also made some progress,
thanks to the French research institutes and the agricultural service of the
Moyen-Congo, but their output was still far below the population's nutri-
tional needs, let alone enough to augment the territory's exports. Of all
the output of the rural economy, that of its forests was the most valuable
to Moyen-Congo in terms of its foreign trade.

In both the volume and the value of its external commerce, Moyen-Congo
was the least prosperous territory of FEA, although the range of its exports
was more diversified and its commercial network the largest. Among its imports, the large proportion of consumer and equipment goods reflected the
concentration in Moyen-Congo of the Federation's European community and its
excessive urbanization. Partly because of these factors and partly because
of a flourishing contraband trade with Léopoldville, living costs rose faster
there than elsewhere in FEA, and price controls were harder to enforce. As
in the agricultural sector, the roster of Moyen-Congo's industries was impressive but their output was small. Most of them were processing industries
that produced only for the domestic or federal market, which was very limited.
Some were profitable and capable of expansion, such as those manufacturing
cigarettes, beer, soap, and textiles, but only the oleaginous and wood industries could be described as even relatively large in scale.

In the domain of minerals, Moyen-Congo again seemed to have greater
variety than volume, and though petroleum and potash had been discovered in
the western region, the extent of their deposits was unknown at that time.
However, their location near the port of Pointe Noire and not far from the
site of what might become a huge hydroelectric dam on the Kouilou River
raised hopes that a large industrial complex might be developed there. The
realization of such a project, or of any large-scale development of the
Congo's economy, depended on extensive foreign aid, overall planning, and a
stable and efficient administration. To varying degrees Moyen-Congo, along
with the other FEA territories, had acquired all of these since World War II,
as well as its first labor organizations and elective political institutions.

The Political Framework

Before 1946, FEA had no political institutions or parties, its administrative structure was a replica of that of French West Africa, and it was
represented in Paris by only one appointed member of the Conseil Supérieur

des Colonies and an economic agency. The governor-general of FEA was named
by the French government, and he was the depository of the powers of the Republic for the Federation. He alone could correspond with the Minister of
Colonies, and he controlled the four territorial governors as well as the
local civilian, judicial, and military services. Aiding him were a
secretary-general and an administrative council. The council, a purely advisory body named by the governor-general, was made up of eight federal officials, together with four French citizens selected by the Chambers of Commerce and four French-speaking Africans chosen to represent the native population. The administrations of the four equatorial colonies were similarly
structured and centralized.

Although the delegates to the Brazzaville conference of 1944 were exclusively French officials, their recommendations aimed at markedly reforming the prewar regimes of the two Federations. They laid down the principle
that thenceforth native welfare should be the primary objective of French
colonial policy, but they specifically rejected the possibility of self-
government by the Africans. Indeed, the unity of the empire, now to be
called the French Union, was affirmed, although they suggested that its
overcentralization might be corrected through working out some federal formula for all France's overseas dependencies. The Brazzaville delegates further proposed that the two Federations should elect representatives to the
assembly that would draft the constitution for France's Fourth Republic and
to its future parliamentary bodies, as well as to local councils. They envisaged that in such local councils Europeans and Africans would deliberate
together but be chosen by separate electoral colleges.

Thus, even before World War II ended, the basis was laid at Brazzaville
for the chief issues that were to dominate the political evolution of francophone Africa for more than a decade. These issues were the elimination of
the dual college system, an extension of the suffrage, and the federalization
of the French Union. It was not until 1956 that the first college for Europeans was abolished and universal adult suffrage achieved, and two more years
were to pass before the Africans began their attempts to achieve some form of
interterritorial unity that would replace the moribund Federations. By the
end of 1960, all the African territories had achieved sovereign status and
the plan to federalize the Franco-African Community (as the French Union had
been renamed) had died stillborn.

It was to the first constituent assembly for the Fourth Republic of
France, elected in November 1945, that French Black Africa owed major liberal
reforms. That assembly abolished forced labor (law of February 11, 1946),
proclaimed freedom of meeting and association (decrees of March 13 and April
11), abolished the system of administrative penalties known as the indigénat
(decree of February 20), granted French citizenship to all the inhabitants
of Overseas France (law of May 7), gave the courts applying French law juris-
diction over all penal cases (decree of April 30), and laid the foundation
for application of France's Plan for Modernization and Equipment to the overseas territories (law of April 30).

It is noteworthy that the constitution drafted by that assembly, which
was rejected by the French people in May 1946, won a majority of overseas
votes. Its defeat opened the way for a resurgence of conservative opinion
in France, which was reflected in the less liberal terms for French Black
Africa embodied in the second constitution, which received an affirmative

vote the following October. Félix Tchicaya, who had been elected to represent Gabon as well as Moyen-Congo in both constituent assemblies, joined the French West African representatives in their vain protest against the retention of the dual college system and the restrictions placed on the size of the African electorate.

A series of decrees, also issued in October 1946, allotted FEA six seats in the National Assembly, eight in the Senate (or Conseil de la République), and seven in a wholly new advisory parliamentary body, the French Union Assembly. Jointly the first colleges of Moyen-Congo and Gabon chose 1 deputy, as did those of Oubangui-Chari and Tchad (see table 2). Concurrent decrees gave each territory an elected representative assembly, in which the prevailing ratio was two representatives of the first college to three of the second college (see table 3). Almost a year later, a law of August 27, 1947, created a Grand Council of 20 members, each territorial assembly electing five members and voting as a single college. These assemblies and the Grand Council were required to hold two regular meetings a year and to elect a permanent committee of three to five members to carry on work between sessions.

Although the territorial assemblies acted as an electoral college in voting for FEA's representatives in the Senate, the French Union Assembly, and the Grand Council, their most important powers related to financial matters. Subject to cancellation by the Council of State in Paris if they should contravene the law, the decisions of the local assemblies were final in respect to the budgets submitted to them by their respective territorial governors. Furthermore, they were obligatorily consulted on such matters as local land concessions, loans, the organization of the administration, labor and social security, the register of vital statistics (état civil), and public works. The governor could submit other questions to the assemblymen for their advice; the assemblymen were also permitted to pass resolutions and to address directly to the high commissioner (called the governor-general beginning in 1947) or the Minister of Overseas France any observations in the general interests of their territory. However, they were forbidden to discuss political questions or other subjects considered to be the province of the administration. On the federal level, the Grand Council had the same prerogatives as did the assemblies on the territorial level. It also had to be consulted on all matters affecting two or more territories; it set the fiscal duties for imports and exports; and it allocated subsidies and rebates from the federal budget, whose revenues derived very largely from the customs service.

The main issues on which all the FEA elected assemblies locked horns with the French administration were their right to investigate government projects, euphemistically called "missions of information," the reapportioning of financial revenues between the federal and territorial budgets, and the overstaffing of federal services with high-paid Metropolitan officials. On such subjects, it is interesting to note that voting did not always follow ethnic lines, for the European and African members usually worked together against what they considered to be the administration's authoritarianism. Until about 1950, the African assemblymen generally looked upon their European colleagues as mentors and guides, and they elected the more experienced among them to be presidents of the assemblies and chairmen of technical committees. Perhaps one reason for this era of good feeling was the small size of the electorate during the first postwar decade.

TABLE 2

FEA REPRESENTATION IN PARLIAMENTARY BODIES
AS OF NOVEMBER 1947

Territory	National Assembly		Council of the Republic		French Union Assembly
	1st college	2d college	1st college	2nd college	
Gabon..........	1	1	1	1	1
Moyen-Congo.....		1	1	1	1
Oubangui-Chari..	1	1	1	1	2
Tchad..........		1	1	1	3

Source: Minutes of the Grand Council session of November 24, 1947.

TABLE 3

TERRITORIAL REPRESENTATION IN FEA ASSEMBLIES

Territory	Representation in 1946 by college		Total no. of members		
	1st college	2d college	1946	1952	1956
Gabon.................	12	18	30	37	40
Moyen-Congo...........	12	18	30	37	45
Oubangui-Chari........	10	15	25	40	45
Tchad.................	10	20	30	45	60

Source: E. Trézenem and B. Lembezat, La France Equatoriale, Paris, 1950.

In 1946, the franchise was extended to members of both sexes who were twenty-one years of age or older and belonged to one of the 12 categories specified by the law—civil servants, members of native courts, Notables, soldiers and veterans, persons holding honorary decorations, and the like. On April 24, 1951, the National Assembly voted in favor of a law adopting the single college for Moyen-Congo and Oubangui-Chari and for an appreciable increase in the whole electorate of FEA. But the Senate rejected the principle of the single college for any of the FEA territories, and for the Federation accepted only three new categories of voters—mothers of two or more children, heads of households, and recipients of pensions.

The Loi-Cadre of 1956

Although Tchicaya characterized the new electoral law as one "shameful to the Parliament," it effected about a fivefold increase in the number of registered electors in FEA. The following November, the Parliament also voted a substantial enlargement of the membership of the territorial assemblies (see table 4). Finally, the loi-cadre (enabling act) of June 23, 1956, instituted the single electoral college throughout French Black Africa as well as universal adult suffrage, and it also increased the membership of the elected assemblies (see table 3). Of the political innovations in the loi-cadre, the most important in African eyes were the creation of government councils that would share executive power with the territorial governors and in time develop into cabinets the downgrading of the governments-general and grand councils and a marked extension of the competence of the territorial assemblies in the legislative field, especially in its control over the civil service.

It is perhaps indicative of the tribal and personal character of FEA politics that these changes did not perceptibly alter the existing political situation either in the Federation or in the territories. Unlike their West African colleagues, the FEA deputies in Paris took no outstanding part in the debates on the loi-cadre or on the decrees applying its provisions. The Equatorial Africans were principally concerned with maintaining and increasing France's financial and economic aid and with preserving some of their interterritorial ties. Later, continued French assistance was to be assured by means of bilateral agreements between the territorial and Paris governments. And although the reluctance of Gabon to commit itself to any revival of the federal administrative structure prevented the proposals for interterritorial unity made by the Congolese and Oubanguian premiers from materializing, some forms of their former economic and technical cooperation were salvaged.

Because of France's long neglect of the Equatorial territories and their inhabitants' sense of inferiority to the French West Africans, the impact of the postwar innovations was felt only gradually in FEA. However, the first of its four territories to undergo fundamental changes was Moyen-Congo, which was the most politically and economically evolved among them. Passage of the loi-cadre coincided with the rise to power there of Abbé Fulbert Youlou, under whose leadership party politics and trade unionism grew apace. It was during his tenure of office that Moyen-Congo voted in the referendum of September 28, 1958, to join the amorphous Franco-African Community proposed by General Charles de Gaulle, opted for the status of an autonomous republic the

TABLE 4

THE ELECTORATE IN FEA

Territory	Population (round numbers)	Registered electors (second college)				Percentage voting
		Nov. 1946	June 1951	Mar. 1952	Mar. 1953	
Gabon.......	409,000	26,530	70,843	86,530	87,365	47.8(1946) 41.7(1951)
Moyen-Congo.	684,000	23,119	118,523	176,711	186,509	67.7(1946) 44.3(1951)
Oubangui-Chari.....	1,072,000	32,716	111,204	187,908	192,891	70.1(1946) 60.9(1951)
Tchad.......	2,241,000	27,664	250,341	307,970	317,646	64.5(1946) 66.2(1951)
Total.......	4,406,000	110,029	550,911	759,119	784,411	

Source: Adapted from La Documentation Française, L'Evolution Récente des Institutions Politiques (etc.), March 11, 1954.

xxv

following December, and achieved independence in August 1960. Since the three other Equatorial states did likewise, the subsequent divergencies in Moyen-Congo's evolution must be attributed to other factors. Among these factors were the abbé's personality and, even more, his territory's historical, geographical, and ethnic situation.

Moyen-Congo's Individuality and Evolution

What made Moyen-Congo unique among the FEA states were its exceptionally sharp tribal and regional divisions, the high percentage of school-educated and of unemployed young people in its southern towns, its comparatively well-developed industrialization and urbanization, and its receptivity to foreign influences. One of the most striking consequences of the internationalization of the Congo basin by the Act of Berlin was the transplantation from the Belgian Congo of movements of political protest in the form of messianic religious sects, which took deep root among the Lari of the Brazzaville area and, to a lesser extent, among the Vili of the region of Pointe Noire.

These phenomena gave Moyen-Congo a marked individuality and accounted for its distinctive evolution even before it became an independent republic. While it had a favorable geographic location, an active transit trade, a high literacy rate, and the institutional equipment of a democratic state, it also had handicaps that prevented the Congo Republic from utilizing those assets to the full. What Moyen-Congo lacked when it became an autonomous republic in 1958 more than offset the advantages it possessed. It did not have harmonious tribal relations, a well-trained and conscientious African bureaucracy, a skilled wage-earning class, a prosperous peasantry attached to the soil, an indigenous bourgeoisie of traders and industrialists, or good relations with its northern neighbors.

Indeed, during the period of the Congo Republic ethnic violence lay very near the surface, the countryside was neglected, the cities were overflowing with unemployed and unskilled rural youths, the labor unions were weak and poorly led, the republic's finances were chronically in disarray and dependent on foreign bounty, and external trade and local industry were not only insignificant but in the hands of aliens not concerned with developing the country or promoting the population's welfare.

All of these deficiencies persisted during the first years of independence with the result that the Congo became perhaps even more backward and underdeveloped than it had been as an autonomous republic or even as a colony. Not surprisingly, the Congolese, like other former colonial peoples of francophone tropical Africa, had almost no understanding of political democracy or the concept of nationhood, and only a handful of trained officials and technicians was available to take over control from the French administration, despite the high rate of literacy. What, unfortunately, they were unable to produce at that time were leaders who might have transcended these handicaps. As can be seen from the following pages, the men who first came to political prominence were none other than tribal chiefs in modern guise, and they manipulated the new electoral institutions accordingly. They proved incapable of welding the Congolese into a nation and promoting their economic and social evolution.

V. T.
R. A.

Notes

1. The Makoko's status was that of a paramount chief, but French historians have preferred to call him king. In any case, by the mid-nineteenth century his powers had been curtailed by the Batéké Notables and his kingdom drastically reduced in area by aggressive Kongo and Gabonese tribesmen.

   In the late eighteenth century the Mbochi tribe, whose origin is unknown, began to expand southward from the Likouala-Mossaka basin. This brought them into conflict with the Batéké, who tried to defend their monopoly of the trade between the north and Stanley Pool. After their defeat, the Batéké were effectively restricted to the cuvette region.

   The various kingdoms founded by the Kongo tribes were widely scattered in parts of the countries that became the French and Belgian Congos. In the French colony, they lived in the Brazzaville region and took over the area north of the Niari after ejecting the Batéké from it.

2. At the time the Portuguese began to arrive along the coast in the late fifteenth century, the kingdom of Loango stretched from Cabinda to Cap Ste. Cathérine in Gabon. It reached its apogee at the end of the seventeenth century, after which its Vili inhabitants were pushed back to their present area under the impact of migrants from the country now called Gabon.

3. Pointe Noire became the territorial capital in 1950.

CHAPTER 1

CONGOLESE TRIBES AND THEIR POLITICAL LEADERS

Congo-Brazzaville's population of some 850,000 Africans in 1962 was
made up of 14 main tribes and 73 subtribes, almost all of whom were of Bantu
origin. As of that year, they were growing at an annual rate of nearly two
percent and had almost doubled in the course of the preceding 40 years. A
sparse population for the area (two inhabitants per square kilometer for the
whole territory), the Congolese tribes were very unevenly distributed. The
most densely inhabited regions were those near Brazzaville (17 persons to
the square kilometer) and along the coastal plain (5.7). There, 45 percent
of the Congolese lived on 15 percent of the total area, while the inundated
forest zones of the north and the Batéké plateau were virtually deserted.
Furthermore, some 212,000 of the population lived in the southern towns of
Brazzaville, Pointe Noire, Dolisie, and Jacob. Despite their common ethnic
origin and remarkably high literacy rate (80 percent of the school-age children attended school), the Congolese tribes lacked any basic unity.

Of the country's four main ethnic groups, the Bakongo in the south
formed almost half the total population.[1] Next in importance came the Batéké
in the central region (20 percent) and the Boubangui (16 percent), of whom
the outstanding subtribe was that of the Mbochi. Among the western tribes,
which traced their history back to the ancient Loango kingdom, the most advanced were the Vili of the Pointe Noire region. All the tribes living near
Moyen-Congo's frontiers were related to those in adjacent countries.

In modern times, the first tribe in Moyen-Congo to become politically
prominent was the Mbochi. According to semilegendary sources, the earlier
Mbochi immigrants were dominated by the indigenous riverine peoples of the
Congo basin. Within less than a century, however, they had freed themselves
from that yoke and won control of both banks of the Alima River, where they
now live. That region, thanks to Mbochi enterprise, was to become the gran-
ary for a vaster area of inundated forests and very limited resources. Intelligent, talkative, obstinate, and with a penchant for intrigue and a
strong sense of tribal solidarity, the Mbochi are believed to have come
under the influence of the French Catholic mission at M'Boundji in the early
twentieth century.[2] The education provided by that mission enabled the
Mbochi—then less advanced than the coastal peoples, who had been in contact
with Europeans since the sixteenth-century explorations—to become one of
the most westernized ethnic groups in equatorial Africa.

Jacques Opangault, who became the undisputed leader of the northern
populations, was born in 1907 in the Likouala-Mossaka region. His birth coincided with the arrival in Mbochi territory of the first French missionaries
from the Atlantic coast. Like most of his fellow tribesmen who rose to
political prominence, Opangault was trained at Catholic mission schools,

first at M'Boundji and then at Brazzaville, and he entered the administrative service in 1925. This was the period when the Mbochi supplied the African cadres for the French administration, as well as for the private business sector.

After having long been the dominant tribal group in the government at Brazzaville, the Mbochi gradually lost ground during the period between the two World Wars to other tribes. These were the Lari and the Vili, who began later than the Mbochi to benefit by the growing number of mission schools. Those who know Congolese psychology claim that the Mbochi regarded the admittance of other ethnic groups into the administration as a blow to their cultural preeminence. So, in 1938, some Mbochi civil servants formed a Mbochi committee for the joint defense of their common interests. The immediate stimulus for forming that organization may have been the famous Amicale Balali, which gave birth to Matsouanism.[3] On the other hand, it might have been simply an expression of the innate African vocation for communal causes, which explains the multitude of associations that have burgeoned in urban centers over the years. In any case, four members of the Mbochi Committee soon became politically prominent. These were Jacques Opangault, who for many years was to dominate the Moyen-Congo political scene; Charles Kibaht, who was elected in 1958 as deputy in the French National Assembly, only to lose his compatriots' confidence; and Matadi and Eckomband, who never acquired nation-wide renown and wielded influence solely in the small Mbochi area of the Likouala.

The Mbochi Committee might never have aroused more than indifference had not the Apostolic Vicariate of Brazzaville, with the praiseworthy aim of greater efficiency, decided one day to replace Mbochi—until then the language most widely used along the banks of the Congo River—by Lingala. This step was interpreted by the Mbochi leadership as a new affront, and it awakened in the Committee's Brazzaville members anticlerical sentiments that, in turn, engendered the anti-French feeling that was expressed after France's defeat in 1940. The authority of the administration, temporarily shaken by attacks from a few individuals who, without opposition, tried to involve the population, was soon restored by Governor-General Eboué. Although Eboué himself was a black man, he exiled Opangault and the other Mbochi Committee members to Oubangui-Chari, thus ending the Mbochi agitation in Moyen-Congo.

After returning from his exile in 1945, Opangault made amends to both the Catholic mission and the civil authorities. Soon he was able to resume his leadership position, benefiting by the new democratic freedoms that France then granted to the territories of the French Union. Intelligent and shrewd, and aware that he was under close surveillance, Opangault sought the support of an influential French party so that he might have a legal cover under which to promote the Mbochi cause. This was the origin of the local branch of the Section Française de l'Internationale Ouvrière (SFIO). By setting the north against the south, infiltrating the northern electorate through the agency of Mbochi civil servants, creating ethnic cells which have survived to this day, and resisting the nationalism being preached by Abbé Fulbert Youlou, Opangault profited during the next 15 years by every political event to keep his name before the public. As of 1962, Opangault was still the soul of the African socialist party in Congo-Brazzaville and, to a greater degree, that of its Mbochi element. Although his dynamism and congenital impetuosity were calmed with the passage of time and replaced by a statesmanship marred by occasional missteps, he will remain one of the important political figures of his country, regardless of what the future has in store for him.

Again, as a sequel to the postwar introduction of democratic institutions, there arose in the south of Moyen-Congo another popular personality—Jean-Félix Tchicaya, a member of the Vili tribe albeit born at Libreville in Gabon. It may seem surprising that a native of Gabon should come to play a dominant role in Moyen-Congo, but one must remember the ethnic relationships between the two equatorial territories and also that the Loango kingdom, cradle of the Vili tribe, stretched along the Atlantic seaboard from the frontiers of the Belgian Congo to the lagoons of Port Gentil.

More favored than their hinterland brothers, who were related to the northwestern Kongos, the coastal Vili had contacts with the Western world for 300 years. About a century before the first Catholic missionaries reached Loango in 1645, the coastal peoples had already been trading with the Dutch, Portuguese, and Spanish slavers whose ships often anchored in Loango Bay. Such contacts, followed by others with Western sailors, effected changes in the Vili, who later became agents for the slavers in supplying them with their rural brothers, the main victims of that trade.

Tchicaya was born in 1903, and after attending school in Libreville, he completed his studies at the Normal (Ponty) School at Dakar, where he became an outstanding pupil. Upon his return to Gabon, he entered the government service, and then moved to Pointe Noire just after the Congo-Ocean railroad had begun full service. His work as a warehouse accountant quickly brought him into touch with both laborers and educated persons. When war was declared in 1939, he was mobilized as a French citizen and served, successively, in Brazzaville, Tchad, and Algeria. He was in Paris when the Franco-German armistice was signed. In 1945, when the doors of the French Parliament were opened to Africans, Tchicaya's Gabonese and Congolese friends urged him to stand for election. At that time, Gabon and Moyen-Congo were to be represented in the successive constituent assemblies by two elected representatives, one chosen by the European electoral college and the other by the second, or African, college.

Through his family and friends in Gabon and Moyen-Congo, and thanks to his intellectual capacities and military record, Tchicaya fulfilled all the requirements to be a suitable candidate for the African electorate. Chosen from among a dozen contenders, including Opengault and Aubame (long the political adversary of Léon Mba in Gabon), whose popularity in both cases was restricted to their own ethnic groups, Tchicaya was elected from Gabon-Moyen-Congo to the first and second constituent assemblies. In 1946, he became the first African deputy elected by Moyen-Congo to the French National Assembly.

Raised to political prominence by the minority of évolués who were his friends, Tchicaya was soon able to form an alliance with civil servants and customary chiefs through his skillful leadership and tact. Thus, he came to dominate the politics of Moyen-Congo to the exclusion of his rivals, despite his frequent absences from Pointe Noire to stay in France, where he built himself a modest home. Winning over his Metropolitan colleagues by his jovial bonhomie, Tchicaya quickly acquired the knowledge of parliamentary practices that is the key to political success and that enabled him to launch the first wholly Congolese party, his Parti Progressiste Congolais (PPC).

3

Concentrating on southern Moyen-Congo, where the population was much larger than in the north, Tchicaya built up around his person a notably ethnic political following. This enabled him to triumph consistently over his most dangerous northern competitor, Opangault. Nevertheless, after 15 years of spectacular success, Tchicaya lost everything—his influence and his parliamentary mandate—because he preferred Paris to living in the Congo. In his last years, he could count on only a few traditional and uninfluential Notables, for he lacked the vigor required by the new times. In his own Vili region, he had more faithful friends among the Europeans[4] than among his fellow tribesmen, and even there he was replaced by Stéphane Tchichelle, his former right-hand man. Tchichelle, after having worked for a decade in the PPC, chose the right moment to join forces with Abbé Fulbert Youlou to form with him a dynamic movement, the Union Démocratique pour la Défense des Interêts Africains (UDDIA), which became the government party.

When Youlou, as the UDDIA's president, later became head of the Congolese branch of the RDA,[5] Tchicaya, disgruntled and finished as a politician, was forced into the opposition. He then allied himself with Opangault, his longtime political adversary, and turned his back on the RDA president, Houphouët-Boigny, whose faithful friend he had been from 1946 to 1958. After the loi-cadre of 1956 was applied in the French African territories, Tchicaya continued to follow with faltering steps the evolution of the young Congo Republic, which he looked upon with the indulgence shown by a teacher to a bright former pupil. To Tchicaya, who was an idealist and moderate nationalist, the evolution of Africa seemed too rapid and dangerously revolutionary. After an illness lasting several years, Tchicaya died at Pointe Noire on January 16, 1961, having witnessed the first steps toward union among the Congolese political leaders in Youlou's government. For the Congolese, Tchicaya will always be a popular national figure, their first outstanding political leader, and the precursor of the colonial peoples' emancipation.

At the crossroads of the two large quasipolitical groups formed by Opangault in the north and by Tchicaya in the south lies the country inhabited by the west Kongo tribe, usually called Lari or Balali. In Tchicaya's political career, the element of the Lari who were Matsouanists was destined to play a significant role. Matsouanism, sometimes known as Balalism, made its appearance among the Lari living along the banks of the lower Congo River about 1947. It replaced N'Gounzism, a messianic religion which itself stemmed from Kibanguism,[6] a cult solidly rooted on the Belgian side of the frontier since 1918. This religious eclecticism is peculiar to the Bakongo peoples, and Matsouanism has had no influence over other Congolese tribes. It takes on a purely religious, or fetishist, or sociopolitical aspect, depending on where and by whom it is propagated. Around the person of Matsoua, there was woven first a mystique and then a cult.

Matsoua, whose real name was André Grénard, was older than Opangault and Tchicaya, having been born on January 17, 1891, in the Pool region. Reportedly, he was brought up at the Catholic mission of Kindamba, and then, like a good évolué, he entered the administration in the customs service. At Paris in 1926 (where he had status as a war veteran and French citizen), Matsoua founded the Association Amicale des Originaires de l'AEF and absorbed the Marxist dialectic. Perhaps he thought that he had found, in the defense of the nationalist aspirations of the Congolese people, a means of helping all the natives of FEA living in France. Some allege, however, that he used his organization mainly to collect the funds he needed to live in Paris.[7] A few years later, Matsoua's application for membership in the Ligue de Défense de la Race Nègre (formed in Paris by some French West Indian expatriates as an anticolonial movement) attracted the attention of the Ministry of Colonies.

As active as he was in Paris, Matsoua did not lose touch with his own country, and in 1930 he sent two members of his Amicale back to Brazzaville.[8] By a fund-raising campaign and by sowing discord in the Lari region (where they wore a tricolor ribbon resembling a French decoration), they gave rise to alarm in the local administration. They were arrested at Brazzaville, as was Matsoua in Paris, on charges made by the FEA judiciary. Matsoua was tried and deported to Tchad, thus acquiring a martyr's halo and a legend. Escaping from Tchad in 1935, he sought refuge in France, where he was rearrested and returned to Moyen-Congo. In 1942, Matsoua died of bacillary dysentery in the Mayama prison, but his followers refused to believe that he was dead. Abbé Youlou was to say later that Matsoua had died to give his fellow Africans universal suffrage.

When Matsoua was exiled to Tchad, the Lari peasants refused to participate in the campaign to increase peanut production (Opération Arachide), ordered by the administration throughout Moyen-Congo. Governor-general Reste reported:[9]

> The Lari have adopted an attitude that is neither frankly hostile nor
> disdainful. It cannot be compared with that of Gandhi in British India,
> but it derives from the same spirit of passive submission to the admini-
> strative authority, albeit unmitigated by any spontaneous feeling of
> sympathy, goodwill or attachment to us.

In 1940, the Lari moved from passive resistance to action. A Lari village chief and his two companions, heading a band of 18 armed men, attacked a ter-ritorial guard, for which they were sentenced to death and shot. The execu-tion of those three Amicalists unexpectedly led to the first manifestation of hostility to the administration by the Lari of Brazzaville, which was so seri-ous that the police had to intervene to restore order. Despite repressive ac-tion by the authorities, such as the transfer of functionaries involved in the disorders and the deportation of dangerous individuals, "Balalism" crystallized and spread throughout the Pool region.

It might well be asked why the Brazzaville Lari, who normally lived quietly in the Bacongo district, should suddenly become aroused on behalf of men whose behavior, under French law, was culpable. The following explanation is the one most widely accepted at that time: In Brazzaville, the Lari of the Bacongo district constituted the African elite. Matsoua's two emissaries from Paris romanticized their life in that capital and this aroused envy, for they said that in France black and white men lived on an equal footing. Hence, the Lari believed that by imprisoning the "messengers of freedom," the local ad-ministration showed that it intended at all costs to prevent the Lari from en-joying the same egalitarian privileges as those accorded to their compatriots in France.

Among a people who have always dreamed of independence and expansion, no more than that was needed to awaken their hatred and anger. The Lari never tire of repeating that they were neither conquered nor defeated by Westerners. Coming from the south, they installed themselves as conquerors along the banks of the Pool, just as did Brazza and the French. Some claim that the Lari acquired the lands that they hold today by gifts made to the Batéké, while others contend that they inherited them from their predecessors, the Bahumbus. Fired by Matsoua's emancipatory views, the Lari came to believe that they could purchase their independence and equality from France, just as they had earlier bought their land from other tribes. In their eyes, his Amicale was to serve as an intermediary in their negotiations for independence with Paris, and they thought that the membership dues collected by Matsoua's emissaries would be the purchase price. Because they had paid for their freedom à la parisienne, they refused to take back their money even after the emissaries were imprisoned. It was not the return of the money that they wanted but the freedom which they believed had been promised them.

The Lari claim that if European missionaries say that a white savior will come one day to deliver them, there is no reason why Matsoua should not be the black man's savior. Like Christ, they believed, Matsoua suffered and was the Son of God. Matsouanism rapidly crystallized, a church was organized, and missionaries spread far and wide Matsoua's last words—"Pray by the light of candles"—and this is what the Lari have done since 1942. The cult of the dead is a long-established practice among them, and it is usually in cemeteries that Matsouanists gather together by candlelight.

In such ways did Matsouanism enter into the Lari's daily life, and a dogma was built up around Matsoua's name. As a sociopolitical as much as a religious sect, Matsouanism evolved in a very rigid framework, and as such often clashed with the authorities and the law. Generally speaking, a dedicated Matsouanist would take no orders from Europeans, in whom he saw only the usurpers of his land, and he even avoided contact with them. Matsoua's return to his native country was periodically prophesied as a way of sustaining his followers' fervor. Matsouanists used passive resistance to any administrative regulations that ran contrary to their interests or beliefs; they could not be intimidated, and regarded any court judgment against them as a claim to glory. They refused to be vaccinated just as they refused to work on the roads. They would vote for Matsoua and for him alone, and if they must ask anything from the administration, they would deal only with officials at the highest echelon.

The inert Matsouanists remained in a state of permanent opposition to the administration, as could be seen whenever a census of the Bakongo population was taken. Officials charged with this operation found it difficult to obtain the necessary information from a Matsouanist, and he never came to get the identity card they had made out for him. Yet, there were signs in the early 1950s that the Lari were beginning to lose their intransigence, for the young among them, in particular, were beginning to emerge from their long, retrogressive isolation. Abbé Youlou claimed that Matsouanism was a crisis of adolescence and not a xenophobic movement—rather, it was a sporadic socio-economic protest against administrative abuses such as the indigénat.[10] Yet, when one studies the activities of the Matsouanists in recent years, one wonders if, under cover of a religion, the Lari were not trying to dominate the other Congolese tribes and to organize the country for their own benefit.

The first postwar elections gave the Matsouanists an opportunity to transform their "god" into the apostle of universal suffrage and the franchise. Because they were grateful to Matsoua and believed that he had not died but was a prisoner in the Elysée Palace at Paris, the Lari electorate wrote his name on their ballots. Time was to show how profoundly the Matsoua myth influenced the Lari and how the political force they represented came into play on the day when they decided to vote for a living man rather than a corpse.

When this occurred, all forecasts about elections were upset, and the established hegemony of Tchicaya was jeopardized.

In his study of Matsouanism, Abbé Youlou wrote that it had become riveted in the brains of the Lari for psychological and political reasons. "All the attempts made thus far to dam up the current of Matsouanism have failed, so it seems wiser not to try to destroy it but to channel its course."[11] Five years later, when he was head of the Congolese government, Youlou was to learn that it was not so easy to find a political solution for the Matsouanist problem as he had thought. After having placed Matsoua on a pedestal, the Lari a few years later elevated Youlou politically. In the 1956 elections, Youlou was a serious threat to the outgoing deputy, Tchicaya, and also to his valiant adversary, Opangault. A few months later, Youlou was elected mayor of Brazzaville, and within two years he became head of the Congo Republic's government. Youlou's rapid rise revealed the strength of the static political force represented by Balalism, which had been only a socioreligious movement 25 years earlier. It was to become the basis of the UDDIA, the party which, under Youlou's leadership, came to control the Congo government.

Notes

1. This division of the Moyen-Congo tribes is not followed by all French scholars of the area. J.-D. Wagret, for example, divided them into the Kongo, Batéké, and Mbochi (see his Histoire et Sociologie Politique de la République du Congo (Brazzaville), Paris 1963, p. 123). He believed the Kongo, some 350,000 in all, to be the most important tribe but less cohesive psychologically than some of their many subgroups. Among the latter, he placed the Vili (about 37,000) and the Bayombé, both vassal tribes of the king of Loango (or Ma Loango), as well as the more independent Bacougni, who occupy the region of Dolisie and Loudima. The name Bakongo, Wagret claimed, usually was given to three related tribes—the Basundi, Bakongo, and Balali or Lari. (This nomenclature is confused further by writers who refer to all tribal members of the Kongo family as Ba or Mba, which in the Bantu language simply indicates the plural of the tribal name to which it is attached.) If Wagret's classification is accepted, it would make the Bakongo the largest tribe of Moyen-Congo and the Balali (about 75,000) their most sizeable subgroup. The Balali include the Babembé of the Mouyoundzi region (about 40,000), the Bakamba of the Madingo area (some 18,000), and the Badondo of the Mindouli region (approximately 13,000).

   According to the same authority, the Batéké numbered about 80,000 in 1962. Wagret also identified the Mbochi with the Kouyou and, together with some related tribes, estimated their total at nearly 100,000 persons in the two prefectures of Likouala-Mossaka and Alima. Sometimes that group is called Boubangui, a name given them by their first European discoverers, who thus recognized their Oubanguian origin.

   Since each Congolese tribe has its own distinctive dialect, there have developed two vehicular languages that are spoken widely throughout the territory. The northern tribes speak Lingala, and those of the south Monokutuba. Those languages are closely related, and their grammar is rudimentary.

2. European religious penetration of the French Congo followed soon after the explorations. In 1881, Father Augouard became the second Frenchman to reach Stanley Pool, and nine years later, the Oubangui vicariate was established. By the beginning of the twentieth century, 10 mission stations had been founded in the country, of which that of M'Boundji (in 1899) was the third. The first Protestant mission, at Madzia, near Kinkala, dates from 1909.

3. See pp. 6-7.

4. In francophone Africa, the term "European" is used for all whites.

5. Rassemblement Démocratique Africain; see note 3, p. 15.

6. The name N'Gounzism derived from the surname of Simon Kimbangou, a Belgian Congolese who proclaimed himself in 1921 to be a prophet and the Son of God. His cult, which combined African traditions with Christian ritual, spread rapidly across the Congo River into French territory. By stressing those Biblical passages that incited the oppressed to revolt, he alarmed the Belgian officials, who arrested him and deported him to Katanga, where he died in prison soon afterward.

   For similar reasons, the French colonial administration forbade the practice of N'Gounzism among Kimbangou's Bakongo converts, but it survived as a clandestine protest movement. In 1939, it was revived by another Belgian Congolese, Simon M'Padi, who claimed to be Kimbangou's heir. When the Belgians tried to arrest M'Padi, he fled to French territory. There the name of Kakism was given to his sect from the color of the uniforms worn by his followers. M'Padi continued to proselytize until 1949, when the French arrested him on charges of swindling and handed him over to the Belgian authorities.

7. For differing accounts of Matsoua's life and activities, see G. Balandier, _Sociologie Actuelle de l'Afrique Noire_, Paris 1955.

8. Matsoua's emissaries, Pierre N'Ganga and Constant Balou, were initially so persuasive that they favorably impressed Governor Antonetti at Brazzaville. He even granted an annual subsidy of 1,000 francs to aid the educational work of the Amicale. (See Wagret, _op. cit._, p. 43.)

9. "Etude Du Balalisme" (unpublished typescript), C.H.E.A.M., n. d.

10. The _indigénat_ was a native-status legal "code" that enabled administrators to impose arbitrarily certain penalties on noncitizens for offenses other than statutory ones.

11. _Le Matsouanisme_ (pamphlet), Brazzaville, n. d., p. 1.

CHAPTER 2

THE DAWN OF CONGOLESE POLITICS

Alongside the two ethnically oriented groups formed by Tchicaya and Opangault, there existed a third party. This was the Congolese branch of General de Gaulle's Rassemblement du Peuple Français (RPF), founded by the local association of Free French. It was a white man's party, but had subsections made up of the Africans who had fought for Free France and who consequently were regarded as subservient to its European members. Perhaps one should see in this attitude of the Congolese not so much an incipient xenophobia as the expression of their disorientation. They were passing through a period of over-rapid transition from a policy of paternalism without civic rights to forming an electorate that, albeit still restricted, was potentially democratic.

Elections to the French constituent assemblies, in October 1945 and June 1946, were followed by still another election in November of the latter year. This last vote made Félix Tchicaya the Moyen-Congo's first deputy to the French National Assembly. More significant, however, were the elections held on December 15, 1946, when a limited electorate, voting in two colleges, chose members of the first territorial assembly, as envisaged by a law passed by the French Parliament on the preceding October 25. This election clearly showed the nature of the outstanding political forces that during the next decade were to divide the country into two rival blocs.

Far more than any doctrine or ideology, it was the personality and the ethnic origin of the candidates that determined the choice of the electorate, which then numbered only 23,035 of a total population approximating 750,000. This first local election, however, aroused no enthusiasm, for only 9,617 of the registered voters actually went to the polls. Such widespread abstentionism was attributable mainly to the African prejudice against what is new and especially against what the native himself calls "the white man's ways."

As expected, Opangault's socialist party[1] won all eight seats in the northern circumscription, while the PPC,[2] headed by the deputy, Tchicaya, took the south's allotted 10 seats. Between these two politicoethnic blocs, constituted respectively by the Sangha-Boubangui in the north and the western Kongo in the south, lay what was the apolitical no-man's-land of the Lari. Its inhabitants continued to offer passive resistance to all the administration's actions, and only sporadically did they express their continuing confidence in Matsoua, their immortal idol. Other minuscule parties, labeled "Independents" or "Evolués," used this election to take their first political steps, but the personality of their leaders made it clear from the outset that they had no real chance of success.

From this democratic jousting among the elite, one needs to remember only the names of the few individuals who were already emerging from the mass of parliamentary apprentices. For many years to come, they were to be the driving force behind all political activity in Moyen-Congo. Among the socialists,

Opangault—faithful to his convictions and his tribe—was to remain the pillar of that movement, whereas his listless early collaborators were to be replaced in the coming years by younger, more dynamic, and perhaps less stable elements. Among the PPC members, Tchicaya, Dadet, Goura, and Tchichelle were to survive the winds of change. Some of them underwent a temporary eclipse, but they remained the bulwark of southern politics in the years between 1946 and 1962. Among those defeated in 1946 but who later rose to prominence, one should note the name of Abbé Fulbert Youlou, who ran on the Evolué ticket along with his mentor, Mambéké-Boucher. The latter, some 10 years later, joined the Mouvement Socialiste Africain (MSA) to become minister of education and the political opponent of his former collaborator.

The African branch of the SFIO, to which the parent organization in France gave only moral support, was to remain for several years a movement with limited funds and restricted to certain tribes. Although its membership included a significant percentage of the French residents in Brazzaville, it was never to acquire any ideological influence in Moyen-Congo, and it survived among the northern Congolese only because of the personal influence of Opangault and a few of his militants. The PPC, on the other hand, through its majority in the territorial assembly, got all its candidates elected to the three French parliamentary bodies. (Malonga became a member of the Conseil de la République, Dadet of the French Union Assembly, and Tchicaya was deputy in the National Assembly.) From its foundation, this movement had its own press organ, a novel luxury overseas, which conferred on it the trappings of a big party in the eyes of the FEA population. Later, after the second congress of the RDA, the PPC became the Congolese section of that movement and tried to imitate the West African parties by organizing itself on the Metropolitan models. Only his lack of sufficient funds prevented Tchicaya from fully realizing that aspiration.

The RDA, launched at the Bamako congress of October 11-13, 1946,[3] was initially regarded, at least by Frenchmen, as a cryptocommunist movement because of its affiliation with the Metropolitan communist party and, even more, because of its determined attacks on the colonial administration. Under the leadership of Houphouët-Boigny, it became the fastest-rising party in French West Africa, whereas in the equatorial federation, even its African members who had been elected to office were isolated and still feeling their way. Nevertheless, on the eve of the elections to the second constituent assembly, in 1946, the Africans who were elected from both federations (albeit ideological rivals) agreed on a common platform. Its theme was the eviction of the colonial system by constitutional means. All wanted the rights of the overseas peoples, which had been written into the first constitution (rejected by the Metropolitan electorate), to be retained in drafting its successor, but in this they were disappointed.

Tchicaya, who was opposed in all the elections of 1945-1946 by Opangault and his socialist party, could find in the RDA a haven for his own embryonic movement. In 1947, therefore, after some months of observation and contact with his Metropolitan and West African colleagues, Tchicaya jumped on the RDA bandwagon. He brought along with him the cadres of his PPC, now reduced to its elected territorial assemblymen and a few faithful friends. (In the other equatorial territories, the RDA was headed by the deputy Gabriel Lisette in Tchad, Antoine Darlan in Oubangui-Chari, and Léon Mba in Gabon.)

In August 1948, there appeared the first issue of A. E. F. Nouvelle, the RDA's organ for equatorial Africa, whose manager was Jean Malonga and its political editors Tchicaya and Lisette. Later, the French Union Assemblyman, Darlan, joined its editorial board as representative for Oubangui-Chari. Because it lacked an office and material equipment, this monthly was printed in Paris. It was supported by voluntary contributions from the RDA parliamentarians, notably Houphouët-Boigny, the only one among them who possessed a personal fortune.

A. E. F. Nouvelle immediately attracted attention by its open attacks against the administration's "colonialism" as well as by its racist tendency to treat all its RPF and SFIO adversaries as "valets of the white man." Echoing the Metropolitan communist daily L'Humanité, it espoused so wholeheartedly the anticolonialist causes that it more than satisfied a readership unaccustomed to such xenophobic dissidence and open attacks on the government. In FEA, where there exists a certain distrust of anything bearing the communist label, A. E. F. Nouvelle did not circulate among the masses as Tchicaya and his friends had hoped that it would. Nevertheless, it enabled the local assemblymen and évolués, eager to acquire more political information, to follow the activities of the RDA in France and in French West Africa during its struggle for "the emancipation of the African people." It also permitted Tchicaya, in particular, to maintain a hold on his Congolese following from Paris, where, by then, he was living permanently.

The PPC continued to dominate the local political arena, where its leaders disseminated their progressive views among the slowly awakening masses. Utilizing every grievance, legitimate or otherwise, they tried to convince their political opponents that they alone were qualified to deal with the administration. Indeed, because they were the only ones to protest and to allege persecution by the colonial administration, they consistently had an audience. Raymond Barbé, an important French communist, came to Brazzaville on a lecture tour in November 1948. His visit increased the élan of the PPC assemblymen and local militants, who were delighted to have a Metropolitan parliamentarian show so much interest in their small problems.

Tchicaya attended the second RDA congress at Abidjan in January 1949. There he was elected a vice-president of the movement, an honor he shared with Mamadou Konaté, deputy from Soudan; Ruben Um Nyobé, general secretary of the Union des Populations Camerounaises; and Doudou Gueye, secretary of the Union Démocratique Sénégalaise. Two other delegates from Moyen-Congo attended the Abidjan congress—Michel Kouka and Louis Vouama, who had no future in politics although they were both active PPC militants. After the Abidjan congress, the PPC called itself the local branch of the RDA, was reorganized, and formed subsections throughout Moyen-Congo. At about the same time, an RDA group was organized in each of the three French parliamentary bodies, where the movement was aligned with the communists, and a similar pattern was followed in the overseas assemblies wherever RDA branches were formed.

In the overall reorganization program laid down at Abidjan, the central committee of the PPC-RDA was to be replaced by a directorate from which all of the local assemblymen were excluded. Among the new directors were Vouama, Kouka, and Germain Bicoumat, all active party members but lacking a popular mandate. Under this directorate's impetus, an attempt was made to form subsections in all parts of Moyen-Congo. Consideration was also given to complying with another of the Abidjan congress's directives—that of forming "committees for the defense of workers," which were to be ethnic and vocational cells. The PPC did try to carry out the communist doctrine of infiltrating both the administration and the private sector, but this was only partly successful. As to its internal organization, it can be said that the teachings of the communist party were beginning to bear fruit. At the doctrinal level, however, its success was less spectacular, for it took longer for ideas and concepts to make headway.

Within the PPC, it was not long before questions of personal prerogatives created considerable discontent, and in consequence, Malonga and Dadet resigned from it. In the African districts of Brazzaville, the SFIO opposition was hard at work among the population, where those who had voted the socialist ticket expected substantial material rewards that were impossible to satisfy. Furthermore, the RDA leaders throughout the Black African territories, as in France, were being severely criticized for their alignment with the communist party. In short, it looked as if the African was resisting Marxism. The Indépendants d'Outre-Mer (IOM)[4] profited by the RDA's impending crisis to extend a hand to their "misled brethren" so as to revive the unity among Africans that had foundered lamentably at the first RDA congress in Bamako. Houphouët-Boigny, however, did not respond to their overtures and persisted in working with the French Communist Party.

The shaken RDA then tried to save face. To counter the rumor that Tchicaya and his movement were losing momentum in Moyen-Congo, it was decided to hold a mass meeting at Brazzaville in April 1949, which all the RDA leaders of FEA—Tchicaya, Lisette, and Darlan—would attend. At about the same time in Paris, Gabriel d'Arboussier, general secretary of the RDA, attracted attention at the World Peace Congress by his attacks on colonization and the imperial powers. If the RDA was still going strong anywhere in FEA, it was in Tchad and Oubangui-Chari, where the activity of Lisette and Darlan, respectively, was outstanding. It should be recalled in passing that Lisette was from the Antilles and Darlan was a mulatto of Portuguese descent, whereas Tchicaya and Mba were natives of the territories they represented.

At Brazzaville, personal and ethnic antagonisms were creating difficulties for the movement. Tchicaya, preoccupied by his parliamentary duties in Paris, became a target for his opponents in the PPC, who reproached him with a lack of aggressiveness and with ethnic favoritism. The party's shock troops, virtually abandoned by leaders concerned only for their personal interests, began to lose their zeal and to hold ever fewer meetings. To this disaffection and neglect were added the growing financial difficulties that threatened the party organ, A. E. F. Nouvelle. The FEA leaders kept insisting that subsidies would arrive at any moment from the RDA coordinating committee, but these promises were unfulfilled. To maintain the role of a big party requires funds, and it is a well-known fact that in Africa money is not voluntarily forthcoming without the prospect of immediate benefits. Africans see no reason to pay for the pleasure of playing politics.

For different reasons, the RDA in French West Africa was undergoing a decline, and the consequent loss of its prestige there affected its influence in FEA, particularly in Brazzaville. Dues owed by members to its local sections, always hard to collect, now ceased entirely. In general, it could be said that the mass of the population, albeit devoted to some of its leaders, remains indifferent to the politics practiced by demagogues who have nothing to offer them, for slogans do not feed people. As the country developed, the

Congolese voter experienced one disillusionment after another. He kept hoping that his ballot would bring him substantial benefits, but they never material-ized, at least for the poor of the population.

In the face of the PPC's apathy, rumors ran rife that the dissident Dadet and Malonga had made contact with a certain Abbé Youlou of the Brazzaville diocese, with a view to creating an independent progressive party and one not aligned with the communists. It looked as though they were moving from a state of static discontent to a position of active opposition. Tchicaya, how-ever, would not admit defeat, for he had the poise of an experienced soldier and great confidence in his own destiny. He spent the last four months of 1949 in Moyen-Congo, where he tried hard to put his demoralized movement back on the right track.

Because no elections were held in Moyen-Congo in 1950, it proved to be a nonpolitical year. Experience had shown that the Congolese became interested in politics only during electoral campaigns, and thereafter lapsed into apathy. This behavior reflects the African taste for interminable, diffused, and confused palavers, which leave the participants unsatisfied but still hopeful. The African palaver has no decisive outcome, whereas the Western electoral "palavers" cut discussion short by proclaiming one side the victor and the other the vanquished.

The PPC, like the SFIO, had drowned in its own lethargy. Although both had their quota of militants, there seemed to be no compelling reason why they should become active. For lack of a political stimulus, which could come only from the socialist opposition, the PPC continued to stagnate if not to retrogress. Tchicaya, despite his personal propaganda efforts, could not but regretfully recognize during his many tours the electorate's lack of enthus-iasm for a militant policy. The long-expected demise of the bankrupt A. E. F. Nouvelle deprived his movement overnight of an easy medium for propaganda and for attracting the évolués.

The crisis that threatened the RDA in French West Africa was hardly pro-pitious for ending the persistent dissensions among the PPC leaders. There the historic decision reached by Houphouët-Boigny on October 17, 1950, to dis-sociate his movement from the communist party, following violent clashes in Ivory Coast, was not accepted by all the other RDA leaders. In FEA, Lisette, Darlan, and Tchicaya, suddenly left to their own devices, needed some time to mend their political fences. The year 1951, in contrast to 1950, saw a re-vival of political activity due to the legislative elections. In Moyen-Congo, the same candidates as before sought to win the territory's sole African seat in the French National Assembly, and this indicated how little new blood was available. For the fourth consecutive time, Tchicaya successfully defended his mandate against his tenacious northern adversary, Opangault.

The administration exerted itself to revise the electoral rolls, and the number of those eligible to vote rose from 23,035 in 1946 to 121,581 in 1951.[5] In the Pool region in general and at Brazzaville in particular, the unexpected increase in registrations among the Lari suggested that a candidate claiming to be Matsoua's heir would enjoy a clear advantage. Yet nothing of the sort occurred. The Lari maintained their former attitude and remained impervious to the appeals made by men who had nothing in common with their idol. For the Matsouanists, Matsoua was still living in exile at Paris, and the Lari refused to vote for anyone claiming to represent him. Three-fourths of the registered voters who failed to vote in the Brazzaville circumscription were Lari.

As before, the elections of June 17, 1951, were held under the dual-college system. Among the European first-college candidates, the outgoing RPF deputy Bayrou was reelected, receiving nearly twice as many votes as his two rivals together. In the second college, the three candidates were Tchicaya, Opangault, and Dr. Sambat-Dalhot, the last-named running on the RPF ticket. Of the 53,579 votes cast, only slightly more than half were valid ballots. Tchicaya received 23,213 votes, Opangault 13,176, and Dr. Sambat-Dalhot 9,048. It should be noted that the balance of the electorate who cast valid ballots voted for Matsoua and that they came exclusively from the Pool region and the circumscription of Brazzaville (see table 4).

Despite his clear-cut victory, Tchicaya's election was invalidated by the National Assembly because of protests from Opangault based on the high proportion of abstentions. On November 4, the same candidates again competed. The local administration expected that Tchicaya's invalidation by the French Parliament would have strengthened his position. On the contrary, the PPC leader's following declined, and the election was marked by a few insignificant racial incidents in the main towns. In this run-off, Tchicaya won 20,844 votes, Opangault 15,172, Sambat-Dalhot 4,054, and 12,307 blank ballots were cast. Again, it should be noted that the Matsouanists' blank ballots represented 23.5 percent of the total, and this once again demonstrated that the Lari would not accept as their representative even one of their fellow tribesmen, Sambat-Dalhot.

The fact that only 42.8 percent of the registered electorate actually voted showed the indifference and disillusionment of the mass of the population following the preelectoral campaign, as well as the Lari's uncompromising attitude. Furthermore, the 2,000 or so votes that Tchicaya lost in the run-off were picked up by Opangault, and in the township of Brazzaville Opangault clearly defeated Tchicaya. This new and significant development was due to Tchicaya's obvious alienation from the Congo. In the Pool region and in Brazzaville, where 9,354 electors turned in blank ballots, Matsoua remained the great victor, and Balalism again had confirmed its existence and strength. Yet, it is noteworthy that in the districts of Mouyondzi, Madingou, and Mindouli, wherever the Lari actually participated in the election, their votes went to Tchicaya. This was because he was regarded there as an experienced African politician, whereas Sambat-Dalhot, albeit a native son, was a newcomer to politics and had also been sponsored by the RPF, which was regarded as the party of the whites and consequently of the administration. Although Tchicaya was a clever propagandist, he had made no effort to dissuade the Matsouanists from voting for their "god," for he knew that a mass of blank ballots would help his cause, since they did not go to Opangault.

In the political annals of French Black Africa, the year 1951 was disastrous for the RDA. In Tchad, Lisette was defeated, and in Oubangui-Chari, Boganda, founder of the Mouvement d'Evolution Sociale en Afrique Noire (MESAN) and unallied with any Metropolitan party, was reelected. Antoine Darlan, Boganda's RDA rival, not only failed to run but abandoned the party. Only in Moyen-Congo did Tchicaya win by a few thousand votes over the SFIO candidate. Despite its financial weakness, the local SFIO branch was slowly making headway. From Paris, word reached FEA that the RDA had made a parliamentary alliance with the Union Démocratique et Sociale de la Résistance (UDSR),[6] and once again Tchicaya followed in Houphouët-Boigny's wake and teamed up with that party on February 6, 1952. This alliance enabled Houphouët-Boigny to make a spectacular comeback in the years thereafter, but this was not true for Tchicaya, who managed to remain the political leader of his territory only with the greatest difficulty.

Notes

1. This party was a branch of the Metropolitan Section Française de l'Internationale Ouvrière, or SFIO. In 1936, the SFIO had come to power in France as a Popular Front government headed by Léon Blum, and had founded branches in French West Africa. It was not until January 1946, however, that it sponsored a party in Brazzaville. In 1957, the African branches of the SFIO merged to form an autonomous group, the Mouvement Socialiste Africain (MSA).

2. The PPC was a branch of the Rassemblement Démocratique Africain (RDA), but it was not officially recognized as such until 1949. See note 3.

3. The defeat in May 1946 of the first constitution for France's Fourth Republic alarmed the Black African deputies in the French National Assembly. Five of them, including Tchicaya, signed a manifesto inviting all organizations in the two federations that were seeking to achieve political and economic democracy to meet at Bamako, the capital of French Soudan. There 600 delegates formed the Rassemblement Démocratique Africain (RDA) under the leadership of the Ivorian deputy, Félix Houphouët-Boigny, and with the sponsorship of the French Communist Party. The RDA's avowed purpose was to achieve a "real French Union—that of different peoples who are free and equal in their rights and duties," and to participate in the "antiimperialist struggle led by the people of the whole world." In regard to French Black Africa, the delegates denounced the institution of the double electoral college and all other evidences of racial discrimination. In 1950, however, Houphouët-Boigny drastically altered the RDA's policy by severing his affiliation with the French Communist Party and by collaborating with the local French administration.

4. Léopold Senghor of Senegal and Dr. Louis Aujoulat of Cameroun founded the IOM at Paris in 1948 as an alternative organization to the RDA for African parliamentarians. Its program was less radical than that of the RDA at the time and, as its name implied, it was linked to no Metropolitan party.

5. The figures cited by Gauze do not tally with those given by an official source in table 4, which doubtless represent the final count.

6. In 1945, the UDSR was founded by René Pleven, a French businessman who had been one of de Gaulle's earliest followers and who became the Free French Overseas Minister after France was liberated. When the Gaullists formed the RPF, the UDSR began to decline slowly in power, although Pleven held cabinet posts throughout the Fourth Republic and was prime minister in 1950-51. During his premiership, his overseas minister, François Mitterand, persuaded Houphouët-Boigny to dissolve the RDA's ties with the French Communist Party and to become loosely affiliated with the UDSR in the Parliament.

CHAPTER 3

THE PARTIES AND THE MESSIANIC SECTS

In the 1952 elections to the territorial assembly, the RPF candidates encountered virtually no opposition in the European college and won all 13 seats. Among the Africans of the second college, the two rival blocs of the PPC and the SFIO competed as zealously as before, and eliminated all newcomers to the political arena. Tchicaya, who was an abler propagandist than his adversary, Opangault, also benefited by his recent reelection to the National Assembly. His PPC party won 16 seats, leaving only the eight seats of the four northern circumscriptions to be held by the socialists. Thus, after six years, the old political division between the north and the south was confirmed. Among the outgoing assemblymen, only four were reelected— all of them members of the PPC. These were Tchichelle in the Kouilou region, Goura in the Niari, and Albert Lounda and André Kitoko in the Pool. In the last-mentioned region, Opangault himself was beaten; and Dadet, the French Union Assemblyman who had deserted the PPC, was also defeated.

Tribute should be paid to both Opangault and Sambat-Dalhot, who, despite their defeat at the hands of Tchicaya in the legislative elections, were courageous enough to offer their candidacy again to the Matsouanist Lari electorate, even though they knew it was a losing game. In particular, Opangault bravely did his duty as head of the Congolese socialist party by running in the Brazzaville circumscription, for if he had been a candidate in his native Likouala-Mossaka, he would have been sure of reelection. Although he was defeated in the Lari area as a whole, Opangault had the consolation of winning in the township of Brazzaville with 4,227 votes against the 3,905 cast for Matsoua. Already, in the 1951 legislative election, it had become clear that the two African districts of Brazzaville were politically divided: Poto-Poto, which was a mosaic of tribes, voted socialist, whereas Bacongo[1] voted for Matsoua. Throughout the Pool region, the ticket headed by Lounda and backed by Tchicaya won by the narrow margin of 15,572 to 15,075 votes cast by the Matsouanists.

In 1952, the prestige of the RPF fell rapidly during the year, despite its decisive victory in the first-college elections. The return of Senator Coupigny from Paris during the parliamentary recess did nothing to revive that party, for he virtually abandoned its African subsections. The SFIO, on the contrary, pulled itself together, albeit defeated at the polls, and intensified its propaganda campaign. Its leaders sought the support of the socialist trade unions (Force Ouvrière), as well as an alliance with the Matsouanists. Encouraged by his success in Brazzaville, the resilient Opangault did not hesitate to attack the PPC strongholds in the Pool and Niari regions.

During this period, the PPC was racked by continuing internal dissension. Tchicaya was reproached by his militants for aligning his party with

16

the UDSR and for his alleged subservience to the administration. Further-more, Dadet had not only resigned from the PPC but had sought an understand-ing with Abbé Youlou, who was considering founding a new party based on the theses of Senghor and Tchichelle. Youlou was able to profit by Tchicaya's difficulties and absences from the territory to bolster his own popularity. Nevertheless, the PPC continued to dominate the local political scene, as was shown by the 1953 elections to the French Union Assembly. On that occa-sion, party discipline in the territorial assembly was respected by the PPC majority, and Lounda won by 20 votes to seven for the socialist candidate (Fourvelle) and five for that of the RPF (Lann).

In January 1953, the RPF seemed on the verge of a reorganization fol-lowing a year of inactivity, and in a by-election, its candidate, Etienne, defeated his almost equally conservative rival. The RPF deputy, Bayrou, also made a tour of the territory to revive both its European and African sections. And at Pointe Noire, the RPF Africans were especially active in holding propaganda meetings. But all this activity proved to be the RPF's swan song. Attacked by all the African political parties and by the left-wing parties in France, the RPF in FEA was virtually abandoned to its fate and finally faded away when the dual-college system died with the first municipal elections in 1956.

The year 1954, which brought a surcease in elections, was used by all the parties to prepare for the much heralded municipal elections, even though these were two years away. The SFIO continued to be very active, and it un-dermined the PPC by welcoming as members that party's dissidents at Brazza-ville and Pointe Noire. The socialists' propaganda was directed at capturing the municipal bastions. The local évolués took a marked interest in the draft bill for municipal reform, currently in its first reading before the National Assembly in Paris, because it would widen African political respon-sibilities by promoting the mixed communes of Pointe Noire and Brazzaville to the status of full communes.[2] Although the SFIO had little influence in the territorial capital of Pointe Noire, it tried to draw all the non-Vili population into its ranks. In so doing, the socialists risked heightening ethnic antagonisms in a town where frequent clashes evidenced the perennial hostility between the Vili and outsiders.

This tactic intensified the internal malaise of the PPC, which for more than a year had been sporadically manifest. In the elections for the presi-dency of the territorial assembly, held in April 1954, Goura flouted party discipline by insisting on running against Tchicaya's candidate, a European named Istre, and with the support of other PPC assemblymen, Goura was elected president. Clearly, a break-away movement was shaping up, and Tchicaya was reproached increasingly by his colleagues with being "the white man's deputy." A few weeks earlier, the election of the Lari Lounda to the French Union Assembly had also been viewed as a challenge to Tchicaya and the Vili tribe. Lounda went so far as to accuse Tchicaya publicly of collaborating with François Mitterand, president of the UDSR, for his personal advantage, and the PPC assemblymen exerted pressure on Tchicaya to break with that Met-ropolitan party and join the IOM. As the months passed, it became increas-ingly apparent that the PPC was losing its mass support, although Tchicaya still held his own, for his parliamentary experience and his cooperation with the administration offset the steady decline in his personal popularity. Less and less was heard of the RPF in African circles; it had become the party of a few Metropolitan Frenchmen, and nothing more.

The events of 1955 sorely tried the PPC, whose great fault was to have too many able men pursuing divergent policies. Although Tchicaya's position was becoming increasingly shaky, he was still far from being dethroned. In both the territorial and federal capitals, intrigues flourished and the tempo of defections by PPC members accelerated. At Pointe Noire, Tchichelle, like Opangault, cultivated the nonindigenous tribes, as well as the Vili minority in his native canton, but most of all, he leaned for support on the N'Zambie Bougie sect, described below, and he began to make a frontal attack on Tchicaya. For some months more, the incorrigibly optimistic Tchicaya continued to bear with his inconstant disciple, and then expelled him from the PPC. For propaganda purposes, Tchicaya played up this expulsion, but it had no effect on the electorate of the Kouilou region, for everyone there had long known that Tchichelle was annoyed with Tchicaya and publicly disapproved of his policy.

At this point it is worth digressing in order to throw light on the N'Zambie Bougie sect, a messianic cult which Tchicaya had courted and which Tchichelle had more discreetly and effectively won over. It was a new and prophetic African religion, similar to the other syncretic sects of N'Gounzism and Matsouanism that had taken root in the Lari area and in the Belgian Congo.[3] N'Zambie Bougism, or Lassyism, first came to the notice of the police on September 22, 1953, when a group of some 100 persons was seen praying by candlelight in the African district of Pointe Noire. Inquiry brought out that it had been created, or rather plagiarized, by a Congolese called Lassy Zépherin.

Born about 1908 at Pointe Noire in a family of Vili Notables, Lassy had begun his travels at the early age of thirteen. He is said to have enlisted in the Belgian merchant marine as a stoker, and subsequently became a sailor, an acrobatic dancer, and a professional boxer, living for some time in Antwerp. During World War II, he enlisted to serve on ships of various nationalities, which touched at Dunkirk and Dakar, and he also participated in the Allied landings in Italy. Such, at least, was his story, and he wove about his person a legend that defied verification. All that is known with certainty is that he was a Vili by birth and, unlike his coastal compatriots who never sailed outside their territorial waters, had an unusually adventurous life. It gave him perspective and sophistication, though not from book learning, as well as a practical outlook that made him appear shrewd and resourceful to his compatriots.

In 1946, after deserting from the Belgian army, he returned to his native land. He lived successively in Pointe Noire and Brazzaville and, in 1947, at Dolisie in the Niari valley. There Lassy claimed that he was visited by the Holy Spirit just before midnight on July 5, 1948, while he was reading the Bible. He saw a great light and heard the voice of Jesus Christ—and no one contradicted him. In 1951 he joined the Salvation Army, and two years later became one of its soldiers, but this remarkable Vili could not long remain satisfied with a secondary role. With the aid of Tchicaya, who saw in Lassy the makings of a second Matsoua, he was installed at Tchicaya's expense on a coffee plantation near Hollé in the Kouilou region. There he built his first chapel, using some planks and corrugated iron. From this forum, he exhorted the disciples who flocked to hear him to recite their prayers and destroy their fetishes, just as Simon Kimbangou had done before him. Because he dared to destroy fetishes, his disciples concluded that he must be a powerful magician, and they revered him as such. His reputation spread from village to village throughout the Kouilou region, and his name became associated with the performance of miracles which no one actually saw but in which all were ready to believe.

Soon Lassy's help was sought from all directions, and the holy water which he distributed for its healing properties reputedly wrought miracles. It was said that this water could bring the dead to life, restore sanity to madmen, make the paralyzed walk, and cure sterility in women. Villagers called on him to deliver them from ill fortune, and even the Ma Loango, king of the Vili, asked him to exorcise one of his wives. As a prophet, Lassy was no philanthropist, and he hired out his services as healer and magician. In 1954, the Ma Loango accused him of demanding 30,000 francs for effecting imaginary cures among his followers. He collected an estimated 150,000 francs in contributions from converts to his new religion, and Lassy was charged with even selling the candles given him by his worshippers.

Intelligent as he was, Lassy realized that his "profession" involved risks, and he knew that in Africa disaffection comes as rapidly as does notoriety. Mindful of Kimbangou's misadventures and those of Matsoua nearer home, he began to curtail the number of his "miracles," simply suggesting to those who consulted him who were the persons responsible for their troubles. Usually he designated either sorcerers or village chiefs, who soon reaped the consequences of such denunciations.

Claiming to be a prophet of Christ, Lassy founded his church on Christian dogma, but he was careful to take over from Christianity only those aspects that demanded the fewest sacrifices and were the most assimilable to the traditional beliefs that are the way of life for rural Africans. The acts of faith that Lassy advocated were contrary to those he had been taught from childhood by the Christian missionaries in Moyen-Congo. Lassy won followers because they found in him their Black prophet, and they saw in his cult a great African religion. His church spread throughout southern Moyen-Congo,[4] and it was based on an ethical code inspired by the Bible and the Koran, both of which he interpreted very freely.

Nevertheless, because some of his doctrines ran counter to custom, Lassy at times found himself in conflict with the traditional chiefs, who often maintained their authority through the fears inspired by fetishist practices. Yet even if Lassy encountered such hostility, he enjoyed the support of the great mass of his followers. His church services always ended with a "dance of allelujah," and they attracted regular attendance. In such meetings, the participants experienced the mystical experience that they sought, and they also shared in sacred rites that harmonized with their traditions. Not infrequently at the end of the dance, men and women entered into a trance and fell to the ground in ecstasy, just as they did during pagan village rites.

Contrary to what one might expect and to what Matsoua did, Lassy was careful to respect the administration's regulations. Furthermore, he never gave any signs of xenophobia, and even welcomed the presence of Europeans at his services. For Lassy, the Congo-Ocean railroad served as an easy means of penetrating the countryside, and his reputation spread from one station to the next, carrying his legend to remote areas. Liberal-minded, Lassy closely followed the political evolution of his country. Whereas the Matsouanists adhered to a policy that long kept them away from the polls, Lassy made it a duty for his disciples to vote. His followers could seek election, but neither Lassy nor any of his catechists became candidates. In this way, Lassy, who in a short time made thousands of converts, became an interesting pawn on the chessboard of Congolese politics.

To turn now to other developments in the PPC's evolution, Decorade, one of that party's assemblymen, campaigned in the Batéké region against Tchicaya. The immediate effect of his propaganda was to strengthen the SFIO's position in that area. Imitating Goura, Decorade became a candidate for election to the assembly presidency and was successful. Like Tchichelle, he challenged the authority of his superior and was similarly expelled, as were Toundé, Néré, and Kitoko at the same time. But this purge did not stop the party's hemorrhage, for in the Niari valley, Kikhounga-Ngot in turn attacked the PPC leader and his local representatives.

Faced with this open dissidence that was sapping his popularity, Tchicaya backtracked, and followed more strictly the "progressive" beliefs voiced by Lounda. In the senatorial elections, Tchicaya not only forgave Goura his dissidence but actually supported his candidacy, and this gave the PPC a fresh victory. Tchicaya's confidence was thereby restored on the eve of the legislative elections of 1956, and he tried to rally his forces. During the parliamentary recess, which he spent in Moyen-Congo, Tchicaya paid lengthy visits to all his southern electoral fiefs, but he assigned to his spokesmen that same task in the northern regions because he knew that they were wholly in Opangault's camp. Although Tchicaya was elected deputy for the third consecutive time, he won by a hair's breadth, and this proved to be his last victory.

The socialists were busy making propaganda among both Europeans and Africans. Opangault, taking advantage of the PPC's internal troubles, allied himself with the Batéké and also reinforced his hold over the militants of the Mbochi area. There he was confronted by Dadet, a native of Impfondo, who had just founded the Front Démocratique Congolais, which seemed to be taking root there. Poto-Poto, Brazzaville's most populous district, was already under Opangault's control, and in the Bacongo quarter, he tried to win over the obstinate Lari Matsouanists. Even while the SFIO was assaulting Tchicaya's southern clientele, its militants were not neglecting the northern electorate. Its members were loyal but demanding party supporters.

In Brazzaville, the socialists were so confident of their lead that they already saw themselves taking over control from the quarreling PPC militants. From the vantage point of hindsight, it can be seen that the socialists' optimism blinded them to the rising popularity of Youlou. At that time, however, few could imagine that the Lari, after so many years of passivity, suddenly would be reactivated politically. The somnolent RPF made no effort to profit by the appointment of its deputy Bayrou, as secretary of state for overseas France, to make a fresh start. Actually, that movement existed only at the level of its Metropolitan parliamentarians and first-college assemblymen, and even they had given their votes to Tchicaya's adversaries. Dadet's new party, born in 1955, was to have only an ephemeral existence, despite the inclusion in its membership of such able politicians as N'Zalakanda, Malonga, Kibaht, and Indoh-Baucot—all of whom were to become close collaborators of Youlou in 1961. At Pointe Noire, the socialist grand councilor of FEA, Mathurin Menga, formed the Union Démocratique Municipale, with a view to competing in the forthcoming municipal elections, and he had the moral support of Tchichelle, who now belonged to no organized party. Nevertheless, this new movement had a very limited scope, for the municipal elections did not take place as soon as expected.

The last months of 1955 were taken up with campaigning for the legislative elections to be held in January of the next year, in which it seemed that the chances of the traditional rivals Opangault and Tchicaya were about equal. Opangault was encouraged by the number of candidates, former members of the PPC, who were running in the south, where they were likely to split Tchicaya's vote. Among them were Tchichelle, Dadet, Vouama, Malekat, Kikhounga-Ngot, and now also Abbé Youlou. Since Youlou had been inactive politically since the 1946 elections, he caused general surprise by the ease with which he knew how to turn the neutralism of the Lari to his advantage. Because of their potential dynamism and numerical preponderance, the Lari became the politically determinant force in the territory after emerging from their apathy. Except for a few uncompromising individuals, they unexpectedly participated in the legislative elections of January 2, 1956, and gave strong support to Youlou as Matsoua's worthy successor.

The legislative elections of 1956 were the last held in French Black Africa under the dual-college system. Bayrou, the outgoing deputy of the first college, was reelected by a majority of 2,938 votes, whereas his four opponents divided 3,114 votes among them. The fact that half the registered electors abstained was due to ideological considerations. They preferred not to participate in the election rather than to vote for either the RPF candidates or the others, who in their view lacked serious objectives. As to the second college, never before had so many candidates run for office. Of the total, numbering 10, many were Tchicaya's former followers and friends, and only one—Christian Jayle—was a Frenchman.

The spectacular growth in the registered electorate, from 23,035 in 1946 to 233,544 ten years later, was to some extent a testimonial to the administration's efforts in updating the rolls. Of the 154,363 who went to the polls, the ballots cast by 6,332 were not valid. Tchicaya was elected with 45,976 votes, Opangault received 43,976, Youlou 41,084, and of the remaining seven candidates, Tchichelle topped the list with 4,746. Neither Tchicaya nor Opangault won as large percentages as in the 1951 elections, but it was noteworthy that the deputy retained his seat.

The most striking features of this vote were the success of Youlou and the nascent antagonism between the Lari who remained staunch Matsouanists and those who had transferred their loyalty to the abbé. Now the electorate was divided into three blocs corresponding to the territory's main geographic and ethnic regions. Youlou controlled the Lari area in the southeast, Opangault the northern Likouala-Mossaka and Alima-Léfini regions, and in the southwest Tchicaya dominated in the Niari and Kouilou. The number of nonvalid ballots had declined, but 35 percent of the total still bore the name of Matsoua. (See table for comparative figures on voting percentages in the elections from 1951 through 1953.) This campaign had revived the old charges against Tchicaya to the effect that he had sold out to the administration, had become the white man's deputy, and was concerned solely for the welfare of his Vili fellow tribesmen.

Youlou conducted an effective campaign, for which he had made careful preparations by establishing personal contacts among the Lari and other Bakongo. But so closed to outsiders was that tribal society that few realized until the campaign opened how great was the ascendancy that he had acquired over its members. Other native sons, such as Dr. Sambat-Dalhot, had failed conspicuously in a similar effort to breach the Lari's neutralism. In the early stages of his campaign, Youlou had made the most of his status as a priest, but after his ecclesiastical superiors publicly disapproved of his candidacy, he knew how to exploit their refusal. He also knew how to reawaken Lari mysticism, and at least among the young Lari, he was accepted as the living reincarnation of Matsoua. Those who rejected such a claim now numbered no more than 4,000, whereas in the 1952 elections they had totaled well over 15,000.

These stirrings of the Lari after their long lethargy gave rise to racial agitation in the African districts of Brazzaville, and incidents occurred there that had had no parallel since the time of Matsoua. According to a press dispatch, groups of Youlou's young fanatical supporters went early to the polling booths in Brazzaville, where they intimidated the voters and stoned the police when the latter tried to prevent violence being done to the abbé's adversaries and damage to their property. Buildings and motorcars were set afire and street fighting broke out, and reinforcements had to be sent there to restore order. The day's casualties included some 30 persons wounded and one woman killed. A delay in announcing the results of the second-college vote heightened the political tension, and the fighting, destruction, and looting were resumed the next day. The police and armed forces were caught between the hostile groups, who forgot their mutual antagonism, however, and joined together in molesting the members of those services. Nearly 500 persons were arrested, of whom only about 30 were detained, and all of them were acquitted when tried the following August because there was no conclusive evidence against them.

Aside from several clearly anti-European occurrences, such as the lynching of two missionaries of the St. Pierre mission in Bacongo, the incidents marking this election were, on the whole, tribal in character. They were further aggravated by the political antagonism which for generations had opposed northerners to southerners, the population of the plateaus to those of the river valleys, and the savannah tribesmen to the forest peoples. On January 5, Opangault and Youlou simultaneously issued appeals for calm. In pleading for unity among all Africans of good will, the abbé took the press to task for implying that these incidents were racially inspired. He attributed the journalists' misapprehension to their ignorance of Africa, and he resented their insinuation that Africans were incapable of political idealism. Youlou sincerely wanted an emotional union that would raise all the Congo's political problems above tribal strife.

As to the immediate situation, both Youlou and Opangault tried to get Tchicaya's election annulled. They based their arguments on the allegedly defective distribution of ballots, which had disenfranchised many of the electors who had voted in 1951, and on the "irregularities" of Tchicaya's electoral campaign, notably the "moral pressure he exerted on the electorate." Obviously, such charges were weak, but Tchicaya's defeated opponents hoped to save face, cause his election to be annulled, and force a run-off in which they could apply the lessons they had just learned with possibly more favorable results. Despite their efforts, Tchicaya was proclaimed deputy for Moyen-Congo, to the displeasure of the Lari of Bacongo and the socialists of Poto-Poto. This caused a certain tension in Brazzaville, but Youlou, undiscouraged, sought to turn the election to his advantage by uniting his followers in a new political organization.

Notes

1. Bacongo is the name of a district of Brazzaville; Bakongo that of the tribe that inhabited it as well as neighboring areas. See chapter 1, note 1.

2. Mixed communes, such as those of Brazzaville and Pointe Noire until 1956, were administered by elected councilors but headed by officials appointed by the territorial governor as mayors. Full communes, on the other hand, had elected mayors as well as elected councilors.

3. The religious freedom permitted the signatories of the Congo Basin Treaty of 1885 led to the proliferation in French territory of alien movements such as Jehovah's Witnesses and the Salvation Army, as well as those imported from the Belgian Congo. Lassyism and Ngolism in Moyen-Congo, and the cults of Bwiti and of Mademoiselle in Gabon, were among the relatively few indigenous messianic sects in FEA.

4. An administrative report of 1955 gave the number of Lassy's followers in the districts of Pointe Noire as 27,225, in Madingo Kayes as 6,690, in M'Vouti as 4,660, in Dolisie as 1,210, and in Portuguese Cabinda as 6,500.

CHAPTER 4

THE UDDIA AND THE MESAN

The Union Démocratique de Défense des Interêts Africains (UDDIA), which
Youlou organized, had a dual origin. It was born of Youlou's success in the
1956 legislative elections and also of the determination of Barthélemy
Boganda and Roger Guérillot to have their Inter-groupe Libéral Oubanguien
(ILO) take root in Moyen-Congo. This movement, whose aim was to bring Europeans and Africans together, was founded by Guérillot, a French businessman
who represented Oubangui-Chari in the FEA grand council and who had become
the friend and adviser of Boganda, that territory's deputy. Some of Brazzaville's French residents who had been favorable to Youlou were won over by
Guérillot's idealism and persuasiveness, and they agreed to form a group
called the Union du Moyen-Congo. Youlou, backed by Boganda, who was president of both the MESAN and the ILO, then organized his followers into a
political party, the UDDIA, which he founded at Brazzaville.

Showing remarkable political astuteness, Youlou convinced the members
of his UDDIA that he was not discouraged by his defeat in 1956 and would
crush the PPC and SFIO in the forthcoming municipal elections. In a tract
he wrote about the UDDIA, Youlou stated that his organization would not be a
party but a "movement uniting all persons pursuing a common ideal of justice
and progress." By this, Youlou meant to show Tchicaya that he did not intend
to depend on the support of the Lari, the single ethnic group that had given
him 41,000 votes in the January elections, nor on any ideology, nor indeed
even on the Matsoua mystique as his opponents claimed, but on the totality
of the Congolese people. Despite the papal interdiction under which he
labored, this priest was a true leader of men, and his recent electoral success led him to believe that he could create in Moyen-Congo the same mystical
force that had made Boganda's reputation in Oubangui-Chari. Full of good
faith and the will to succeed, Youlou translated his words into deeds. He
immediately appealed for cooperation to his socialist adversaries and to
such PPC dissidents as Tchichelle, Kikhounga-Ngot, and Decorade.

His many and earnest efforts to persuade the socialists and all the
other major politicians to join the UDDIA were doomed to failure. First of
all, it was inconceivable that Opangault and his followers, who had fought
to dominate Moyen-Congo politically for 10 years, would accept being swallowed
up in a new organization whose future was uncertain. Furthermore, the tribalism that has characterized many African political parties made such a rapprochement unthinkable. Despite such rebuffs, Youlou went ahead, and on May
20 had the statutes of his UDDIA duly registered with the authorities. Since
he could count only on his friends and fellow tribesmen in the immediate
future, Youlou gave his party a temporary organization that left the door
ajar for admittance of the new members he hoped to attract. Many wondered

what could be the future of a unity movement formally launched through the medium of tracts and the press. Would the UDDIA survive, or would it die stillborn like so many other African parties? The administrative authorities, very circumspect in their attitude, were skeptical of its survival, given the mercurial behavior of African politicians and the electorate's inconstancy. So many promising movements headed by worthy leaders had lasted only for the duration of an electoral campaign.

The UDDIA's optimistic founder brushed aside the defeatists and the men who advised him to be prudent. He organized his movement by forming regional committees, which he placed in the hands of Lari. Disregarding regional sentiments and ethnic jealousies, Youlou continued zealously to cultivate contacts with an eye on the forthcoming municipal elections. In May 1956 he went to Mayama, where his first visit was to the tomb of Matsoua. In this way, he visibly expressed his gratitude to the "apostle" of the Congolese, indicating that his political strategy was directed at becoming Matsoua's successor. Without trying to destroy the Matsouanist myth that was deeply entrenched among his fellow tribesmen, Youlou cleverly utilized Matsoua's supernatural quality so as to make him the first hero of Congolese independence. Well acquainted with the rites that bound the Lari to their "god," Youlou adopted a line of conduct that combined Christianity with animistic practices. An illustration of this approach was his pouring palm wine on Matsoua's tomb, following the example set by the dead leader's most devoted followers.

Youlou's utterances and deeds, spread by word of mouth, were aimed at creating an image of himself as both a political leader and a true chief, for he knew from his own study of Matsouanism that the Lari felt the need for such a personality. This policy was well timed, for the National Assembly in Paris had just passed the loi-cadre of June 23, 1956, thus granting to the African territories the large measure of autonomy that was to pave the way for the Congo's independence, for which Matsoua allegedly had died.

In the meantime, political alliances were formed and broken in an atmosphere of intense activity and intrigue. The local press reported rumors of "deals" between politicians that were promptly denied. Local prophets variously predicted an alliance between Opangault and Tchicaya or a reconciliation between Tchicaya and Tchichelle, and in this mass of Congolese fantasy there was more fiction than fact. Yet, one new rumor had some basis in truth and this was that Kikhounga-Ngot, after three months of hesitation and multiple contacts, had decided against collaborating with the president of the UDDIA. This became evident when he organized in his native Niari region a new party, related to the SFIO, called the Groupement pour le Progrès Social au Moyen-Congo (GPS).

At Pointe Noire, the dispute between Tchicaya and Tchichelle, which had seemed to be settled, erupted anew. Its revival took the form of a traditional palaver before the Vili Council of Notables of Diosso, which acted as a tribal court of final appeal. By relying on the paramount Vili chief, the Ma Loango, Tchicaya had thought that he could make Tchichelle listen to reason or at least discredit him seriously in the eyes of the Vili people. Tchichelle, treated like a naughty child, refused even to put in an appearance. In retaliation, he undertook an intensive campaign among the Vili on behalf of the UDDIA, in which organization Youlou had shrewdly promoted him to the post of vice-president. Tchicaya surprised his friends by remaining relaxed and passive in the face of Tchichelle's provocations, simply saying that "since he who has the last word is always proven right in Africa, I have plenty of time."

At Brazzaville, Youlou persuaded Dadet and his Front Démocratique Congolais to join the UDDIA. Although this did not appreciably increase the number of UDDIA voters, and although Dadet's political influence was limited to a few of Brazzaville's évolués, nevertheless it brought into the movement a man of some stature and of parliamentary experience gained in the French Union Assembly. Then in August, the Brazzaville Criminal Court acquitted all those who had been arrested for rioting during the January legislative elections. To be sure, Youlou had failed to recruit as their defense lawyer Maître Hector Rivierez—the senator of Oubangui-Chari and Boganda's close friend—yet some credit for the defendants' acquittal rubbed off on the abbé.

Within six months of its founding, Youlou's zeal had transformed the UDDIA, in association with the Union du Moyen-Congo and the ILO, into an organization that could hope to compete on equal terms with the SFIO in the municipal elections of Brazzaville. While touring the Niari region two months before that election, Youlou ran into trouble from the militants of Kikhounga-Ngot's GPS, who prevented him from making a speech. This was enough to convince local observers that the UDDIA was losing momentum. As to the municipal elections in Pointe Noire, the UDDIA seemed to be making no headway despite Tchichelle's activity, for the Lari there were a minority hated by the Vili, who were strong partisans of Tchicaya's PPC. By October 1956, therefore, it looked as if the municipal elections were wide open in Moyen-Congo's two main towns.

Despite his failures with Opangault and Kikhounga-Ngot, and still convinced of the need for union, Youlou tried to win over the main ethnic groups in the territory. Clearly he was trying to follow in the footsteps of his elder, Boganda,[1] who by his nationalist propaganda had created unity among the Oubanguian tribes. Youlou, however, had no greater success with the Bakoukoya[2] than he had had with the Bambouba,[3] who were traditionally hostile to the Lari. Such setbacks were regarded by Youlou as only temporary, and, indeed, he now appeared to be forging ahead. A few weeks before the municipal elections were held, even the most pessimistic forecasters admitted that the UDDIA could at least hold its own against the other political parties in Brazzaville—the SFIO-PPC and the Independents. At Pointe Noire, given the personal influence of the incorrigibly hopeful Tchicaya, the outcome was anybody's guess.

At this point, one must consider the role of Boganda, the controversial leader whose influence had spread beyond the tribes of Oubangui-Chari as far as Brazzaville. Abbé Barthélemy Boganda was born on April 4, 1910, about 90 kilometers north of Bangui. He was a member of the M'Baka tribe that lives along the banks of the Oubangui River and whose members in the nineteenth century were reputed to be cannibals. In June 1946, the small Oubanguian electorate made him deputy, but his success was chiefly due to the backing he received from the mission of the Holy Spirit Fathers. At Bangui, where he had never lived, he was virtually unknown. As soon as he reached France, the orthodox Mouvement Républicain Populaire (MRP)[4] took this priest and apprentice-deputy under its wing. He came to the attention of French officialdom when he published a small mimeographed newspaper called Pour Sauver un Peuple, whose scathing diatribes certainly did not reflect the views of his Catholic mentors. In them, Boganda criticized the French colonial regime by attacking the allegedly "colonialist" methods of the local administration, particularly those practiced by French officials in Oubangui-Chari.

Having observed the tactics of certain of his African colleagues who were affiliated with the French communist or socialist parties, Boganda realized that demagogy paid off. Certainly his attacks might have been frustrated by African lethargy had not the local administration decided to counterattack. In accepting this challenge, Boganda became the number one enemy of the administration and attracted widespread attention. In a territory where the entire economy depended on cotton culture, it was a necessary evil—as Boganda later came to realize—for the administration to compel the population to farm this difficult crop. Rather than earn a miserable pittance from growing cotton, however, the Oubanguian peasants much preferred hunting—a more congenial occupation and one that also gave them food. Although the authorities used all the legal means at their disposal to see that the farmers cultivated their cotton scientifically, this was not always done. In the enforcement of official orders, regrettable abuses occurred, and Boganda exploited them thoroughly for his own purposes.

During his first term in the National Assembly, Boganda was wholly inactive, and so strong was the criticism of his passivity that it seemed unlikely that he would be reelected on January 10, 1951. A few weeks before that election, Boganda was arrested in a market place by the French head of the M'Baiki district on charges of breaking certain administrative regulations. For some time, Boganda deliberately had skirted the limits of legality, and the exasperated administration, seeing in this incident its chance to chastise him, chose the wrong moment to do so. He was kept under surveillance in a comfortable temporary dwelling for 24 hours, then released with a legal reprimand. This incident gave him the halo of a martyr to French colonialism and assured him of reelection to the National Assembly for another five-year term, with a greatly enhanced reputation. (On March 20, 1951, a court for minor offenses sentenced him to two months in prison, but the sentence never was carried out.)

In the National Assembly, few of Boganda's colleagues could claim to know him personally or even to have seen him at its sessions, and he soon left the MRP to join the ranks of the Paysans Indépendants. On the other hand, the officials of the Ministry of Overseas France in Paris were well informed about Boganda and his tirades, which grew more numerous in the course of time and often caused difficulties for the Oubanguian administration. All the governors of Oubangui-Chari between 1946 and 1958 had reason to keep close track of his activities.

Unlike Tchicaya, who preferred Paris to his native land, Boganda—who had abandoned his cassock and married his French secretary—spent less and less time in France and devoted himself increasingly to his Oubanguian constituents. After his election to the territorial assembly in 1952, he concentrated on the MESAN, the party which he had founded, and installed branches throughout the territory. His consistent opposition to the administration and his flamboyant anticolonialism pleased the elite. He also found zealous propagandists among the lower ranks of African government employees, who sent him written memoranda about what was going on in the administration. Playing the martyr's role, Boganda seemed to be the leader who could hold his own against the whites, especially the highest-ranking French officials. He refused to recognize their authority during his tours of the country, and dared even to talk back to the governor. Boganda carefully cultivated an image which gave him a mystique much appreciated in the rural areas and especially by his women admirers. In 1957, thousands of his compatriots gathered on the banks of the Oubangui River to see him walk on the water. When, after hours of vain waiting, he did not appear, the administration was blamed for his failure.

From that time on, all that Boganda had to do was to cultivate his legend. He pursued the only policy effective among Africans—that of personal contacts—and left to his wife the task of replying to the many letters sent to him. In all the villages that he visited, he never failed to criticize the administration. He blamed it for forcing the population to work, punishing those who worked badly, and failing to provide enough schools and dispensaries. For this demagogic deputy, Oubangui-Chari was a gold mine. The peasantry, bemused by the Boganda legend, were more willing to pay a tax to their deputy than to the district officer. Boganda's tours proved to be an excellent investment, for they brought him the funds needed to maintain his coffee plantation in Bobangui.

In the territorial assembly, Boganda and his followers opposed on principle the proposals made by their colleagues of the first college and by the handful of African members of the RPF. The sometimes scurrilous demagoguery of the MESAN assemblymen often led them to attack France and the local administration on the charge that never was enough done for the Africans. Everything not initiated by the MESAN was colonialist in their eyes. What France had done to promote social progress was denigrated, and the Metropole was accused of living off the wealth of Oubangui-Chari, stealing its best lands for the benefit of European planters, causing Africans to go hungry by forbidding them to kill wild animals, and exploiting the country's mineral resources without any benefit to the natives. It must be said, however, that such charges were not peculiar to Oubangui-Chari but often were used against European colonial regimes in Africa.

The rebellion started by Boganda spread beyond the confines of his territory as far as the boundaries of FEA. The Oubanguian grand councilors, meeting at Brazzaville, were effective propagandists among their colleagues from other parts of the federation. Having learned how to promote the cult of his personality, Boganda used his influence with Oubanguian emigrants to spread his renown in Moyen-Congo, Tchad, Cameroun, and even the Belgian Congo. The ILO, which he founded with the aid of Guérillot when the single college was about to be instituted under the provisions of the loi-cadre, aimed at effecting a rapprochement between the white and black populations. Although it was not welcomed wholeheartedly by the Europeans, who feared being ostracized as traitors to the white man's cause, it acquired enough support to expand Boganda's influence throughout FEA. Even more, it helped to attenuate the reputation for xenophobia that he had acquired because of his speeches in the territorial assembly. (Later, when the territories were moving toward independence, Boganda launched his proposal for a republic of African peoples comprising the four states of FEA, Cameroun, and some parts of the Belgian Congo.)

At Brazzaville, Boganda found Youlou receptive to his ambitious scheme, and the latter agreed to head the Moyen-Congo branch of the ILO. Because of Youlou's undeniable popularity there, Boganda could be sure of a responsive audience among the évolués of the federal capital. After his victory in the January 1956 legislative elections and his even greater success when he ran for mayor of Bangui 10 months later, Boganda became the undisputed leader of the only territory in FEA where political, not to say national, unity over and above ethnic groups had been achieved. Boganda's election to the presidency of the Grand Council in March 1957 confirmed his position as FEA's outstanding political leader. His skill as a debater, together with his political experience, enhanced his popularity among the Brazzavillians, where the fair-sized colony of Oubanguian expatriates provided him with an excellent medium for his propaganda.

From then on, Boganda divided his time between Bangui and Brazzaville. His increasingly frequent attacks on the administration were as warmly received in the federal capital as in Bangui. Under the loi-cadre, Boganda became the Federation's premier spokesman in dealing with the French government. Although the passage of that law justified his decade-long attacks against the administration, Boganda was not satisfied with this half measure, and he remained in the background the better to continue the struggle, or so he claimed. Without assuming the slightest responsibility, Boganda was the behind-the-scenes manipulator of the Oubanguian government council during the short period when the loi-cadre was in force.

With the birth of the Central African Republic as an autonomous member of the Franco-African Community in 1958, Boganda became the vice-president of its first government council. Thus, within the span of 13 years, this once timid and colorless rural curé of the Holy Spirit Mission had achieved his ambition and had become a star in overseas politics. Unfortunately, he did not long enjoy the power that wisdom, moderation, and a sense of African realities had brought to him, for he died in an airplane accident on March 29, 1959, a few weeks after becoming prime minister.

Notes

1. See below and the biographical appendix.

2. The Bakoukoya, to the number of some 15,000, were a subgroup of the Batéké tribe who lived in the Djambala region, north of Brazzaville. Unlike most of the Batéké, who were hunters and fishermen, the Bakoukoya were skillful farmers.

3. Bambouba, or Bambamba, was an alternative name used in French sources for the Ambété tribe, whose habitat extends from the Okondja-Franceville region southward to the area between Sibiti and the Niari.

4. The Mouvement Républicain Populaire, a liberal Catholic party, was influential in French politics during the early post-World War II years.

CHAPTER 5

MOYEN-CONGO ELECTIONS AND THE RDA
IN FRENCH EQUATORIAL AFRICA, 1956-57

At Brazzaville, the intransigence of the socialist leaders was responsible for the failure of their negotiations with the radicals on the issue of sponsoring a common list of candidates. For the same reason, the plan for a large-scale coalition against Youlou, comprising the SFIO, radicals, PPC, Independents, and RPF, proved abortive. At about this time, however, the UMC (the ILO's branch in Moyen-Congo) was able with some difficulty to present a mixed slate of candidates which included European members of the UMC and Africans of the UDDIA. During the lively campaign that preceded the Brazzaville municipal elections of November 1956, the chances of the UMC-UDDIA coalition and those of the PPC-SFIO candidates seemed to be about even.

The somewhat surprising outcome was a victory for Youlou and the eight Europeans and 14 Africans who ran on his ticket. Opangault's SFIO carried 11 seats and the PPC only three. In the numerical tally, the coalition candidates captured 20,907 of the 38,519 votes cast in the first municipal elections held under the single-college system in Brazzaville. Consequently, the post of mayor went to Youlou as head of the UDDIA, and 11 of the 47 new councilors were Europeans. Of the five men who became assistant mayors, three were members of the UDDIA and two belonged to the UMC.

At Pointe Noire, Tchicaya was so confident of victory that he did little active campaigning, and this left the field open to his active young rival, Tchichelle. Five outstanding Europeans belonging to the public and private sectors ran on Tchicaya's ticket, whereas Tchichelle had chosen less well-known Frenchmen. Contrary to the tactics used by the SFIO of Brazzaville, the Pointe Noire socialists, inexplicably, had joined forces with the UMC and the UDDIA. As a result of these elections, nine seats on the Pointe Noire municipal council were awarded to the PPC, nine to the SFIO, and eight to the UDDIA. This overwhelming victory for Tchichelle and his followers astonished even the local officials. Only in the districts where Europeans formed a majority of the electorate did a party affiliated with the PPC win. Elsewhere, Tchichelle's tidal wave had so shattered the position of the overconfident Tchicaya that there could be no doubt of a complete reversal in the attitude of Pointe Noire's electors. The 7,483 votes cast for Tchichelle's party (compared with 3,653 for the PPC) gave him 22 of the council's 31 seats, as well as the post of mayor. His three assistants were also among the successful UDDIA-SFIO candidates.

In Brazzaville, Youlou lost no time in preparing for the March 1957 elections to the territorial assembly. The UDDIA leaders, soon after their municipal victory, decided to reorganize the movement by enlarging its central committee. Two of the newcomers—the Batéké Marcel Ibalico, and the

Mbochi Jean Kibaht—were deserters from the Front Démocratique Congolais, and they were named, respectively, general secretary and treasurer of the party. Still pursuing his goal of national unity, Youlou renewed his efforts to win support from all the territory's ethnic groups. Equally concerned for the emancipation of African women, he now planned to appoint a woman to the party's technical council.

Stepping up his contacts with the Lari, on whom he continued to rely, Youlou again journeyed to Mayama, where he once more decorated the tomb of Matsoua and those of three Matsouanists who had been executed. He was careful to see that the tributes he paid to those men as responsible for the grant of universal suffrage to Africans reached the ears of the French administrators. Westerners gave different interpretations to this tactic. Some believed that in this way the new mayor of Brazzaville was courting the uncompromising Matsouanists. Others, however, thought that by placing a wreath on Matsoua's tomb he was shrewdly intent on proving that Matsoua was dead, so as to benefit from destroying the legend of Matsoua's immortality.

On his propaganda tours, Youlou adopted the strategy that Boganda had used so effectively. This consisted generally of denigrating the French administration and especially its officials, whom he derisively called "petits lieutenants de brousse" instead of commandants, the term by which they were known to the rural population. By espousing the cause of the Matsouanist resistance, Youlou probably was consciously cultivating nationalist sentiments among his auditors. It was in this same Lari milieu that N'Gounzism had taken root in 1921 with the slogan "Africa for the Africans."

The attractive prospects of a membership in the territorial assembly, and especially of the perquisites that came with it, made Youlou's followers into ardent propagandists for the UDDIA. Kibaht founded a branch of that party among his fellow tribesmen of the north. Not daring, however, to be a candidate in Mbochi territory, which was solidly prosocialist, he ran in the Djoué district of Brazzaville. (At the time there was talk of founding a UDDIA section in Léopoldville, but nothing came of this because the Belgian authorities would not have tolerated it.) Youlou persisted in his attempts to win over tribes other than the Lari, and in order to make headway with the Batéké and their "king," Makoko, he enlisted the services of the king's nephew, Prosper Gandzion.

While Youlou was busily promoting his own movement, great changes were taking place in the ranks of the French West African socialists. In June 1956, the Senegalese branch of the SFIO had voted in favor of autonomy from its parent organization in France, which already had encouraged such a move. Decisive action to this effect was taken at a congress held in Conakry, Guinea, on January 11, 1957, at which an autonomous Mouvement Socialiste Africain (MSA) was constituted for all French Black Africa. During this meeting, Lamine Guèye, the newly elected president of the MSA, came out strongly against forming a single party for the two federations. (At about the same time as the MSA was formed, the IOM under Senghor's auspices held a congress at Dakar which gave birth to another autonomous interterritorial political movement, the Convention Africaine.)

No delegate from FEA attended the Conakry congress, but that Federation's SFIO leadership telegraphed its support in principle to the new MSA. However, since Opangault and Kikhounga-Ngot remained, respectively, president and vice-president of the local socialists, there was no fundamental change made in their status or in that of their party. Actually, FEA's socialist leaders were far more preoccupied with the forthcoming assembly elections. In the party organs—L'Indépendance of the MSA and Le Progrès of the UDDIA— polemics were written and personal quarrels aired in an atmosphere of growing tension. Tchicaya's PPC now seemed to be out of the running, for that party's following was more and more restricted to the Vili of Pointe Noire.

Despite the mutual animosity displayed by Brazzaville's two political groups, attempts at a rapprochement were made by the more conciliatory members of both blocs. Once again, Youlou agreed in principle to meet with the MSA leaders in the hope of reaching a preelectoral understanding. And once again, due to the intransigence of those militants who would have nothing to do with the PPC and former members of the RPF, no working agreement could be reached. Already, it could be seen that Youlou was caught on the horns of the same dilemma. He was torn between his ambition to play a wider leadership role and his desire to satisfy his bigoted Lari tribal militants. So again, it was with the European members of the UMC that Youlou came to an understanding as to the list of candidates which they and the UDDIA would jointly sponsor.

As in November 1956, the territorial assembly elections were held with all the registered adult Congolese voting in a single college. In a total population of 759,767, the number of voters on the rolls had grown from 189,936 in 1952 to 400,847 in 1957. As to the distribution of the 45 assembly seats to be filled, one was assigned to the Likouala circumscription, two to Sangha, six to Likouala-Mossaka, seven each to Djoué and the Pool, four to Niari-Bouenza, eight to Niari, and five to Kouilou. In this election, 73.68 percent of the registered electorate participated, whereas in that of 1952, only half of the second-college electorate had voted. Of the assemblymen elected, nine were Europeans, two mulattoes, and the rest Africans.

As in the other FEA territories, a large number of candidates had been induced to compete due to the considerable material benefits accruing to the post of assemblyman in the form of salary, perquisites, and patronage. Consequently, when Youlou was drawing up his slate of candidates, he was besieged by more than 200 applicants, and for both sentimental and political reasons, he found it difficult to say "no" to his militants. Among the socialists, there were fewer aspirants. In general, the electoral campaign passed off calmly, and although emotions reached fever-pitch during the final week, the situation never got out of hand. Very few candidates voiced xenophobic slogans, and only a handful tried to gain popularity by denouncing Europeans for monopolizing their ancestral lands—a strategy that had been used by Boganda during his preelection tours.

The Congolese electorate gave 22 assembly seats to the UDDIA-UMC, as against 20 to the MSA, one to the PPC, and two to Independents. In the territory as a whole, the UDDIA won in four regions and the MSA in five. After the UDDIA's success in the municipal elections, Youlou and his followers had expected better results, especially in the Sangha region, where the socialists' victory surprised them. Just to keep up appearances, Youlou naturally claimed another triumph for his movement, but he had no illusions as to the slenderness of his majority.

Once the assembly elections were over, the outstanding question was that of the UDDIA's affiliation with Houphouët-Boigny's RDA, but for this

Tchicaya remained a serious obstacle. Since 1946, the Congolese deputy had been the supporter and friend of Houphouët-Boigny. On the level of local politics, Tchicaya's PPC, affiliated with the RDA, nevertheless had allied itself with the MSA the better to combat the UDDIA. To ask an elder states-man like Tchicaya to yield his top rank and play second fiddle to his junior, Youlou, was unthinkable. For its part, the RDA, viewed in the over-all scene of African political alliances, had every reason to welcome the overtures made to it by the UDDIA, of whose importance there was no longer any doubt.

It was well known that Houphouët-Boigny had long cherished the plan of creating a Franco-African Community, for which the RDA would serve as springboard. Although the territorial elections of March 1957 had been favorable to the RDA, Houphouët-Boigny was clearly worried by the growing activity of Senghor's Convention Africaine and Lamine Guèye's MSA; hence, he sought support in FEA. In Tchad, Houphouët-Boigny could count on Lisette, and in Gabon on Léon Mba (neither of whom favored the primary federation of African states advocated by Senghor). But in Moyen-Congo, he was reluctant to sacrifice his friend Tchicaya in order to gain the support of Youlou, even though Tchicaya was no longer of any political value to him. As to Oubangui-Chari, Boganda had no intention of allying his MESAN with the RDA, despite the efforts made by Lisette to convert him. To Boganda, the loi-cadre represented no progress for Black Africa—in fact, it perpetuated colonialism. In a speech before the Oubanguian assembly on October 5, 1957, Boganda claimed that he was loyal to France and "obsessed" by its revolu-tionary spirit of 1789. He also said, however, that that spirit had been betrayed by the loi-cadre, or at least by the way it was being applied in Africa by the local French administration.

As far as the RDA was concerned, the Oubanguian leader considered him-self the equal of Houphouët-Boigny and had no desire to be his second-in-command. He further disagreed with the Ivory Coast leader's refusal to ac-cept an elected federal executive in the place of the governments-general. If Houphouët-Boigny wanted to unite all French West Africa under the RDA banner, Boganda aimed at bringing all the FEA parties together in his Inter-groupe. To Boganda, both Federations were part and parcel of Black Africa, but each of them had its own character and required different types of gov-ernment. Because their economic problems were dissimilar, political unity between them was to him inconceivable.

Long and difficult negotiations between Houphouët-Boigny and Youlou were carried on successively by two RDA envoys, Dr. Sylla and Ouezzin Couli-baly, and also by the UDSR's special emissary and Lisette. Finally, on May 20, 1957, Youlou agreed to sign a request for the UDDIA's membership in the RDA-UDSR. It was left to the RDA congress, scheduled to be held later in the year at Bamako, to decide whether the PPC should be evicted from the movement or be integrated into the UDDIA, and in the latter case, what post should be offered to Tchicaya by way of compensation. The semiofficial affiliation of the UDDIA with the wholly African RDA and with the Metropoli-tan UDSR posed another problem on the local level: what was to be done with the European members of the UMC, who had run on the same ticket as those of the UDDIA and among whom there were some whose personalities were antipa-thetic to the UDSR leadership? Thus, an issue that appeared at first to concern only Moyen-Congo was transformed into a problem for all of French

Black Africa. Finally, it was decided to sweep the whole matter under the rug, maintain the status quo, and hope that time would resolve the difficulty.

At the RDA congress held at Bamako, Soudan, in September 1957, which was ignored by Boganda and his MESAN, FEA was represented by about 20 delegates, a handful compared with the 800 from French West Africa. All the RDA delegates unanimously favored a large political and economic grouping for Black Africa, and a democratic Franco-African Community to be created on the basis of equality among its members. The question of creating executive governments at the federal level was not on the agenda, but this question divided Ivory Coast and Gabon from the majority of RDA delegates, who favored such governments. Strongly criticized by some of his own militants, Houphouët-Boigny threatened to resign from the presidency of the RDA, and a breakup of that movement was barely avoided.

A compromise was reached in an ambiguous resolution advocating a democratization of the existing federal executive organs. With the delegates' tacit agreement, the question of a regrouping of African parties was discussed. At that juncture, Lamine Guèye, who had defended the multiplicity of parties as recently as January, appealed for unity, and to this Houphouët-Boigny immediately acquiesced, since it was the goal set by the RDA as long ago as 1946. The RDA's insistence on its exclusive and "permanent vocation to unite all the living forces in French Black Africa" was incorporated in the final resolution passed by the Bamako congress. The ways and means of reaching that goal, however, were to be determined by another conference on the regrouping of parties, which was to be organized by the RDA's coordinating committee. Although the Bamako congress did no more than pass ambiguous resolutions and the RDA subsequently failed to unite the Black African parties, it nevertheless marked a turning point in the emancipation of the African colonies.

CHAPTER 6

MSA-UDDIA RIVALRY

Moyen-Congo's first government council was elected on May 15, 1957, by its newly installed territorial assemblymen. Since they were divided into almost equal blocs, the governor urged them to give proof of their civic spirit when choosing the councilors.

From the outset, the 22 assemblymen belonging to the UDDIA ran into opposition from the 20 MSA members, who allied themselves with the three remaining colleagues who had belonged to neither party when elected. This working agreement gave the MSA a majority of one vote in the new assembly. If the governor were to permit the majority party to form the government council, he risked transforming the UDDIA assemblymen into a permanent opposition. After long negotiations, the governor agreed on the assignment of five portfolios to each of the two blocs, with the vice-presidency[1] going to one of the MSA ministers. In Western terms, this was a logical solution, but in African eyes, it was a very precarious one because of the bigoted attitude of the two parties. It was severely criticized by both the UDDIA and the MSA militants, to whom ethnic predominance was more important than other considerations.

This tribal hostility, against which Youlou and the administration had struggled ever since the incidents of January 2, 1956, was to cause a rapid deterioration of the territory's political stability. Looking back on this decision, one now wonders if it might not have been better to experiment with a homogeneous council, for that would have placed the minority clearly in an opposition stance and one that conceivably might have become constructive. In trying to appease both parties, from neither of which good will could be expected, national interests were certainly sacrificed and the budding strength of subversion encouraged.

After many palavers, the UDDIA was awarded the portfolios of labor, health, and housing (which went to Tchichelle), budget (Vial, the European UMC assemblyman from Djoué), agriculture, livestock, water, and forests (Youlou), and finance (Zakété, not a member of the assembly but spokesman for the Babembe[2] in the UDDIA). To the MSA were allotted the ministries of economic affairs (Kikhounga-Ngot), education and youth (Mambéké-Boucher, a member of the Jeunesse MSA but not of the assembly), civil service (Nardon, a European socialist who had been elected on the UDDIA ticket from Kouilou), and industrial production (Kerhervé, a European who described himself as an Independent but who had been elected on the MSA slate) as well as the vice-presidency of the council (Opangault).

Inside the government council, the behavior of both rival blocs was marked by random agreements and quarrels occurring in rapid succession and within the restricted radius of Brazzaville, Pointe Noire, and Dolisie. During the first few weeks of the council's existence, there was no calming of political passions that would have enabled its members to work together harmoniously in the country's general interest. Instead, their mutual animosity even found fresh stimulus in the hotly disputed election of Boganda as president of the FEA grand council, despite the concerted opposition to his candidacy from the territorial branches of the RDA.

By this time the UDDIA, whose demise had long been predicted, was one year old. Now the leaders of that nascent movement had to cope with experienced adversaries who subjected them to a war of nerves—alliances followed by ruptures, agreements alternating with discord. The ILO and UDDIA press organ, Le Progrès,[3] encountered grave financial difficulties. Then the European members of the UMC, who had been elected on the UDDIA ticket, were systematically denigrated by the UDDIA militants who wanted to take their places. Among the young people, the spirit of nationalism and tribalism grew apace. The flexible Youlou did not permit such difficulties to trouble his serenity. He tried to control his own followers as well as the administration, which was still "colonialist" in his eyes despite the loi-cadre. He even cold-shouldered Boganda, whose expanding influence caused him concern. At Brazzaville, where the growing number of unemployed was daily heightening social tension, the problem of collecting taxes became especially acute for him as mayor. Yet, alongside these difficulties, Youlou enjoyed compensations that gratified his ego. During a trip to Paris, he was made president of the mayors' association of Overseas France.

Ignoring his militants, who wanted him to jettison the European members of the UMC, Youlou succeeded in having a Frenchman, René Mahé, elected president of the UDDIA bloc in the territorial assembly. This determination to govern, come what may, was characteristic of Youlou. To intrigues he reacted by making his own decisions, which were often contrary to those advocated by his entourage. He tried to remain loyal to those who had early befriended him, and when he yielded to external pressures it was never done on impulse. By temperament, Youlou could not remain inactive, and he was far better at proselytizing and handling controversy than he was at administration and desk work. Hardly had he returned from Paris than he started out on a tour of his constituencies. His main objective was to win political control of the Niari region, formerly a PPC stronghold but currently the preserve of Kikhounga-Ngot, whose refusal to join the UDDIA Youlou could not soon forgive. Relying on Senator Goura and on Senator Sathoud, a former territorial assemblyman whom he had persuaded to join the UDDIA, Youlou went after Kikhounga-Ngot until he had rendered him harmless. During one of his many tours of the Mayombé area in September, Youlou was involved in an automobile accident which some believed to have been an attempt on his life by Kikhounga-Ngot.

As time went on, the tension between the UDDIA and MSA became aggravated, for the need to give the country a good government failed to check the politicians' intrigues. Youlou was torn between his desire to attend the RDA congress at Bamako, where the UDDIA's alliance with that movement was to be discussed, and that of promoting construction of the Kouilou dam as zealously as were his political rivals. In the end he went to Paris, accompanied by Tchichelle and Vandelli as members of a delegation that also included the socialists Opangault, Nardon, and Kerhervé. This clearly showed that Youlou gave priority to local over wider problems, even those that were to be debated at such an important congress as that called by the RDA. Nevertheless, Moyen-Congo was represented at the Bamako congress—which opened on September 25, 1957—by Mahé, Joseph Goma, and Philippe Bikamou.

Concurrent reports of growing dissensions among Youlou's followers naturally delighted members of the MSA, who did not try to hide their satisfaction. Although the reports were probably exaggerated, there was no doubt that a persistent malaise plagued the government council—a phenomenon common to many other francophone Black African countries. An example was the refusal by the UDDIA ministers to attend the November 21 assembly meeting on the ground that their leaders had been libeled by the MSA, but neither party showed restraint in showering abuse on its rival. A few days later, Georges Yambot, the MSA assemblyman from Niari, defected from his party to join the UDDIA, a move that surprised everyone. Since this now made the UDDIA the majority party in the assembly, Youlou immediately insisted that he should head a new government council.

The "Yambot affair," as it came to be called in Moyen-Congo, has been much written about.[4] It shook both parties to their foundations, exacerbated emotions, and so troubled the atmosphere in Pointe Noire, the territorial capital, that it risked causing trouble in the assembly, which was then holding its budgetary session. The militants of both parties were stirred up to such a point that only a spark was needed to set off the powder keg. Yambot, as the precious embodiment of the UDDIA's one-vote majority, was heavily guarded by his new masters, and it was even rumored that to keep him safe he would be sent to a comfortable place in the Lari region. The hide-and-seek game played around the person of Yambot for more than a month transformed Pointe Noire, according to the journalists who covered this story, into the setting for a Western movie. It culminated in an official reconciliation between Youlou and Opangault, and in the governor's presence they stated their desire for a "union in which we can work together for the welfare of Moyen-Congo without regard to personal considerations." Once again, political calm seemed to be restored, and by mutual agreement the "Yambot affair" was pushed into the background. In the absence of the turncoat assemblyman, who lived under the watchful eyes of his new friends, the budgetary session resumed its normal course.

In its evolution and growth, the UDDIA underwent ups and downs. Vial, as a European and journalist, was criticized sharply, as was Dadet because he was not a Lari. Youlou himself was not immune from attacks by his militants, who charged him with encouraging a "cult of personality." There was also friction between the party's executive committee and its parliamentary group, and between the former body and the regional committees. The atmosphere became oppressive with tribal quarrels, to which were added personal animosities and material difficulties. All these developments confirmed the truth of the saying that "if politics feeds a man, it also whets his appetite." Youlou seemed to be unaffected by his followers' intrigues, and the year 1957 ended with a highly optimistic proclamation issued by the UDDIA's executive committee.

The year 1957, in which the institutions decreed under the loi-cadre began functioning and Opangault and Youlou were apparently reconciled, was marked by two other significant events. Briefly, these were the disappearance from the political scene of Tchicaya's PPC and the rapid rise of Youlou's UDDIA. The PPC was now represented in the assembly by only two members, one a European and the other an African, and they had been elected on the slate jointly sponsored with the MSA. In part, the PPC's steady decline since the elections of January 2, 1956, was due to a change in the voting system. Had the system of proportional representation been retained, the PPC could have counted on winning from six to eight seats in the assembly. It is noteworthy that until the Fifth Republic was born in September 1958, the three seats allotted to Moyen-Congo in the French parliamentary bodies were held by members of the PPC, a party virtually unrepresented in the territorial assembly. This paradoxical situation hardly facilitated the work of the Congolese parliamentarians, cut off as they were from the elected assemblymen and from the mass of the population, who claimed that they were unrepresentative.

Logically enough, the disappearance of the PPC left room for the rise of the UDDIA, which—with 23 seats in the assembly and control of the municipal councils of Brazzaville and Pointe Noire—became the premier party of Moyen-Congo. The political rise of Youlou also seemed to sound the death knell for Matsouanism, or in any case for Balalism, since it was the Lari who had become aroused from their apathy to elect him. Between 1946 and 1960, the number of Lari voting for Matsoua declined from 4,422 to 535, an undeniable testimonial to the UDDIA and especially to its leader. Another development indicated by the March 1957 elections is significant. This was its highlighting of the role played by the traditional chiefs and Notables in influencing the choice of candidates to be sponsored by the various parties. In recent years, the French administration had seriously underestimated the authority of the chiefs, who in some rural areas had maintained sufficient influence with the population to play the role of "Great Electors."

In analyzing the political forces still active in 1957, the situation in the Kouilou region deserves mention. There, very exceptionally, the PPC retained a nucleus of supporters who served as a base of operations for its ally, the MSA, which was still having trouble in gaining a foothold among the urban population of Pointe Noire. By this means, the PPC-MSA coalition could oppose the UDDIA—which only recently had become active in that region—on almost equal terms. However, from the African viewpoint, it would be more accurate to speak of the followers of Tchichelle and those of Tchicaya rather than use party labels that were almost meaningless. Since the municipal elections of November 1956, Tchichelle, as leader of the UDDIA in that area, for all practical purposes had forged ahead of his former master. Tchichelle should be given credit for devoting himself wholeheartedly to the UDDIA cause without trying to benefit personally by his popularity with the Vili. Just as Youlou had attracted the Lari, including a goodly proportion of the diehard Matsouanists, so Tchichelle allied himself with Lassy, who had founded the N'Zambie-Bougie sect. Lassy had induced his followers to vote for Tchichelle in the March 1957 territorial elections, in retaliation for which Tchicaya's Pointe Noire partisans destroyed many of his sect's chapels.

The situation in the Niari region was quite the reverse of that in the Kouilou. In the former area, the PPC militants not only opposed the MSA but were drawing closer to the UDDIA under the local leadership of Goura and Sathoud. Although by the end of 1957 there was still no formal merger between them, the results of the March elections indicated the trends: 29,489 votes were cast for the MSA compared with 29,685 for the informal PPC-UDDIA alliance. Apparently the political forces arrayed against each other in the Niari were in balance, but it could not be assumed that party discipline would be effectively maintained in regard to that "coalition" in the next elections. It depended on the way in which the relatively recent and flourishing N'Zambie sect would move, and this could not be foreseen. Kikhounga-

Ngot and his fellow socialists followed very closely the activities of the highly opportunistic Lassy Zépherin, to see if he would come out openly in favor of the UDDIA in the Niari as he had done in the Kouilou.

Despite the MSA's activity in the Niari-Bouenza region, it seemed likely that the UDDIA would long be able to maintain its ascendancy there. In the March elections, the UDDIA, with 17,494 votes, had won handily over the PPC-MSA alliance, which received only 6,883, for the Mouyondzi district alone remained loyal to Tchicaya. Although some chiefs who formerly had been pro-Youlou later came to favor the PPC, Youlou remained the undisputed leader of that region, as he was of the Pool and Djoué. The propaganda activity of the assemblyman Lounda on behalf of the PPC did not avail against the control maintained by the UDDIA in all the Lari districts, where the Matsouanist irreconcilables had been reduced to a few hundred. If it could be said almost without reservation that the UDDIA commanded a majority throughout the south, it was equally true that Opangault's MSA was as firmly entrenched in the north.

In Opangault's native Likouala-Mossaka, where the UDDIA had boldly tried to form some branches, the MSA's influence was not breached, and Youlou's followers had nothing to show for their efforts. To be sure, the top UDDIA leaders never risked appearing in person there, where the Lari were known to be highly unpopular. In the March assembly elections, the MSA had won 39,518 votes to 3,395 for its adversaries, and such local opposition to Opangault as existed in Likouala-Mossaka had no ideological basis but derived from contests between his individual partisans. Much the same situation prevailed in in the Batéké region of Alima-Léfini, where the ascendancy of the MSA remained unassailable despite the intensive propaganda undertaken on behalf of the UDDIA by two popular native sons, Ibalico and Gandzion. In the March 1957 elections, the MSA-PPC coalition won 27,008 votes and the UDDIA only 1,698.

Turning to the Likouala region, where the Mbochi were a numerical minority, the MSA could count on the votes of no more than half of the electorate. That region's vote in March 1957 was split four ways, the MSA winning 4,662, the MESAN 3,027, the Independent Socialists 1,376, and the Independents 780. That the MESAN took only second place was due to the greater accessibility of Bangui than of Brazzaville to some of the Likouala villages. Finally, in the Sangha region, the MSA maintained its control of about a third of the population, although the UDDIA had been very active in Ouesso and Souanké. Again the dispersal of votes between the candidates of four groups enabled the socialists to chalk up a modest victory.

Summarizing the political situation during the crucial last months of 1957, it could be said that all the area south of Alima-Léfini was dominated by Youlou's party, and that the north was controlled by the MSA. This rough division provides the explanation for Youlou's gerrymandering tactics on the eve of the June 14, 1959, legislative elections.[5] Politicians concentrated their attention on the three towns of Brazzaville, Pointe Noire, and Dolisie. At year's end, the reconciliation between Youlou and Opangault brought about an easing of the tension, long hoped for by all and especially by the French administration, thus enabling the government council to deal with pending business and the assembly to complete its budgetary session.

Nevertheless, the truce between the two main political leaders, played up in the local press, once again drew sharp criticism from both the MSA and

UDDIA militants, who were as disinclined as ever to make mutual concessions. Since this also had occurred when the government council was announced, it looked as though the rank and file never agreed with their leaders. In view of such partisanship, which stemmed more from tribalism than from political ideology, it was obvious that the respite achieved at the top echelon could not last very long, and proof of this was soon forthcoming.

On January 11, 1958, during a three-day meeting of the UDDIA at Dolisie, there were serious incidents that abruptly ended the modus vivendi recently reached by Youlou and Opangault. While the UDDIA delegates were assembled in the courtyard of a private building, a sudden rain of stones, sticks, and bottles caused them to panic. This attack came from some faithful followers of Kikhounga-Ngot, who were determined to break up the meeting. The UDDIA delegates had to fight their way out, and a free-for-all ensued in which the local police had to intervene immediately and then send for reinforcements to prevent further incidents. Throughout the day, the fighting continued in the African quarter of Dolisie between the militants of the two parties or between tribal enemies. When it was over, the score was one death, a few individuals slightly wounded, and some houses burned down.

In the socialist stronghold of Dolisie, each party held the other responsible for this outbreak. The MSA considered it the result of deliberate provocation, whereas the UDDIA viewed it as an unjustified and unqualified act of aggression. In any case, it led to a complete rupture between the two movements. Had Opangault not categorically refused to meet with Youlou, as the latter proposed, the incidents might have been explained away, or the antagonism between the two parties at least might have been attenuated. As matters turned out, their hostility created still further difficulties for the government council, and the ensuing impasse paralyzed the territory's administration.

Upon the advice of the territory's secretary-general, who was acting governor at this time, each of the two parties sent a delegation to talk with the Minister of Overseas France in Paris in the hope that he could arbitrate the dispute. Nothing came of this encounter because the UDDIA could expect no concessions from such political adversaries as the minister and the governor, both of whom were socialists. The two delegations returned to Pointe Noire as divided as when they had left it. The government council, presided over by the secretary-general, continued to function in an atmosphere of such discord that the hostility between its members surfaced even during its meetings. The only possible solution would have been to hold fresh elections from which a clear-cut majority might emerge, but for the time being that was out of the question. The UDDIA's one-vote majority was so precarious that the MSA naturally tried to undermine it by surreptitiously courting some UDDIA assemblymen.

So deep was the mutual distrust among the assemblymen that the leaders kept a close watch over their followers. Yet this was the time when the UDDIA actively challenged its opponents by conducting a propaganda campaign in predominantly socialist circumscriptions. Every member of the government became absorbed by playing politics to such an extent that he neglected his administrative duties, and urgent matters received no attention or were deliberately lost to view in the discussion of trifles. Ministerial offices were turned into propaganda centers from which poured out tendentious directives and vituperative pamphlets.

The conference on the regrouping of African parties, held at Paris in February 1958, had no influence at all on political developments in Moyen-Congo. The MSA leaders who attended showed not the slightest inclination to follow their West African colleagues in striving for unity among the Congolese parties. In their view, there was no possible area of agreement with the UDDIA, or so they felt at that time. The MSA-UDDIA struggle dominated all general as well as local issues. Because the RDA by then had committed itself to admitting the UDDIA to its membership, Tchicaya and his friend and adviser Lounda formally resigned from the RDA. In leaving the RDA, these two men had no choice but to throw themselves into the arms of the MSA. As a matter of fact, the split between Tchicaya and Youlou had occurred after the legislative elections of January 1956, just as the alliance between the PPC and MSA had been a reality since the territorial elections of March 1957. Now the unanswered question was whether or not Tchicaya's official membership in the MSA would hurt the position of the UDDIA in the Vili region. To this question, the by-election of July 6, 1958, was to provide an answer.

While Youlou and Tchichelle were attending the RDA colloquium in Abidjan, Opangault and Tchicaya sealed their alliance at Brazzaville. This took place during a PPC congress at which Goura, Sathoud, and Hazoumé, not surprisingly, were expelled from that party because they had joined the UDDIA. The UDDIA leadership, strengthened by this addition to the party's membership, undertook an intensive propaganda campaign in the Niari region, where they hoped to weaken the hold of Kikhounga-Ngot and the MSA. At the same time the UDDIA organized a meeting in Brazzaville, whose purpose was to confirm officially its integration with the RDA. Just then there arose a crisis in the French government, in which Houphouët-Boigny was a minister, and this prevented him from coming to Brazzaville. Therefore, the congress was postponed indefinitely, with the result that the UDDIA had not yet become a formal member of the RDA by the time the constitutional referendum on the Fifth French Republic was held. However, Youlou and Tchichelle were invited regularly by Houphouët-Boigny to attend all the RDA meetings and ceremonies, thus unofficially confirming the UDDIA's membership status.

In April 1958, three months after the Dolisie incidents, the sudden death in a road accident of Georges Dumont, a UDDIA assemblyman, troubled the political situation anew. His elimination brought the opposing forces in the assembly once again into balance, each party holding 22 seats, and it gave the MSA another chance to win control. It also gave rise, however, to very serious clashes at Kakamoeka, a small hamlet near Pointe Noire in the Kouilou region from which Dumont had been elected. The death of their assemblyman so stirred its few hundred villagers, led by some agitators, that they went in a body to stone the house of Peiffer, the French manager of the local sawmill, whose automobile had caused Dumont's demise. The local gendarmerie intervened, but this incident was followed by threats and bodily harm to several Europeans living in Kakamoeka, including Peiffer's wife. Police reinforcements restored order within 48 hours, and several of the troublemakers were arrested. The Europeans of Brazzaville saw in these incidents the first serious manifestation of hostility, which they took to be a sign of the times and especially of the current political mood. As to the UDDIA leaders, they publicly accused their socialist opponents of responsibility for what had happened.

Local politics were relegated to the background temporarily by the in-
surrection at Algiers in May 1958,[6] for in the main Congolese towns, the grave
French political situation absorbed the attention of Europeans and Africans
alike. Reacting as they had done during the somber days of 1940, the European residents were deeply concerned over the danger of civil war in France.
They quickly came out in favor of a government of national union under General
de Gaulle, as the only man who could create unanimity among the French. This
attitude was expressed by Governor-general Pierre Messmer in a cable sent to
President René Coty on May 28. His action soon dispelled local fears and,
above all, clarified the situation in central Africa, where rumors had been
circulating to the effect that if republican freedom was threatened the reforms effected by the loi-cadre might be in jeopardy. At Brazzaville and
Pointe Noire, vigilance committees were formed, although some extremists there
also talked of the need for a Committee of Public Safety. Both the local
Europeans and Africans approved wholeheartedly of the vigilance committees,
especially as their leaders refrained from making any irresponsible moves or
holding meetings that might have troubled public order.

On May 31, Opangault appealed to Guy Mollet, president of the SFIO, to
vote for General de Gaulle's investiture. The more cautious Youlou did not
commit himself until June 2, at which time, speaking in the name of the RDA,
he expressed his confidence in the general. A few days after coming to power,
De Gaulle reassured the African community by indicating that his government
would undertake overseas reforms more liberal than those of the Fourth Republic. The appointment of Bernard Cornut-Gentille[7] as Minister of Overseas
France was welcomed enthusiastically in FEA, where his term of office as head
of that Federation had been marked by liberalism.

As soon as the political crisis in France had been virtually settled,
the Congolese politicians turned their attention to the local scene, although
they continued to follow closely the policies of the new French government. A
press dispatch of July 3 announced the formation at Pointe Noire of a Mouvement Congolais d'Union Civique et Républicaine under the aegis of Tchicaya and
Opangault. According to its communiqué, the new group proposed to support
General de Gaulle so that all Moyen-Congo would accept the constitution he was
drafting, which would confirm the ties between that territory and France and
also define them. It further promised to dissolve itself as soon as the new
constitution came into force. This move surprised the Brazzaville MSA militants and even Tchicaya himself, for it was to a large degree the work of
Opangault, and even more that of his chef de cabinet, inspired by analogous
movements that recently had been formed in France.

Motivating this initiative, praiseworthy in itself, was a local competitive spirit attributable to the imminence of the Kouilou by-election. In
making a display of its loyalty to the French Republic, the MSA aimed at
stealing a march on the UDDIA-RDA, whose leader had lagged behind Opangault in
declaring his devotion to General de Gaulle. However, by chance there appeared in the same press dispatch as the MSA's communiqué a statement by the
UDDIA favoring a reform of article 8 of the constitution[8] and the creation of
federal executive institutions. Some observers thought that this was a local
move by the UDDIA to outbid the MSA, while others interpreted it as a response
to rumors (reportedly emanating from the government-general) of impending
changes in the status of the overseas territories. Acccording to those
rumors, FEA could not expect an evolution like that of French West Africa

because it was a more backward region and one that had never asked for either internal autonomy or the institution of a federal executive. Certainly the rumors circulated by UDDIA militants could not be taken seriously, but in propagating them among the electorate Youlou was playing a political long shot. It should have caused no surprise, inasmuch as every African congress held since January 1957—those of the MSA, Convention Africaine, RDA, and PRA[9]—had asked for a revision of the relations between France and its overseas territories.

In the more immediate foreground was the by-election of July 6, when the population of the Kouilou was to choose a successor to Dumont. The stakes were high, for their choice would determine whether the PPC-MSA or the UDDIA would become the majority party in the assembly. Inevitably bitter disputes marked this electoral campaign, and the government was concerned lest some incident spark disorders. Because this election took place after Tchicaya's decision to merge the PPC with the MSA, it was also a test of strength for that coalition. Despite the strong language used by the rival parties in their tracts and a generous distribution of wine, the election passed off calmly because the population showed a sense of civic duty and political maturity. The UDDIA candidate, Jean Makaya, received 13,208 votes, and the candidate of the PPC-MSA, Jean-Aimé Makosso, won 11,383. This evident equilibrium between the local political parties was the more disappointing to the socialists in that at M'Vouti, birthplace of the Makosso family, they sustained their most crushing defeat.

Another noteworthy feature of this contest was that the Kouilou electorate, probably for the first time, voted for a party and not for an individual. Makaya's victory restored to the UDDIA its one-vote majority it had lost with the death of Dumont. Despite the significance of the election, the victors could claim only a modest success, while the socialists found consolation in an increase in the number of their followers over that in the previous election. Furthermore, the UDDIA's success had not of itself resolved the problem of Moyen-Congo's political instability, which was basically due to the equal strength of its two parties. In commenting on this election a few days later to the editor of the _Petit Journal de Brazzaville_,[10] Youlou said that it had given him special pleasure in that

> it brought me further confirmation of the confidence I have inspired in the population of Moyen-Congo. Moreover, I include among my supporters an important European element, who have come to realize more and more that our policy is the same as that laid down by the RDA president, Houphouët-Boigny, within the framework of the Franco-African Community.

Youlou's expression of gratitude to the European residents was designed to offset the impression of xenophobia left by the Kakamoeka incidents, for which some of those residents had held the UDDIA responsible. He also aimed to prevent European voters from moving into the socialist camp. Such fears were more than justified by the support known to be given to the MSA ministers by the French socialist governor, and his predilection was shared by many of the European civil servants.

Thenceforth, the growing weight of local political problems was to be aggravated by far larger constitutional issues, in which the Congolese politicians, like all their Black African colleagues, were soon to become involved.

1. Under terms of the loi-cadre of 1956, the president of the government council was ex-officio the territorial governor, and the vice-president was the African minister who had received the largest vote in the assembly.

2. The Babembé were a subtribe, about 40,000 strong, living in the Niari region.

3. Early in 1956, Youlou founded Cette Semaine—A. E. F., a monthly, to publicize his election campaigns. After a few issues, it ceased publication when René Mahé, editor of Le Progrès, gave the support of his fortnightly to the abbé. Soon, however, the circulation of Le Progrès dropped from 4,500 to 1,200 copies, and in 1957 it, too, disappeared. Its place was taken by France-Equateur, which had been founded in 1952 as an apolitical triweekly news bulletin. France-Equateur became the semiofficial organ of the UDDIA when its owner, Vial, and its chief editor, Jayle, entered politics as partisans of Youlou (see Wagret, op. cit., p. 218). After Europeans were eliminated from the government in February 1960, still another UDDIA party organ was founded. This was L'Homme Nouveau, which was launched with Benjamin Indoh-Baucot as editor in July 1960, shortly before the Congo became independent.

4. For an amusing account of this episode, see Le Monde, January 23, 1959.

5. See chapter 10.

6. On May 13, 1958, a stormy demonstration in Algiers by the French settlers and army against the Paris government's weakness in dealing with the Algerian revolt eventuated in the downfall of the Fourth Republic. Civil war in France, itself, was barely averted by General de Gaulle's success in asserting control over the settlers and the French armed forces, after he was invested as head of the government by the Parliament on June first. That body also granted him exceptional powers to carry out drastic changes in France's constitution and in its policy toward its African dependencies.

7. A former prefect in France, Cornut-Gentille had distinguished himself in the Resistance movement during World War II. He was governor-general of FEA from January 1948 to October 1951.

8. In the constitution of October 1946, article 8 defined the relations between the Fourth French Republic and its overseas dependencies.

9. The Parti du Regroupement Africain (PRA) was formed at Dakar in March 1958 by all the major French Black African parties except the RDA. It advocated the replacement of the governments-general by primary federations of francophone Black African autonomous republics, which would be associated with France in a confederation. Its program was essentially that of Senghor's Convention Africaine.

10. See issue of July 7, 1958.

44

CHAPTER 7

LOCAL REACTIONS TO THE CONSTITUTIONAL PROBLEM

During mid-1958, the all-absorbing topic of conversation in Moyen-Congo, as in the rest of Black Africa, was the new constitution. In all the talk about it, the words that most frequently recurred were integration, federation, and confederation. Black African party leaders were invited to attend the Bastille Day celebrations in Paris and also to participate in political discussions with the new Overseas Minister, Cornut-Gentille. Youlou and Opangault accepted the invitation, but the abbé did not stay until the constitution was drafted in its final form. Nevertheless, he wrote a short account of his trip to France, in which he commented on the joint resolution of the PRA and RDA which their spokesmen handed to General de Gaulle.

This resolution[1] expressed the desire of the leaders and parliamentarians of those movements for the establishment of a federal French republic, comprising France, the two former African federations, and the individual overseas territories,

> based on free cooperation, total liberty, and the right to independence. They also ask that these territories be endowed with a central autonomous government responsible to the legislature, which would have all the attributes of internal sovereignty except direct and exclusive control over foreign relations, defense, currency, higher education, and the magistracy, which would be reserved for the government of the federal republic.

Although the full text of this resolution was not published, it is believed to have contained nothing more than the foregoing statement. It was also utilized mainly by the UDDIA militants and especially by certain radicals who, since the Bamako RDA congress of September 1957, had tended to align themselves more with the Parti Africain de l'Indépendance (PAI)[2] than with the RDA or PRA.

During one of the public meetings held by the CGAT[3] in Brazzaville, its leaders proposed that a plebiscite be held to ascertain the wishes of the Congolese concerning federalism or independence. Queried about this proposal, Youlou was said to have replied that such a plebiscite was out of the question. General de Gaulle, he added, "leaves us free to choose our own path after consultation with the population, so we are quite at liberty to take a stand in favor of independence." This reply satisfied the CGAT leaders, but the UDDIA militants held a meeting in the Bacongo district on July 28 at which they voted for autonomy, as defined by Youlou in his speech to that gathering. Autonomy, declared the abbé, meant that power would pass into African hands, when the post of a prime minister possessing authority analogous to that of a territorial governor would be created. His statement was made the day after

45

the PRA had closed its constituent congress at Cotonou, where the delegates had rejected the Franco-African Community and had opted for independence.

After the Cotonou congress, the political leaders of FEA, like their West African counterparts, took their stand on the independence issue. The Gabonese deputy, Aubame, declared: "Independence does not mean secession, for it simply implies that responsibility for the full and complete management of our own affairs will be dealt with in a confederal framework with France." Dr. Abel Goumba, president of the Oubanguian government council, stated that "the final resolution of the Cotonou congress cannot be interpreted as secessionist, let alone an expression of hostility toward France. It merely affirms our wish to have the African personality recognized, our will to enjoy independence, and the desire of the overseas territories to belong to a French grouping based on the principle of freedom."

At Brazzaville, the CGAT leaders responded enthusiastically to the Cotonou resolution and at the same time voiced their approval of a "unification of Black Africa and the elimination of artificial colonial frontiers." By championing the cause of immediate independence, the CGAT spokesmen at Brazzaville were acting together with the procommunist Union de la Jeunesse Congolaise (UJC),[4] and they jointly asked Youlou that the UDDIA opt for total independence. Replying with some humor to this request, the abbé snubbed his interlocutors by saying that "since you represent a movement that is more involved with political than with labor issues, you alone can raise the question of independence."

In Moyen-Congo, as at Cotonou, the Black African students home on vacation from France came forward to align themselves strongly with the UJC and with the CGAT in criticizing France and in demanding unconditional independence. "Independence first, and the rest will follow," declared Matsika Okoko, the UJC leader, in a Marxist-inspired diatribe. Much the same happened at Pointe Noire when Tchicaya was objectively outlining to the electorate the various options offered by the constitutional project. There, a student was warmly applauded by his PPC listeners when he demanded "independence for the Congolese."

By that time, all the organizations in Moyen-Congo—political, cultural, labor, and even religious—were closely following the constitutional issues. At Brazzaville, a temporary committee was formed among members of the council of tribal representatives (Conseil Coutumier),[5] and a few days later it came out in favor of a confederation. Also in the federal capital, the small Parti Socialiste Démocratique, which had neither influence nor militants, sent a message to General de Gaulle on August 20, denouncing the resolution of the Cotonou congress and the activities of the PAI extremists, adding that it would approve the constitution regardless of the form it finally took. In a speech on August 8, 1958, to the constitutional advisory committee in Paris, General de Gaulle already had made it clear that an affirmative vote by the overseas populations in the referendum would be interpreted as an acceptance of federation, whereas a negative vote would mean secession with all its consequences, of which the most important would be an end to France's economic aid. His words were brutally frank but at least not ambiguous.

While the advisory committee in Paris was debating the terms "federation" and "confederation" and finally adopting "community," all the political leaders of Black Africa were broadcasting their views on the subject. Youlou stated that the UDDIA wanted a federal French republic, to which all the overseas territories could belong as national states and on a footing of equality. The MSA awaited the return of Opangault from France before taking an official position. Its militants in Pointe Noire, influenced by Kikhounga-Ngot, expressed a preference for the independence-in-a-confederation formula, but those in Brazzaville declared themselves opposed to immediate independence.

On August 14, the advisory constitutional committee handed to the government its report on the draft constitution. Yet the final form it would take depended on the conclusions that General de Gaulle would reach after the journey to Black Africa, which he began on August 20. This gave the FEA politicians another chance to state their positions. At a reception given in honor of Yvon Bourges, the newly appointed high commissioner of FEA, Youlou declared, inter alia, that "none of us would dream of building the Moyen-Congo apart from France and without benefiting from French aid as in the past." He followed this up with an appeal for African unity, stressing that only in this way could the balkanization of the continent be avoided.

At Bangui, Goumba admitted that he was disappointed in General de Gaulle's conception of the future relationship between France and the overseas territories. Koulamallah, spokesman for the MSA in the Tchadian assembly, said that becuase autonomy would lead to increased financial burdens for the population, "Tchad favors a prolongation of the status quo until we win independence." His political adversary, Lisette, also expressed a qualified approval of the new constitution.

On the eve of General de Gaulle's arrival in FEA, its leaders were running a high political fever. Aubame, the PRA leader of Gabon, invited Koulamallah, Boganda, Tchicaya, and Opangault to meet at Brazzaville to discuss the resolution passed by the Cotonou congress in favor of independence. Youlou, on the other hand, proposed a round-table conference of all the FEA leaders, at which equatorial unity would be the subject. But it was around Boganda, champion of FEA's emancipation, that political activity crystallized. On August 21-22 at Brazzaville, he received visits from all the federation's political and labor leaders, as well as representatives of cultural and youth movements.

This rash of meetings in the federal capital gave Youlou the opportunity to address the main leaders of FEA's political parties in the name of the UDDIA, as follows:[6]

> I have asked you to meet so that before General de Gaulle arrives we can exchange views and express the different desires of our territories. We are living through historic times for Africa, and the next few days should determine what will be our new statute. After we have established the position that each of our territories will take in regard to the referendum, we should decide how to live together in the future, and, if we reach such a decision, decide what it will mean for each of our countries. If my information is correct, General de Gaulle is thinking in terms that go beyond the recommendations of the constitutional committee. He is considering the possibility that the territories will gain independence before the end of the 5-year transition period laid down in the first draft.
>
> If such latitude is given us, it would be nothing short of a recognition of independence and we would have a wide range of choices, ranging from maintaining the status quo to "departmentization" and ultimately

to independence. Also our ties with France would be more or less flexible, depending on the juridical form that the Community might assume.

The first hope I want to express is that all our territories make the same choice of their statutes so that we may achieve genuine homogeneity. I don't think that we will have much trouble in reaching a common decision. What will be harder is the kind of links to be forged between autonomous territories that would be free to form a group, if they so desire. For my part, I would like to preserve the unity that has been gradually achieved between us, for I do not believe that any of our territories has the potential to go it alone in a world that is being drawn ever closer together in large groups.

This trend, whether we like it or not, leads us to envision an organization that would hold the powers of the group at the level of a primary federation. So as to avoid creating a supranational power independent of the member territories, we could set up a council that would bring together at regular intervals the presidents of the government councils and the relevant ministers of each territory. In the intervals between its meetings the council's decisions could be executed by a permanent secretariat. We might also consider setting up a federal assembly composed of representatives from the states' legislatures, as well as those of the National Assembly and Senate at Paris.

No decision has yet been reached as to the site of such a federal assembly, though many would immediately opt for Paris. But I myself would prefer an African capital and, if you agree with me, I should like to propose Brazzaville. In any case, it would be desirable for at least one annual session to be held in Africa, so as to facilitate the expression of local views and enable the Metropolitan delegates to have a better grasp of the African scene as a whole. Brazzaville's historic past, tradition of freedom, and its geographical location enable it to fulfill all the requirements of a federal capital....[7]

The next day, Opangault expressed his views about the constitutional proposal, but he said nothing about Youlou's project for maintaining organizational unity among the FEA territories. The equatorial Africans' natural desire for independence, he said, should not be construed as hostility toward France. Indeed, the many ties that could be established between a united and independent central Africa and France would be the stronger because they were freely accepted by the two partners:

It is precisely because I love France that I want, with all my heart, to see written into the new constitution these words: "The overseas territories will become independent when they so desire, and thereafter no constraints on them shall be exercised by the Metropole. All that will be required is a unilateral declaration by their assemblies for them to be recognized as sovereign states...

The inclusion of such a statement, he added, would lead to a unanimous affirmative vote by the overseas populations in the referendum, assure France of their permanent love and devotion, and prove to the world that France's colonialist policy was a phenomenon of the past. Furthermore, it would end the present ambiguity, for the overseas populations are now being asked to vote upon a constitution whose terms offer them the choice between a very hypothetical independence in the distant future if they vote "yes," and an immediate independence tantamount to secession if they vote "no." We do not want secession, but neither have we the right to mortgage the future of our children.

From all the meetings and discussions at Brazzaville, there emerged on August 23 a memorandum that was given by Boganda to General de Gaulle upon his arrival there. Its authors first expressed regret that FEA had not been more widely represented on the constitutional advisory committee, regarding this as the unjustified downgrading of a federation that had chosen in 1940 to "fight so that France would live." With some exaggeration, they went on to say that the francophone African territories, and especially FEA, risked being "stifled," surrounded as they were by independent African states, and were suffering from an inferiority complex vis-à-vis the former British colonies, which now had acquired sovereign status. Their concluding plea to the effect that the African territories' right to independence be written into the constitution repeated almost verbatim Opangault's arguments and thesis. Among the signatories of this memorandum were the outstanding political, labor, and youth leaders of the four equatorial countries, including Youlou, Opangault, and Tchicaya.

Early in the afternoon of August 23, General de Gaulle reached Brazzaville by plane from Madagascar. If the enthusiastic welcome he received at the Maya-Maya airport by the Brazzavillians caused the reason for his visit to be forgotten temporarily, the hour of truth came the next day. Then the general made the first of his political speeches in French Black Africa, addressing a crowd of some 25,000 persons. Before he spoke, Boganda made a short address, calling on De Gaulle to "calm the winds of independence that are blowing over all Africa. Today, as in 1940, you are our last chance, and it is you who must save us. Speak frankly, Mr. President, and we will respond in kind on September 28."

In an impressive silence, General de Gaulle rose and came forward to speak on the immense podium of the Eboué stadium, where thousands of Africans were waiting to hear him. In confident tones, he offered the choice of independence to the French equatorial Africans, just as later he was to give the same option to the Guineans, Ivorians, and Senegalese. At the sound of the magic word "independence," which the political and labor leaders were so eager to hear, it might be assumed that the authors of the above-mentioned memorandum would proclaim immediately their intention of voting affirmatively in the referendum. Unfortunately, some of them were neither wholly satisfied nor reassured.

At the Maya-Maya airport, even before the general's plane took off, Boganda, Aubame, and Tchicaya voiced their reservations, which they intended to express to the French government in the form of a resolution. In their view, the general had not been explicit enough, and it would be unwise to make a definitive decision and commitment before seing the final draft of the constitution. Boganda wanted Youlou and the other equatorial RDA leaders to adopt the same stand. Not only did they refuse to do so but after a meeting chaired by Youlou on August 24 announced through the press that they would cast an affirmative vote on September 28. This RDA declaration surprised and annoyed the PRA leaders and Boganda, who then gave up the plan to send to the Paris government their resolution expressing mistrust of De Gaulle's intentions. Instead, they drafted an unsigned press communiqué explaining their reservations in more ambiguous terms. Its authors were Boganda and Aubame, for Opangault, tired of their beating about the bush, would not participate. Youlou, for his part, restated his position in writing to the governor. At the same time, he protested against publication of the August 23 memorandum, claiming that the printed text was not the same as the one he had signed.

General de Gaulle's speech in Paris on September 4 and the publication of the final text of the constitution impelled the FEA leaders to take definitive stands. The UDDIA opened the referendum campaign by repeating its approval of an affirmative vote, "for in saying 'yes' we will hold the key that opens all doors, and we choose the community of African states, associated with each other and with France."[8] In Oubangui, although the embryonic branch of the RDA was inclined to side with Sékou Touré more than with Houphouët-Boigny, it decided to vote "yes." Boganda did likewise, and in a speech to 5,000 persons at Bangui, he told them of his decision. His stand induced the Brazzaville branch of the MESAN to follow suit.

As to the MSA, Opangault and his Brazzaville militants opted for an affirmative position, but when the referendum campaign opened, no one knew for certain how Kikhounga-Ngot would act, for his labor union followers favored a negative vote. How Tchicaya would move was also unknown, for he said that he would await the decision of the PRA congress at Niamey before making up his mind.[9] On September 9, following the congress of his party, Aubame finally came out for an affirmative vote. In Brazzaville, the head of the Islamic community asked his fellow Muslims to vote "yes" "for the sake of both Africa and France."

Thus, on the eve of the referendum, it was clear that the four FEA territories would vote affirmatively, despite some reservations, especially on the part of the CGAT union members.

It will be recalled that before the memorandum of August 23 was drafted, representatives from Moyen-Congo's radical groups, as well as politicians, came to consult with Boganda. Among them was Jean-Gaston Bagana, spokesman for the CGAT unions. In describing to its members his two meetings with the Oubanguian leader, Bagana said[10] that "independence" was the only significant word included in the text of the memorandum,

> because we want and demand independence. Don't let yourselves be lulled by the fine phrases of journalists, who can twist the meaning of words as they please. You are being told that Madagascar has chosen the federal formula. That is false. I urge you to vote against De Gaulle's referendum if he doesn't include the word "independence" in the constitution. It is only by offering opposition that we will obtain satisfaction. France must negotiate with us....

Such an outburst marked a turning point in the history of the Congolese unions, which for many years and in successive elections had remained politically neutral. The announcement of the constitutional reforms in France and of the impending referendum impelled their leaders to enter the political arena. They realized that they could no longer stand apart, for the future of their country was now at stake, and if they remained on the sidelines they would be blamed by generations to come. Moyen-Congo's politicians viewed this decision with mixed feelings. In principle, they agreed that the labor and youth movements should be involved in so vital an issue, but they deeply distrusted the men who claimed to represent the toiling masses. It is worth considering just what organized labor represented in Moyen-Congo in the year 1958, when the country was moving toward administrative autonomy and even independence.

Elsewhere labor unions were based on the mass of workers, but in Moyen-Congo the movement was formed only of leaders. Except for a small militant nucleus built up 10 years earlier for political purposes, the overseas labor movement had had an overrapid development after application of the 1952 code. In most instances, however, this had redounded mainly to the benefit of the Metropolitan labor federations. Prior to gaining autonomy, Moyen-Congo appeared to have a solidly structured labor movement, but in reality it was only a hollow shell that lacked true leaders and militants. Union membership in Africa, generally speaking, bears no resemblance to that in Western nations. Throughout FEA and notably in Moyen-Congo, workers are members of a union only for as long as they find it to their interest, or because in a dispute with their employers they prefer to seek advice from a union official rather than from the Labor Inspector. Beyond that, it is rare for them to persevere as active members, and it can be said that only their immediate gain induces them to frequent the Labor Exchange (Bourse du Travail). Indeed, the elections held to choose the personnel delegates of an enterprise show clearly the Africans' indifference to, or lack of confidence in, unionism. So it is not surprising that a mass labor movement has never become truly significant and that only the few leaders appointed by the big Metropolitan federations have been consistently active. Furthermore, conscientious as such leaders have been, they often hold meetings that are sparsely attended.

In underdeveloped countries with shaky economies, labor inevitably has many grievances, but because the workers lack interest in their unions, the latter are never very aggressive and strikes are highly localized. In Moyen-Congo's overcrowded towns, the fact that unemployment is endemic has made the threat of a work stoppage ineffective. Paradoxically, the concept of union solidarity has not yet made headway among the Congolese, although a communal spirit at the tribal level is an essential element of their attitudes and customs. In brief, the labor movement in Moyen-Congo stems mainly from competition between the Metropolitan labor federations. A possible exception is the CGAT (Confédération Générale Africaine du Travail), which was founded for political reasons, albeit disguised.[11] Despite some CGAT leaders' not disinterested commitment to the communist party, the political influence of Moscow is almost nil among the Congolese members of that federation. This is even truer of the other labor unions, in which ideology has no appeal for their members. Their only driving force is the spirit of nationalism, which has developed during recent years and which creates an atmosphere propitious for promoting labor's demands.

51

The three Metropolitan federations—Confédération Française des Travailleurs Chrétiens (CFTC), Confédération Générale du Travail (CGT), and Force Ouvrière (FO)—founded branches in Equatorial Africa after the Brazzaville conference of 1944. These branches generally developed into federations under African management, although they still received financial support from their parent organizations. The oldest—the CGT—was implanted in 1946, in the wake of the RDA, whose well-known political role in Africa from 1946 to 1950 was played with help from the communist party. The RDA's recognized leaders in FEA—Tchicaya, Darlan, and Lisette—transformed organized labor into a political mass movement. Despite considerable disillusionment, the CGT's activities in the long run continued to benefit the same individuals, and the distrustful masses remained as aloof from trade unionism as they were from politics.

When the RDA broke its ties with the communist party in 1950, the CGT was forced to revise its methods and activities so as to retain such political hold as it had acquired over the generally passive workers. It was then that the World Federation of Trade Unions (WFTU), to which the Metropolitan CGT was linked, promoted an AEF-Cameroun Coordination Committee, to which theoretically the Congolese CGT unions were subordinated. Until 1957, the French CGT maintained its direct ties and its political and financial tutelage over them, and in this way it tempered the influence of the WFTU. At the local level, the CGT unions' activities were confined to a few meetings held by their leaders and to forming many subsections, but these had almost no members.

The communist party's directive of infiltrating groups of workers was fully grasped by the African leaders but was difficult to carry out. Employers, supported by the administration, kept a watchful eye on them. Because of the administration's hostility to union proselytizing, African labor leaders preferred making trips to Europe, especially to the Iron Curtain countries, for which their expenses were paid by the party (see table 5). In the many reports they made to the Paris headquarters, which was well aware of the African leaders' lack of success, the latter claimed to have control over the working masses. Unfortunately for them, the reality was clearly revealed at the traditional May Day parade, when only about 50 of a wage-earning population numbering some 100,000 participated. This parade, which was regularly authorized by the public powers, failed to attract even onlookers, who, in Africa, are easy to attract. The bicycle races that often occurred on the same day drew far larger crowds.

The autonomy movement engendered by the loi-cadre of 1956 also gave birth to the Confédération Générale Africaine du Travail (CGAT). In principle, administrative autonomy was to be matched by an autonomous labor movement, but in reality the CGAT continued to receive funds as well as directives from the CGT. This was still the case at the time of the September 1958 constitutional referendum, when the CGAT received a flood of propaganda material from the WFTU at Vienna as well as from Russian, Hungarian, and Chinese unions. The CGAT's Congolese stars were Matsika, Boukambou, and Thaulay-Ganga, all of whom had been trained at the Marxist labor union school at Gif-sur-Yvette in France. Parallel to their union activities, which were disappointing, these men formed the Union de la Jeunesse Congolaise (UJC).[12] This became a dynamic, communist-oriented movement which flourished notably among the Lari of Brazzaville. (By 1960, it had begun to contaminate some members of the UDDIA youth organization.) For the most part, the CGAT's union activities served as a cover for the subversive political action undertaken by the UJC.

52

TABLE 5

PARTIAL LIST OF VISITS BY EXTREME LEFT CONGOLESE LABOR LEADERS
TO COMMUNIST COUNTRIES AND MEETINGS, 1955-58

Date	Name	Organization	Destination	Occasion
May 1955	Matsika, A.	CGT Brazzaville	Vienna	WFTU subgroup meeting
June 1955	Thaulay-Nganga, A.	CGT Brazzaville	Prague	WFTU Congress
June 1955	Kikhounga-Ngot, S.-P. Ngouah, S.	CGT Niari	Helsinki	World Peace Council
July 1955	Bouesso, V.	UFA Brazzaville	Geneva	International Congress of Mothers
July 1955	Matsika, A.	CGT & UJC Brazzaville	Warsaw	World Youth Festival
May 1956	Bagana, J.-G. Bemba	CGT Brazzaville	Moscow	May 1 celebration
July 1956	Thaulay-Nganga, A. Mouanda, N.	CGT Brazzaville CGT Niari	Sofia	8th session, WFTU Council
July 1956	Mouanda, N.	CGT Niari	Prague	WFTU Congress
Aug. 1956	Mongany	CGT Brazzaville	Bucharest	Rumanian national holiday
July 1957	Boukambou, J.	CGT Brazzaville	Moscow	Invited by Soviet labor
Aug. 1957	Mouanda, N.	CGT Niari	Colombo	World Peace Council
Nov. 1957	Mouanda, N.	CGT Niari	Moscow	40th anniversary, October revolution
Nov. 1957	Mouanda, N.	CGT Niari	Leipzig	WFTU Congress
Dec. 1957	Thaulay-Nganga, A.	CGT Brazzaville	Peking	Chinese students congress
Feb. 1958	Matsika, A.	CGT & UJC Brazzaville	Vienna	—
July 1958	Matsika, A.	CGT & UJC Brazzaville	Moscow	Invited by Soviet labor
Aug. 1958	Tchicaya, R. Malanda, F. Makosso, T.	CGT Pointe Noire	Prague	WFTU Congress
Aug.-Nov. 1958	Mbi, A. Boukambou, J. Matingou, F. Boukambou, J.	CGAT	U.S.S.R., China	Invited by Soviet and Chinese labor
July 1958	Bandiagana, A. Gamavelle, M. Matsecoto, L.	CGAT Brazzaville UFA Brazzaville Student	Vienna	World Youth Festival
Oct. 1958	Bissambou	CGAT Brazzaville	Leipzig	2d International Civil-Service Congress

Source: Wagret, J.-D., Histoire et Sociologie Politiques de la République du Congo (Brazzaville), Paris, 1963, p. 186.

To prevent an eventual take-over of the labor movement by the communists, the Catholic missionaries helped to establish African branches of the CFTC, for they never had lost their interest in African politics. In principle, membership in the CFTC unions was open to all workers regardless of their religious faith, and this brought Muslims and animists as well as Christians into their ranks. Despite the weakness of its propaganda and financial means, the CFTC took root in Moyen-Congo, where it competed successfully with the CGT in regard to the number of its members. Even though the CFTC was an apolitical movement, its leaders were demagogues who would not let the CGAT outdo them in voicing labor's grievances. Such activities undermined the CFTC's legitimacy as a labor movement, so that it often proved to be a disappointment to its sponsors.

In 1957, the FEA section of the CFTC took the name of Confédération Africaine des Travailleurs Croyants (CATC), and linked itself to analogous international organizations.[13] These were the labor federation of the Franco-African Community and the Union Panafricaine des Travailleurs Croyants, whose parent organization was the Confédération Internationale des Syndicats Chrétiens. Its leader in Moyen-Congo was Gilbert Pongault, whose influence and following soon spread as far as the Belgian Congo and anglophone Africa. In choosing the workers' representatives in labor negotiations, many more members of the CATC than of the CGAT were elected, but this did not mean that the influence of the CATC was paramount.

Alongside the two federations mentioned above, the Force Ouvrière (FO) constituted still another element.[14] Its members were mainly European civil servants and railroad employees, who found in the FO a politically neutral organization which promoted their interests, although it was by no means able to match the financial resources of either the CGAT or the CATC. Under the leadership of men sent from France to head the African FO, that federation was soon subjected to not disinterested pressures from the Anglo-American-dominated International Confederation of Free Trade Unions (ICFTU), which aimed at substituting its own ideology for that of Marxism. Thanks to the autonomy acquired by the African labor movement, the ICFTU obtained an ascendancy over the overseas FO unions, and in 1959, they became full-fledged members of an African counterpart, the African Confederation of Free Trade Unions. Of the three labor federations in Moyen-Congo, the FO had the smallest following among the local wage earners. In time, control of it passed from the hands of Europeans to those of secondary indigenous leaders, who had little influence among the Africans.

It is obvious from this brief survey of Congolese trade unionism that its importance cannot be gauged either from the size of union membership or from its affiliations. Perhaps the only valid criterion would be the caliber of the union's delegates in negotiations with employers and the government, for in the eyes of the membership, these men carry more weight than any doctrines that the labor leaders proclaim. As of 1961, about 20,000 Congolese workers voted in the elections of personnel delegates, but this did not mean that all of them were active union members nor even that they paid their dues.

On the eve of the constitutional referendum, the union leaders certainly were cognizant of the issues involved, and because of their ideology, this awareness increased in the days to come. At the time, it was difficult to foresee whether or not this consciousness would be extended to the rank and file of wage earners or, indeed, what might be the role of organized labor in an autonomous or independent state.

When the constitutional referendum campaign opened, many groups in Moyen-Congo besides the main parties had already opted for an affirmative vote. Among these were the Committee of Civic Action, the Youth Council of Moyen-Congo, the Council of Customary Chiefs of Brazzaville, the CATC, the FO, officials of the public school teachers' union, the Veterans' Association, the Niari section of the CGAT, and "King" Makoko, speaking for the Batéké tribe. Advocating a negative vote were the Brazzaville branch of the CGAT, the UJC, the Matsouanists, and the Congolese students in France. Those still on the fence included some young members of the UDDIA, more or less affiliated with the UJC, and certain elements of the PPC.

Considering that the overwhelming majority of the Congolese had already declared their intention of voting affirmatively, the campaign might well have been low-keyed. On the contrary, it was taken more seriously than any previous electoral campaign. For the leaders of the major political movements, this campaign had a special character. First of all, it gave them the opportunity to be seen by their followers. Secondly, it enabled them to take stock of the electorate's political maturity, for this was the first time in the history of Black Africa that a population had the opportunity to declare itself on a matter of principle. Because the electorate was used to voting for a man, a party, or simply an ethnic group, the propagandists' main task was to make the illiterate masses grasp the meaning of the referendum and the importance of their vote. A surprisingly strong negative reaction was less to be feared than was the electorate's abstentionism. The population, for its part, was astonished at being asked by its political leaders to make an affirmative gesture, without regard to party or to tribe.

It was mainly to combat apathy that leaders and militants alike spontaneously abandoned their usual occupations throughout the month of September and traveled to the most distant parts of the territory by road, track, or river. The presidents of the UDDIA and the MSA were active mainly in their traditional electoral constituencies, but this did not prevent representatives of the two big parties from establishing contact almost everywhere with their political minorities. Over the radio, UDDIA spokesmen explained that their party approved of the new constitution because the Fourth Republic, despite the loi-cadre, had not promoted African emancipation. Opangault told why the MSA, after its initial hesitation, had decided to vote "yes," and in the same broadcast he advocated unity for FEA, lest the isolation of its four territories leave them exposed to the two dangers threatening Africa—the Arab League and communist imperialism. In mid-September, word reached equatorial Africa that Sékou Touré of Guinea and Djibo Bakary of Niger had decided to vote against the constitution, but this did not affect the positions already taken by the most important FEA leaders.

Not surprisingly, the CGAT leaders showed their true Marxist colors by urging all the labor unions and youth groups to vote "no." At the same time, a similar undercover campaign, financed by the French communist party, was conducted by the UJC and Congolese students on vacation from France. Mimeographed tracts, couched in the Marxist terms used by Matsika and Boukambou, as well as brochures emanating from the Paris headquarters of the communist party, were distributed among the African residents of Brazzaville. The rural areas were virtually untouched by this propaganda, as was the population of Pointe Noire. At Dolisie, where the CGAT advocated an affirmative vote, some communist tracts were discreetly circulated, but they had no

55

effect. In any case, propaganda by means of tracts affects only a fraction of the public in Africa, where the masses are far more influenced by verbal persuasion.

Another characteristic of this campaign was the competition between parties that reflected local pride in the rural settlements. At Ouesso, the socialists asked their constituents not only to vote "yes" but also to induce the Sangha electorate to do likewise, and provided transport to the polling booths. Ouesso never before had known so much political activity. The next day the local leader of the UDDIA urged his followers to roll up the maximum affirmative vote. Thus, the small-scale warfare between the parties continued without let-up behind the screen of a nation-wide plebiscite.

As the date of the referendum neared, the elements favoring an affirmative vote throughout FEA were reinforced. The one discordant note in this generally harmonious chorus was sounded by Boganda who, like all the other equatorial leaders, had said "yes" but could not leave it at that, and in a broadcast over Radio Brazzaville, he once again harshly criticized the administration. Perhaps because of Oubangui's strategic geographic location and his fear of communism and of Pan-Islam, Boganda was even more apprehensive than other Black African leaders of being outflanked from the left. Distrustful of such local political opponents as Darlan, and even of the friendly overtures made to him periodically by the Tchadian socialist Koulamallah, Boganda believed that they would undermine his authority unless he maintained his popularity by fiery diatribes against colonialism. Often, when the extremism of his words outran his real views, he thought that he could explain them away "among friends," as he expressed it. Referring to the youthful Oubanguian communists, Boganda said, "I have pronounced the word 'independence' to show the extremists and students that they have no monopoly of that term, and in this way I cut the ground from under their feet." Boganda always had been the champion of Oubanguian nationalism, and now it looked as if he were about to launch a campaign for the emancipation of all FEA.

In accordance with an official directive, all the top administrators of Moyen-Congo toured the territory to explain the reasons for holding the referendum and what would be the consequences of the vote. The governor himself visited the regions of Alima-Léfini, Likouala-Mossaka, the Sangha, Niari, and the Pool, everywhere stressing the significance of the referendum and the imperative duty of each citizen to vote. The results of the concerted efforts of all the advocates of an affirmative response exceeded the most optimistic expectations. Of the whole federation, Moyen-Congo was the territory where the fewest negative votes were cast. In large part, credit for the outcome in FEA could be given to the administration's outstanding organizational work.

In preparation for the referendum, the authorities had revised the electoral rolls and engaged in an intensive campaign to induce all eligible citizens to register. However, the vote showed that the rolls were not up to date in all the territories, and increases in the registered electorate (see table 4) were far from uniform.[15] More polling booths than before were installed to enable voters in isolated regions to do their civic duty without traveling many kilometers to vote, but again the results were spotty.[16] More generally successful was the campaign to inform the public about the issues involved in the referendum. Moreover, a marked improvement in the means of communication enabled the population to learn sooner the outcome of the vote. Reports from polling booths were sent in promptly, so that by early in the morning of

September 29 the overall results were known. The official figures for Moyen-Congo showed that 339,436 affirmative votes had been cast as against 2,122 negative ones. The corresponding statistics for Oubangui were 487,033 to 6,009; for Gabon 190,334 to 15,244; and for Tchad 804,355 to 14,032.

Notes

1. Published in France Equateur Avenir, July 20, 1958.

2. The Parti Africain de l'Indépendance (PAI) was a small, short-lived party founded in 1957 by some orthodox Marxist intellectuals in Senegal, whose goals were independence, unity, and scientific socialism. It formed even more ephemeral branches in a few other francophone Black African territories.

3. See pp. 50-52, also note 11.

4. See pp. 52-53, also note 12.

5. Founded to constitute a "national repository of customs," the Conseil Coutumier gave its support to Youlou in 1956. The constitution of the Congo Republic required that two members of that council be consulted by the national assembly whenever a law regulating tribal customs was being drafted by that body.

6. As reported in France Equateur Avenir, August 23, 1958.

7. Ibid.

8. Ibid., August 30, 1958.

9. At that congress, it was decided that each territorial branch of the PRA should vote on the referendum as its members saw fit.

10. Reported to the author by an observer present at the meeting.

11. The CGAT was formed at Libreville in October 1957 by delegates of the equatorial branch of the Metropolitan communist labor federation, the CGT. Although its members proclaimed their independence from the French parent organization, they voted to affiliate with the World Federation of Trade Unions (WFTU). From the outset, the CGAT was divided both ideologically and geographically. In general, the leaders of the Pointe Noire unions were more moderate than those of Brazzaville, who favored joining forces with Sékou Touré's UGTAN. Among the "hardliners" was Dominique Sombo-Dibele, whom Youlou included in his government of December 1958 to neutralize the CGAT's opposition to his regime. By June 1959, when he had persuaded some MSA members to become ministers, Youlou felt strong enough to drop Dibele from his cabinet. From then on, the CGAT adamantly opposed Youlou's government. See pp. 82-83.

12. The UJC was unique among the Congo's youth organizations in that it owed its allegiance to no political party and was able to infiltrate the youth branches which the parties had established. The weakest among the party youth organizations was the Jeunesse MSA, founded in 1957 as the successor of the Jeunesse Socialiste among the northerners living in Poto-Poto. More dynamic and better organized was the Jeunesse Catholique,

which was also the strongest in Brazzaville but which also had branches in Madingou, Dolisie, and Jacob. However, the UJC made its strongest inroads in the youth branch of the UDDIA, and in 1960 they caused that party to forbid its members to belong both to the JUDDIA and to the UJC (see Wagret, op. cit., p. 215). See also pp. 83-85, 218.

13. Although the CATC continued to receive aid from its parent organization in France, it developed an indigenous leadership earlier than did the other nominally autonomous labor federations in FEA. In the Congo, its outstanding leaders were Jean Biyoudi and, above all, Gilbert Pongault, who became the promoter and organizer of the Pan-African movement among Christian wage earners in 1956.

14. The FO's Congolese branch was established by two French employees of the Congo-Ocean railroad and another of Radio Brazzaville. The chronological advantage enjoyed by the FO as the first Metropolitan labor movement to establish a branch in FEA was offset by its dilatoriness in eliminating its European officials and in severing its ties with the parent federation in France. It was not until 1959 that the FO transformed itself into the Confédération Congolaise des Syndicats Libres (CCSL) under local leadership. Internationally, it was affiliated with the International Confederation of Free Trade Unions (ICFTU), and nationally it was dominated by the CGAT, notably after it accepted the latter's proposal to form a single labor union in the Congo.

15. Since the March 1957 elections, the registered electorate in Gabon had increased by 11.7 percent; in Moyen-Congo, by 25.8 percent; in Oubangui, by 5.7 percent; and in Tchad, by 65.5 percent.

16. Between 1957 and 1958, the number of polling booths in Gabon had grown from 196 to 305; in Moyen-Congo, from 380 to 441; in Oubangui, from 544 to 732; and in Tchad, from 783 to 900.

CHAPTER 8

FIRST STEPS TOWARD EQUATORIAL UNITY

As soon as the constitutional problem was settled, the thoughts of all
territorial leaders turned to the question of setting up a federal state for
FEA. Shortly before the referendum, Boganda, Opangault, Youlou, and Aubame
had met and discussed the principle of establishing a united FEA so as to
prevent at all costs the balkanization and isolation of that Federation. It
already was known that only Léon Mba disapproved of the proposal, and that
Boganda and Youlou were its most enthusiastic supporters.

Immediately after the referendum, Boganda sent his legal adviser,
Senator Rivierez, accompanied by David Dacko, to explain to the heads of the
three other equatorial states his plan for creating a single central African
nation. Boganda's prognosis was that Africa must become a unit but would be
divided into three blocs, of which the first would be that of "Latin African"
countries. To create this unit, the four FEA territories must be grouped
into a single state, uniformly subject to the legislating emanating from a
central assembly. Its sole executive organ would be a council of ministers,
but there were also to be various services and budgets at the state, depart-
mental, communal, and rural levels. In short, Boganda proposed to revive—
without France's tutelage—the FEA as it had existed prior to the loi-cadre,
but with significant additions. The new state should immediately have a
national anthem and flag, and be represented in international bodies as a
united and independent equatorial Africa. In support of his thesis, Boganda
argued that, with the elimination of France as the external power that had
held FEA together, unity must be created by indigenous African nationalism.
Tribalism having become outmoded, the immediate task was to unite all the
equatorial tribes so as to form a single nation.

At Pointe Noire, Boganda's "Operation Union" drew unqualified approval
from such MSA leaders as Tchicaya, Kikhounga-Ngot, Nardon, and others, but
the UDDIA leaders—Youlou, Jayle, and Tchichelle—had reservations. Indeed,
the RDA leaders in FEA whom Boganda contacted were skeptical about the feasi-
bility of his proposal. Léon Mba, for his part, simply refused to receive
the Oubanguian envoys, asking them to postpone their visit. Nevertheless,
Boganda's project was far from moribund, for Lisette said that he and his
friends recognized the need for establishing strong bonds between Tchad,
Oubangui, and Moyen-Congo. Nor did Boganda despair of reaching some working
agreement with Gabon, even though its leaders had stated their preference
long ago for a direct federal tie with France.

Even those FEA politicians who agreed on the principle of unification
were not in accord as to its form. Various formulas for federation that, at
first glance, seemed quite sound were proposed. However, in FEA generally,
and in the other African territories, the cult of personality is no myth,
and questions of leadership and domination often determine the behavior of

individuals toward each other. Alongside fundamental problems that deeply concern all of Africa, minor considerations of local predominance and often of ethnic domination inspire blind partisanship and bigotry in some men. Furthermore, as the Oubanguian envoys stressed in the report on their mission, there existed undeniable centrifugal forces. Since the indispensable will to unite existed, they believed that in time an effective counteracting central authority could be created.

When the UDDIA leaders were asked for their reactions to Boganda's proposal, Youlou to some extent sidestepped the main issue. He emphasized the difficulties arising from the lack of a working majority in Moyen-Congo's government, and this gave him the chance to attack the local administration once again. On several occasions, Youlou had tried to get rid of the territorial governor, who favored the MSA ministers, and he continued to press the issue in Paris until he obtained the governor's recall. Now Youlou accused local French officials of such partiality that they would not permit the free play of democratic institutions. In brief, Youlou contended that it was essential to resolve Moyen-Congo's internal crisis before proceeding with the unification of FEA. It was quite true that the complete political harmony reached at the time of the referendum had not eliminated the malaise that still plagued the Moyen-Congo government.

At this juncture, Youlou and Tchichelle went to Paris to attend a meeting of the RDA coordinating committee. There they agreed with Houphouët-Boigny in regard to choosing the statute of member state in the Community at the territorial level, while at the same time working toward an effective collaboration among the future African states. This was not yet tantamount to balkanization, but it meant the rejection of any federal formula until after national entities had been created. Progress toward a federal constitution by groups of territories was not wholly abandoned but only stymied for the time being.

Oubangui's strong man, Boganda, having failed to push through his project to set up a unitary state for FEA, gave up the plan to negotiate it through another mission of good offices. He tried the new tactic of utilizing the last session of the Grand Council, of which he was the president and in which all the territories were represented. Speaking at the opening meeting, Boganda launched his proposal for a central African state, just as President Nkrumah of Ghana had done a few years before in urging the formation of a United States of Africa. In Boganda's views, the establishment of a central African state would lead not only to the elimination of all the boundaries between the four FEA territories but also to a revision of the international frontiers set up by the Act of Berlin in 1885. In other words, he wanted the left bank of the Congo River to be included in his new state. In declaring that FEA was outmoded and that "the Africa of tomorrow must be organized on the basis of ethnicity, geography, resources, and evolutionary prospects,"[1] Boganda was dreaming of building a great Bantu state in which the FEA territories would play the leadership role. Henceforth, "our primary objective will be to build an Africa based on the community of language and inspired by French culture."

Regardless of whether Boganda was moved by sudden inspiration or by excessive ambition, his remarks attracted attention. They disagreeably surprised the authorities in the Belgian Congo, who, nevertheless, decided to remain silent. Boganda was regarded as a superman by his colleagues in Tchad,

Gabon, and Moyen-Congo, but they were afraid of him and considered him autocratic; hence, it was with some mistrust that his political friends greeted his bold proposals.

Among the Congolese, there was no chance of Boganda's weakening the close ties that bound the UDDIA leaders to Houphouët-Boigny, but in Opangault he found a fervent admirer. So zealously, in fact, did Opangault support Boganda that he wanted to move ahead faster than was consistent with the provisions of the newborn constitution. Opangault appealed to the elected representatives of FEA to meet no longer as territorial assemblymen but as a national constituent assembly for a united FEA state. He even offered Boganda his services in convening such an assembly for the purpose of setting up a temporary government for the new nation. Opangault's proposal, which was publicized in the local press, drew a reprimand from the French high commissioner on the ground that it contravened the constitution. Above all, it seriously embarrassed Boganda, who had not foreseen such a rapid evolution for his plan. In a communiqué, he disavowed Opangault's initiative, pointing out that such a decision was legally the prerogative of the territorial assemblies, but he could not completely backtrack. He therefore invited all the FEA leaders to a round-table conference to discuss his project. And to win over public opinion to his cause, he published and distributed a series of statements in the form of ten tracts that he entitled "Pour une République Centrafricaine."[2]

Collected after Boganda's death as his political testament, these tracts show that he considered the equatorial state to be only the first step toward a much larger—and for the time being, utopian—project. In a second stage, he envisaged its union with Cameroun and the left bank of the Congo River, and in the more distant future, the creation of a Latin Africa[3] formed of the two Congos, Cameroun, Ruanda-Urundi, Angola, and even Somalia.[3] His most immediate concern was to take over the left bank of the Congo, "which here and now we regard as part of the Central African Republic, because our historic and official frontier is that river and not the Oubangui."

In his haste, Boganda must have forgotten all about his political ally, Koulamallah, Muslim leader of the Tchadian socialists, whom he placed in an embarrassing position. By basing his proposed political entity on peoples of Bantu origin, Boganda was implicitly stressing the dangers of Pan-Islam. His project contained few details concerning the administrative structure of his united central Africa, but because he proposed large-scale groupings of black peoples, he appealed to the imagination of the African masses, as did many other advocates of Pan-Africanism. While it might be said that Nkrumah made Pan-Africanism into a political concept and Senghor made it a cultural concept, Boganda's Pan-Africanism was an ethnic and spiritual concept and, as such, it was opposed to Pan-Islam.

Youlou was the first to reply to Boganda and Opangault, and in a broadcast, he stated that it would be a "mistake and an illusion" to believe that a highly centralized government and single state could bring about unity in the "great FEA family which we are forming."[4] He also stressed the illegality of efforts to "eliminate all our old institutions, as well as the constitution, on which the ink is barely dry." Only after the territories had been transformed into states could they sign a "durable and lasting common charter for the purpose of maintaining the ties that unite them and managing together their joint interests in the great Community founded by General de Gaulle." This declaration gave the UDDIA press organ a chance to attack Boganda and Opangault.

Seeing in Youlou a convert to his views, Léon Mba of Gabon spoke darkly to a journalist about "very bold and premature" political stances and hinted that they might lead to interference in the affairs of neighboring states and even become an incitement to disorder. After having long been drained of its financial resources, Gabon should not also be asked to surrender its autonomy. In reviving this old complaint and in protesting against the claims of an adjacent territory to his country's manganese and iron, the Gabonese president hardly endeared himself to Youlou. To these "secessionists" and to those who had attacked him personally, Boganda retorted in strong terms. In an article that appeared in the sixth issue of L'A.E.F. Face à l'Avenir, he denounced "some territories that for two years have indulged in a policy of sterile polemics, whose disastrous consequences are becoming more evident each day...Neither Oubangui nor myself has any personal interest in creating a single state with Moyen-Congo which, if it is separated from the territories to the north, will become just a little Congo of 400,000 inhabitants. What then will become of Brazzaville's 100,000 residents, and its present and future unemployed?" (The Marxist CGAT unions used this quarrel among the major FEA leaders to demand once again the creation of a central African ensemble made up of independent states.)

The real reason for Youlou's refusal to participate in the round-table conference proposed by Boganda was that he did not want to commit himself on the eve of a meeting at Brazzaville of the RDA coordinating committee. It was scheduled to open on November 26, 1958, and to be attended by the principal RDA West African leaders. Everything about Youlou's behavior at this time indicated that he believed there would emerge from the Brazzaville meeting a policy acceptable to all the delegates present, and one which the RDA would strongly support in all the Black African territories where it was in control. Then, just at the time when Youlou was making preparations for that meeting, Opangault was attacked in a well-organized press campaign. This was the UDDIA's retaliation for a proposal that Opangault had made, in connection with his support for Boganda, that northern Moyen-Congo secede and be united with Oubangui-Chari. Actually, Opangault, realizing that his term of office as president of the government council was nearing its end, was practicing a form of political blackmail. Once again, verbal war was declared between the MSA and UDDIA, and the press was used as the medium for washing their dirty linen in public.

Tchicaya's return from Paris to Moyen-Congo did nothing to calm the tense atmosphere, especially at Pointe Noire. Realizing that his influence was now very limited and that the end of his parliamentary term was fast approaching, Tchicaya at once rallied to Boganda's project for a united central African state, although he disagreed with him as to the procedures to follow. Tchicaya's main hope of making a comeback in Moyen-Congo lay in new elections following a dissolution of the territorial assembly. Opangault had already made a similar appeal to General de Gaulle, in the event that Boganda's equatorial African state failed to materialize.

Experienced political strategist as he was, Tchicaya knew that a major crisis must occur if the assembly were to be dissolved under circumstances not provided for by the constitution. In brief, he knew that only violent public disorders would provide the necessary justification. If Moyen-Congo were no longer governable because of the hostility between the two parties in power, only a few public demonstrations were needed to attract the attention of the French government to the territory. (This had been the case in Niger, where, after serious incidents in November 1958, the assembly had been dissolved.) Tchicaya saw in the official visit of Houphouët-Boigny, formerly a minister in successive French governments, a chance to carry out his plan. Given the current political climate, the prospect of Houphouët-Boigny's appearance at Brazzaville to attend the RDA meeting exasperated the MSA militants. What was worse, Houphouët-Boigny's arrival at Pointe Noire would coincide with the opening of the territorial-assembly session, at which the UDDIA, as the majority party, intended to insist on controlling the presidency of the government council. Whereas the UDDIA saw in Houphouët-Boigny's visit only the moral confirmation of that party's popularity with the Congolese people, the MSA-PPC coalition viewed it as a plot and a provocation. Deliberate distortions of the news heightened tension in both Brazzaville and Pointe Noire, and it spread from the active militants of the two parties to the apolitical masses. In the process, ethnic quarrels became indistinguishable from partisan conflicts.

In the three other FEA territories, quarrels over leadership were aggravated by the question of unification, and feelings ran high, but the situation in Moyen-Congo seemed to be more serious. To prevent an explosion or, at least, to gain time by temporizing, the high commissioner called all the FEA leaders to Brazzaville so that together they might find some generally acceptable compromise formula. This conference lasted three days, and although no formal agreement was reached, recommendations were made that led to the formation of union governments in Tchad and Gabon. The conference and the postponement of Houphouët-Boigny's visit slightly relaxed the atmosphere. But in Moyen-Congo, the intransigent positions taken by both sides left little hope of finding even the smallest area of agreement. The test was to come on November 28, the day on which the territorial assembly would open its next session.

Notes

1. Minutes of the Grand Council of FEA, October 17, 1958.

2. Published in L'A.E.F. Face à l'Avenir, Brazzaville, n. d.

3. Boganda's inclusion of Somalia in his "Latin Africa" scheme is surprising, given his fear of Arab and Islamic imperialism. It is possible that he knew so little about Somalia that he was not aware it was a Muslim country.

4. Reported in a special undated issue of France Equateur Avenir.

CHAPTER 9

THE BIRTH OF THE REPUBLIC

When the territorial assembly session opened on November 28, 1958, the administration expected trouble, because the UDDIA clearly intended to assert its recently confirmed position as the majority party and take over the presidency of the government council. Its members, though somewhat apprehensive, were generally optimistic about the outcome, whereas the MSA suffered from a premonition of certain defeat. Tchicaya, Opangault, and their friends therefore decided to take strong action, which, they believed, alone could save them.

In a speech at Pointe Noire on the eve of the assembly session, Tchicaya stigmatized Yambot[1] as a traitor who must be prevented at all costs from taking his seat in the assembly. In the early hours of November 28, before police reinforcements appeared, MSA commandos and Mbochi—some of whom had come from Brazzaville for the occasion—gathered in front of the assembly hall, shouting demands that the traitor Yambot be handed over to them. They were encouraged by a number of curious onlookers, and the crowd grew rapidly. Not surprisingly, the session opened in a stormy and emotion-charged atmosphere. At once the MSA assemblymen protested strongly in the name of freedom against keeping all the public except some officials out of the hall. Indeed, admitting the public was part of the MSA's strategy, which required action by the dozen or more agitators who had been waiting outside the building yelling insults and threats.

Out of respect for the regulations, President Jayle yielded to the pleas of the MSA, and the doors of the hall were opened to admit the MSA-PPC commandos. Within minutes, they invaded the auditorium, broke up the meeting, overturned tables, hurled chairs, and brushed aside the officials who were trying to protect Yambot. Responding to Jayle's appeal, the city police immediately intervened, and gendarmes cleared the entrance and drove the intruders from the hall. Sufficient calm was restored for the president and governor to make their opening speeches, and this spelled defeat for the MSA in the first round of the day.

After the governor and his entourage had left, the discussion of the territory's future statute began in an atmosphere that was still very tense and in the presence of a small selected audience. After an hour's debate on the principles involved, the assemblymen unanimously voted in favor of an autonomous status. Thus, inauspiciously but solemnly, Moyen-Congo became a member state of the Community and took the name of the Congo Republic. Outside the building, the gendarmerie, in battle dress, kept at bay thousands of African onlookers, including the militants still prepared for action. At noon, during a ceremony at the governor's residence, the MSA and UDDIA assemblymen were superficially reconciled.

The afternoon session, at which the formation of a union government was to be debated, was immediately interrupted by the same paid agitators. Within a few minutes, the MSA group, claiming that the constitutional project proposed by the UDDIA was unacceptable, withdrew as a unit. This left only the 23 UDDIA assemblymen, but they were numerous enough to form the necessary quorum and still had their one-vote majority. A few of them made the gesture of proposing some amendments, but they unanimously passed the constitutional project which became the Congo Republic's first law. The only MSA assemblyman present was Opangault, who had returned to the hall as an observer.

Next, by a show of hands, Youlou was invested as premier, and he promptly named Tchichelle as his minister of interior. After thanking the assemblymen for the honor done him, the new prime minister said that his government must be one of union. In order to be able to form such a government, he would wait before appointing the other members of his cabinet. He went on to say that it should include not only politicians of the opposition but also representatives of the labor unions and of social and cultural organizations. While on his way to present his respects to the governor, Youlou and his convoy of cars were pelted with pebbles only a few meters away from the assembly hall. That same night, the UDDIA assemblymen left Pointe Noire for Brazzaville, which became the temporary seat of what was thenceforth to be called the legislature, but Youlou and Tchichelle did not leave for the federal capital until the next day. Profiting by the absence of all the UDDIA assemblymen, their MSA colleagues met at Pointe Noire in the afternoon of November 29. It was rumored that Opangault then intended to form a "free government of the republic," but this meeting lasted only a few minutes and nothing conclusive emerged from it.

Unfortunately, the advent of the Congo Republic gave rise to racial conflicts and attacks on individuals between November 28 and 30, resulting in five deaths and the serious wounding of 20 other persons. Despite the vigilance of an unusually strong police force aided by the army, many huts in the African quarter of Pointe Noire were pillaged or burned. Whereas the republics of Tchad and Gabon were proclaimed in a happy atmosphere, that of the Congo was born in bloodshed. This was caused by the cupidity and selfishness of some ill-advised leaders who, from being minor civil servants, had become lavishly paid ministers and clung to their new prerogatives. The miracle wrought by the loi-cadre, which was also the miracle wrought by the French taxpayer, had raised ten-fold the living standards of only a handful of évolués, elected by an ethnic constituency rather than a political party. And this miracle had been accomplished at the expense of the masses, whose standard of living was exceptionally low.

Then, as now, the politicians called themselves leaders because they had adopted an ideology that served their personal advancement. Alongside them lived the individual Congolese who had left his family and village to make his own way, and who swelled the mass of urban unemployed. In the town, he lived at the expense of his brothers or of his sisters, for whom prostitution had become a profitable means of livelihood. Such men, uprooted and deprived of their traditional ties, formed the new proletariat, which became an easy mark for eloquent politicians. They were untouched by party doctrines and rootless in the towns, and because they clung to their fellow tribesmen there, they were especially sensitive to ethnic appeals. It was by playing on such sentiments that the politicians formed their electorate and their shock troops, dividing the peoples of the Congo into large racial blocs to which they gave political labels. Then Mbochi attacked Lari, the Vili of Diosso those of St. Paul, and the Babembé the Boucougni.

Not until the first day of December 1958 did the violence that marked the birth of the Congo Republic subside. That last troubled weekend might well have set off a nationwide conflict between rival tribal groups had not the army and police restricted the outbreaks to certain areas. At Pointe Noire, the psychosis of fear that had gripped the population gradually gave way to a wait-and-see attitude. On the other hand, Brazzaville, which had remained calm, began to experience some agitation. Youlou, after entering the federal capital with fanfare, held a press conference on December 2, at which he outlined his government's policy. But more than this, his efforts to form a union government immediately attracted the attention of all the political, cultural, and labor organizations, and especially of the tribal groups. The bargaining for ministerial posts took place in Brazzaville, whither Tchichelle and the UDDIA assemblymen had been transported as a precautionary measure. Reports of the progress of these negotiations reached Pointe Noire in the form of wild rumors, and the atmosphere this engendered was hardly one of optimism.

The UDDIA membership was not sparing of its criticism of Opangault, claiming that it was his intransigence and partisan attitude that was impeding the formation of a union government. Some top officials of the MSA anticipated the inclusion of socialists in Youlou's government, while others opposed such participation because they would be offered only minor posts. The attitude of most of the Congolese was one of curiosity rather than concern, even though the country's future would be in the hands of the new government. After a week of uncertainty, Premier Youlou announced the composition of his government, which he described as "provisional."

The reaction of the MSA militants was strikingly inconsistent. After having demanded, in the press, five portfolios for the MSA-PPC, they expressed disappointment and, even more, their criticism of those who had agreed to collaborate with Youlou in defiance of party discipline. Such attacks, combined with threats, were directed particularly at Fourvelle (named minister of state) and Kerhervé (minister for industrial production). The latter, although describing himself as an Independent, had long been considered as emotionally committed to the socialists. As to the choice of Odicky as minister of "customary affairs," it did not surprise his friends, who had regarded him as a dubious member of the MSA. Some of the appointments of UDDIA partisans, such as those of Biyoudi (minister of youth) and Sombo-Dibelé (minister of labor), were contested. The latter being secretary of the UJC, a communist movement related to the World Federation of Democratic Youth, his nomination gave rise to contradictory interpretations, the more so as he was Oubanguian by birth.

At Pointe Noire, the composition of the new government created some discontent among the Babembé because their most popular fellow tribesman, the former minister Zakété, had been dropped from the cabinet. That ethnic group, which had held the balance of power between the MSA-PPC and UDDIA parties in the preceding elections, had consistently supported Youlou. But even more than Youlou's choice of individual ministers, it was his proposal to transfer the seat of the legislature and government from Pointe Noire to Brazzaville that caused uneasiness among the port's wage-earning class, who feared that it would increase unemployment, and among its retail merchants, already affected by the economic recession. In the nick of time, however, a declaration by Tchichelle publicized by the local press gave renewed confidence to Pointe Noire's inhabitants.

Rumors circulated in Brazzaville as well as at Pointe Noire that Opangault and his friends were going to create a dissident government for the Congo, whose capital would be at Fort Rousset. The tension then gripping the socialist leaders was probably the cause of such a surmise, but it was unlikely that Opangault himself was seriously considering setting up a rebel government. In any case, the validity of Youlou's rule was confirmed when he and Tchichelle were received officially by General de Gaulle. During their absence in Paris, Opangault left Brazzaville to reestablish contacts with his northern constituents. He was probably preparing the ground for the next elections, and also perhaps consulting with his followers about the possibility of attaching the northern province to Boganda's Central African Republic. At Brazzaville, where the atmosphere was tense, it was said that a revolt was brewing in the north, and the posting of an UDDIA official to Fort Rousset was interpreted as an attempt by the new government to infiltrate the administration there. Such reports gave rise to a few local incidents and to fantastic stories, circulated notably by the Mbochi of Poto-Poto. In actual fact, however, unrest was widespread in the north.

In the general malaise deliberately cultivated by the opposition, the new cabinet began to function, after a period of adjustment and groping. Youlou's first move was to reduce the pay of his ministers and their chefs de cabinet, probably with a view to convincing the public that his government was determined to remedy a budgetary situation that was well known to be critical. At the level of party politics, the UDDIA leadership was frustrated in late January 1959 by another last-minute postponement of the RDA coordinating committee meeting. However, the presence at Brazzaville of two of its outstanding members, Dr. Sylla and Mamadou Coulibaly, permitted holding a two-day study meeting which revived the flagging zeal of the UDDIA militants, who had begun to have their doubts about the benevolent attitude of the top RDA leadership.

Another event earlier in that same month was the riots that took place at Léopoldville. The capital of the Belgian Congo was too near to Brazzaville for that town's inhabitants to remain indifferent to such unprecedented outbreaks, the more so as they were incited by members of the Abako,[2] an organization of Bakongo who were ethnically related to the UDDIA Lari. After the Belgian authorities suddenly refused to permit the Abako's president, Joseph Kasavubu, to hold a meeting which they had previously authorized, the police were attacked by openly antiforeign demonstrators. This abrupt awakening of the Belgian Congolese was watched closely by the UDDIA militants. They expressed their sympathy with the Abako's liberation movement by giving its refugees shelter in Brazzaville and by helping some of its leaders to flee to Ghana and Guinea with false identity papers. The MSA, on the other hand, feared that the Abako "revolutionaries" might be cherishing expansionist aspirations and trying to create a Bakongo kingdom that included their fellow tribesmen living in the other Congo, as well as in Portuguese Cabinda. Indeed, the MSA attributed this objective to Youlou, who was a close friend of Kasavubu.

Thus it can be seen that although the UDDIA leaders preached calm and hard work so that the government could get off to a good start, the MSA membership was not similarly motivated. They had not been sobered by the casualties they had suffered at Pointe Noire, especially since many of the MSA ringleaders there had been freed and now felt themselves immune from prosecution. Kikhounga-Ngot went to France, where he vainly pleaded with the SFIO leadership to espouse the cause of the Congolese socialist ministers who had been dropped from Youlou's government. After the failure of his mission, the MSA-PPC militants concentrated their propaganda on the need to hold assembly elections in March 1959. At first, Kikhounga-Ngot claimed he had received formal assurances from General de Gaulle and the SFIO president, Guy Mollet, that such elections would be held in the Congo on March 15. A few days later, however, he seemed less sure of his ground, and at Dolisie declared that it was up to the electorate to demand this. Opangault also stressed to his Pointe Noire militants the necessity for holding elections soon, and to exert pressure on the UDDIA to this end, he raised the specter of the north's secession and its union with the Central African Republic. Substance was given to his assertions by Boganda's concurrent announcement at Bangui that elections would be held in his territory in mid-March. At the same time, Boganda urged the other equatorial republics to do likewise so as to reassure their populations.

If some of the more aggressive MSA-PPC militants held the illusion that new elections would bring them control of the legislature, the general public seemed less eager to go again to the polls. Some of the population feared that an electoral campaign in the near future would be an invitation to violence, whereas others thought that the refusal to hold elections would lead to a trial of strength between the rival parties. In any case, a détente seemed improbable.

At Brazzaville, Youlou was installed in the modest office of the agricultural service. There he was playing the role of St. Vincent de Paul by distributing alms to the mendicants who filed in to see him, and by promising jobs in the government to members of his shock troops. All these developments stirred up rather than calmed a population already overwrought by conflicting propaganda, and it was expected that a conflict between the abbé's Bakongo partisans and the northern socialists would break out any day. Before leaving for Paris to attend the first meeting of the Community's executive council, Youlou appealed to the patriotism of the Congolese and denounced the handful of agitators who were deliberately compromising the government's constructive operations. In an editorial inspired by the premier and printed in the January 20, 1959, issue of the weekly, France-Equateur, the activities of Kikhounga and his friends were castigated and the official view on the elections upheld. This editorial maintained that the UDDIA was not afraid of holding elections, which it was sure to win by a large majority, but believed that the country's best interests would be served by a period of calm in which the Congo could make progress and take its rightful place among the Community states. The MSA, lacking a press organ,[3] could reply only through the voice of its militants, who found a fertile field for their propaganda among the unemployed of Pointe Noire.

To such local political jousting, two external developments came to add their weight. One was a new move by Boganda to promote his Central African Republic through a union of the four equatorial states. The other was a revival of the historic San Salvador empire of the fifteenth century that would

unite the Bakongo peoples now under French, Belgian, and Portuguese rule.
All these maneuvers simply widened the gulf between the northerners and Youlou's followers, and paved the way for a head-on clash between them. The
MSA leaders stepped up the number of their meetings and harangued their
troops so as to force the UDDIA to hold elections. Opangault, always ready
for a fight, talked of calling for a mass demonstration in which placards
demanding elections would be brandished before members of the government.
The rising tension in the Congo alarmed the French Community authorities,
who strove to make the socialist leaders listen to reason and avoid a catastrophic showdown. They succeeded in persuading Opangault to give up mass
demonstrations in favor of a peaceful parade aimed at proving to the government that the population was restive. Opangault tried to give the impression that he was fully in control of his followers, but he did not succeed
in winning their wholehearted support. The local authorities, for their
part, did everything they could to prevent even small crowds from assembling.

On the Congolese scene, the most important forthcoming event was the
opening meeting of the legislature on February 16, when the MSA members would
surely demand that a date be set for new elections and might stage the same
disruptive demonstrations as they had on November 28. A few minutes before
the meeting opened, some Mbochi members of the MSA clashed mildly with the
police, who controlled all the approaches to the assembly hall. Finally, a
providential rainstorm caused the demonstrators to disperse. Inside the
hall, the MSA minority lost no time in trying to force the election issue,
but they were frustrated by the UDDIA bloc's adroit use of procedural obstacles. This initial confrontation ended in a draw, and discussion of the
agenda was postponed until the afternoon meeting. Then, when most of the
urban police were stationed in front of the hall and the deputies were beginning their debate, it was announced that outbreaks were taking place in Poto-
Poto.

Poto-Poto is Brazzaville's most populous district, whose inhabitants include peoples of the Pool region as well as tribesmen from the north. Since
early afternoon, the MSA militants, who wanted to avoid a repetition of the
morning's encounter with the police, had been meeting at the Bouya bar in
Poto-Poto, where they were expecting word to be brought them as to the legislature's decision in regard to an election date. At 3:00 p.m., the MSA emissary from the assembly, speaking to a crowd of 400 to 500 persons, told them
that they could expect nothing from the UDDIA, whose deputies remained opposed to holding elections. He ended his harangue by saying, "Under such
conditions, act as you please." His speech gave the MSA militants the green
light they had been waiting for.

Five minutes later, in the middle of a noisy and excited crowd, the
first Lari fell to the ground. He had been stabbed by a Mbochi commando, who
then ran through the streets of Poto-Poto, haphazardly seeking new victims.
As soon as a Lari was sighted, a howling mob brandishing spears, daggers, or
simple sticks pursued him until he was struck down. Within two hours, nearly
40 Lari were thus attacked, and eight of them died from wounds inflicted by
side arms. Any person who failed to reply in the Mbochi tongue to a question
asked in that language was automatically considered a Lari and therefore to
be killed. After the first attack, the police intervened, but they could not
come to grips with an enemy who disappeared into labyrinthine enclosures and
then emerged in bands after the forces of order had gone away.

After the massacre of February 16, in which the only victims were Lari, the police expected a reaction from the UDDIA. This did not occur until the afternoon of the next day, when the Lari commandos of the Bacongo district wreaked their revenge on the Mbochi of Poto-Poto. With the first dagger thrusts, the political causes of the riots were forgotten, and it became a war between northerners and southerners. All the rites of traditional tribal warfare were reenacted, beginning with the planting of a spear in front of the enemy's hut. There followed scenes of dreadful savagery that spared no one. Corpses were strewn in the streets, and the overwhelmed medical personnel used all their resources to save as many as possible of the wounded, who were carried to the hospital in jammed ambulances. Despite appeals for calm issued by the premier and the governor, the manhunt lasted for three days, during which Brazzaville was the scene of numerous atrocities. The murdering of women and children and the burning of huts caused the African population to flee to the area inhabited by Europeans, who gave them shelter. Panic seized all the Brazzavillian Africans, especially those who had never been involved in politics.

In the huge maze of Poto-Poto, the police did what they could to curtail the damage, which, unfortunately, was great. The sad balance sheet of the bloody days of mid-February 1959 included 100 dead, 200 wounded, and 300 dwellings destroyed. A few days later, Youlou called a press conference at Brazzaville "so that French and world opinion should be accurately informed" by his official version of the events. Naturally, he exonerated his own party, blamed the opposition for stirring up racial discord, and stressed his own role as the elected, impartial, and constructive leader of all the Congolese.

While the sorely tried population was licking its wounds, the police arrested nearly 300 persons, who were charged with crimes ranging from murder to carrying forbidden arms, pillage, and arson. During this time, the MSA and UDDIA deputies resumed their debate on the issue of holding general elections. Ibalico, the UDDIA's general secretary, insisted that his party was not opposed in principle to holding elections but refused to do so in the near future. Elections, he affirmed, concerned only members of the legislature and those who aspired to become deputies, whereas the population as a whole wanted to live in a peaceful atmosphere untroubled by political disputes. Since Opangault faced legal charges in connection with the recent outbreaks, the MSA spokesman was Kikhounga-Ngot, who had been interrogated at length by the police but was not under arrest.

Kikhounga-Ngot told the press that his party would not enter into negotiations with the government until the latter had set a date for the elections, for to do otherwise would be a betrayal of the cause for which MSA members had died in the riots. A few days later, Youlou replied that the election date depended on the opposition's prior pledge of good behavior. Both sides refusing to make any concessions, there was no solution in sight for the problems raised by the government's instability. Brazzaville's African population continued to be apprehensive, as well as puzzled by the behavior of the Congolese politicians. The riots of mid-February, which followed many similar episodes in Black Africa, made French and world opinion wonder if the new African republics had not become victims of their independence before being able to enjoy any of its benefits.

The UDDIA deputies, who now sat alone in the legislature, voted three emergency laws to prevent a resurgence of tribal conflicts. These concerned the possession of arms and ammunition, house searches by the police, and the verification of the population's identity cards. Inevitably these laws impelled the opposition to claim that the government had given itself the legal means to establish a dictatorship. On February 22, the assembly accepted a constitution which it characterized as democratic despite the absence of the MSA deputies at the time it was voted. As matters turned out, this constitution proved to be only a temporary measure, for the Congo Republic, like most of the other African states, soon moved from a parliamentary to a presidential regime.

Notes

1. See p. 37.

2. Members of the Association des Bakongo (Abako) looked on the UDDIA as their "brother party." For some months in 1959, its president, Kasavubu, took refuge with his family in Moyen-Congo, where they lived in Youlou's country house. Reportedly, the Abako leaders asked Youlou to make a formal offer of hospitality to a provisional government for the Belgian Congolese. The abbé, however, was apprehensive about the political consequences of such a move and gave them only an evasive reply. See chapter 15.

3. Soon after the MSA was formed in May 1957, it founded a fortnightly, L'Essor, as its party organ. This publication soon encountered financial difficulties, and despite successive efforts to revive it, L'Essor finally disappeared early in 1959.

CHAPTER 10

LEGISLATIVE ELECTIONS AND THE MATSOUANIST REVOLT

A few days after the gory incidents in Poto-Poto, Tchichelle told a re-
porter that as soon as peace was restored, the government would hold elections to the legislature in conformity with the new constitution. Youlou,
for his part, castigated the instigators of the February riots in a broadcast, and again stated his determination to punish them. He held Opangault
personally responsible for the crimes and deaths which Brazzaville was still
mourning, and said that if it were up to him alone, Opangault would be
swiftly punished. Out of respect for democratic procedures and the independence of the judiciary, however, he would leave this up to the law courts.

In another well-publicized speech, early in March, Youlou again said
that he was not against holding elections in principle, but that they must
be carefully prepared lest trouble break out anew. In the background, Youlou's advisers were quietly working on a gerrymandering plan so that the
electoral circumscriptions would be revised in a way wholly advantageous to
the UDDIA. To calm the impatience of the MSA, they urged him to set a date
for the elections, no matter how far in the future. The premier listened to
them, reflected, and then acted as he thought best—a procedure he was to
follow throughout his official career.

A few days later, the public was surprised by Youlou's announcement,
not of a date for the elections as was expected but of his intention of
holding a plebiscite in the north as soon as possible. Its purpose, he
said, was to learn the northerners' real wishes as to remaining a part of
the Congo Republic, since the MSA had been campaigning there in favor of
secession. This announcement had the effect of a bombshell, especially on
members of the MSA. Some of its militants were pleased because they thought
that Youlou had fallen into the trap set by Boganda and Opangault, but
others protested energetically against his proposal, for two reasons. First,
they felt that the plebiscite was no substitute for general elections, and,
secondly, they thought that party members who lived elsewhere than in the
north would not be consulted. Yet, on March 12, the top socialist leaders
agreed to the plebiscite, on certain conditions. The MSA communiqué noted
that the abbé's "sudden decision" contradicted statements he had made recently in Paris, and they attributed it to difficulties Youlou was having
inside his own party concerning a date for the legislative elections and in
forming a new government. It was further implied that the unity of the
young republic might be disrupted if the northerners, who formed nearly half
the country's total population, were asked to answer "yes" or "no" to the
question of remaining in the Congo as currently constituted. Nevertheless,
they would agree to a plebiscite provided it was conducted in a free and
democratic manner, and under the supervision of observers sent to the Congo
by the president of the Community.

At Pointe Noire, those favoring such a plebiscite could be counted on the fingers of one hand, and even the inhabitants of Alima-Léfini could reach no agreement on the subject. In general, the PPC opposed a partial plebiscite such as Youlou proposed, and in the UDDIA, opinion was divided. After a week's discussion of this proposal, the talk in the main towns turned again to the elections which, it was rumored, would be held within two months. The socialist militants were sure that they would take place in May because the premier and his ministers were busy visiting their constituents, and their exceptional activity had all the earmarks of the first stage of an electoral campaign. There were also other signs that a date for the elections had been decided upon, but Youlou himself would neither deny nor confirm this. And no amount of insistence by the socialists could induce the government to break its silence. The only important local event at this time was the signing, on March 13, of the provisional protocols for a transfer of powers to the Congolese government.

On the wider African scene, the outstanding event at the end of March 1959 was the sudden demise of Barthélemy Boganda, killed in an airplane accident while returning from an electoral tour of the Haute-Sangha.[1] The news of Boganda's death, shocking as it was, only temporarily deflected the Congolese from their preoccupation with the subject of elections, about which there was still no definite word from the government. It was expected that Youlou, in the speech he was scheduled to make in mid-April inaugurating the Square Charles de Gaulle at Brazzaville, would at long last announce the date, but again he failed to do so. The tension was slightly reduced, however, by his designating May 10 as the date for Dolisie's municipal elections, which marked that town's promotion to the rank of a full commune.

The only hint of the government's intentions was contained in a press article written by Christian Jayle, couched in general terms but drawing on examples taken from current events in francophone Africa. In it the president of the assembly argued that both Western-style democracy and dictatorship were equally inappropriate to Africa, and he praised the political system in which the opposition would be contained inside a single party. Within such a framework, the executive and legislative powers would be concentrated in the hands of an elected leader, who would interpret the nation's wishes and have sufficient authority to carry them out. There was little doubt but that this article was officially inspired, with a view to preparing the Congolese for an eventual transformation of the current parliamentary regime into an "African-type" democracy.

Absorbing and important as were such discussions of political theory, the UDDIA government could not afford to ignore the economic and social malaise from which the country was suffering. So rapid had been the political evolution of the young African republics and so unstable were their governments that new capital investments were not forthcoming. In recent years, the Congo's trade had remained stationary, and there was unemployment in the industrial sector. Popular resentment expressed itself against the leaders who had made false promises, and those leaders, in turn, blamed their own inexperience and also France for not giving them more aid. All hopes for the country's future prosperity were centered on building the Kouilou dam,[2] although it was improbable that that project could fulfill their exaggerated expectations. It might in the immediate future provide jobs for some thousands of young men, but it would not prove to be a sovereign remedy. Yet some

Congolese leaders had the illusion that constructing the Kouilou dam would lead to a large-scale industrial development that could absorb the 20,000 to 30,000 youths who would flood the labor market within a few years. The only hope of raising the masses' living standards lay in concentrating on the Congo's essentially agricultural vocation and, after that was fully developed, perhaps supplementing it by a gradual industrialization.

In a speech to Pointe Noire's Chamber of Commerce on April 15, Youlou gave his views on the economic future of the Congo. He assured his audience that his government had drawn up a plan to give the country a balanced economy and that he intended to ask the help of experts in allocating the funds for this purpose which he expected from France. To cope with the current recession, his ministers were trying to inspire confidence in private investors in the hope that an influx of capital would "regenerate the economic circuits." To do this, Youlou felt that he must give proof of his authority and ability to govern. New regulations, therefore, were drafted to supplement the exceptional powers which the government had assumed following the incidents at Pointe Noire. The assembly duly passed a law which, in effect, enabled the authorities to remove well-known political agitators from circulation in the capital by placing them under house arrest. To counter the probable reaction to such a coercive measure, the assembly at the same time passed another law permitting the government to amnesty the political prisoners arrested at Dolisie and Kakamoeka early in 1958. In this way, Youlou played all the trump cards at his command to win the forthcoming elections. On the one hand, he repatriated the northern MSA militants who had caused trouble in the south, and on the other, gained popularity by freeing the political detainees. At the administrative level, he shifted officials about so as to assure his control over certain centers.

At the end of April, the cabinet finally set the date—June 14—for the legislative elections. Naturally, this pleased the MSA-PPC militants, although they did not fail to complain that if the government had acted sooner the February massacres would have been avoided. The news was received with satisfaction by most town dwellers, who hoped that the election of a new legislature would put an end to the perennial party conflicts. Now that the long-awaited date had been set, the socialists became apprehensive about the terms of the new electoral law, especially as to how it would divide the country into electoral districts. No one expected that the boundaries used in the March 1957 elections would be retained, but some socialist deputies actually believed that the government would not revise the districts in such a way as to assure itself of a victory that would totally eliminate the opposition.

When the terms of the electoral law became known, the MSA leaders rapidly calculated that at best they could win 16 seats in the legislature compared with 45 for the UDDIA. Consequently, they at once wired energetic protests to the president of the Community, the French government, and the high commissioner of FEA. Their next reaction was to preach abstentionism to the electorate and to demand that the whole country be divided into two electoral districts. After reflection, however, they decided to urge a massive vote on the part of their constituents so as to give proof of their party's strength. Above all, it was the breakup of the old electoral districts in the regions of the Pool, Djoué, and Alima-Léfini that aroused their strongest resentment, but the government stood firm. Then an attempt made by the opposition parties to agree on a joint list of candidates also proved abortive. All that the UDDIA would promise to appease its opponents was to form a government representing all shades of Congolese opinion if it won the election.

Opangault was still in prison but Tchicaya returned to Pointe Noire for the electoral campaign. There his PPC militants asked Tchichelle to join them in drawing up a single list for all the Vili candidates, but when Tchicaya insisted that half of them be members of his party, this compromise proved unacceptable. In fact, neither Tchicaya nor his right-hand man, Germain Bicoumat, was included among the candidates sponsored by the MSA-PPC. Since Tchicaya must have known that he no longer enjoyed the confidence of the Kouilou electorate, the only explanation of his attitude was that he wanted to prove to his militants that he could still take his revenge on Tchichelle.

Dolisie's municipal elections took place calmly, a month before those of the legislature. The UDDIA won 13 seats on the town council to 10 for the MSA. Although the local socialists had lost by only a small margin, they reacted as if they had suffered a major defeat and refused to take part in the election of a mayor, with the result that that post went to Senator Goura. The UDDIA made no secret of its pleasure in now controlling the municipal councils of the Congo's three main towns. Tchichelle congratulated the Dolisie electorate on the "political maturity" it had shown in electing Frenchmen along with Africans as its councilors. The fact that Europeans were still participating politically in Congolese affairs was to be evidenced again when three French candidates were included in the UDDIA slate for the legislative elections. The MSA, however, sponsored only African candidates in the Likouala district, where it was sure of winning six seats in the legislature.

Despite the MSA's continuing protests against the UDDIA's gerrymandering moves, its leaders appealed for calm, and, indeed, no violence troubled the elections of June 14, 1959. Then the UDDIA won an even greater victory than had been expected, capturing 51 seats to 10 for its opponents. Perhaps the greatest surprise of all was the defeat of Kikhounga-Ngot in the region of Nyanga-Louesse. As expected, Opangault and Bazinga won in the Likouala region. Analysis of the popular vote showed that the UDDIA had no more than a slight edge over the MSA, winning by 198,815 to 145,273, and under a system of proportional representation, Youlou's party would have won only 33 seats to 28 for the socialists. On the other hand, if the boundaries and number of seats assigned to the electoral districts of 1957 had been retained, the UDDIA would have won 31 as against 14 for the MSA. Therefore, it appeared that the changes made by the government in 1959 had had little or no influence on the outcome of the election. By and large, the MSA's grip on northern Congo had weakened slightly, following the defection of Fourvelle and Itoua to the UDDIA, and at Brazzaville the socialists lost six percent of their followers to Youlou's party. In the Kouilou region, the UDDIA gained a larger majority than in 1957, thanks to Tchichelle, but in Pointe Noire itself, the two parties ran almost neck and neck, with a margin of only 2,106 votes going to the UDDIA.

The new legislature comprised 58 African and three French members, its European contingent having been reduced by the elimination of Mahé and Jayle from the UDDIA's slate. Of the new African deputies, 16 were Lari, six Vili, and 11 Mbochi, and the rest were divided among representatives of smaller tribes. Geographically, 12 of them were northerners, seven from central Congo, and 30 from the south. The African members included 33 civil servants (in majority, primary school teachers), 10 clerks, six manual workers, and 10 traders or planters, and the remaining two fitted into no vocational category. Ten of the Africans had been active in the labor movement—seven in the CATC and three in the CGAT. Thirty-nine of the 61 deputies were newcomers, and of the seven former assemblymen who were defeated, six were members of the MSA and one of the UDDIA. Assured of 51 votes in the new legislature, Youlou now felt strong enough to consider making some concessions to the opposition.

Suddenly, the political stability that apparently had been assured by the election was shaken by grave incidents, albeit not comparable in violence to those of February 1959. For three days following the election, the Bacongo district of Brazzaville was troubled by clashes between the Lari members of the UDDIA and the Matsouanist irreconcilables. Youlou, in a broadcast about these incidents, denounced the anticivic behavior of those Matsouanists who for many years had resisted integration into the Congolese community by collectively refusing to pay taxes, apply for trading licenses, and register births and deaths with the authorities. Neither the administration nor public opinion had been able to alter their negative attitude, and since the elections, it had become deliberately provocative. Consequently, this had awakened a fiercely hostile reaction on the part of the Brazzavillians in the districts and markets frequented by the Matsouanists. To be sure, the Matsouanists always had been intractable to French rule, but after the February 1959 massacres, they had placed the blame on their compatriot, Youlou. Now they publicly expressed their regret at not being able to take the measure of the UDDIA militants in open combat. Naturally, this angered Youlou's Lari followers, who recently had proved their prowess against such renowned fighters as the Mbochi of Poto-Poto.

Because the bad example of the Matsouanists was beginning to spread to all the main towns, the premier decreed penalties for all Congolese citizens who refused to pay their head tax. The Matsouanists, realizing that they were the main target of this regulation, held a meeting in the Bacongo district to organize their defense against the government. The French administration had always had so much trouble in collecting this unpopular tax that it had had to use forcible means, notably by cordoning off the main towns so as to prevent defaulters from fleeing to the countryside. Inevitably, Youlou's new law aroused protests from the unemployed of Poto-Poto. They claimed that Youlou was simply trying to line his own pockets, and they demanded that he arrest the recalcitrant Matsouanists before victimizing his own jobless supporters. Nevertheless, in spite of these difficulties, a fair proportion of the head tax was actually collected.

Rumors began to circulate in the Bacongo district to the effect that those Matsouanists who had paid their taxes would turn on their fellows who had failed to do so. Such rumors were attributed to the UDDIA youth groups and therefore did not intimidate the Matsouanists into complying with the law. Having long succeeded in evading the French tax collectors, they saw no reason to change. Furthermore, by appearing en masse at the police commissariat to register their protest, they openly challenged the government headed by their fellow tribesmen to penalize them. This show of defiance, which Youlou considered humiliating, led some Congolese to urge that he arrest the Matsouanist ringleaders, in the belief that the rank and file would then submit to the authorities. In mid-April, 12 of the Matsouanist standard-bearers were ordered to leave Brazzaville, but they did not do so. It looked as if they could be moved only by force, but the government was still unwilling to use it.

Throughout the Pool region and especially in the Kinkala subprefecture, the authorities encountered the same resistance as in Brazzaville. The civic-minded Lari therefore renewed their pressure on the government to take stern measures, threatening to withdraw their confidence from the administration if it failed to use force. Neither threats nor legal charges had any effect on the obstinate Matsouanists, and, indeed, such moves actually increased the number of those who went to register their formal refusal to pay taxes. One group, called "kakis," even marched to police headquarters in military formation, and the jails began to be filled with Matsouanist prisoners. Clashes between the Matsouanists and young UDDIA Lari grew apace, and in some parts of the town, the former were not allowed to draw water from the public fountains. Such facilities, the UDDIA militants asserted, had been financed by taxpayers, and they even manhandled the Matsouanists who tried to use them. On the same grounds, the Matsouanist dissidents were barred from using the paved streets, and Matsouanist merchants who tried to sell their palm wine in the public market were stoned.

Such minor but frequent incidents, mainly provoked by children and adolescents egged on by their parents, reached a climax in the days following the election. After Youlou's victory was announced on June 17, these escapades became widespread in the Bacongo district, where many Matsouanists were molested, their clothes torn off, and their huts pillaged. Despite the publicly expressed disapproval of Youlou and Tchichelle, the tempo and intensity of these attacks increased the next day, with the result that 200 dwellings were badly damaged, 15 were burned down, and 200 Matsouanists had to be treated for wounds. This widespread assault caused all but the most fanatical Matsouanists to give in. Those who still held out said that they would pay their taxes only in the presence of Matsoua himself.

To end the conflict, Youlou toured the Bacongo district in person, preaching calm and tolerance to his Lari followers. He told them that the government would severely punish not only those who refused to do their civic duty but also all who created disorder by taking the law into their own hands. Youlou's attitude indicated that the government had now decided to take swift action, and soon it did so. Eleven of the Matsouanist leaders were apprehended and taken by truck to an abandoned factory in the M'Pila district of Brazzaville, where they were kept under surveillance and underwent "psychological treatment." They were soon joined by their families, who feared to stay in their homes lest they be subjected to reprisals.

During the next few weeks, while Youlou was preoccupied with external affairs, the Matsouanist prisoners turned their center of detention into a redoubt. They refused to let the authorities interfere in any way, and neither civil servants nor the police could enter their bastion without being jostled and insulted. This development made the government realize that it must move quickly if it were to avoid a repetition of the June 17 incidents. Again it was the young Lari who forced the authorities to take action, for every day they came to attack the M'Pila center with volleys of bottles and stones. The climax came on July 22, when the young militants turned on the police who tried to arrest their leaders, and they launched such an assault on the M'Pila bastion that the Republican Guard had to be called in to restore order.

This fresh outbreak finally convinced the authorities that the existence of a Matsouanist stronghold in the heart of Brazzaville simply encouraged its hard-core element to further resistance and the young Lari to engage in a trial of strength with their "misled brethren." Hence, it was decided to remove the Matsouanists from M'Pila and disperse among the rural settlements those who still resisted integration into Congolese society. This was done at dawn on July 29, but in the process 36 persons died accidentally from suffocation. When ordered to get into the trucks that were to carry them away, the most fanatical refused to obey. According to the official version of this tragedy, when force was used they stampeded, and about 200 of them were trampled on by a crowd of some 2,000 persons. When the authorities finally succeeded in gaining control of the situation, it was found that 36 had died and about 100 others required hospital treatment. Those not injured were duly carried away to their exile, and a committee of deputies was appointed to ascertain who had led the irresponsible crowd to commit such "acts of collective despair."

By nightfall, two truck convoys had taken between 250 and 290 Matsouanists to Fort Rousset and Djambala, while others carried 200 more to Sibiti, Mossendjo, and M'Vouti. At the same time, the wives and families of the exiles who had been living at M'Pila returned to their homes. At the end of the day, seven persons had been arrested, all but 17 of the wounded had been discharged from the hospital, and calm reigned again in Bacongo and Poto-Poto. In reply to some critical articles about this episode that appeared in the French press, the Congolese minister of information denied that the Matsouanists had been victims of discrimination, asserted that the problem was a strictly localized one involving less than one percent of the population, and claimed that the government had emerged strengthened from this trial of force. Naturally, he did not mention that the Matsouanist dilemma had not been solved but had probably only shifted its ground.

Forty-eight hours later, one of the M'Pila Matsouanists who had escaped from the police ran amok in the Bacongo district, killing seven persons and wounding about 40 others with his dagger. Because this seemed to be an act of reprisal, it created a panic among the Brazzavillians, and a curfew was immediately imposed and the police were reinforced. However, appeals issued by Youlou and Opangault, who recently had been freed from detention, calmed the population, which soon realized that the incident was an isolated gesture and not the beginning of an organized Matsouanist vendetta.

At an extraordinary session of the legislature on August 16, Youlou used the Matsouanist revolt as leverage for asking the deputies to declare a state of emergency and grant him exceptional powers. The legislators unanimously acceded to his request, although the MSA deputies urged that the new law be applied impartially and solely to maintain order, and that it not serve as a partisan weapon against the opposition. Forthwith a state of emergency was decreed for the regions of Djoué, Kouilou, Niari, and Sangha, and no one in Brazzaville protested. A few days later, however, a strike at the sugar refinery in Jacob, followed by a fire that destroyed 20 hectares of canefields in the Niari region, impelled the government to extend the state of emergency to cover that part of the Congo.

<u>Notes</u>

1. Some claimed that Boganda was the victim of a plot, others that the plane had crashed because of a mechanical failure. The truth probably never will be known. Boganda's body was found in the cockpit, and, as the plane fell in a forest adjacent to his native village of Babangui, he was probably trying to get a good view of his own plantation. There were no survivors of this accident.

2. Kouilou was the name given to the lower course of the Niari River. Ninety kilometers from its mouth and 75 from Pointe Noire, it flowed through the Sounda gorge, over which a dam could be built that would generate enough electric power to process the manganese ore of Franceville and also create a large industrial complex in the Pointe Noire region. Construction was thought to be technically easy, entailing the displacement of only about 3,000 persons, and the large artificial lake formed behind the dam would give access to a rich forest region.

    In 1954 a study mission was sent from France, and two local organizations were formed to promote the industrial development of Pointe Noire, whose flat terrain and well-equipped port seemed propitious. The vistas opened up by the whole project excited the Congolese but did not arouse the same enthusiasm in France. Opposition there stemmed from the huge cost of the enterprise, estimated at more than 300 billion francs, and from the prospective competition of two other similar projects. Of these, the more serious was that of building a hydroelectric dam at Inga, 40 kilometers from the Belgian Congo port of Matadi and 300 from Kouilou. The Inga scheme was much more grandiose than that of Kouilou, the current generated there was likely to be cheaper, and the range of local raw materials available in the Belgian Congo for processing was far greater. Although the French and Belgian authorities failed to reach a compromise on a joint scheme, and the cost of financing the Kouilou project was still an unresolved problem, France nevertheless began preliminary work on constructing the dam in February 1958.

CHAPTER 11

THE OPPOSITION TO YOULOU'S GOVERNMENT

Two weeks after the elections of June 14, 1959, the new legislature met and unanimously reinvested Youlou as prime minister, and he at once reappointed Tchichelle as minister of the interior and Vial as minister of finance. Thenceforth, in the legislative assembly, whose mandate ran for five years, the opposition was effectively muzzled, and Youlou's opponents either had to resign themselves to this situation or be wholly eliminated from the political scene. That the socialists were fully aware of the dilemma was shown by the fact that two of their members occupied posts in the new government. As his first step toward a general reconciliation, Youlou proposed an amnesty law that led to the liberation of Opangault and 35 other political prisoners.

Youlou's next move was to form a government of national union, but one from which were eliminated all those MSA leaders who had been deeply compromised in the February incidents, and for this reason neither Opangault nor Kikhounga-Ngot was taken into his cabinet. His new government, which comprised 11 ministers and four secretaries of state, gave the MSA two portfolios. Bazinga was named a minister of state and Okomba minister of labor, the latter replacing Sombo-Dibelé, who was dropped from the cabinet. With a comfortable majority in the legislature and with some socialist participation in his government, Youlou had nothing to fear from the MSA, at least in the way of active opposition.

The eclipse of the MSA in the legislative elections had caused a serious internal crisis in that party. Its militants demanded a settling of accounts, and its leaders gave the impression of not knowing which way to turn. The most aggressive party members, who had seen their comrades arrested, were especially disillusioned with Opangault, who, since his liberation, had lapsed into passivity and resignation. Kikhounga-Ngot, more resilient, was active among the Bacougni, but to the northerners he was not acceptable as a true representative of the MSA. As for Antoine Léthembet-Ambily, who as a trade-union leader and an economic councilor could get publicity in the local press, he seemed to be using his party's disarray for his own personal advantage. The most dedicated socialists placed their hopes in the contacts which the highly respected and conciliatory MSA minister, Bazinga, made with French socialists during his trip to Paris.

The rank and file of the MSA had not yet grasped the truth about their party's position. The UDDIA's assumption of power had eliminated all the material advantages and opportunities enjoyed by the socialists when they were well represented in the cabinet, and when they also could count on their political ties with Metropolitan SFIO officials. The eclipse of the SFIO in General de Gaulle's government had not improved the position of the Congolese socialist party in the local scene. With old-timers still holding the top party posts, and unable to rely any longer on help from the Metropolitan socialists in Brazzaville and Pointe Noire (who had withdrawn from active politics upon the advent of the republic), the MSA had quickly become only the shadow of its former self. Consequently, a reorganization of the party structure could not revive the movement in the immediate future. The tribal influence of the redoubtable Opangault probably would enable the MSA to survive in certain areas, but that it could ever again become one of the Congo's major parties was unlikely.

By the end of the Congo Republic's first year of existence, during which virtually all the executive and legislative power had passed into the hands of the UDDIA, the opposition was made up of five blocs, each with its distinctive character. Sometimes they worked against the government separately, at others together, and they operated more often openly than sub rosa. The most important of these opposition groups was the MSA-PPC coalition, albeit represented in the cabinet. The political opposition offered by the MSA-PPC bloc was intensified by ethnic animosity. As a party, it was represented in the cabinet by two ministers, Bazinga and Okomba; on August 15, 1960, they were joined by a third socialist, Opangault; and three months later, two more members of the coalition—Kikhounga-Ngot and Bicoumat of the PPC—were added. Furthermore, there were 10 socialist deputies in the legislature, who had been elected from the Likouala and Likouala-Mossaka regions.

As to the ethnic aspect of this opposition, it could be said at the end of 1958 that the Mbochi were as strong as ever, in contrast to the political framework in which it then operated—the MSA-PPC party—which was shaken to its foundations. Indeed, that coalition was held together largely as a means of self-defense against the Lari, who formed the majority element in the UDDIA. The Mbochi and Sangha constituted the militant backbone of the MSA, while a few Vili and Bacougni were the last remnants of the PPC. Traditionally, all those tribal groups were strongly anti-Lari. "Anti-Balalism" was widespread among all the Vili of the Kouilou region, although most of them were political supporters of the former PPC leader, Tchichelle, who had become vice-president of the UDDIA. This racial antagonism stemmed partly from the sudden change of heart by the Lari, who in 1956 became active opponents of the northern electorate (composed of Mbochi, Sangha, Kouyou, and Téké tribes), and also of some of the southern electors (Vili, Bacougni, and Babembé tribes). By giving their support to Youlou—halfheartedly in the legislative elections of January 2, 1956, and fully in those from Brazzaville's municipal council the following November—the Lari had completely changed the geopolitical situation in the Congo.

A second and longer-established cause of anti-Balalism aggravated the political antagonism between the Mbochi and the Lari.[1] For many years, Mbochi clerks and secretaries, notably those educated at the M'Boundji mission, had formed the backbone of the local administrative personnel in both Brazzaville and Pointe Noire and also in the Congo-Ocean railroad company (CFCO). Naturally, the Mbochi resented the admission of Lari into the civil service, particularly in Brazzaville, where the Lari were on their home territory and more numerous. It also should be mentioned that the Lari were probably more competent and experienced, having benefited by their long contact with the French residents there. Furthermore, in Brazzaville, the Lari were concentrated in the Bacongo district whereas the Mbochi lived in the

midst of many other equatorial tribes in Poto-Poto—a geographical situation
that sharpened their mutual hostility. Political quarrels may have sparked
the riots at Pointe Noire in November 1958 and at Brazzaville in February
1959, but soon tribal enmity took over. Because those outbreaks had shown
the difficulty of controlling a rampaging mob once blood had begun to flow,
both parties made moves toward a reconciliation.

Nevertheless, the tribal hatred between the two rival blocs still persisted below the surface. After Youlou became head of the Congo government,
the Mbochi socialists boycotted Lari officials in all the areas controlled
by the MSA. Their antagonism was strengthened periodically by rumors of an
ethnic entente between the UDDIA and the Abako which, after the Belgian Congo
became independent, would result in the creation of an autonomous republic
composed of all the Bakongo in central Africa. Such fears inspired the MSA-
PPC to charge Youlou, in collusion with the Abako, with some responsibility
for the Léopoldville riots of January 1959.[2]

Lari-phobia was less marked among the Vili than among the Mbochi, thanks
to Tchichelle's moderating influence. Nevertheless, the Vili people, jealous
of their area's mineral wealth, have drawn closer on occasion to their Gabonese brothers in self-defense against the "Lari peril." Fanned by a disillusioned Tchicaya and a dyspeptic Kikhounga-Ngot, both openly hostile to the
government, a secessionist wind sometimes has blown over the southern region
of Kouilou and Niari, though less strongly than in the northern area of
Sangha-Likouala. In the latter region, the full-scale secessionist campaign
organized by the MSA early in 1959 impelled Youlou to consider holding a
plebiscite there on the issue. Well aware of the danger of secession for the
country, Youlou, aided by Tchichelle, constantly preached unity to the Congolese and tried to induce the socialists to share with the UDDIA responsibility
for the government.

The organized left-wing opposition to Youlou's government comprised two
principal groups—the CGAT unions and the radical youth movements. That element among the wage-earning members of the CGAT which properly could be called
proletarian resembled a coalition of adversaries to the government rather than
labor unionists. Without any basic organization, they had become dangerous
puppets in the hands of unscrupulous individuals, who either looked upon union
leadership as a job like any other or were Marxist ideologues. In the latter
case, they used unionization as a cover to keep up agitation among the working
class and to persuade union members that Youlou's government was antidemo-
cratic. Had control of the Congolese wage-earning class come into the hands
of trained and dedicated union leaders, the labor movement might have become
a dynamic force for the government and a stabilizing element in the country's
economy. Unfortunately, however, this was not the case. Even before wage
earners had been trained in unionization at the local level, there was talk
of a world or Pan-African labor movement, as well as of a single African labor
federation.

Because the demand for trained cadres exceeded the supply, an African
could move without transition from the status of a dues-paying union member
to that of a leader. A few weeks of rapid training in Europe could not teach
him the tactics required to lead a mass of turbulent and ignorant workers. In
recent years, the result has been a spontaneous burgeoning of embryonic
unions, which in Africa usually surface only when it comes time to make demands. When the Overseas Labor Code of 1952 came into force, these inchoate

unions were headed by men claiming to be valid representatives for negotiating with the _patronat_, which found them easy to handle. It should be noted, however, that the FO and CATC, despite the inexperience of their leaders, tried to instill in their African members a genuine trade-union spirit. The CGAT, on the other hand, initiated its membership in Marxist ideology by advocating anticolonialism, an easy form of propaganda in underdeveloped countries.[3]

In the Congo Republic, the predominantly political activities of the CGAT leaders were financed far more by the WFTU, the trade unions of Communist China, and the Soviet-African Friendship Association than by the French CGT. Those leaders became missionaries for international communism, using the poverty and precarious position of the laboring class to create unrest. The CGAT leadership never missed an opportunity to stress the bourgeois living standards enjoyed by the UDDIA ministers, deputies, and officials, contrasting them with the misery of the unemployed and the despair of the rural populations, and their criticism was the more telling because it had a basis in fact. Considering this situation, it seems inaccurate to describe the Congolese proletariat of that period as an opposition group, especially as the bulk of the working population was not fundamentally against the government and even understood the latter's difficulties in solving the unemployment problem. Certainly the workers wanted to raise their own living standards, but also would have liked to have found among the authorities some worthy examples of industry and responsibility. Among them, the only genuine opponents of the government's policy were a handful of indoctrinated individuals who, in the name of patriotism, would have subjugated the population in the process of achieving their goals.

The mystical-religious opposition to the government on the part of the hard-core Matsouanists cannot be described as truly radical, and it will inevitably die out within a few generations as an anticivic movement. In the meantime, it appeared to be an inoperable cancer for the republic, as well as a "shameful malady" for those Lari who were the most dynamic force in the Congo and on whom the government largely depended. Currently it was a danger for the UDDIA in that the young Lari who were hostile to Matsouanism might persist in viewing it as a racial problem to be suppressed by force—that is, by applying their customary laws rather than democratic procedures. As was seen in the Bacongo district and in the Pool region in June 1959, the hostility could easily have degenerated into a massacre had not Youlou intervened personally.

More to be feared than Matsouanism itself was the possibility that the radical Lari of the UJC would utilize the Matsouanist fanatics to prove the government's inability to enforce its own regulations. (They already had done this among the unorganized wage earners where they operated hand in glove with the CGAT leaders.) Such an instance occurred during the referendum campaign of September 1958, when they helped circulate a Matsouanist tract demanding unconditional independence for the Congo. In the same way, and especially at international meetings, the UJC stressed the repressive character of the government's measures against the Matsouanists as a new form of neocolonialist oppression. Consequently, it was as an instrument in the hands of an ideological minority that the few remaining Matsouanist die-hards could be considered a threat for Youlou's government.

By all odds, the most dangerous element of opposition to the government was that of the Marxist UJC, which the young Lari dominated. Its sphere of influence was restricted to Brazzaville, and its ties with the French communist party, and especially with the WFTU in Vienna, were well known. In conformity with the directive of international communism, the UJC's objective was total independence for the Congo, for by evicting the French administration its leaders hoped to take over the reins of government. Generally speaking, the UJC's activities were clandestine and its propaganda was spread by word of mouth, especially among the Lari, whose leaders could make use of their ethnic and family relationships to transmit directives. On such international issues as nuclear testing and the Algerian war, however, they took a stand openly, for they were sure of support from foreign countries and from many Pan-African movements. In some local matters, they also acted without concealment, as when they participated in the drafting of Boganda's memorandum to General de Gaulle in August 1958 and insisted that the word "independence" be written into the constitution, and also when they actively campaigned for a negative vote in the referendum. More recently, they joined in the chorus of opposition to French nuclear tests in the Sahara.

On the other hand, it has never been established that they played any role whatsoever in the February 1959 incidents, nor in those of the following June which involved the Matsouanists. Nevertheless, there was every reason to believe that collusion existed between the UJC and the Matsouanists. Through their family ties with members of the UDDIA youth organization and of the government, the UJC leaders were well informed about the activities as well as the weaknesses of both groups. As its model country, the UJC looked to Guinea, whose president, Sékou Touré, had a strong appeal for the young. He was also head of the Union Générale des Travailleurs de l'Afrique Noire (UGTAN), the CGAT's West African counterpart, and through that channel the UJC was in regular touch with the Guinean leaders, on whom they counted for unlimited aid. The UGTAN was used by the UJC to procure Guinean passports for its members to visit Iron Curtain countries, after the Congo government had refused to give them exit visas. They were also successful in obtaining a scholarship in Guinea for one of their members.

Both perforce and by ideology, the UJC youth were xenophobic, for in the Congo, the white man was a capitalist if he belonged to the private sector and an anticommunist if he were an adviser to the government. Their immediate goal, therefore, was Africanization of the administration, with the elimination of all French officials. Not only would this paralyze the administration, they believed, but by automatically weakening the government would make it more vulnerable to attack. The second step in their program was Africanization of the private sector, which would lead to the nationalization of trade and industry. To pave the way for such developments and also to promote their ideology, the UJC exploited the discontent of workers and functionaries. (It only needed the Léopoldville riots of January 1959 for the UJC leaders to offer their services as intermediaries between the Abako and certain communist countries which were delighted by the "Congolese rebellion.") By infiltrating the whole administrative apparatus, the UJC was dangerously undermining Youlou's government. Apparently he was well aware of the scope of their operations, and the year 1959 was to show how far he would let them go.

Bracketed with the UJC as ideological opponents of the government with a Marxist veneer were the Congolese students in France. Most of them worked inside the radical Fédération des Etudiants d'Afrique Noire Française (FEANF), but compared with the UJC militants they were lukewarm Marxists.[4] Indeed, the majority of African students in France have opposed their own governments simply on principle. Because they found their elected African representatives not aggressive enough about emancipating the colonial peoples, upon arrival in France they aligned themselves with the communist party, which alone was promoting independence for the underdeveloped countries. Anticolonialist while on vacation in Africa, these students became less so in France, where they could fraternize with the French. They regarded themselves as the elite of their country—and this was partly true because they had acquired a certain veneer of Western culture—and as such they were in opposition to a government headed by what they called "puppets of the French colonial administration." Yet when Youlou visited Paris, they quickly flocked around him to shake his hand, hoping that he would lend them small sums so that they could repay their personal debts.

For all their self-importance, these students had a serious handicap to overcome if they were ever to become locally a "valid opposition." Uprooted for some years from their country and divorced from their tribal background, they had for all practical purposes lost contact with the mass of the population and even with their own families. Having adopted, despite the small means at their disposal, a Western-bourgeois style of living, they could not readapt themselves to African ways of life for the short time when home on leave. To keep in touch with their home territory while abroad, they established contacts with the UJC. The UJC leaders were gratified by such a show of confidence, but they had no intention whatever of moving into the background and letting the students take their place.

The students who return to Africa after completing their studies in France find themselves submerged in the mass of their compatriots. The latter's indifference makes them lose their aggressiveness, especially as the difficulties they experience in readapting themselves absorb all their time. For those who bring back white wives, the adjustment is even harder because it complicates their family life. If, despite all such disadvantages, the activities of the Congolese students deserved attention, they were definitely less dangerous to Youlou than those of the UJC. This was because the latter group had a mass following among the young Lari, and by increasing it and by using Marxist methods, they could exploit the discontent of the masses.

To summarize, it could be said that the MSA-PPC coalition, despite its obvious weaknesses, remained the government's chief opponent. Next in importance came the left-wing labor unions, but their opposition was directed primarily against the increasingly bourgeois character of the UDDIA's leadership; although still without an authentic ideological base, it was tending to become more and more politicized. The pseudoreligious and mystical nature of Matsouanism made its hard-core members hostile on principle to any government, regardless of its nationality or its policy. Sometimes in association with the Matsouanists, there followed the numerically small but obstreperous UJC, whose ideology was definitely Marxist. Finally, there were the Congolese students assimilated to the UJC but lacking that organization's local power base and its more doctrinaire Marxist orthodoxy.

From the foregoing observations, it can be deduced that in taking its first steps the Congo Republic had to avoid falling into the traps laid for it by unscrupulous and tenacious opponents. The authoritarian character of Youlou's administration gave rise to various criticisms, but to impartial local observers his was the only possible policy if the country were not to fall a prey to anarchy and chaos. Naturally, the opposition's first reaction was to denounce Youlou as a dictator, but his behavior was more that of a paternalistic monarch than that of a despot. Toward his adversaries, Youlou's manner resembled that of an authentic African chief. He gave orders and took action but with the population's support, and this became evident as the legislature began building up the republic's institutions, stone by stone. Symbolic of this evolution was its adoption, six months after the republic was born, of a flag (red, yellow, and green), an anthem ("La Congolaise"), and a national motto (Unity, Work, and Progress).

As the legislature was winding up its extraordinary session, the cabinet drafted two laws. One concerned the creation of a special criminal court that would rapidly judge all cases affecting the state's internal security. The other laid the groundwork for instituting "civic service," by creating centers for training unemployed youths and utilizing their services. In October 1959, not only did the legislature approve these laws but even its socialist members joined in giving the government a vote of confidence. Thus Youlou had the legal basis as well as the determination to govern, and could now cope forcefully with both internal and external problems.

A week before the Congo Republic celebrated its first birthday on November 28, 1959, Youlou surprised both the Congolese and France by a sudden move. Instead of announcing a long-expected reshuffle of his cabinet, he presented to the legislature an important constitutional law that had been drafted by the UDDIA's executive committee. In essence, this law authorized the premier to assume immediately the title of president of the republic. Its unanimous acceptance by the deputies testified to the desire of all factions to cooperate with Youlou in bringing about unity among the Congolese people. Opangault, in seconding the motion, added that the premier thereby would become not only the head of state but its first magistrate, and as such would belong to no political party. At the republic's birthday celebrations one week later, Youlou appeared for the first time in public wearing the Grand Cordon of the Congolese Order of Merit. He thanked his "Congolese children" and all those who had worked for the nation's unity, and he included France and the Frenchmen who had helped to build the Congo.

Thus, the year 1959 ended in an atmosphere of apparent reconciliation, in contrast to that of 1958, which had known bloodshed, exasperation, and tension. It now seemed that all Youlou's efforts to achieve unity and harmony had not been put forth in vain. The socialist deputies had freely consented to Youlou's elevation to the presidency of the republic, and had shown their willingness to collaborate with their UDDIA colleagues. Even such radicals as Sombo-Dibelé and Jean-Gaston Bagana had left the extremist UJC movement to serve the government of the republic. And, finally, the young Vili, who had been Tchicaya's faithful supporters, also had chosen to follow the path of national union. Consequently, as the momentous year 1960 began, Youlou knew that he could count at least on the passivity of his opponents and on the desire of most Congolese politicians to rise above ethnic, religious, and political quarrels so as to strengthen the republic's institutions.

<u>Notes</u>

1. See pp. 1-21.

2. See p. 67.

3. As of 1958, the FO comprised 23 unions, the CATC 31, and the CGAT 19. During the preceding decade, membership in the autonomous unions had declined, the Christian unions had expanded, and the others had remained fairly stationary. Passage of the French Overseas Labor Code in 1952, probably more than union organization, had spurred the militancy of Congolese wage earners. According to Wagret (op. cit., p. 207), the number of workers on strike had more than doubled by 1960, as compared with 1950, rising from 925 to 1,878.

4. As of 1959, there were 85 Congolese studying in France.

CHAPTER 12

INDEPENDENCE

In 1959, the Congo's external relations were focused on the evolution
of the Franco-African Community. The long-standing dispute between the RDA
and PRA, which had not been settled by the referendum of September 1958, was
brought to a head by the formation, early in the year, of the Mali Federation by Modibo Keita of Soudan and Léopold Senghor of Senegal.

Youlou headed a large UDDIA delegation that attended an extraordinary
congress of the RDA held at Abidjan in September. His speech there sug-
guested a modification of his views on the Community, although he continued
to support it as a collective venture by culturally homogeneous states concerned to promote social and economic progress. Increasingly, Youlou was
moving away from Houphouët-Boigny's antifederalist position, and he now
seemed to be advocating a confederation of independent African states associated with France. In this, he was influenced by General de Gaulle's new
stress on the "evolutionary character" of the Community, which paved the way
for the Mali Federation's acquisition of a sovereign status.

A few weeks later, Youlou's speech to General de Gaulle and his colleagues—assembled in Paris on the eve of the fifth meeting of the Community's executive committee—reflected the reasons for this change in his
views. He insisted that the "malaise now affecting the Community" was not
due to any faltering in its members' belief in that organization's basic
concept or in their attachment to General de Gaulle himself, but to their
disillusionment with the "haughty and dilatory" behavior of highly placed
French officials toward the needs and aspirations of the new African states.
In this respect, his sharp criticisms echoed those of many of the heads of
the other francophone African states.

As a matter of fact, Youlou's views on confederation and independence
for the Community states were not rooted in any political ideology but had a
highly practical motivation. For him, political sovereignty was meaningless
without economic independence. To reach the latter goal, the Congo required
an increase in France's financial aid, and so Youlou continued to lavish
praise on General de Gaulle, who held the key to such grants. Some of Youlou's audience felt that he was using the threat of seeking independence for
the Congo as a weapon to force a French decision favorable to construction
of the Kouilou dam. The concurrent visit to Paris of the Congolese finance
minister seemed to confirm this strategy. Thus far, France's grants-in-aid
had been far smaller than the amount that Youlou deemed necessary for his
government, the more so as some of its expenditures were sumptuary. In a
wider perspective, the Congo's financial stringent and malaise were due to
the stagnation in production which, in turn, led to unemployment and social
unrest.

All the country's hopes for improving the economic situation had come to be centered on construction of the Kouilou dam and on the industrialization of Pointe Noire. Youlou, for his part, had staked his whole political future on carrying out this project. Early in September, this obsession with the Kouilou dam had been intensified by a ceremony in which the Congolese and Gabonese authorities jointly inaugurated the initial work on the railroad that would carry the manganese of Franceville across the Congo to the port of Pointe Noire.[1] While this railroad would certainly help to open up an inaccessible region of the Congo, it foreshadowed a major development of Gabon's economy, and as such was galling to Youlou. On more than one occasion, he was moved to imply that the Franceville mines belonged to the Congo rather than to Gabon, and such talk was hardly pleasing to the latter's president, Léon Mba. While Gabon was forging ahead, the Kouilou project had not yet progressed beyond the stage of "studies." In view of the world economic situation at this time, about which Youlou professed ignorance, French financiers were reluctant to take the risks involved.

In the Congo Republic, the word "Kouilou" was more magical than that of "independence," for in that project all the Congolese, of whatever political stripe, had placed their hopes. This was particularly true of the rising generation, which was strongly influenced by radical ideology. Youlou feared for the stability of his government unless he could offer the Kouilou project as an outlet for the energies of Congolese youth and as a means of enabling it to work for better living conditions. His bitterness was increased by the likelihood, at that time, that the Konkouré dam in Guinea would be built before that of Kouilou.[2] "What can I say to my young people who look up to Sékou Touré, for he will have his dam although he left the Community?" he asked in a speech of September 16, 1959, and went on to say, "Since the Congo is the gateway to central Africa, France should realize that it has every interest in keeping our country in the Community."

Nevertheless, Youlou issued a warning at a press conference held on September 20, 1959, to those Congolese who were pleased by the prospect that he might break away from the Community in a moment of despair. "The Congolese nation is a reality and it controls its own destiny. Under the constitution of the Community, which we accepted by an overwhelming vote in the 1958 referendum, we can choose total independence if we so desire. But being able to declare ourselves independent is quite different from making such independence a reality. Colonialism exists in many forms, and one of them is the dictatorship imposed by an ideology..." By such words, Youlou was also trying to calm the fears that had been awakened among the resident French businessmen by his veiled threat to leave the Community. A few days later, he tried another tactic in addressing the members of a visiting French parliamentary mission. In introducing the subject of his country's economic difficulties, he stressed the "red threat" that menaced Africa, claiming that the communists were using investments there as a means of undermining Europe from its southern flank. He ended his speech by appealing to both the white and black peoples to form a genuine Community.

Youlou's conciliatory gestures toward France were to some degree countered by the president of the legislature, Massamba-Débat, in his address opening the budgetary session in November. Massamba-Débat blamed the colonial regime for disrupting Congolese unity by creating a "diversity of parties," and the present French government for failing to satisfy the "just" needs of the country. French officials, "many of whom no longer have any place in our states," must be made to realize that time was running out and that "hunger leads to anger." It would be disastrous, he added, if the Community should break up because of France's pettiness and niggardliness. The 16 billion francs that France had spent in the four equatorial territories in 1959 were, in Massamba-Débat's words, "far below what we expected and what is due us from the Community." At the celebrations of the republic's first anniversary later that same month, Youlou poured some oil on the troubled waters by praising General de Gaulle as "one of the greatest statesmen of our times, and a benefactor of humanity to whom we can never express enough thanks."

General de Gaulle's historic decision to permit an independent Mali Federation to remain a member of the Community, and thus continue to receive French aid, was announced on December 12, 1959. It drastically altered the course of the Community's evolution, as well as the attitude of its member states toward both France and each other. Upon returning to Brazzaville, Youlou praised France for its liberality and General de Gaulle "as the instrument of God's will." He was also visibly impressed by the warm welcome that had been given him by the Senegalese and, even more, by the lavish ceremonies that took place at Dakar. The new aspect given to the Community soon wrought a change in Youlou's attitude toward independence and in the Congo's relations with the other territories of former French Equatorial Africa. At Pointe Noire, Youlou prudently said that he favored the formation of a

> small community of sovereign equatorial states provided they achieved their independence in unity and by hard work, the two cornerstones of the Congolese structure....We, too, are a nation, with the requisite organs of a presidency of the republic, a national assembly, and a government. It now remains for us to assume international responsibilities.... The path lies clearly before us, and we have not a minute to lose....[3]

In his messages to the nation at Christmas and on New Year's day, Youlou repeated his exhortation to hard work and, as a requisite for construction of the Kouilou dam, it became the leit-motiv of his government's policy.

Among his more specific policy objectives outlined in these messages, Youlou cited an accelerated Africanization of the cadres in both the public and private sectors, increased production, a campaign to lower prices so as to raise the population's living standards, and closer links between the four equatorial states. Youlou's stress on economic goals and the necessity for hard work to attain them was echoed and reinforced by Vial, his minister of finance. In a speech on January 16, 1960, closing the legislature's budgetary session, Vial described the Congo's three-year plan. He said in a speech to the legislature on January 17, 1960,

> it must not be a simple catalog of operations to be financed, but an overall instrument for promoting future economic development. To be feasible, it must be envisaged in the setting of a geographical group that includes those neighboring countries which exercise a decisive influence on the Congo's economy. The plan concentrates on three main sectors: Pointe Noire, where a free-trade industrial zone is to be created; the regions north of the Niari, which will certainly be affected by the Comilog railroad; and those of the north, about whose economic potential little is known.

Youlou's publicly announced stand in favor of national sovereignty for the Congo and close relations with other equatorial states cut the ground from under the UJC radicals, who had always claimed a monopoly in demanding independence for the country. This deprived Matsika, Boukambou, and other nationalists of the chance to denounce his government again for failing to set a goal on which all the population was agreed. It also provided Youlou with another opportunity to exhort the Congolese on February 17, 1960, to "work and serve. Exert yourselves for the benefit of all. That is the law of the Congo."

All these appeals for individual and collective effort fell on deaf ears. The unemployed of Brazzaville responded by asking the government to find them jobs, but not one of them wanted to return to the land, whose cultivation alone could rescue the country from its economic stagnation. The Congolese felt none of the "mystique of human investment"[4] which Sékou Touré, by force or by persuasion, had instilled in the Guineans.

Youlou's next move was political and authoritarian. At a three-day congress held in a Brazzaville suburb, the UDDIA ruled that no member could belong to both that party and the UJC. It further warned the party's youth who had been seduced by the demagogic promises of the UJC leaders that they had become unwitting propagandists for Marxist ideology. During January 1960, there was much talk of an imminent cabinet reshuffle, and this impelled Opangault to make a statement to the press. He said that he never had been asked by the premier, nor had he ever sought, to occupy a ministerial post and that his only concern was to work in the interests of the country.

The abortive coup d'état at Algiers on January 24, in which 20 persons were killed during a clash between the police and the partisans of a "French Algeria," had repercussions in the Congo only upon its French residents. Nevertheless, the incident provided the Congolese leaders with food for thought, because it showed that even so popular a figure as General de Gaulle was not firmly in power. Perhaps the possibility that he might be overthrown made Youlou more determined than ever to wrest from France a pledge that the Congo would be granted independence. Certainly other factors caused him to seek the same assurances as had been given to Mali and Madagascar, and of these factors, the most compelling was the precarious situation in the nearby Belgian Congo.[5]

As for the internal political situation, Youlou had long been considering changes in his cabinet. By reducing the number of his ministers from 15 to 10, he hoped to make his administration more efficient and also to nip in the bud criticism from his opponents as to his government's expenditures. But it proved difficult to eliminate five ministers without playing into the hands of the opposition, inasmuch as most of his cabinet had been selected to represent specific ethnic groups. Finally, he solved the problem by giving important civil-service posts to Dadet and Bikoumou, the two ministers who had the smallest constituencies, and also dropping his three French cabinet members, Vial, Jayle, and Bru. This reshuffle proved to have greater psychological than financial significance. In the new government, Youlou took the portfolio of justice and Tchichelle retained that of the interior. The other ministers were Bazinga (information), Gandzion (education and youth), Mahouata (health and population), Okomba (labor), N'Gouala (public works and transport), Goura (economic affairs and finance), Samba (agriculture and livestock), Ibouanga (industrial production), and Sathoud (civil service).

No noticeable adverse reactions on the part of the electorate followed the announcement in mid-February of the new cabinet's composition. Consequently, Youlou was able to attend a summit conference of the equatorial states at Bangui, followed by a tour of France, without feeling apprehensive about the local situation. Yet, while he was absorbed by international affairs, trouble was brewing at home. Early in the year, the time came to renew some important collective labor agreements, and this prompted wage earners in the main towns to demand better terms. The campaign they conducted under orders from their leaders had barely disguised antiforeign overtones. Through petitions and demonstrations, most of the unions demanded that some French employers, whom they called "bad whites," leave the territory for good. Inasmuch as most of the charges against them were patently false, it seemed that this demand had been motivated by a desire for personal revenge on the part of some incompetent employees. Regardless of their justification, such accusations created an atmosphere of distrust and caused some businessmen and top-ranking cadres to worry about losing their jobs. Since their precarious situation soon became known to their head offices in France, there was little likelihood that the latter would respond favorably to the Youlou government's solicitation for new capital investments in the Congo.

The French lack of confidence in the territory's stability, on the one hand, and the problem of unemployment among the Congolese, on the other, created a general malaise. To dissipate it, Youlou could think of nothing more than to appeal once again to the "courage and enthusiasm" of Congolese youth, and to Westerners to finance the Kouilou project. He asked a visiting group of American journalists to "come and build the dam and transform Pointe Noire into an industrial town. You are practical men and businessmen, and please tell America for me that this is the moment of decision." Merchants and industrialists, however, felt that there was too much oratory and too little realistic action. Furthermore, they were worried about the deterioration in the Congo's economy, which perhaps could be ascribed to its uncertain status, midway between autonomy and independence. As to the reaction in France, economic leaders there simply proposed that Youlou make a "friendly study tour" of their country as a means of countering the Congo's xenophobia and social unrest.

While Youlou was enjoying his tour of France, the UJC and MSA forces were working in the Congo to undermine popular confidence in his government. Well aware of the dangers, his cabinet drafted a series of laws "for the defense of the republic," which were passed by the legislature on May 11, 1960. Among such measures were one that required all associations to register with the authorities, who would dissolve any that they considered to be working against the national interests, and another that instituted a censorship which, in effect, empowered the government to arrest or expel any individual who wrote or voiced sentiments they judged to be "dangerous." Upon returning from France, Youlou did not wait for the legislature to take action as authorized under these laws but ordered sweeping arrests of all the UJC and CGAT leaders in the main towns.[6]

Among those charged with intent to harm the internal security of the state was Kikhounga-Ngot, whom the government had long suspected of collusion with the UJC leaders. Although he always had been on good terms with the CGAT leadership and openly opposed to Youlou's methods of government, his arrest was probably due to the machinations of some of the abbé's semiofficial political advisers. Later the CGAT leaders published a memorandum denouncing the authorities' arbitrary victimization of the members of the unions and the UJC on trumped-up charges. Time was to prove the validity of such accusations, for the charges of plotting were never brought before the courts and, what was more, Kikhounga left prison to become a minister in Youlou's cabinet. Notwithstanding the dubious legality of the arrests, the deliberately provocative actions of the police, and the publicity given to the whole operation in the official press, the sequestration of the procommunist Congolese elements had a calming effect on the urban wage earners and business circles.

The driving force behind Youlou's recourse to such extreme measures was his obsessive fear of communism. This was shown when he seized the opportunity to stigmatize the local "fishers in troubled waters" in a press conference on April 24, 1960, reporting on his trip through France. He then spoke of

> the ease with which our people can be manipulated by idealists thirsty for power...Everyone knows that misery gives birth to faith in communism, and that hunger deafens understanding. Unemployment is a social danger, the greater because it influences the uneducated classes, who are unprepared to make use of their leisure time. Soon I hope to heal this gaping wound from which our young republic suffers.

A few days later, before an audience of Pointe Noire businessmen, he again stressed the "dangers of communism." On May 10, 1960, he told the legislature that "certain of our misled compatriots...who dream of a new people's democracy, take their orders from professional foreign agitators. I have proof of this in the many telegrams sent from Prague, Peking, and Moscow protesting against the measures we have taken."

The Congo's impending declaration of independence inspired in Opangault fears of a wholly different kind from those of Youlou. He told the legislature on May 10 that even if the presidents of France and the Congo were in agreement, theirs was only the opinion of two men, for no plebiscite on the issue had been held either in France or in the Congolese republic. He himself considered independence per se to be normal and even desirable, but he had grave doubts about its evolution in the Congo.

> Can we talk about genuine democracy in a country where most of its citizens rarely know enough to formulate their own opinions about the problems that confront the nation? Should we sacrifice the material wellbeing of our people to our passion for power? What good will the sovereignty to which we aspire actually do us, if it is associated with such poverty that it generates riots and a dictatorship?

Opangault's misgivings were shared by other members of the MSA, who also feared that the UDDIA government would make use of independence to further reduce their small share of governmental responsibilities. In mid-June a wide-ranging attack on the UDDIA government was led by Leyet-Gaboka, the MSA rapporteur in the legislature. He reproached the government for failing to live up to its promises to the people, and singled out its "ruinous" financial and social policy for special criticism. Youlou replied to these accusations and threats by a recital of the accomplishments of his administration.

Then Biyoudi, speaking in the name of the UDDIA, attacked Leyet-Gaboka as a defender of colonialism, denounced the MSA as "the African branch of the materialistic and Marxist SFIO," and finally asked all the deputies to unite, for "it is not by stirring up tribal hatreds that we shall build the Congolese nation." Before the meeting adjourned, he proposed a vote of confidence in the government, which the socialists supported to show their good will and spirit of cooperation.

In early July 1960, Youlou went to Paris to sign the documents relating to the transfer of powers to the Congo. Upon his return to Brazzaville, he found the population preoccupied by the violent outbreaks in the Belgian Congo. He concerned himself with the plight of the European refugees from Léopoldville, and visited the centers in Brazzaville where they had been given shelter. The hospitality extended to these refugees by Europeans and Africans alike received favorable comment in the world press, where journalists contrasted the humanitarian action and calm of the Brazzavillians with the anarchy prevailing on the other side of the Congo River. This redounded to the credit of all the Congo Republic, whereas the disorderly flight of the Europeans from Léopoldville certainly did not enhance the white man's prestige.

The situation in the ex-Belgian Congo after it became independent inevitably awakened the fears of some European and foreign residents in the former French Congo, and fantastic rumors heightened their tension as August 15 approached. This was the day set for the Congo Republic's proclamation of sovereignty. To what extent were such apprehensions justified? Aside from some embittered individuals who heedlessly talked about revenge, expulsions, and even punishment, the behavior of the Congolese toward the Europeans living in their midst was not aggressive. The situation was not the same, however, when it came to their attitude toward the resident alien Africans, notably Dahomeans, Ghanaians, Togolese, and Malians—who generally held the best posts, thanks to their knowledge of accountancy and their mercantile competence, while the native Congolese occupied inferior positions. Because of the West Africans' monopoly of the top jobs, they also enjoyed higher living standards than did the Congolese wage earners. The latter's latent jealousy risked becoming exacerbated with the proclamation of independence, because those advocating a "Congolization" of all employment were busy stirring up the masses. In Libreville and Abidjan, similar ethnic antagonisms had already led to serious incidents.

To calm the population and to revive the confidence of the alien African residents, Youlou and Tchichelle toured the main towns. They urged that the country's independence be proclaimed in a harmonious atmosphere of union between whites and blacks and between Africans of every ethnic origin. They also tried to explain the true meaning of independence, stressing that it entailed obligations as well as privileges. Then Youlou, accompanied by Opangault, visited the northern regions for the first time. In this traditional MSA fief, his reception could not have been called cordial, but neither was it hostile. Moreover, some northerners expressed their willingness to support a government headed by Youlou, especially as Opangault was to join his cabinet on independence day as a minister of state.

At the end of July, the legislature met and unanimously ratified the agreements for the transfer of powers, and this gave its president, Massamba-Débat, the opportunity to express the country's gratitude to France and to

General de Gaulle. To make independence day one of special celebration, the government granted to all its employees a bonus of 1,000 francs, and the patronat followed suit for those in the private sector. No effort was spared to make August 15 a day of happiness and harmony. Once again Youlou underscored the necessity for unity among all Congolese, now "free and equal before the law," and he publicly thanked Opangault for the "courage he has always displayed." On the previous day, the Franco-Congolese agreements had been solemnly initialed by André Malraux, representing General de Gaulle, and by Abbé Fulbert Youlou. At midnight, a 101-gun salute announced that the hour of independence had arrived. The official ceremonies, parades, and general festivities, which lasted for three days, obscured the fears that had been widespread a fortnight before.

On the same day that the Congo Republic became independent, it asked for admission to the United Nations. Youlou, on August 16, unveiled a statue of General de Gaulle, erected as a permanent testimonial of the gratitude, respect, and affection of the Congolese people. A few hours later, the high commissioner of France presented his credentials to the president of the Congo Republic in sign of prompt and solemn recognition of a sovereignty that France had offered generously and of its free will. While congratulations poured in from most of the world governments, the sound of tam-tams in the most distant villages announced the birth of a new state—and one that now was face to face with realities. Within a few days of the Congo's proclamation of independence, similar ceremonies were taking place in Tchad (August 11), the Central African Republic (August 13), and Gabon (August 17).

Notes

1. The Compagnie Minière de l'Ogooué, or Comilog, was an internationally financed company formed in 1953 to mine the manganese deposits of Franceville in Gabon. It built an aerial cableway 85 kilometers long, and a 285-kilometer railroad connecting it with the Congo-Ocean tracks between Dolisie and Loudima.

2. Since 1921, a series of studies by the French authorities in Guinea had been made of the hydroelectric potential of the Konkouré River, whose many waterfalls represent a vast source of power. Interest in constructing a dam where its course flows near the large bauxite deposits of Kindia and Boké grew rapidly in the 1950s with the expansion of Guinea's mining industry. However, the economic viability of this technically feasible project has been considered so uncertain that the dam has not yet been built.

3. Reported in L'Homme Nouveau, December 1959.

4. "Human investment" was the term applied to the unpaid services of young Guinean volunteers for the building of public works.

5. See chapter 15.

6. The scope and consequences of these arrests were greater than is indicated by this statement. The detention of 15 CGAT and UJC leaders on charges of plotting was the culmination of a series of anticommunist

measures that began in 1959. That year, Youlou drew up a list of his radical opponents so that the police could check on their movements at home and abroad. At a meeting in December, the CGAT hardliners reacted by expelling all the moderates who had collaborated with the government. Then, in January 1960, Youlou forbade members of the JUDDIA to belong also to the UJC. Four months later, the authorities intercepted a letter written by Boukambou to the WFTU announcing the CGAT's decision to create a revolutionary Congolese party, and this sparked the arrests that demoralized and disorganized the CGAT and UJC. At the same time, Youlou refused passports to Congolese radicals, and banned the circulation of communist publications in the Congo.

CHAPTER 13

A PRECARIOUS UNION

By November 28, 1960—two years after the republic was proclaimed and three months after it became independent—Youlou had brought off his tour de force. He had succeeded in forming a government of national union composed of members of the MSA and the PPC as well as of his faithful UDDIA followers. By bringing first Opangault into the cabinet, then Kikhounga-Ngot (freed from prison on November 20), and finally Germain Bicoumat, Tchicaya's most trusted lieutenant, Youlou at the very least had shared his governmental responsibility with leaders of all the Congolese parties. In this way, he also had publicly demonstrated his desire for political harmony that would transcend party loyalties. Youlou's strategy was clever, for he had prevented his adversaries from openly criticizing his government and, at the same time, calmed the racial antagonisms that had become conspicuous in recent years.

Although, at the executive level, it seemed that personal quarrels stemming largely from jealousy no longer hampered the cabinet's teamwork, the political atmosphere in the legislature was far from being as harmonious as the premier desired. For some time, both the 45 progovernment deputies and the 10 who belonged to the opposition parties had clearly and loudly expressed their resentment at being treated as "anonymous pawns" which Youlou moved about to suit his personal policies. Such policies, they complained, did not always conform to the promises that they had made to their constituents; furthermore, even when they were not completely ignored, they could not exercise the prerogatives that were their due as elected representatives of the people.

The legislators' widespread discontent was voiced in strong terms by their president, Massamba-Débat, at the opening of the budgetary session on November 4. Annoyed by the government's failure as yet to have submitted its draft budget to the legislature, he said that he would register his displeasure by omitting to make the customary opening speech. Changing his mind, however, he scolded the government for the cavalier way in which it treated the deputies, and he also expressed disapproval of its financial policy. His criticism substantiated reports circulating in Brazzaville about the capricious and inconsistent way in which the government dealt with the budget. Massamba-Débat went on to say:[1]

> I am unaware of the reasons for the delay in submitting the draft budget, especially since at the last session we asked that it be presented in a detailed, precise and clear manner. Our discussions and our work will be less productive because of this procrastination. Success in budgeting for the state, as is the case for the family, depends in principle less on the volume of the funds involved than on the way in which they are managed.

Massamba-Débat's caustic criticism was a logical sequel to the reprimand given the government, and especially to Youlou, on September 13, when the deputies had refused to allow the premier the free hand financially that he solicited. The 1960 budget, first estimated at 3,300 million CFA francs,[2] already had been raised twice—to 4,465 million—and Youlou's latest request for another increase was based largely on the cost of the November 28 independence-day celebrations. Fifty million were to be expended on those celebrations and on organizing the Brazzaville group conference,[3] the total being a substantial sum which the unemployed of Poto-Poto and Bacongo felt could be better devoted to them. On the other hand, some deputies criticized the government for taking 100 million CFA francs from the Fonds Routier to pay a few weeks' wages to jobless men for improving the road network. This sum was to be spent partly on roads in the north, but in Brazzaville the money was wasted, for not even that town's drains were repaired.

Because of its adverse budgetary repercussions, Youlou's well-known financial impulsiveness was not relished by the deputies. The people's wishes should certainly be respected, said their president, but the government should be courageous enough to give priority to those that would be most useful to the country. The assembly's rebuke, not to say defiance, gave rise to bitter comments about the government, of which Youlou's adversaries made good use. Youlou had been caught unawares by Massamba-Débat's criticism; hence, he made no allusion to it in his own speech to the legislature. This omission gave rise to fresh rumors, and they reached such proportions that Massamba-Débat, after announcing that the 1961 budget of 5,275 million CFA francs had been voted unanimously by the deputies, added a note of warning. He denounced the rumor mongers for causing "division and confusion" among the Congolese workers, and denied that a rift had occurred between the assembly and the government.

Perhaps Massamba-Débat was right in saying that there was no unbridgeable gulf between the executive and the legislative branches, but intrigues were creating discord in the ranks of the UDDIA. That party was especially vulnerable to such maneuvers because it had been inactive for more than a year. Disagreements among its members could not but benefit the political opposition, particularly the left-wing labor leaders and students, who always had been hostile to Youlou and his government. Actually, the opposition to Youlou was of two types—practical as to finances, and theoretical with respect to the exercise of political power. On both counts, his enemies were united against Youlou. It was mainly the unemployed of Brazzaville and certain deputies who criticized the abbé's spendthrift habits and his sumptuary expenditures, whereas the students and, even more, the president of the legislature were opposed in principle to the assumption of ever greater personal authority toward which Youlou was clearly moving.

In reply to the latter category of critics, Youlou chose his faithful friend, Senator Ibalico, to defend his viewpoint. On January 5, 1961, Ibalico made a speech to his fellow deputies in which he expressed gratitude to both Youlou and Opangault, and then took up the basic issue:

> To make the Congo strong and prosperous, we need to have a leader who wields authority according to African concepts of power. I mean by that, an individual who incarnates all the attributes of sovereignty, which excludes any dual executive or sharing of power. The goal that we

should set for ourselves in 1961 is that of applying African methods to our local situation. We must have a government that enjoys total power, and this means that we must re-think our policy from top to bottom.

Between the lines of his speech, Ibalico was transmitting a sharp warning to Massamba-Débat, whose political principles were those of a French-type democracy. Massamba-Débat took up the challenge and defended his position by saying:[4]

I believe that a complete identity of views could be interpreted as a conspiracy against the nation. On condition that divergencies of opinion are not synonymous with hostility, I humbly suggest that they are very salutary for nation-building. Should the deputies docilely follow the cabinet's lead, they will never form a good working team but, rather, resemble a herd of sheep, and that is not what our people want.

A few months later, Youlou made Massamba-Débat pay dearly for what the abbé regarded as an overliberal interpretation of the principles of African democracy. What is more, Massamba-Débat failed in his essential purpose of promoting parliamentary democracy. On the contrary, and perhaps against his own wishes, Massamba-Débat was providing ammunition to the government's detractors by publicly acknowledging that the assembly which he chaired never had shared in government policy-making. It was Massamba-Débat's belief that a parliamentary opposition could be beneficial to the government without impairing its authority, but in Africa, as Ibalico reminded him, democratic concepts have nothing in common with those of the West. An African country's policy becomes identified with that of its leader, the responsible head of state. The moment opposition to him is publicly expressed, it becomes ineffectual because it sounds a false note in the overall harmony. In the preceding two years, Youlou had done everything he could to throttle the opposition, even by force, and thereafter to make his opponents into allies and associates in sharing governmental responsibilities. In any case, such appeared to be his theory of government, for every minister knew that it was Youlou and Youlou alone who governed and that they held their posts simply as administrators and as the loyal executants of his orders.

Youlou was certainly not unique in Africa, particularly in the equatorial states. In Gabon, Mba did not hesitate to eliminate from his administration Paul Gondjout, his political teammate, intimate friend, and president of the Gabonese assembly. Gondjout had shown too openly that he did not share Mba's views on government, and, after three years of disagreements, he allied himself with Mba's strongest adversary, Aubame. Upon his accession to power, President Dacko of the Central African Republic got rid of his former ally and current opponent, Dr. Abel Goumba, whom he later prosecuted in the courts. Goumba had been the vice-president of Oubangui-Chari's first government council and an early member of the MESAN, but after Boganda's death, he had formed a new party, whose support came from the eastern Banda tribes. Two years later, Dacko banned all parties except the MESAN. In Tchad, Tombalbaye had played on ethnic prejudice to eliminate Lisette, a French citizen of Antilles origin and too shrewd a politician to please him, and he then eliminated all of his Tchadian opponents. A few months later, he dissolved the legislature and then held elections with a single slate of candidates. By this device, he received the votes of 80 percent of the registered electorate, and after revising the constitution, he became president of the republic in 1962.

Thinking in African terms became more and more widespread in the newly independent nations. Their heads of state believed that the mass of their populations could understand only the use of force. In this political perspective, the views of Massamba-Débat were retrogressive. It is no wonder, therefore, that they were used against him, not only by those who, out of revenge, sought to break up the UDDIA and reduce the premier's power but also by Youlou himself who, in the pursuit of his goals, would tolerate no criticism from his entourage. Nevertheless, Youlou was apparently not duped by such intrigues. He simply pretended to ignore them, the more easily to carry out his own objectives. To avoid being placed in a less advantageous position, just at the time when major confrontations were about to occur in Africa, Youlou followed the example set by the heads of the Congo's sister republics.

Youlou's inferiority complex vis-à-vis his peers explains his grand design to achieve a union of parties and also his concern to have only friends among the deputies and the customary chiefs alike. Another consideration was his need to gain time in order to legitimatize his rule by a national plebiscite. For those reasons, he made every effort, beginning in January 1961, to win over his political adversaries. In fact, he made so many concessions to them that his UDDIA comrades-in-arms began to be suspicious of his motives. His partisans were not taken into his confidence, for Youlou believed that after he had attained his objective he could win them back by openly explaining his strategy. Although he judged that the time had not yet come to mention that his goal was to form a single party, all Youlou's behavior indicated that he was moving rapidly in that direction. At the time, it was indispensable that he consolidate a genuine union, for on this would depend his success in a plebiscite which he desired as the popular confirmation of his presidency.

The first major victory in his program was the legislature's acceptance of his plea for constitutional reform. It was opposed by some deputies on principle, but was finally adopted by the assembly on March 2. The new presidential constitution empowered Youlou to govern the country for eight years—that is, three more years with the present legislature and another five years with its successor. Youlou undoubtedly would be elected president but whether he could cope with the growing social malaise was open to question. Under pressure from the African labor leaders, experienced Europeans in the main industrial centers were being forced to leave their jobs and the Congo itself, the alternative being their sudden dismissal upon orders from Youlou himself. His government put up little resistance to the demagogic demand for the replacement of Europeans by Africans that swept over the country.[5]

Despite its evident desire to work constructively, the government unfortunately could not resolve the many problems that face underdeveloped and newly sovereign states. The Congolese people expected miracles from their country's independence, and they looked upon Youlou as their magician. Although he could be credited with having rapidly imposed his authority, calmed agitation, and checked intertribal conflicts which might have plunged the Congo into anarchy, he had failed to solve other equally difficult problems. One of the most critical of these was posed by idle youths, ideologically eager for changes that would provide an outlet for their energies or at least a means of livelihood. Although he had dealt forcefully with the

Matsouanists, Youlou had not been able to hold in check all of the retrogressive messianic cults that might eventually encourage a narrowly nationalistic and antiforeign outlook in the masses. (It looked as though he were actually promoting Kimbangism in the Pool region as an expression of anticlericalism.) Moreover, he had been unable to win the confidence of the intellectual elite. Its members were embittered because they had not been given responsible posts and were therefore deprived of the material advantages that went with government office.

During its first year in power, the government had decreed obligatory civic service to provide work for youths who ostensibly wanted employment but who were very choosy about the jobs they would accept. Its aim was to orient unskilled young men toward rural occupations. For a country where agriculture was a prime necessity and farmers were perennially underemployed, the principle behind civic service was admirable. To carry out this policy, a school for training civic leaders (Ecole des Cadres Civiques) was established, but after it had been in operation for a year, it seemed to have deviated from its original purpose and become a center for training military officers. Unfortunately, the "rural mystique" concept was not fully grasped either by its students or by those in the regular academic institutions. In his address to the first class to graduate from the Civic Cadres School, Youlou noted its students' expressed wish to serve in the army rather than in the rural posts for which they had been trained. He seemed to imply that the recently formed Congolese national army might provide an alternative solution to the problem of finding constructive employment for the youths who rejected agricultural occupations.

Opinion was divided as to the respective merits of these alternatives. Some felt that it would be advisable to cut short a costly experiment that would at best only turn young people into temporary parasites of the state, and in the long run make them more embittered than ever because they had no skills that would provide them with jobs. Others, on the contrary, hoped that the army or the school for civic leaders would transform the youths into disciplined, well-balanced, and responsible men. If such training enabled them to become dynamic leaders of an industrious nation, they might usefully promote the republic's evolution.

In 1960, the outlook for such a transformation did not seem promising, for already there was considerable unrest in the army and gendarmerie. The members of those forces were fully aware of how rapidly soldiers in the army of Colonel Mobutu in the other Congo were being promoted. Consequently, they felt themselves discriminated against in their own country, where independence had brought about no such changes in the military structure and had benefited only civilians.

Their sense of grievance was shared by the local civil servants, who resented the numerous, if futile, trips made by the Congolese ministers and deputies to France and other foreign countries. To calm their jealousy and to meet their demand for a total and rapid Africanization of the administration, the government decided to increase the number of functionaries sent to France for rapid professional training. The result was a mass exodus of the administrative personnel, to whose number Youlou intended adding young African women for training in Paris as social workers or nurses. When the time came for the latter group to leave the country, it was noted that they had been selected not on the basis of their qualifications—in fact, some of

101

them were illiterate—but of their pulchritude. Fortunately, some responsible ministers and deputies were able to prevent this from becoming more than an incipient scandal.

What the young republic needed was not such flamboyant and costly projects but the means of dispelling the specter of underdevelopment and malnutrition. As Tchichelle aptly said during the celebration of his country's second birthday on November 28, 1960:

> Our country, like most other African states, has an agricultural vocation. Perhaps in a few years...it can move to the stage of industrialization, but today is here and it comes before tomorrow. It is today that our poor country must win the battle against underdevelopment, so that everyone can eat his fill. It is not by abandoning the countryside and swelling the number of urban unemployed that we will be victorious over hunger. The earth has always provided food for men who will cultivate it and not give way to despair.
>
> Let everyone look at his two hands and ask himself what he is doing with them. Let all those who have nothing to hope for in the towns return to the countryside, rebuild their villages, and clear the land. Let those who have chosen the easy urban life ask themselves if they would not do better to till the soil and make our national capital, the land, produce.

These words revealed the civic courage of a man who had reluctantly handed over his interior portfolio to Youlou to be left with only that of an embryonic foreign ministry.

No one expected Tchichelle's words to have much effect, and such indeed was the case. The unemployed and unemployable youths of Brazzaville did not see farming as a patriotic or remunerative occupation, and they were even less impressed by their leaders' mystical attitude toward economic development. These "unemployed national parasites," who normally lived by illegal means or at the expense of a relative, had no intention of going into rural exile. They recoiled at the idea of living outside the glittering milieu of Poto-Poto or Bacongo, where girls were numerous and available, bars and dance halls were multiplying rapidly, and money of dubious origin flowed freely. It would have been even more ignominious, in their eyes, if they were forced to cultivate the soil. Youlou's government could hardly hope to find any solution for the problems created by such obstinate inactivity,[6] which also certainly contributed to the growth of urban delinquency.

As for the hopes placed in the Kouilou dam as a means of absorbing the unemployed of Brazzaville, in its early stages it could no doubt offer jobs to some unskilled workers. Obviously, this would require them to leave the towns for the back country, but it was unthinkable for the young Brazzavillians to consider making such a sacrifice. In November 1960, they had already vented their spleen against some deputies and ministers whom they reproached with flaunting their wealth in the faces of their miserable brothers. Not only did they demand punishment for individual ministers caught in "places of diversion," but they demonstrated against them in front of public buildings in Brazzaville, especially that of the labor ministry. No sooner were such groups dispersed by the police than they reassembled, only to repeat the performance, to the annoyance of the authorities. As the date approached for celebrating the republic's second anniversary, which

Youlou wanted to make a solemn occasion, the atmosphere became so embittered that the president and his ministers were uneasy.

Before leaving to plead the cause of Congo-Léopoldville at the U.N., Youlou decided to placate the malcontents by hiring 2,000 of Brazzaville's unemployed to work for a few weeks repairing the town's streets. For a short time, this reduced the tension, and it was followed up by political meetings convened by the deputies. Their appeals to common sense and for confidence in the government helped to create a calmer atmosphere during the anniversary festivities. This coincidence enabled Youlou to point to his own country as a model for an eventual solution to the problems of Congo-Léopoldville. In December, the meeting of the Brazzaville bloc[7] in the former federal capital aroused some interest in Africa and internationally. However, even those to whom Youlou had given temporary employment continued to reproach him with his sumptuary expenditures at a time when the budget deficit had reportedly reached 600 million CFA francs. To all appearances, however, such criticism did not greatly disturb the abbé.

What did cause him concern were the local repercussions of his alleged complicity in the assassination of Patrice Lumumba,[8] which occurred just at the time when he was preparing for his presidential electoral campaign. Despite the adverse reactions of the pro-Lumumba Brazzaville students and some labor leaders, their charges against him seem to have had little effect on the outcome. He counted on time to do its healing work, and also on the exceptional powers he had been given by the legislature to keep his adversaries at bay. Although his desire to be elected president of the republic now topped the list of his priorities, Youlou was patient enough to let a fortnight elapse before convening the assembly and submitting to it his constitutional project for instituting a presidential regime.

By taking over the interior portfolio, Youlou centralized power in his own hands, at the same time as he revealed a certain distrust of Tchichelle, who was his friend and second in command. He also appointed a young Lari cousin, in whom he had confidence, as head of the national security service. His next step was to exert pressure directly on the prefects and subprefects so as to make sure of their support in the election, although he had no reason to be doubtful about its outcome. To make doubly sure of his success, he lavished gifts on the customary chiefs and Notables, whom he liberally entertained in his presidential palace.

In pleading the cause of a presidential regime to the legislature on February 23, 1961, Youlou claimed that the constitution adopted exactly two years earlier was no longer appropriate to a country that had moved from an autonomous status to that of a fully sovereign state. He described a presidential-type regime based on a total separation of the powers, as "modern and complete," and well suited to a country that required "quick, efficacious, and pragmatic" decisions. It was accepted on March 2 by the legislators with only a minimum of objections, except for its preamble. The socialists objected to its containing the statement that "the Congolese people place themselves under divine protection." At their request, this was deleted, against the wishes expressed on principle by the Catholic deputies. By this vote, the Congo became the third state of the former French equatorial federation to give itself a presidential government.

The following day, Massamba-Débat published a denial of rumors to the effect that he was seeking the post of president of the republic. In turn,

Tchichelle made short shrift of reports attributing analogous ambitions to him, and he twice publicly announced his support for Youlou's candidacy. This was an exceptionally courageous and disinterested stand for him to take, inasmuch as he already knew that Youlou intended to replace him as vice-president. Tchichelle had been sacrificed to Youlou's view of national unity, and to that end the abbé had promised to make Opangault his successor. Discounting Youlou's motivation in so doing, this move was impolitic as regards the UDDIA's militants. They felt that Youlou was giving away too much to a former opponent whose sincere desire for national union had yet to be proved. (Opangault, for his part, resigned his vice-presidential post casually in 1962 because he considered it to be a purely honorary appointment and one without real responsibilities. He then accepted a ministerial portfolio, but also gave that up within a few months to retire from political activity.)

In 1961, however, Youlou's openhandedness was rewarded, when his candidacy for the presidency was supported by the leaders of all the Congolese parties, who even campaigned for him actively. On the eve of election day, Youlou played his trump card. This was his inauguration, with great pomp, of the preliminary work on the Kouilou dam, for which he had received a subsidy of 100 million CFA francs from the French government. The timing of this gesture could not but favorably influence the electorate, so eager were all the Congolese to have the dam built. On March 26, therefore, they went en masse to the polls, where Youlou received 97 percent of the 405,437 votes cast by a registered electorate that totaled 458,868. In fact, only 10,000 Congolese voted indirectly against him by turning in blank ballots. Nevertheless, this should have given the government ample warning that an appreciable number of Congolese were impatient for a policy that would lead to an improvement in the economic situation. To bring this about, the leaders and population alike counted on the industrialization that they believed would come from construction of the Kouilou dam. They would not, or could not, recognize that much time was required to study its technical aspects, the market for its power, and the probable competition from similar projects. Even less did they realize the difficulties involved in financing the whole scheme.

Faced with such formidable obstacles, Youlou indefatigably sought the necessary funds from every possible source. So great was his obsession with the Kouilou dam that it affected his political judgment. Later, it was reported that he had threatened to leave the Community if General de Gaulle turned down his plea for the needed funds, and his determination to build the dam became a factor in his alignment with Moïse Tshombe.[9]

Notes

1. Minutes of the Congo National Assembly, November 4, 1960.

2. The Colonies Françaises d'Afrique (CFA) franc was created on December 25, 1945, for France's tropical dependencies in Africa and Madagascar. After the third devaluation of the Metropolitan franc, on October 17, 1948, the CFA franc was given the value of two French francs. Since then, the CFA franc has followed the course of the French franc, notably in the latter's

major devaluation of 1958, when the CFA franc became worth 0.02 Metropolitan francs. It maintained that value following the minor devaluation of 1969. In relation to the U.S. dollar, the CFA franc had the value of 210.80 before the devaluation of December 29, 1958, and thereafter 245.25 until August 8, 1969, when the dollar became worth 259.60 CFA francs.

3. See p. 115.

4. Minutes of the Congo National Assembly, January 16, 1961.

5. The nationalist upsurge also affected the policy of the UDDIA. Its 150 delegates to the party congress in January 1960 passed a resolution denouncing Vial, Mahé and the "whole gang of European ministers, deputies, and politicians," whom they described as "opportunists and undesirables." It was mainly because of such pressure that Youlou was forced to dismiss Vial, Jayle, and Bru from his cabinet in February 1960, but well-publicized bickering among those ministers was also a factor in their downfall. Furthermore, they had incurred the enmity of Youlou's left-wing opposition in general by their converting him to a policy of economic liberalism, and in particular by inducing him to place the management of the social security and workmen's accident funds in the hands of private insurance companies. See Wagret, op. cit., pp. 171, 178.

6. In extenuation of the refusal of urban youths to leave the towns for employment elsewhere, it should be noted that little accurate information about such jobs was made available to them and that they had good reason to distrust the vague promises made by their would-be employers. To justify their preference for hiring Europeans whenever possible and paying them far higher wages than were paid to Africans, employers cited the Africans' lack of skills and their chronic absenteeism.

7. See p. 115.

8. See pp. 128-129.

9. See pp. 127-128, 132-134.

CHAPTER 14

RELATIONS BETWEEN THE EQUATORIAL STATES

From the beginning, the internal debate about independence for the Congo was complicated by its involvement with the wider issue of a federation of all the equatorial states. The premiers of Oubangui-Chari and of Moyen-Congo were the pioneers of the federal movement, and Boganda's death in March 1959 left Youlou as the main promoter of equatorial unity.

Two weeks after his investiture as prime minister by the new legislature elected on June 14, 1959, Youlou felt sufficiently secure to devote most of his time to the Congo's external relations. In midsummer, the heads of the four former FEA states met at Brazzaville in an effort to prevent a balkanization of the equatorial countries. As Youlou said on that occasion, together they represented a total of four million inhabitants, slightly more than the population of Sicily and about half that of London or New York. Léon Mba, the Gabonese premier, defending himself against the charge of seeking isolation, maintained that before talking about a federation, a confederation, or a unitary state, each of the countries concerned should offer proof of its own capacity for self-government. He finished his speech with the warning that if union makes for strength, the sum total of weaknesses has exactly the contrary effect. François Tombalbaye of Tchad expressed satisfaction that the conference ended with an agreement to maintain such ties as still united the four equatorial states. Premier David Dacko of Oubangui-Chari, for his part, characterized the measures that had resulted in a dissolution of the FEA Federation as "political murder." Even though all those present at the conference agreed that some form of unity for equatorial Africa was not yet a lost cause, time was to prove that Léon Mba had been right.

On July 10, Youlou went to Tananarive, where the next meeting of the Community's executive council was to be held. There he avoided becoming involved in the federalist quarrels between the French West African leaders, but he did not want the Congo to become isolated in the Community lest it be cut off from the flow of French funds. Among his compatriots, only the UJC showed any positive interest in the basic issue of African unity, its leaders openly supporting Modibo Keita's insistence on interstate union and on independence for the newborn Mali Federation.

Soon after celebrating the Congo Republic's first anniversary, Youlou went to Libreville, where the heads of the four equatorial states met to discuss a customs union between them. There he expressed confidence that the conference would end in complete agreement, for "if minor revisions have to be made in the legal texts creating such a union, the essentials for common action in this domain have been maintained, if not strengthened."[1] This statement was certainly an optimistic oversimplification of what had happened at Libreville, where divergencies in the views expressed by the four heads of state had almost broken irreparably the weak links that still united them.[2]

After the conference ended, Dacko publicly regretted that "selfish interests sometimes had been placed ahead of the general interest, just at the time when each state has been asked to make more effective efforts to achieve solidarity." The main reason for the latent misunderstanding that marred relations between the equatorial leaders was the shadow cast over their conference by the expectation that France would gratify the Mali Federation's desire for independence at the executive council meeting soon to be held in Senegal.

It was the conviction of Youlou, weighed down by his own economic problems, that none of the equatorial states could go it alone, not even Gabon, whose egocentricity had alienated all the other leaders. After the Libreville conference, each of the four went to the Community council conference in Senegal alone. Their feelings of isolation and weakness were reinforced there by contacts with the Senegalese politicians and the population of Dakar. Consequently, they returned home after the council meeting more convinced than before of the need for unity among their four states and more determined to harmonize their respective positions.

In his New Year's message to the nation on January 1, 1960, Youlou said that the grant of independence to the Mali Federation had

> created throughout Africa a new situation that will determine our future. We have the choice between two paths. Either we can maintain the status quo and be isolated, or we can accept a sovereignty that implies tightening the links between our four sister republics. I believe that only the second alternative will prove beneficial to us, and we might take the European Economic Community as the model for our union. If we fail to follow the present trend in Africa, we shall simply become second-rate states.
>
> However, it is up to each of us to ask individually for the transfer of powers, notably to establish our sovereignty in the international domain. Later we can grant some of our sovereignty to a higher body that we will ourselves form and define. This is to be the primary objective of the conference of premiers that will take place early in 1960.

Youlou's words evoked a responsive note throughout Black Africa. They met with approval especially in Dahomey and Upper Volta, whose leaders, confronted with the chain reactions to the Mali Federation's independence, counseled against moving too hastily. Gabon's Premier Mba said that in view of his country's lack of native technicians and administrative cadres, he did not approve of a "total and nominal independence that would submerge Gabon in neocolonialism." Rather than this, he preferred prolonging the present status of autonomy, for it would give him the time needed to prepare his country properly for the assumption of international responsibilities. Despite the prudence of such views, there was not a single African head of state who could remain deaf to the siren call of independence, and within eight months all of them had opted for national sovereignty.

The purpose of the next meeting of the four equatorial premiers was to devise a common policy that would lead them to sovereignty in the framework of a flexible union. It opened with great pomp on Feburary 22, 1960, and was in itself an exceptional event, since it was the first time that Bangui had played host to such a gathering. Some apprehension was also felt about this confrontation, for shortly before it took place the Gabonese leaders, at the celebration of their national day, had shown themselves very reserved about equatorial unity and even about independence for Gabon. Gondjout, in particular, voiced his fear lest independence plunge Gabon into anarchy.

In toasting Premier Mba and his guests on February 25, 1960, Youlou gave his views on the issues facing the equatorial states in this decisive hour for Africa. During the coming years, he said, they would be surrounded by great blocs of independent nations, and must adapt themselves to this situation.

> While safeguarding the rights of each member state, we must see to it that the economic union we are about to form can move up to a higher level. If we fail to do so, each of us risks such isolation that our voice will carry little weight in the comity of African nations. Even in Europe, the hour for large groupings has come. Reinforcing the ties between us, as we planned to do at Dakar and for which purpose we are meeting here, holds the key to our future.

In this way, Youlou made himself the advocate of African unity, and he had the support of the Tchadian and Oubanguian leaders. Considering the personal animosity between himself and Mba, Youlou showed courage in voicing such sentiments in the presence of the Gabonese premier. It is easy to imagine the atmosphere in which this conference was opened by a long speech from Dacko. After some sweeping generalizations about all Africa's aspiration to independence and higher living standards, Dacko said that it was "our duty as statesmen to define the conditions indispensable for sovereignty so that we may become truly independent." These indispensable conditions as defined by Dacko were to be the theme of the Bangui conference. The basic question for the conference members to settle was whether unity among themselves should precede or follow independence for each of the four states. Oubangui, Tchad, and the Congo preferred the former option, Gabon the latter.

When each head of state was asked to submit his views in writing, Dacko surprised his colleagues by saying that his delegation had nothing to add to what he had already said. Youlou's memorandum simply confirmed the Congo's wish to "work toward unity in the thoughts, aims and aspirations of the four heads of state." Tombalbaye wanted equatorial unity to take a federal form, as defined in a constitution and headed by an executive and a legislature, and he also wanted the transfer of powers to be gradual. As for Mba, he expressed overall agreement with Dacko's program, but proposed setting up a higher committee to study what institutions could best harmonize the requirements for a common international sovereignty with those of national autonomy. This was a graceful way of not formally opposing his three peers and at the same time leaving himself free for future maneuver. In the end, it was the Gabonese formula, somewhat amplified, that was adopted by the conference. The study committee, to be composed of the four heads of state and presidents of their legislature, was also charged with drafting proposals for harmonizing the evolution of the equatorial states within the Community. At a later stage, the committee was to draw up a timetable for the transfer of powers and for concluding cooperation agreements with France, after consultation with their respective legislatures and contacts with General de Gaulle and the French government.

Of greater interest to political observers than the official communiqué issued by the conference were the statements made after its conclusion by each head of state. For the Tchadian, Oubanguian, and Congolese delegates, its most tangible achievement was the preservation—at least in principle—of the tenuous unity of equatorial Africa. The Gabonese premier could not resist reminding his colleagues that his country's national interests were often different from those of their states. For all of them, Mba believed, independence was impossible without very considerable foreign aid, and if for no other reason, this should keep them faithful to the Community and to General de Gaulle. Both legal and practical considerations made it impossible for them at the time to do more than establish the study committee as he proposed. Youlou declared that the conference members had proved their will to seek independence inside the Community and in wholehearted friendship with France, and "the study committee will try to organize our common political relationships within the framework of international sovereignty. Equatorial Africa has been reconstituted according to the program and desires of the late President Boganda."

Even taking into account Youlou's exuberant optimism and the usual reservations of Gabon, it did appear that Boganda's project for an equatorial union would materialize, even if it were to be composed of only three of the four states. This reflected a marked change in attitude, for Boganda's proposal had not been enthusiastically received when he made it soon after the 1958 referendum. At that time, this pioneer of FEA's unity suggested that it should be realized in successive stages, with economic and political solidarity preceding overall unity.

Many Congolese in Brazzaville had misgivings as to Youlou's real intentions. Certainly the ambiguous statements he and his colleagues had made at the close of the Bangui conference were open to varied interpretations. To such skeptics, Youlou said, in a broadcast on February 25, that agreement had been reached at Bangui on a "constructive project which will be jointly drafted by a competent committee but we cannot commit ourselves until we have studied its report." In the meantime, he went on to say, he would work toward the attainment of the Congo's independence.

At a meeting of experts in Paris on May 2, 1960, a proposal for equatorial union was drafted for discussion at the next interstate meeting in Fort Lamy. Anticipating its content, Youlou had hinted in a message to the nation dated April 24 that the future union might take a confederative form, with each member state preserving its sovereignty. Such a union would be concerned only with their common powers, which would be exercised on a collegial basis, and it would in no way alter their individual ties with France.

While Tchad, Oubangui, and the Congo seemed disposed to accept out of hand the principles laid down in the project prepared by the experts in Paris, Gabon insisted that another meeting first be held so that it could make an official statement on two points it regarded as essential. One of these was that all the powers currently exercised by the Community should be transferred to the individual states, which would then be free to retrocede some of them to France by means of an agreement. The second point was Gabon's preference for the name of Union des Républiques d'Afrique Centrale (URAC), which union, furthermore, should be formed without infringing on the sovereignty of each member nation. In order to give the URAC authority to act at the international level, its members should agree to grant certain of their powers to a coordinating committee that would handle their common business.

These conditions showed that the Gabonese, in agreeing to an economic union, would make no concessions in the matter of their national sovereignty, and in particular they refused to accept any joint diplomatic representation abroad. In short, the Gabonese wanted the U.N. to admit their country as an independent state and not just as a member of the URAC. They were willing, however, for the URAC to exercise authority for all the members in the fields of defense, a customs union, and common economic development projects. In the end, the URAC was formed with only three members, although Gabon agreed to maintain close economic ties with them after it had become a sovereign state. At the Fort Lamy meeting, where the Gabonese delegation made known its stand, there were some Congolese who would have liked to take the same position but could not publicly disagree with Youlou's policy. The Belgian Congo's imminent independence, considered humiliating for the former FEA territories, provided ammunition to the opponents of the URAC.

The URAC's charter was modeled after that of the Swiss Confederation, and empowered the union to determine its members' common foreign policy. It was ratified without difficulty by the legislatures of the three contractual states. Nevertheless, in the Congo, where Opangault had already opposed national independence, the MSA refused to approve the URAC charter on the grounds that its terms were "obscure and misleading." Some of the UDDIA deputies, including Tchichelle, also had misgivings about it, but they did not want to disavow openly the position taken by their leader. They felt that it was up to Youlou to decide whether or not to withdraw from the union. Probably the Congolese deputies were so dazzled by the prospect of independence, and were also so politically unsophisticated, that they did not grasp the full purport of some of the charter's provisions. In particular, they seem not to have realized that membership in the URAC obviated the possibility of the Congo's being recognized as a separate sovereign state by foreign nations. (Article 9 of the charter stated that foreign policy would be the domain of the Union, and that all the member republics would participate on a footing of equality in the Union's representation in international bodies.) It is hard to understand so ambiguous a situation in view of the aspirations often expressed by Youlou to his closest friends, to the effect that his most cherished desire was to see his country publicly admitted to the U.N. as the Congo Republic and not under a more general nomenclature that would obscure its personality.

A few weeks before he began negotiating for the transfer of powers, Youlou did admit that he had been tempted to seek a separate sovereign status for his country. He would not do so, however, because he believed that the ties which had so long bound the Congo to the other equatorial states could not be broken and that individual independence for them was not practicable. He continued to advocate an equatorial union until the agreements with France were signed. And, indeed, the Congolese legislature had ratified the URAC charter by a comfortable majority at the end of June 1960, and the national assemblies of Tchad and the Central African Republic did likewise. Consequently, there was every reason to assume that those three countries, after attaining a sovereign status, would retrocede to the URAC authority in the fields of defense, foreign policy, and currency. This was clearly the conviction of Tombalbaye, as he expressed it to the press on the eve of his departure for Paris. On the other hand, Youlou, also just before leaving Brazzaville, announced that he hoped the Congo would be represented at the next meeting of the U.N. General Assembly.

Thus it can be seen that there existed a flagrant contradiction between the respective views of the signatories of the URAC charter, but this did not become conspicuous until after the agreements for the transfer of powers had been signed. Indeed, the French premier, Michel Debré, seemed quite unaware of Youlou's sentiments when he said at the ceremony: "You Congolese, Tchadians, and Central Africans, despite the individuality of your states, want to preserve your ties of friendship and even your political links...."[3]

Before leaving Paris, Youlou told the press how pleased he was by his country's accession to independence, but added nothing about retroceding any of its newfound sovereignty to the URAC. Nor did he make any mention of that union when he reached Brazzaville. Only some French journalists very discreetly wrote of the disagreeable surprise Youlou's statement had caused among the Tchadians and Central Africans. At Bangui, Dacko expressed his disappointment at Youlou's unexpected stand. After this, there was no further talk of the URAC and of its shared powers.

This account of the early relations between the former FEA territories would be incomplete without a mention of the little "war" between Gabon and the Moyen-Congo that broke out in 1962. For many years, Mba had reproached Youlou with sending his emissaries to the Franceville mining area, where many Congolese were employed, to stir up a secessionist movement among them aimed at annexing the Haut-Ogooué region to the Congo. Such subversive activities threatened to break up Gabon's political and geographical unity and, especially, to deprive it of its mineral wealth. To counter them, the Gabonese government instituted draconian measures as soon as it had achieved internal autonomy. These measures affected the migrations of the Congolese living along the riverbanks who had been trading in foodstuffs and miscellaneous merchandise ever since France ruled the federation. Suddenly, the migrants were required to have visas, and this came as a shock to the Congolese, who had no understanding of the reasons that lay behind Mba's action.

Gabon's defensive attitude in all the equatorial interstate meetings placed that country automatically in opposition to the rest. The Congolese blamed what came to be called "gabonitis" for the failure of the URAC. Relations between Gabon and the Congo could not be called tense, but neither were they frank and aboveboard. Gabon's discovery of an important manganese deposit near their common frontier was a source of envy and regret to the Congolese authorities, the more intense because its shipment from the port of Pointe Noire would not bring any permanent benefits to the Congo. Mba's frequently expressed preference for shipping Gabon's ore out of Port Gentil further embittered the Congolese, especially as he added that the existing route by cable airway and rail could not be used for longer than 20 years. This was particularly galling to a country like the Congo, which depended on its transit trade and the traffic of the Congo-Ocean railroad for a large part of its revenue. Moreover, they would decline even more drastically if a branch line to Bangui were built after construction of the Douala-Tchad railroad.

Thus self-interest made enemies out of blood brothers, and each day added to the rancor, bitterness, and jealousy between them. As for the abbé, who undoubtedly cherished irredentist ambitions, he complained in his moments of ill humor about Mba's obvious egocentricity. In mid-September 1962, this latent antagonism came to a head at a soccer game. The Gabonese team, which had defeated the Congolese at Libreville for the Cup of the Tropics, came to

Brazzaville for a return match. The local press reported that the game would have been a national disaster for the Gabonese if the Central African umpire had shown them less indulgence. Although this was only a sports event, the Brazzavillian spectators, on leaving the stadium, vented their anger on the umpire. According to the account given in the Libreville papers, the Brazzavillians attacked the Gabonese players so viciously that the latter had to make their escape from the field in trucks provided by the gendarmerie. These trivial incidents, which were never serious despite the threats of an excited crowd, were blown up in radio broadcasts. In this way, they immediately became known to the Congolese colony in Libreville, which—forgetting that they were foreigners in Gabon—made no secret of its pride and joy. This was all that was needed to fan the flames of latent racial hatred, which in Africa can swiftly and brutally come to the surface even after centuries of peace between related peoples.

If the account given by the Gabonese minister of information is to be believed, Tchichelle had prepared the way for this outbreak 10 days before the match was played. He then made an emotional speech in the Lingala language to an audience of about 100 Congolese, meeting at the cultural center of Libreville. Reportedly, the Congolese there had become so excited that they broke glasses and furniture and even did physical violence to their Gabonese hosts. Youlou himself added fuel to the flame by making an equally provocative speech against Gabon to his compatriots working at the Engaco plant in Libreville.

During the night of September 18-19, some Libreville hoodlums roamed through certain districts of that town attacking the Congolese in their homes and pillaging and damaging their houses. The police at once went into action, and calm was restored after 75 arrests had been made. Mba went in person to the hospital, where he visited both the Congolese and Gabonese victims, but in getting the police to free one of his high officials who had been involved in the fracas, he insisted that all the Gabonese prisoners also be liberated. His intervention, which surprised the police authorities, was interpreted as giving the green light to further aggression, with the result that the violence continued for 36 hours longer. These developments made the government decide to recall a Gabonese defense mission then visiting Brazzaville, expel all the Congolese from Gabon, and repatriate the Gabonese then living in the Congo. The climax came when the Congolese labor minister, then in Libreville to report on the status of the Congolese workers there, was confined to his hotel room under police protection. Despite the Gabonese government's appeals for calm, and intervention by the French embassy, the resident Congolese, as well as some Togolese and Dahomeans, continued to suffer injury to their persons and property at the hands of the Gabonese.

While the Gabonese police were rounding up the Congolese for internment prior to their repatriation, Mba officially notified Youlou that these measures were being taken to safeguard Congolese lives, and he asked that the Gabonese living in the Congo be given analogous protection. Youlou urged his compatriots to show moderation, but the arrival of the first Congolese refugees at Pointe Noire aroused violent reactions there and at Brazzaville and Dolisie. The population's anger was taken out not only on the resident Gabonese but on all the other foreign Africans, many of whom had lived for decades in those towns and were to all appearances thoroughly assimilated. These incidents, in which 16 Congolese were killed and 81 seriously wounded at Libreville and the Mayombé region, brought grief to both Gabon and the Congo. They also caused immediate concern to all the members of the Union Africaine et Malgache (UAM),[4] who regarded them as a threat to that organization. This quarrel between neighbors sharing common interests in the mining of manganese at Franceville, they felt, portended troubled economic and diplomatic relations among the states of former French Equatorial Africa.

Youlou's request to General de Gaulle that he arbitrate the dispute surprised Mba, who forthwith charged the abbé with a "spectacular" volte face in his former views as to the relations between France and its former African dependencies. On the eve of an official visit to Guinea, Youlou retorted by saying that he intended to ask reparations from the Gabon government for its "odious behavior." At the same time, he asserted that "the Gabonese will, nonetheless, remain our brothers."

Both the harsh words exchanged by Mba and Youlou and the violence that preceded and accompanied them were symptoms of essentially economic grievances between the two territories. There is no doubt but that the UDDIA leaders had taken advantage of their presence at the UAM conference in Libreville to stir up their compatriots in Gabon, and that Youlou had been responsible for the publication of an article in the official periodical, L'Homme Nouveau, bewailing their "deplorable living conditions" in the camp where they were housed near the capital. Certainly, too, Mba could legitimately complain that Youlou had sent his labor minister to conduct an inquiry without asking permission from his government, and could claim, with reason, that in employing 300 Congolese at the Franceville mine he was helping the Congo to solve its dire unemployment problem. However, Mba was on shakier ground when he described the "atrocities" committed against Gabonese men, women, and children at Pointe Noire, and hinted that for his public defense of the Katanga secession Youlou had received huge sums from Moïse Tshombe.

The generally unfavorable reports on Gabon's behavior that were appearing in the world press placed Mba on the defensive, and on October 3 he told journalists that he had reluctantly

decided to break my self-imposed silence, solely to reply publicly to the lies and attacks by misinformed persons...No one can deny that Gabon got less than nothing from the Federation, and that for many years our money and our manpower served to develop what was then called the Moyen-Congo, notably by building the Congo-Ocean railroad and the towns of Brazzaville and Pointe Noire. Basically, it was this centralizing and inequitable policy that made us reject joining the URAC in 1959....

I am weighing my words when I say that it was their nostalgia for the past that made some irresponsible Congolese in recent years believe that they could reconstitute the old federation by persuasion or by force. So they sent to our country emissaries provided with money and arms to sound out the Gabonese populations of the Haut-Ogooué, the Ngoumé, and Myonga. Needless to say, such clumsy propaganda met with no response. Indeed, the local inhabitants promptly informed the authorities, who were thus immediately able to prevent those undesirable persons from doing further harm. On this point I have no fear of being called to account, for I can readily supply proof of the moral dishonesty of certain individuals.

To settle the conflict between Mba and Youlou, which threatened to get out of hand, the UAM held an extraordinary meeting. It was called by President Maga of Dahomey, who had a national stake in the issue because 131 of his compatriots had been suddenly expelled from Pointe Noire. A compromise solution was finally found at the round-table conference held a few weeks later in Douala and attended by Mba, Youlou, and the presidents of Cameroun and Tchad, as well as by representatives from Ivory Coast and Niger. The two governments mainly concerned agreed, in principle, on paying damages to all the victims of the conflict and on permitting those who so desired to return to the town from which they had been evicted. In a spectacular ceremony, Mba and Youlou were reconciled, but as of early 1963, none of the material compensation which they had pledged to make had yet been carried out.

Thus ended this particular quarrel between Gabon and the Congo, which was the most noteworthy episode in the latter's foreign policy since independence. It convinced the Gabonese that if the Congolese had been helpful in developing their resources, they were not as indispensable as had been thought, inasmuch as their sudden elimination caused no harm to the economy of Gabon. In all, 7,289 Congolese and 4,396 Gabonese were repatriated. For Youlou, this posed the problem of absorbing 3,000 workers into already overpopulated towns where unemployment had become endemic.

Notes

1. Lettre de Brazzaville, December 1959.

2. This statement seems unduly strong, considering that an agreement perpetuating the existing customs union of the four equatorial states was signed at Libreville on January 17, 1959. At the same time, the signatory heads of state agreed to establish a common service for their means of communication and transport and also a permanent secretariat. Furthermore, they planned to meet periodically with a view to formulating a joint financial policy.

3. Le Monde, July 13, 1960.

4. See p. 122.

CHAPTER 15

THE TWO CONGOS

By early 1961, the Community as an entity was fast disintegrating, and of its six remaining members, the former FEA territories constituted the dominant bloc. In January, Youlou again expressed his desire to cooperate on a friendly basis with France, but added that "in a world undergoing rapid change, some of the terms of the agreements we have signed should be adapted to meet the future needs of the Congo's political life."[1] Soon he was to awaken doubts as to his intention of preserving the ties that still bound his country to what was now called the "renovated Community." Houphouët-Boigny's announcement that he would take his Council of the Entente[2] out of the Community made a revision of France's relations with its former sub-Saharan colonies inevitable.

Independence and admission to the U.N. had reinforced the African leaders' determination to prove the authenticity of their new sovereign status. While continuing to voice their sentimental attachment to France, the African delegates attending the U.N. General Assembly made a point of asserting their independence, not only vis-à-vis France but also their other partners of the old Community. This inconsistency in their views was apparent when some of them supported the resolutions that were sponsored by the revolutionary African states and the Afro-Asian bloc concerning the Algerian revolt and the seating of the Congo-Léopoldville delegation. Notably in the debate on Bizerte,[3] the Congo-Brazzaville's delegate voted in favor of the resolution stigmatizing France's action there.

This development seemed to be in contradiction to the decisions reached at the Abidjan conference called on October 24, 1960, by Houphouët-Boigny, whose aim was to formulate a common foreign policy. Congo-Brazzaville was among the 12 francophone states represented at that conference, which in its final communiqué announced that "unanimity has been reached as to the most effective methods for finding solutions to each problem." Foremost among those unspecified solutions was one for ending the Algerian war, and two missions were named to present it to the interested parties. Youlou was a member of the mission headed by Houphouët-Boigny which went to discuss its proposals, fruitlessly, with General de Gaulle. As to the problem posed by Congo-Léopoldville, at the request of Youlou it was scheduled for discussion at the next meeting of the same group to be held at Brazzaville the following December. Upon his return to Brazzaville from the Abidjan conference, Youlou expressed his conviction that the francophone African states could now play a role in finding pacific solutions to international problems, especially those of Africa. He added that the heads of state gathered at Abidjan had promised to instruct their delegates at the U.N. to follow the decisions reached there. Yet Youlou was to become the first to take a stand opposed to that of his colleages, by supporting the secession of Katanga province from the central government at Léopoldville.

115

For many years, the Belgian Congolese living across the river from Moyen-Congo had been watching French Equatorial Africa move calmly and more rapidly than they toward democratic government. In 1955, when colonial peoples everywhere felt the impact of the Bandung Conference, the Belgians believed that their Congolese population was isolated from such "contamination." Feeling secure within the bastion built by their economic and social policy, they thought that by censorship they could prevent the Belgian Congolese from learning about developments in other parts of equatorial Africa. Suddenly this was disproved by the riots that broke out at Léopoldville on January 2, 1959. At a round-table conference meeting in Brussels a year later, the date of June 30, 1960, was set for the Belgian Congo's independence. The Belgian Congo thus moved without transition from a paternalistic regime to the status of total emancipation. Flanked by such colonies as Angola and the Rhodesias, the Belgian Congo might have remained politically immobile for some time longer had it not had FEA for a next-door neighbor.

In the Belgian Congo, political parties were illegal but the populations of the big towns had formed ethnic groups of a cooperative character. The authorities could not prevent the diffusion of news and ideas, by radio and by tourists, that stimulated political activity among members of these tribal associations. This evolution first became apparent mainly in the administrative capital of Léopoldville, a fast-growing city with nearly 450,000 inhabitants.

The best-known, largest, and most influential of its ethnic groups was the Association des Bakongo (Abako), formed in 1948 and headed by Joseph Kasavubu.[4] Long considered an almost wholly cultural movement, the Abako first showed its true nationalist colors in a manifesto issued in August 1956, and then its political strength in the municipal elections held at Léopoldville in December 1957. Other significant associations that developed at about this time elsewhere in the Belgian colony were the Balubakat[5] in the Kasai and the Mouvement National Congolais (MNC)[6] headed by Patrice Lumumba. General de Gaulle's speech at Brazzaville in August 1958, offering independence to the French Black African territories if they desired it, had a strong impact on all these groups and spurred the MNC to demand immediate and total independence for the Belgian Congo two months later.

Since World War II and especially since passage of the loi-cadre of 1956, the progressive emancipation of the FEA territories had influenced the Belgian Congolese, although they could not show this openly. There were daily contacts between the Bakongo on the two banks of the Congo River, either in their villages or in the bars and sports fields of Léopoldville and Brazzaville. The members of the Abako were especially pleased by the announcement on November 28, 1958, that a fellow tribesman, the Lari Fulbert Youlou, had become head of the autonomous republic at Brazzaville. The local Belgian press, on the other hand, asserted that he had expansionist ambitions, for the Belgians believed that Youlou had espoused Boganda's aspirations, which included the recreating of the fifteenth-century Kongo Kingdom of San Salvador by uniting all the Bakongo living in the area stretching from Loanda to the mouth of the Congo River and as far as Haut-Kouango. As a matter of fact, Youlou was then too absorbed by his own country's internal problems to consider annexing any additional territory. There is no doubt, however, that contacts were increasing between the Belgian and French Congolese, and that the UJC leaders in particular were trying to convert the Abako political leaders to their Marxist creed.

In December 1958, the unrest existing among the "Kinois," as the inhabitants of Léopoldville were called, was intensified by a public meeting at which the MNC leader, Lumumba, gave an account of the Pan-African meeting at Accra, which he had just attended. His auditors clamored so strongly for independence that the MNC officials told the Belgian authorities that they would be unable to control the masses unless this was pledged in the royal declaration of policy that was to be made at Brussels on January 13, 1959. Members of the Abako, wanting to share the limelight with the MNC, planned to hold a rally of their own on January 2. It was the last-minute cancellation of this meeting, previously authorized by the Belgian administration, that provoked the murderous Léopoldville riots of January 4. A week later, Kasavubu, after having taken refuge with Youlou at Brazzaville for three days, was arrested after returning to Léopoldville with other Abako leaders, and the association itself was banned.

The Belgian minister for Congolese affairs, Van Hemelrijck, in analyzing the causes of the riots, attributed some responsibility for them to France and the French Africans. After speaking of the role played by the "tragic events in Algeria and the political reforms in the French territories," he cited in particular a speech made by Youlou on December 1 at Brazzaville, as well as the abbé's comments to African journalists and politicians. Interviewed in Paris on July 12, 1960, about the Léopoldville riots, Youlou said that "as a priest I disapprove of any kind of violence, and I hope with all my heart that calm will be restored through a better understanding between Belgians and Africans. I believe that this violent explosion was in part due to the gap between our rapid political evolution, thanks to General de Gaulle, and the slow progress made by the Belgian Congo." The Belgian premier's declaration on January 13 of the Congo's right to independence and of territorial elections in December did not bring about the "better understanding" that Youlou hoped for. Léopoldville was gripped by the fear of fresh outbreaks, thousands of Europeans went home, and its population remained tense as long as the Abako leaders were held in prison. Thanks to Van Hemelrijck's personal intervention, and despite the strong opposition of the Belgian colonists, Kasavubu and two other Abako leaders were taken briefly to Brussels. They were soon allowed to return to the Congo and to hold the municipal posts to which they had been elected the preceding December.

During Kasavubu's absence in Belgium, political parties sprang up in all the Congolese provinces. Among the most important of these were the Conakat[7] (Confédération des Associations Tribales du Katanga) headed by Moïse Tshombe, and the Parti Solidaire Africain[8] of Antoine Gizenga. The MNC split into two parts, of which one was still led by Lumumba and the other by Albert Kalondji. It seemed that each ethnic group feared being dominated by its neighbors and not getting its slice of the pie. The Belgian authorities also appeared to be promoting the creation of new tribal and political groups. The most aggressive of these was Tshombe's Conakat, which demanded that Katanga province be granted autonomy in a federation with the other provinces of the Congo. The Abako, not to be outdone, also asked that Léopoldville province become an autonomous state, to be called the Republic of Central Kongo. All, however, were united in insisting on independence for the former Belgian colony, but the Brussels government still hesitated about setting a date.

Throughout the summer and autumn of 1959, ugly incidents occurred in many parts of the Congo, some of which were veritable tribal wars, and both

117

Kalondji and Lumumba were arrested. The surprise visit to the Congo of King Baudouin, who wanted to study the situation there at first hand, gave rise to more demonstrations. Finally, a round-table conference on the future of the Congo was held at Brussels on January 20, 1960, and was attended by 44 Congolese delegates representing all the territory's political movements.

At this conference, the Belgian Congolese were divided into two blocs, of which the one advocating a unitary government was headed by Lumumba, and the other, which wanted a federal state, comprised the Abako, the Conakat, and the Kalondji wing of the MNC. Despite their divisions, the conference delegates eventually agreed on June 30 as independence day for the Congo and the government concurred. In his speech closing the conference, King Baudouin issued a warning on January 13, 1960, to the "new state of the Congo. We have strongly defended the integrity of your frontiers. It is now up to you to defend this legacy against the covetousness of foreigners who, under guise of helping you, may well take advantage of your inexperience." Since the king did not specify from what quarter he expected the danger to come, his words were variously interpreted to mean communists, international financiers, or France. Credence was given to the last-mentioned interpretation when a few days later a polemic was published conspicuously in the Belgian press about France's right of preemption to the Congo in the event of Belgium's withdrawal.[9] It looked as though the Belgians feared that France might try to replace the Belgian administration there or that the Congolese might ask for French technical aid.

Wild rumors and tribal clashes throughout the Congo caused a flight of capital and also heightened apprehensiveness about the outcome of the elections to a parliament in May that were to precede independence for the Belgian colony. In those elections, the MNC was clearly victorious and Lumumba became premier, while Kasavubu, temporarily reconciled with him and his policy of a unitary government, was elected president of the forthcoming republic. It was Lumumba's insistence on the name of République du Congo for the new state that brought him into conflict with the Congolese on the opposite bank of the Congo River, to whom he owed a great deal.[10] Some claimed that Lumumba's intransigence in this matter was due to his Belgian advisers, who could not forgive Youlou for having raised the question of France's preemptive rights in their former colony. Others, however, believed that Lumumba had taken his stand to thwart Kasavubu, whom he suspected of sharing Youlou's plan to unite all of the Bakongo in an independent republic. Whatever his motives, Lumumba's insistence on his country's taking a name already assumed by the former Moyen-Congo angered Youlou. On May 22, he had Senator Ibalico register a formal protest with the French parliament on the grounds that the so-called French Congo had been recognized as such in 1882, that is, at a time when the other Congo was still only the private property of King Léopold. In so doing, Ibalico not only accused Lumumba of pursuing an expansionist policy but also of formally posing the question of Africa's existing frontiers:

> Many of our brothers will not be slow to join us when they come to understand the basic problems involved. That is, whether or not we are going to confirm the frontiers of our states as laid down by European explorers in the name of the imperial powers. For our part, we believe that the map of Africa should be revised according to other criteria.

118

Hence we are now asking all the African political leaders to study the problem so that, when the time comes, we can redraw our boundaries on the basis of the natural divisions created by our languages, physical appearance, and traditions.[11]

Upon attaining independence on June 30, 1960, the former Belgian Congo was formally named the République du Congo solely on the initiative of Lumumba's government. To the Congolese on the opposite bank, Lumumba seemed to be throwing down the gauntlet and also trying to cast doubt upon the authenticity of Youlou's republic. Youlou, confronted with a gesture that was discourteous to say the least, lodged an official protest against this usurpation of his country's title with the general secretariat of the Community. In the Brazzaville legislature, a motion was passed denouncing and denigrating Lumumba as a dictator in the pay of Moscow. Nevertheless, Youlou decided, after long hesitation, to attend the independence celebrations at Léopoldville. Because he was the only African head of state present, he was repaid for his gesture by being placed on King Baudouin's left and receiving the plaudits of the crowd, for his white cassock was as popular in Léopoldville as it was in Brazzaville.

The euphoria created by the declaration of independence and the truce between Lumumba and Kasavubu did not last long, for less than a week later, the Force Publique mutinied against its Belgian officers and Lumumba's government. Xenophobic attacks spread panic among the white residents, and within a short time, more than 8,000 Europeans had taken refuge in Brazzaville. To offset the presence of Belgian troops flown in to restore order, Lumumba and Kasavubu called on the U.N. to send an expeditionary force to the Congo. Of the 10,000 soldiers sent there, Africans formed the great majority, Westerners being only a small minority. Tshombe did not hesitate to hold Lumumba publicly responsible for the mutiny of the Force Publique with a view to establishing a dictatorship allied with communism. On July 12, Brazzaville heard rumors to the effect that Tshombe had just declared Katanga to be an independent state, refused the aid of the U.N. forces, and asked for the protection of Belgium. In the meantime, Lumumba had requested the U.S.S.R. to send technicians, and soon they were using Brazzaville as a point of transit en route to Léopoldville.

Youlou's principal concern over developments in the ex-Belgian Congo was lest its growing chaos lead to large-scale foreign, and especially communist, intervention. Upon returning from Paris, where he had signed agreements for the transfer of powers, he offered his good offices in helping to restore peace there. Youlou was under no illusions as to the sentiments Lumumba felt toward him personally, and he explained his offer by saying publicly on July 18, 1960, that it was made "in the cause of humanity and without ulterior motives." Skepticism in this regard was fed by rumors that circulated after the announcement in July of Katanga's secession, to the effect that either the Bas-Congo or Léopoldville province would ask to join Youlou's republic. Senator Ibalico's call for a revision of African frontiers in June had already increased talk of a union among all the Bakongo peoples. It was further recalled that as early as 1958 Boganda had laid claim to the left bank of the Congo River as part of his own republic.[12]

As for the Bakongo, who had become the focus of political intrigues, all the proposals to merge them ignored the ethnic rivalries that existed in the regions they inhabited. To be sure, in the former French Congo a certain degree of political unity had been reached, but it had not yet eliminated such ethnic antagonisms as those between the Lari and Vili. This rivalry was equally true of the relations between the Bakongo and the other tribes in the ex-Belgian Congo and in Angola. Therefore, it was most unlikely that Youlou, Kasavubu, and the Angolese rebel leader, Holden Roberto,[13] would surmount their personal ambitions in order to further a national Kongolese resurrection. Even the unity that had resulted from the combined efforts of Youlou and Opangault was far from perfect and was even less so across the river, where Kasavubu was losing his influence in the Abako. As for the Bakongo in Angola and Cabinda, there was no indication that the Portuguese intended to change their colonial policy. Under all these circumstances, it was hard to believe that a nation could be resuscitated solely on the basis of historical nostalgia for a period 500 years in the past.

Aside from such political considerations, the subdivisions as well as the number of Bakongo living in those countries would be a determining element of any potential union. In Congo-Brazzaville, 350,000 of its inhabitants, or a little less than half the republic's total population, were northwestern Kongo, and they occupied about 15 percent of its whole area. Across the Congo River, the same ethnic group totaled 470,000, and accounted for 60 percent of the inhabitants of Léopoldville province. Cabinda's total native population of some 50,000 were much more closely related to the Vili than to the Lari. Numbers being decisive in a democratically governed state, it was improbable that the 350,000 politically divided Bakongo in Youlou's republic could absorb and control the 470,000 Kongo in the former Belgian colony who, moreover, were far from being politically united. Even supposing that this proved feasible, it was further unlikely that Congo-Brazzaville's 37,000 Vili, 15,000 Yombé, and 21,000 Kongo would accept domination by 75,000 Lari. If through exaggerated ambition the Lari "nationalists" actually tried to carry out their expansionist aspirations, as suggested by Ibalico, they in all probability would awaken a strong defensive tribal reaction that could disrupt the precarious unity of Youlou's republic. Already that unity had been undermined by Opangault's efforts to promote a secession of the north. What is more, any move to create an independent Bakongo republic would break up the unitary state headed by Lumumba and his allies, which Kasavubu, albeit reluctantly, had finally sworn to support.

During the summer of 1960, such basic questions as those of a Bakongo union or the revision of central African frontiers did not come to the fore. Instead, the latent conflict between the two Congos was overshadowed by the comparatively minor dispute over the name of République du Congo. On July 6, the former Belgian Congo had been admitted to the U.N. as the République du Congo, so Youlou found that name had been preempted when, after independence, his republic also became a member of the international organization. As it was obvious that two countries having the same name would cause confusion, the U.N. recommended that their leaders get together and reach an agreement before the fifteenth session of the General Assembly opened on September 21.

Profiting by this respite, Youlou's foreign minister, Tchichelle, returned to Brazzaville, where he initiated talks with his counterpart in Léopoldville to find a solution to the problem. Lumumba's foreign minister could not be pinned down, and he asked for more time to reflect on such a "delicate" subject. His procrastination came as no great surprise to the

Brazzaville government, for Youlou had long realized that he could not count on even the slightest gesture of good will from Lumumba. The latter had been carrying on a radio campaign against France and especially against Youlou, whom he accused of having adopted the expansionist aims of the French colonialists. Then, too, Lumumba was fully preoccupied at the time by his quarrel with Kasavubu and the secession of Katanga.

By mid-September 1960, the positions of both Lumumba and Kasavubu had changed drastically since their country had been granted independence. Although the Abako was not fully united behind him, Kasavubu had reverted to his previous profederalist views, and on September 5 he dismissed Lumumba as premier and replaced him by Joseph Ileo, dissolved the government, and asked the U.N. to restore order. Lumumba retaliated by declaring that Kasavubu was deposed as president of the republic and by claiming that he alone ruled the country. The ensuing confusion was heightened by the support given to Lumumba by the gendarmerie, whereas the army, commanded by Colonel Joseph Mobutu, sided with Kasavubu. On September 13, the parliament at Léopoldville granted Lumumbu unlimited authority, whereupon Kasavubu suspended that body. The next day Colonel Mobutu announced that the army would assume full powers until the end of the year and would cooperate with the U.N. Inasmuch as the former Belgian colony by that time had three rival governments, each claiming legitimacy, it was no wonder that Tchichelle could make no headway in his negotiations with Léopoldville.

To find a solution to the impasse, Youlou again called the legislature to meet in extraordinary session and listen to Tchichelle's account of his abortive efforts. The deputies then voted their confidence in the government "to defend in every way the name of République du Congo, to which the Congolese people attach great psychological importance." Armed only with this resolution, the Congolese delegates perforce returned empty-handed to New York, where Dag Hammarskjold, the U.N. secretary-general, gave them a chilly reception. He favored the sizeable Afro-Asian bloc in that organization, which gave its full approval to Lumumba, as did also the Iron Curtain countries. From various quarters, the Brazzaville delegates learned that in the dispute over nomenclature Lumumba's supporters believed that his country, by virtue of its earlier acquisition of sovereignty, had prior rights to the name of République du Congo.

Not wholly discouraged by this rebuff, Youlou's representatives continued to defend their cause behind the scenes in the U.N. They tried to win over those of its members who, out of ignorance or indecision, had not yet taken a firm stand on the issue. To bolster their argument, they contrasted the calm reigning in their country with the increasing chaos in the former Belgian colony, of which many reports reached New York. Their strategy proved effective, and finally it was agreed that one of the contestants should call itself the Republic of Congo-Brazzaville and the other the Republic of Congo-Léopoldville, leaving it up to the two parties to settle their dispute at a later date.

This decision proved to be a dual victory for Youlou, inasmuch as his delegation was immediately seated in the U.N. while Congo-Léopoldville's three rival delegations had to await a decision by the committee on the verification of credentials. The Congolese of Brazzaville could now afford to be magnanimous; hence Tchichelle, in his maiden speech to the General Assembly on September 21, asked that Congo-Léopoldville be admitted to that body as soon as possible. Two weeks later, in the same session, he defended the legitimacy of Kasavubu's government, insisted that the latter's compatriots alone should settle their own problems, and asked that the U.N. forces stationed at Léopoldville be replaced by troops that had never served there before. Despite the support quietly given to Tchichelle's plea by most of the francophone African states, and particularly by Cameroun, no decision was then reached about the admission of Congo-Léopoldville.

In mid-November, Kasavubu flew to New York to plead personally for the admission of his delegation. A few days later, Youlou, in turn, flew to the aid of his "brother" Kasavubu. At the same time as he supported Kasavubu, Youlou, speaking to the General Assembly on November 18, 1960, warned the great powers in the U.N. to stop interfering in African affairs, regardless of their offers of assistance. "I tell you as a Christian and as a black man that we need aid desperately, but we are not ready to sell our souls for it." Two days later, Tchichelle again defended the cause of Kasavubu, and, alluding to Ghana and Guinea, he censured all those who used Congo-Léopoldville's unhappy plight to impose their views on the Congolese people. At long last, after 60 days of discussion, Kasavubu's delegation was seated in the U.N., but despite all the efforts by Youlou and Tchichelle on Kasavubu's behalf, relations between Brazzaville and Léopoldville remained chilly.

Meanwhile, the situation in Congo-Léopoldville had taken another dramatic turn. In late November, Mobutu's alliance with Kasavubu made Lumumba fear for his life in their stronghold of Léopoldville, and he tried to escape from there and return to his Stanleyville bastion. On December 2, however, he was intercepted by an army patrol and was held prisoner by Mobutu at Thysville. He was still there when invited by Youlou to attend the conference of mid-December at Brazzaville, where the 12 francophone heads of state who had met at Abidjan two months earlier were planning to discuss the problems of Congo-Léopoldville. Lumumba's captors told him that he might go to Brazzaville, but he declined Youlou's invitation by saying, "I don't want to be your Opangault."[14]

After a prolonged debate at Brazzaville on the Congo-Léopoldville situation, during which spokesmen for the various political parties represented there expressed their views, it was agreed that "the solution to this problem can be found only at a round-table conference, at which all political parties without exception should be represented."[15] Then the Congolese leaders actually agreed on the date and place for such a conference—but it was never held. Thus both the Abidjan and Brazzaville meetings could be put down as having accomplished little in regard to Congo-Léopoldville, but from those conferences, there did emerge the important organization of francophone states that was to be called, successively, the Union Africaine et Malgache (UAM), the Union Africaine et Malgache pour la Coopération Economique (UAMCE), and the Organisation Commune Africaine et Malgache (OCAM). Of its four operative sections, that of the post and telecommunications department was to be located at Brazzaville.

Notes

1. L'Homme Nouveau, January 1961.

122

2. Formed in May 1959, the Council of the Entente comprised Ivory Coast, Niger, Upper Volta, Dahomey, and—from 1966—Togo.

3. In July 1961, Tunisia's attempt to force France to evacuate its base at Bizerte was repulsed by French paratroops with a great loss of Tunisian lives. An agreement to return to the status quo was reached after the U.N., by an overwhelming majority, had denounced France's action.

4. Under Kasavubu's presidency, beginning in 1955, the Abako was transformed into a political party. In the first municipal elections held in the Belgian Congo, in December 1957, he became mayor of Dendale, a suburb of Léopoldville.

5. The Balubakat, or Association des Baluba du Katanga, was an important constituent group of the Conakat (see note 7) until it broke away in November 1959 under the leadership of Jason Sendwe.

6. The Mouvement National Congolais (MNC) was organized in 1956 by a small group of intellectuals who favored national unity. In 1958, it became an important political movement under Patrice Lumumba, who advocated independence and a strong unitary government for the Congo. The MNC was weakened by a split in July 1959, when a group of moderates led by Joseph Ileo, Cyrille Adoula, and Albert Kalondji formed what came to be called the MNC-Kalondji. The latter group became identified with the Baluba tribe and the main MNC with that of the Lulua.

7. Baluba immigrants in Katanga province organized the Conakat in 1957. Two years later, under the presidency of Moïse Tshombe, it became largely a Lunda tribal organization and one openly supported by the Belgian government and the Union Minière, the company that controlled the copper mines of Katanga province. An analogy existed between the policies pursued at this time by Tshombe, Mba, and Houphouët-Boigny. All three leaders wanted to sever the ties of their exceptionally rich territories with the former colonial groupings to which they had belonged, so as to preserve their wealth for self-development.

8. The Parti Solidaire Africain, founded in 1959, was a splinter group of the Fédération Kwango-Kwiloise, which drew its support from many small tribes of the Kwilu region. Its president, Antoine Gizenga, initially favored the Abako's formula of a federal government for the Congo, but after independence he increasingly supported Lumumba's views. Late in 1960, he formed a strong provincial government at Stanleyville, where he perpetuated the Lumumba regime. Gizenga claimed to be a left-wing nationalist, but his visits to and support by Marxist countries earned him Mobutu's enmity and the reputation among Western nations of being a communist.

9. This right was granted by King Léopold to France on April 23, 1884, in return for its benevolent neutrality toward his International Congo Association.

10. During the brief period when Lumumba cooperated with Kasavubu, he received considerable material aid from Brazzaville. Youlou, in particular, helped provide Lumumba with a false passport so that he could attend the Pan-African conference at Accra in December 1958.

11. Minutes of the Congo territorial assembly, May 22, 1960.

12. See pp. 159-160.

13. See note 15, chapter 21.

14. Quoted in L'Express, June 22, 1961.

15. Le Monde, December 20, 1960.

CHAPTER 16

YOULOU AND THE KATANGA SECESSION

When Youlou was host to the Brazzaville conference in December 1960, his attitude toward the problems of Congo-Léopoldville was generally regarded as unequivocal. During the preceding year, there had been frequent comments in the world press on the emotional and ethnic ties that united the two Bakongo leaders. The many courtesy calls made by Kasavubu to Youlou at Brazzaville were invariably interpreted as proof of Youlou's influence over his tribal brother of Léopoldville. It was true that Kasavubu owed much to Youlou, whose advice he had often sought. This debt had been increased by the outstanding role played by the Brazzaville delegation in pressing for the admission of Kasavubu's delegation to the U.N. against the opposition of that organization's pro-Lumumba members. In addressing the General Assembly on November 19, Youlou had stated categorically that the U.N. had misconceived its role in the Congo by preventing the country's legitimate president from arresting Lumumba, whom he described as a "rebel and a malefactor."

For the Afro-Asian bloc in the U.N., and especially for Mali, Guinea, and Ghana, Youlou was not only anti-Lumumba but was responsible for Kasavubu's decision to eliminate his dangerous rival. It was only natural to suppose that Youlou would support a fellow Bakongo against a native of the Province Orientale, especially when in his eyes the latter incarnated communism and the former anticommunism. What was less probable was that Youlou had urged Kasavubu to eliminate Lumumba forcibly, and in any case that was a secret known only to those two men. From experience, Youlou knew that the unity of the former Belgian Congo, as laid down by the Fundamental Law of May 15, 1960,[1] was not viable—at least in the immediate future—in a large territory where 14 million Africans were divided by ethnic rivalries. Furthermore, he had seen at first hand the difficulties encountered by leaders of the four FEA states in preserving even their economic ties, and he stated publicly that that was why he did not believe in the formula of a unitary state for Congo-Léopoldville at the time.

Consequently, no one was surprised to learn that, along with the central government authorities, Youlou had invited Moïse Tshombe and Albert Kalondji to the Brazzaville conference. To those who claimed that his invitation was tantamount to recognizing the legitimacy of the two secessionist movements in Katanga and Kasai, Youlou replied imperturbably that he had asked Tshombe and Kalondji to come on the same basis as he had asked leaders of other political parties to attend. What was even more astonishing to observers was Youlou's proposal, made with the utmost discretion to be sure, that Lumumba be invited to participate in a round-table conference on the future of Congo-Léopoldville. Youlou justified his gesture by citing the spirit in which he had conceived his Council of the Great African

Family, through which he had a slight hope of effecting a national reconciliation among the Congolese leaders.

To Youlou, who was both realistic and well versed in African psychology, it would be impossible to build a Congolese state, regardless of the juridical form it might take, if Lumumba's influence were ignored. Since the proclamation of independence, the radical dynamism of Lumumba and his followers had won the widespread support of youth, even among the ethnically hostile Bakongo. This was the more true since the alternative to Lumumba was Kasavubu, whose vaunted wisdom seemed to many of his compatriots simply flabbiness. Youlou was well aware that Kasavubu's apathy was incompatible with the executive powers conferred on him as president of the republic. In the melting pot formed by Léopoldville's 450,000 inhabitants, the exuberant and nationalist "Kinois" youths identified themselves far more with Lumumba than with "King Kasa," as they called Kasavubu. All this Youlou knew full well, for he faced the same—albeit less acute—problem in Brazzaville and Pointe Noire. Motivated either by personal ambition or by his determination to immunize his own country against influences which he regarded as subversive, he knew that he must not alienate the young people of Léopoldville. Furthermore, to continue playing the role of arbiter in their country, he also realized that he must maintain his contacts with Kasavubu, Tshombe, and Kalondji.

Adroit diplomacy was necessary if Youlou was to change his policy within the short span of one month, from the support for Kasavubu that he had voiced in the U.N. to pleading the cause of Lumumba, without at the same time alienating his anti-Lumumba friends. He found the opening he needed through contacts with Madame Lumumba, who sometimes came to Brazzaville to obtain from Opangault the moral and material support which she had not found in Léopoldville. In January 1961, he decided that it would be politically expedient to intervene indirectly by persuading Opangault to use his influence with the Association des Femmes MSA of Brazzaville. In a well-publicized petition which Opangault induced that association to sign, Youlou was asked to work for the liberation of Lumumba so that the latter could attend the round-table conference of African leaders. In so doing, Youlou was counting solely on his influence over Kasavubu, but he failed to take into account the attitude of Colonel Mobutu, whose sentiments toward Lumumba were anything but amiable. One jump ahead of Youlou, Mobutu delivered Lumumba and two of his ministers to Tshombe, who had no intention of letting them escape from his grip alive.

Students of the political history of Congo-Léopoldville are sometimes astonished to learn that of all the African countries which strongly supported nationalist causes, Congo-Brazzaville was virtually the only one that faithfully defended to the very end the secessionist policy of Moïse Tshombe. Indeed, Youlou was the sole African leader who, often against the wishes of his own ministers, followed his emotional impulses by championing the cause of the Katanga secession. So strongly did he do so that later in 1961 he was described in a French newspaper[2] as Katanga's itinerant ambassador. The question naturally arises as to why he pursued a policy that brought him into conflict with the central government at Léopoldville and especially with his tribal brother, Kasavubu. Many years may pass before this question can be fully answered.

Youlou liked to play a lone hand, and from the outset he pursued a foreign policy that accorded with his personal views and ignored opposition.

An explanation may possibly be found in viewing Youlou as a Christian before considering him as a politician. From the time he abandoned his apostolic calling for politics, Youlou acted as if the latter occupation derived logically from his previous vocation. In other words, he believed that he had a messianic mission to save the Congolese people from ideologies that threatened the Third World, and this belief was intensified by Boganda's tragic death. Now the only priest among the heads of the francophone African states, Youlou remained deeply impregnated with the spiritual prestige conferred on him by his cassock, despite the papal interdiction to say the mass. He carried this conviction with him into the domain of top-level world politics, just as he had done for some years in the Congo itself, and often also beyond his own country's frontiers. This belief in his humanitarian mission dominated his whole personality and prevented his feeling any sense of personal inferiority.

Some analysts of Youlou's domestic and foreign policies saw behind his sometimes muddled decisions the influence of his close, strongly anticommunist advisers. It was sometimes said in Brazzaville that these advisers were simply the puppets of their Parisian masters, who were missionaries of world anticommunism. Such was the view of Eric Rouleau, Le Monde's expert on the Congo-Léopoldville imbroglio, when he wrote[3] about the influence of certain international lobbies in Katanga and of the "France-Katanga Group" in the French Parliament, whose main objective was to build up support for the pro-Western and anticommunist regime of Tshombe. In circles close to the Brazzaville government, it was even said that some of Youlou's secret advisers for several years were the agents of a nonofficial anticommunist organization and were implicated in Lumumba'a assassination. This charge was made before the Security Council of the U.N. in April 1961 by Guinea's permanent delegate. He cited Maurice Delarue as "one of Youlou's advisers who formerly had been condemned to death in absentia for collaboration with the Nazi police, and then sent to Elisabethville as head of the Katanga sûreté at the time of Lumumba'a death." This charge was not wholly accurate, for Delarue, after leaving Brazzaville and his friend Youlou, remained for only a very short time in the service of Kalondji, the "king-emperor of South Kasai."

On ideological grounds alone, Youlou would have been attracted to the pro-Western Tshombe, but their rapprochement was furthered by Lumumba's groundless hostility to the Brazzavillian leaders and by Kasavubu's weakness and equivocation. Kasavubu let himself be influenced by such opponents of Youlou's policies as Lumumba, Mobutu, and Bomboko. Aside from those factors, however, nothing else seemed to favor an understanding between Tshombe and Youlou. Tshombe was a practicing Protestant, reared in that creed, and Youlou remained a strong Catholic although not permitted to perform his priestly functions. Tshombe was a member of the Lunda tribe, whereas Youlou was a Bakongo. Tshombe was fortunate in not having had to run any risks in fighting for the Congo's independence, and he had never sought advice or aid from Youlou, whereas both Kasavubu and Lumumba owed a great deal to him. Brazzaville was 1,500 kilometers distant from Elisabethville, and before Congo-Léopoldville became independent, Youlou had never met Tshombe, whereas there had been innumerable encounters between the heads of the two Congo governments. Youlou invited Tshombe to attend his republic's second birthday celebrations more to annoy the Léopoldville leaders than out of self-interest. He was as surprised and beguiled by the amiability, easy smile, and dynamism of the young nationalist, Tshombe, as he was by his forceful-ness and political insight. Youlou was not similarly attracted to Kalondji, although the latter was also a secessionist. When one realizes to what lengths Youlou let his emotions carry him when he first met someone who pleased him, it is easy to understand the ties of friendship that thence-forth bound the two men together. One might also suggest that Youlou was deeply impressed by the prosperity of Katanga's economy, and this admiration increased every time he compared Tshombe's budget with the minuscule re-sources of Congo-Brazzaville. (Gossips in Brazzaville used to say that every morning Tshombe found on his desk a check for 100 million francs as a gift from the Union Minière du Haut-Katanga.)

During the Brazzaville conference of December 1960, Tshombe made a re-markable speech on behalf of nationalism, expressed in wholly African terms, in which he gave an unqualified endorsement to Youlou's foreign policy. He praised its author for sponsoring the Great African Family Council as a center for discussion of all matters concerning the African states. This glowing tribute from Tshombe went straight to Youlou's heart, and thereafter he personally "adopted" Tshombe, defending him against all comers and even against international opinion. After the conference ended, Youlou showed Tshombe a signal honor which he reserved for only his closest friends. He received Tshombe along with Kasavubu and Kalondji at his home in his native village of Madihou. In talking with these men who "understood" him, Youlou felt that his role as spiritual arbiter for central Africa had been rein-forced. It was at this time that he decided to do everything in his power to bring about a reconciliation between Tshombe, Kasavubu, and Lumumba.

By early January 1961, Lumumba already had been Mobutu's prisoner for some weeks. Youlou hoped to have him freed by persuading Kasavubu to exert his presidential authority, for once, over Mobutu and Bomboko. If this proved successful, Youlou was prepared to welcome Lumumba to Brazzaville, away from the troubled atmosphere of Léopoldville, where he could easily use his diplomatic prestige to organize a summit meeting of all the Congo-Léopoldville leaders. Then doubtless that whole country could be saved not by the U.N. and its thousands of troops and technicians of all nationalities but by the little Abbé Youlou of tiny Congo-Brazzaville. This, no doubt, is what Youlou told himself in the silence of his small house at Madihou, where he liked to withdraw for meditation on his problems. At the international level, such a momentous development would certainly bring to Youlou and his country more appreciable and less materialistic benefits than the arms traf-fic for which the left-wing press in France[4] and Lumumba's faithful friends in the U.N. attributed responsibility to his government.

Youlou had been encouraged to think that a solution to the problem of the Congo was imminent because of the decision reached at the Brazzaville conference to hold a round-table meeting of representatives from all the Congolese parties—without any U.N. participation—to determine Congo-Léopoldville's future statute. He was particularly eager to play a role in such an outcome after he had learned that some of Gizenga's followers were exerting themselves to reconcile Kasavubu and Lumumba, and also asking sup-port from the U.N. to disarm the "armed bands" of Mobutu and of the Katanga gendarmerie. Soon, however, Youlou heard that Lumumba had been handed over to the Katanga authorities on January 18. This prompted him to send Hazoumé, his Dahomean director of political affairs, on two occasions to negotiate with Tshombe for the liberation of Lumumba. At the same time, Youlou in Brazzaville continued to prod Kasavubu into taking energetic measures to make the Mobutu-Bomboko tandem toe the line, for despite their promises, those two men continued to act independently of Kasavubu.

Unfortunately for Youlou's high hopes and the success of his efforts, there was no ground for optimism. At the beginning of February 1961, two rumors circulated in Brazzaville. One of them reported that Kalondji in Kasai had followed Tshombe's secessionist example, and the other that Lumumba had been assassinated. On February 3, Mali's delegate at the U.N. strongly denounced to the Security Council Congo-Brazzaville's "aggressive intervention," which he believed was to prepare the ground for military operations in the former Belgian colony. He also reported a "plot" allegedly hatched by Mobutu and Bomboko with the complicity of various Belgian and French politicians, whose objective was the murder of Lumumba. All these allegations were made without offering any proof, and in some cases they were contradictory.

The Katanga situation caused Youlou increasing concern, especially in view of the failure of his emissary's missions and the persistence of rumors about Lumumba's assassination. Suddenly, on February 10, Youlou made the surprising announcement to his ministers and to the press that he was immediately leaving for Elisabethville where, as a private person, he was going to take a rest cure at the home of his friend Tshombe. In confidence, he told his friends that he was sure that Lumumba was still alive and that he would bring him back to Brazzaville in his plane.

At Elisabethville, Tshombe in person received Youlou as a head of state making an official visit. He was given red-carpet treatment and acclaimed by the crowds, whose display of enthusiasm had been well rehearsed by a leader who was fully aware of what he was doing. A few hours after his arrival, the "bomb" burst with the announcement by the Katanga government that Lumumba and two of his imprisoned companions had escaped. It is impossible to say whether this synchronization was pure chance or calculated, and Youlou himself made no public comment about the strange "coincidence." After a remarkably short rest cure of two days, Youlou left his friend Tshombe and returned to Brazzaville. There the Congolese students declared themselves to be the "defenders of Lumumba's cause," but they staged no public demonstration.

Youlou lost no time in making a frontal attack on the U.N., but without alluding to the "Lumumba affair," which for once he seemed to regard as an internal Katanga issue. Speaking as a "Congolese of Brazzaville,"[5] he described the military intervention of the U.N. in Congo-Léopoldville as catastrophic:

> It has enabled the foreign powers to quarrel over Africa, and has brought disorders, civil war, and famine to some places. Here and there terror reigns because subversive influences have gained a foothold in provinces that were formerly prosperous. A policy is to be judged by its effects, and that is why my friend Tshombe and I denounce the UN's policy in the Congo.

By these words, Youlou was revealing his anticommunism and also unreservedly condemning the U.N.'s action and aligning himself with Tshombe.

To Youlou's charges against the U.N., the Afro-Asian group in that organization replied by implicating Youlou in Lumumba's assassination. Dadet, Congo-Brazzaville's ambassador, retorted with a spirited defense of his government in a speech to the Security Council on February 12, 1961:

> We have never had any conspirators in the Congo giving support to any person whatsoever, unless one can so define the help we gave a few years ago to Kasavubu in his struggle with the Belgians, that is to say, against their colonialism. How can you make such charges against President Youlou when every week members of Lumumba's Mouvement National Congolais have been coming to Brazzaville from Léopoldville to consult with us on how best to cope with their situation? Recently Madame Lumumba with two of her husband's relatives came to Brazzaville, where she stayed for more than a month. Abbé Youlou himself arranged for her lodging there, and saw to it that one of Lumumba's younger brothers was admitted to the Lycée Savorgnan de Brazza.

All of Dadet's eloquence, however, did not dispel suspicion of Youlou among U.N. members. In particular, he was reproached with having placed the Brazzaville radio station at Tshombe's disposal for making attacks on the Léopoldville government, and for permitting private planes carrying arms to Katanga to touch down at Brazzaville. Tshombe, in return, was said to have promised Youlou financial aid in the building of the Kouilou dam, although he had consistently refused to meet the Léopoldville government's budgetary deficits.

Amidst the general confusion prevailing in Congo-Léopoldville, the most fantastic rumors gained credence. At Pointe Noire, where the Congo drama was closely followed, some mysterious vessels were reported near the mouth of the river. Local sailors claimed that they were craft of Russian origin disguised as fishing boats, and this was accepted by those who had long believed that Accra and Conakry were serving as Soviet naval bases. A few days later, some ships of the American navy "coincidentally" stopped at Pointe Noire for refueling, and they were followed by some vessels from France's Mediterranean fleet on a courtesy visit to the African states of the Community. In France itself, the left-wing press again stressed Youlou's expansionist ambitions and asserted that he planned to realize them with the aid of the Portuguese in Angola, French "ultras," Tshombe, Kalondji, and Mobutu. Allegedly they dreamed of organizing a group of Catholic African states as a last bastion against the communism that was being propagated by the Casablanca bloc.[6] If this were to be believed, it looked as if Boganda, as the first promoter of a Bantu "Latin Africa," had made genuine converts.

Such an inference was not substantiated by the reactions of the government or the population of Congo-Brazzaville to the struggle for emancipation in the neighboring Portuguese colonies. To be sure, they could not ignore such developments, for an incessant and massive stream of refugees poured into the frontier region of the Kouilou. In 1961, Youlou addressed a memorandum to the Portuguese ambassador urging that Portugal cease its vain opposition to the freedom of its subjects and negotiate with their representatives. His move was an official confirmation at the diplomatic level of the various appeals that he had been making to the Lisbon government through his delegates to the U.N. Tchichelle's early speeches to the General Assembly were marked by strong denunciations of Portugal's policy in Africa. There he became the advocate for the 50,000 Vili living in Cabinda, whom he described as "our brothers who suffer under the yoke of Salazar's police." Commenting on his speeches, the French press noted the unexpected vigor with which Tchichelle had posed the problem of the Portuguese colonies, which, until then, had received only passing attention. In Brazzaville, on the other hand, the local newspapers were not surprised by Tchichelle's attacks, and they even stressed the "moderation" of his denunciations of the Salazar government. In defending Kasavubu, Tchichelle was simply carrying out his government's orders, but he was himself emotionally moved when defending his fellow tribesmen in Cabinda.[7] (Incidentally, it was during one of Tchichelle's speeches on Portuguese policy that Khrushchev caused a sensation by beating on the desk with his shoe.)

The Brazzaville government, although an ardent defender of the Cabinda nationalists in the U.N., did not care to encourage too active a revolutionary movement in Africa. Its leaders feared that violence there might have undesirable local repercussions, for a sizeable Portuguese community lived in Brazzaville and Pointe Noire. Whereas the exiled Angolans and Cabindians living in Léopoldville could and did agitate openly and turbulently there, those in Congo-Brazzaville chose not to behave so conspicuously. The Association of Natives of Cabinda, which operated clandestinely in that enclave, had branches in Brazzaville and Pointe Noire, but its members preferred to show solidarity with their brothers fleeing from Portuguese repression by helping them discreetly to find refuge in villages near the Cabinda frontier. This prudence reflected partly the ambivalent policy of the Brazzaville government and partly the attitude of the population of the Kouilou and Niari regions. Although the Vili and Yembé of that area were ethnically related to the indigenous Cabindians, they remained indifferent to the latters' appeals for aid in their fight for freedom. In brief, it seemed unlikely that Youlou was planning to annex Cabinda, although eventually it might become a bone of contention between the two Congos. In the meantime, his attention, like that of all the Brazzavillians, was fixed on events in much nearer Léopoldville.

Lumumba's death, for which Tshombe, Kasavubu, Mobutu, and Youlou all bore shares of the blame, inevitably wrought profound changes in the positions of the various protagonists in the Congo drama. His radical foreign supporters transferred their loyalties to Antoine Gizenga, Lumumba's self-appointed heir, who declared himself head of the republic, of which the capital would be temporarily located at Stanleyville. In retaliation for Kalondji's shooting six pro-Lumumba deputies in South Kasai, Gizenga had executed six anti-Lumumba members of a good will mission sent by the central government to Stanleyville. This reciprocal savagery prompted the Security Council to pass a resolution on February 21, envisaging the eventual use of force to prevent the outbreak of civil strife and to end the Katanga secession. Tshombe, interpreting this as a declaration of war that would lead to the U.N.'s taking over Katanga, ordered a general mobilization of its population but, at the same time, he opened the door to negotiations with his local adversaries.

After forming a military alliance with Kalondji and Ileo at the end of February, Tshombe agreed to attend a conference of all the Congolese politicians except Gizenga that was held in the neutral capital of Tananarive, Madagascar, on March 5. There an agreement was signed transforming the

Congo into a confederation, of which Kasavubu would still be the president, and Kasavubu forthwith asked the U.N. to postpone application of the resolution authorizing the use of force in the Congo. Soon, however, Cyrille Adoula, minister of the interior, and Jason Sendwe, head of the Balubakat, expressed their opposition to the Tananarive agreement because it sanctioned the secessionism of Tshombe and Kalondji, and they succeeded in converting the vacillating Kasavubu to their views. At another conference, which met at Coquilhatville in April to devise ways of carrying out the Tananarive agreements, the rupture came when Kasavubu insisted on collaboration with the U.N. forces. Tshombe walked out of the meeting after having called Kasavubu an "incompetent and a beggar" in a moment of exasperation, and he was arrested the next day when he was about to board a plane for Elisabethville.

Eventually Tshombe was released after having made formal concessions to the central government, but his arrest outraged Youlou, who again rushed to the aid of his friend, bombarding Hammerskjold and Kasavubu with telegrams demanding Tshombe's release. At a press conference on May 4, 1962, at Brazzaville, Youlou asked all the UAM heads of state to meet in his capital, "where people are not arrested or killed," to protest against the "act of banditry perpetrated at Coquilhatville," but he succeeded only in angering Premier Ileo. Declaring that Youlou was "meddling overmuch in the Congo's internal affairs," Ileo lodged a formal protest with the French embassy, which was then representing the interests of Congo-Brazzaville at Léopoldville. A few hours later, all air and river traffic between the two capitals was suspended on orders from Youlou. At the same time, he lodged a counter-protest with the U.N. against the low-altitude flights of its planes and armed patrols on the Congo River, the purpose of which, he surmised, was to prevent Congo-Brazzaville from sending an "imaginary invasion force" to land on its left bank. In a message to the nation on May 6, Youlou denied ever having entertained any such bellicose designs against "our African brothers, even those of whose politics we disapprove. As always, we are the fervent partisans of a reconciliation among all Congolese."

The conference of African heads of state held at Monrovia later that month gave Youlou still another forum in which to defend at length the Katanga secession and to plead for Tshombe's liberation. In addition to presenting his familiar arguments against a unitary state for Congo-Léopoldville, Youlou proposed that the African states send a mission composed of nurses and teachers and establish a fund for "Congolese Restoration" that would be in keeping with his concept of the Great African Family Council. Youlou's eloquence, however, met with no response from the neutralist leaders assembled at Monrovia. The final resolutions of that conference ignored all of his suggestions except his expressed wish for a rapid solution of the Congolese problem. Youlou could hardly have expected more, for he knew that the majority of those present at Monrovia favored Lumumba's thesis of a unitary state for the Congo. Moreover, had they gone along with him, they would have disavowed Kasavubu, whom they had long recognized as the sole head of that state, as had Brazzaville's own ambassador in the U.N. To Youlou's great joy, Tshombe was freed by Mobutu soon after the Monrovia meeting ended, but his liberation did not end the Katanga secession.

In mid-July, the Congolese parliament reconvened and invested as premier Cyrille Adoula, a left-wing but anticommunist leader. His government of national union, which included Gizenga and Sendwe, met with the approval of the U.N. and the United States and further isolated Tshombe and his Katanga. After Adoula announced his intention of drafting a constitution for a unitary state, but one that would take regional diversity into consideration, Tshombe tried to establish contact with the new premier through intermediaries sent to Brazzaville. But Adoula refused to meet Tshombe on neutral territory until Katanga accepted integration into the Congo, and said that to achieve it he would use force if necessary. When the U.N. forces tried to do so in mid-September, they encountered a much stronger Katanga resistance than they had expected, and this inspired Youlou once again to rush into the breach. In Paris at that time, he asked the ambassadors of Ireland, India, and Sweden to order their countries' troops in the Congo to cease fire, and through the press[8] he appealed to the nations of the world to demand a withdrawal of the U.N.'s "forces of aggression" in Katanga. "Those who do not heed this appeal," Youlou added, "must assume the terrible responsibility of starting a war of independence, in which those African nations who have had the honor of winning their sovereignty in peace would feel it their duty to aid their unfortunate brothers in Katanga." The Léopoldville government reacted to this challenge by closing the Congo River to commercial traffic between its two banks.

Youlou, upon his return to Brazzaville, held another press conference at which he denounced the U.N. in even stronger terms than before. He also reproached Moscow and Washington for their intervention, claiming that the two superpowers acted only when they wanted to "put niggers in their place." It was at about this time that Opangault, on his own initiative, forbade Hammerskjold to pass through Brazzaville en route to Léopoldville, and Youlou endorsed this gesture by threatening to expel within 48 hours all the Swedes living in his country.[9] He did not do so, however, and within a few hours he learned of Hammerskjold's death in an airplane accident on his way to meet Tshombe at Ndola in Northern Rhodesia.

The death of Hammerskjold was soon followed by a temporary cease-fire agreement, but the Katanga crisis was still not settled. Nevertheless, on the advice of Tchichelle, Youlou did not pursue his denunciation of U.N. policy in the Congo. Tchichelle, being on the spot, could better judge the temper of the General Assembly, and he also argued that it would be useless to antagonize further the Léopoldville authorities. In turn, Léopoldville's foreign minister, well aware of Tchichelle's counsels of moderation, made no allusion to Youlou's attitude in his speech at the U.N. denouncing Tshombe's secession. Tchichelle replied in kind, and simply asked that the U.N. forces in the Congo strictly follow the Security Council's directives. These directives emanated from a much-amended resolution of the Afro-Asian group, accepted by the Security Council on November 24. The U.N.'s new secretary-general, U Thant, was instructed by that resolution to reduce the Katanga secessionists by force. Inevitably the U.N. move aroused Youlou to action, and he cabled 20 heads of state to put an end to the fighting. He also refused to let U.N. planes carrying troops to Katanga to fly over his territory. U Thant reminded Youlou that his actions violated the terms of the U.N. charter, but Youlou ignored this rebuke, perhaps because on six occasions U Thant had refused to grant an interview to Congo-Brazzaville's delegate.

The year 1962 was marked by intermittent negotiations between Adoula and Tshombe, minor clashes between the U.N. forces and the Katanga gendarmerie, and the customary protests against foreign intervention from Youlou, who never ceased preaching the need for national reconciliation through agreements between the Congolese leaders. By midsummer, however, Youlou's defense of Tshombe had lost its pristine vigor, for by then the abbé seemed to have finally concluded that he could do nothing against the growing determination of more and more of the world's governments to force Tshombe into line. On July 23, the Léopoldville government's triumphant announcement that the UAM had agreed to supply it with middle and higher administration cadres made Youlou realize the extent to which his support for Tshombe had isolated him from all the other African heads of state.

For the U.N., the Katanga secession was virtually ended on January 23, 1963, with the surrender of the Katanga gendarmerie, which had controlled the mining center of Kolwezi. Six months before that, however, the handwriting on the wall was clear when Tshombe departed for Europe. Upon his return to Africa on August 17, 1962, Tshombe paid a courtesy visit to Youlou to show that although the abbé was now powerless to help him Youlou nevertheless remained his friend.

Notes

1. Based on the recommendations of the round-table conference of January-February 1960, the Loi Fondamentale was a transitional constitution for the Congo voted by the Belgian parliament. It created a central executive, a bicameral parliamentary regime, and provincial legislatures. But it did not settle the basic issue concerning the form of government—unitary or federal—for the Congo Republic, nor did it clearly define the respective competences of the national and provincial governments.

2. L'Express, November 23, 1961.

3. Le Monde, January 8, 1962.

4. L'Express, February 2, 1961.

5. Reported in L'Homme Nouveau, February 1961.

6. The Casablanca bloc was formed in January 1961 by five so-called "revolutionary" African states—Morocco, Ghana, Guinea, Mali, and Egypt—and the Algerian Front de Libération Nationale.

7. According to Wagret (op. cit., p. 177), Tchichelle had built a country house near the Cabinda frontier on which he conspicuously flew the Congolese flag. He also inspired a pan-Kongo appeal to the Cabinda Africans in the form of an article entitled "Quel est le Vrai Congo?" It was signed by Ibalico and appeared in the June 1960 issue of France-Afrique.

8. L'Homme Nouveau, June 1961.

9. The Swedish Evangelical Mission was established in Moyen-Congo in 1909. As of 1960, it had a European staff of 77 missionaries, 50,000 or so church members, and about 13,000 African pupils in its schools.

CHAPTER 17

THE CONGO REPUBLIC OF FULBERT YOULOU

In reviewing the history of the Congo Republic's first four years of
existence, there can be no doubt but that it had got off to a most unpromis-
ing start. Autonomy in 1958 brought bloodshed to Brazzaville and Pointe
Noire, which other equally turbulent capitals of francophone Black Africa
were spared. The roots of the violence lay in conditions for which Youlou
could not be held responsible, and he sincerely endeavored to calm exacerbated political passions and to create at all costs the unity required for
the young nation to "take off." Youlou was a politician and a diplomat,
like many of his African colleagues, and at times his personality and ability seemed equal to the task of fostering the climate of opinion propitious
for national union. But in making his first decisions, he had at his side
no economist, administrator, or businessman who could have helped him to
keep the ship of state firmly and steadily on the right course. With all
his strong and weak points, Youlou identified the country with himself, and
he could see its future only in terms of a single party—his own.
     The presidential regime and the single party have become the two pil-
lars of the young African states, whose leaders think of themselves as democratic although in Western eyes they appear to be virtual dictators. All
observers are agreed, however, that the chief drawback to such systems is
that when a mistake is made at the top it causes a chain reaction that extends to the lowest echelon. Among francophone Africa's politicians—many
of whom were his friends—Youlou was the only one who for three years resisted the temptation to have recourse to a single party. It was not until
September 1962 (when, during a tour of northern Congo, he found his socialist opponents there still indifferent or hostile to him) that he became convinced that such a party was indispensable. Using all the familiar arguments, he then maintained that it would cement national union, mobilize all
the country's vital forces, and hold in check demagogic attempts to sow the
divisions that were being encouraged by the multiparty system.
     Although Youlou's proposal was accepted by his main opponent, Opangault,
it could not be said, as Youlou affirmed, that setting up the single party
reflected the popular will. How could that have been so, when only three
months earlier he had forbidden the propagation of racialism or regionalism
and dissolved all the organizations that were "tending to divide the people"?
There seems little doubt that in instituting the single party, Youlou intended to make full use of the powers it would bring him to put an end to
the activity of all those individuals or groups that refused to agree with
his government's policy.
     By a generous distribution of well-paid ministerial posts, Youlou could
be said to have created a certain degree of unity among the country's political leaders, but he still had not united the population behind his

135

government. How little this had been done was shown in September when his minister of the interior found it necessary to remind the public that any person using abusive language to or about a minister, deputy, or officer of the law would be penalized. The Congolese had come to distrust the many declarations of official good intentions because they could see no tangible beneficial results therefrom. When Youlou asked them to make sacrifices and show a civic spirit, they noted that the members of his entourage thought that austerity should apply to everyone but themselves. For the preceding four years, the Congo Republic had been sliding dangerously downhill because its government always took the easiest course. By favoring one segment of the population, it sacrificed the peasantry—the backbone of that impoverished country and the only element in its current stage of evolution that could have served as the basis for its economic development. The insatiable pride and blind egoism of the privileged urban caste, never satisfied and always demanding more, had erected a wall between itself and the masses. Behind that barrier, the Congolese peasant vainly tried to make heard his cries of distress and despair.

This privileged urban caste was composed of politicians and civil servants. Under a tropical sky, they dressed in jackets and neckties the whole day long, and lived in an artificial world of telephones, air conditioners, automobiles, bars, dance halls, and cocktail parties. Alongside them lived 400,000 peasants belonging to a wholly feudal era, who earned barely enough to buy a single garment a year and ate wild produce and, as meat, rats and reptiles. They did not farm because they saw no reason to produce food for the nylon-shirted caste. They were even worse off than during the colonial period, for with independence they had lost the incentive to rebel. In the capital, they were represented by a sartorially elegant deputy who, according to the official statistics, was paid during the six months he attended the legislature as much as one of his peasant constituents earned in a lifetime of labor.

Today the Congo has its television station, which diffuses throughout the countryside a false picture of "the good life." Bemused by what he sees on the small screen, the peasant can now compare his miserable rural existence with what goes on daily in Brazzaville. What can be the reactions of a rustic who walks barefoot and almost naked along the tracks left by wild animals, to the televised vision of his compatriots attending a reception in the presidential palace wearing evening dress and holding glasses of champagne in their hands? He may well conclude that all the fine speeches urging him to work are nothing but lies. So his initial revolt as a free man is to abandon his fields and his misery to garner the wealth of the towns. Once there, he is condemned to suffer real hunger, whereas formerly he had known only undernourishment, and he now feels the weight of a genuine servitude instead of the freedom that he experienced before.

The privileged town dwellers often boasted that they were supporting in their homes able-bodied relatives who refused to perform degrading manual labor. Deputies and civil servants consistently enjoyed easy credit for the purchase of automobiles and refrigerators, but the peasants had only their hands and the sweat of their brows to offer as collateral. The government was never willing to grant them the loans with which they might have purchased rudimentary furniture or agricultural or fishing equipment. With these, they might have been able at least to feed themselves adequately if not to prosper, and therefore would have been more firmly rooted in the land.

136

Many of the deputies, civil servants, and students who visited Israel admired that country's communal productivity, but they were unwilling to imitate the austerity and sacrifices made by the highest Israeli officials. Among the Congolese, there was virtually not one civil servant who was willing to live exiled in the bush, where he might have performed conscientiously a constructive task, but where he also risked being forgotten. If he stayed in Brazzaville, clever intrigue might get him a job as director in charge of a government department or even a ministerial post. In the capital, it was well known that the best-educated African civil servants did everything in their power to avoid being posted outside Brazzaville. Consequently, it was often the French technical advisers who were sent to upcountry posts, perhaps as a way of making the country's former masters atone for the colonial past.

The Congolese deputies, perhaps because they depended on popular votes for their mandates, seemed more conscious of the disparity between the living standards of the privileged elite and those of their constituents. In January 1962, Marcel Ibalico, a former theological student and currently president of the legislature, felt impelled to reply to criticism of his colleagues' status. He justified their salaries on the ground that the post of deputy entailed many more "burdensome moral responsibilities" than the public was aware.

> In a country like ours, which is prone to oratory, the electorate is tempted to blame the government and parliament for everything, and to criticize us severely, especially our personal position. The public does not always realize that if we are to carry out our parliamentary duties we must enjoy certain moral and material advantages. I hardly need to add that, after deducting our indispensable expenditures, a deputy's salary comes to only that of a minor civil servant.

The self-sacrifice displayed by Ibalico and his colleagues was unlikely to win much sympathy from the rural population and the unemployed of Brazzaville, who might well wonder if such a statement was not a deliberate slight to them in their misery.

Youlou himself was not wholly impervious to the inequities of this situation, and he tried to make his officials realize that they owed the public something in return for their privileges. When the civil servants began airing their grievances, he sometimes chided them for their "unjustifiable absenteeism," adding, "you have a privileged position compared with the bulk of the population, and you should merit it by being industrious and respectful of discipline." Yet, when he frequently urged the Congolese to work harder because they would derive benefits from their zeal, he could not have been deceiving himself. Youlou knew full well that not a single minister would renounce his prerogatives for the benefit of his constituents, just as he knew that he could not force the unemployed to return to their villages because they had now become inveterate idlers in Brazzaville. Furthermore, no official action followed his exhortations, for no one was willing to roll up his sleeves and get down to work.

By its negative as well as its positive policies, the government itself was largely responsible for such general inertia, because Youlou consistently and weakly yielded to the demands of the elite. In a speech on July 1, 1962, he spoke of the great pressures exerted upon him to grant favors to a village or a ministerial post to a particular family. When he was forced for reasons of state to sacrifice a minister, he realized how precarious, not to say fictitious, was the national unity he had built up—against his will—on the basis of material self-interest. To prevent strikes by the civil servants, Youlou increased their pay. Between 1960 and 1962, the average monthly salary of a functionary rose from 29,000 CFA francs to more than 37,000. Although the pay for wage earners also had been increased during that period, a Brazzaville laborer, as of mid-1962, earned slightly more than 5,000 CFA francs for a 40-hour working week, and in the smaller towns only 3,200.[1]

Another unfortunate aspect of Youlou's consistently indulgent attitude toward an already privileged minority was not only an overrapid Africanization but a "Larization" of the administrative cadres. When trouble occurred and the budget defict grew, there was a natural tendency for the Congolese to blame the white businessman's arrogance or the French technical advisers, although the latters' services were supplied by France free of charge. To win popularity, Youlou had quickly Africanized the administration, beginning at the top echelons, with the result that the French technical adviser became subordinate to a more or less competent Congolese official. In some instances, the latter was a career civil servant, but this was not true of the directeurs de cabinet, who were newcomers to services in which they had never before worked. Sometimes farseeing Congolese protested against the unfortunate consequences of the situation. Such a view was expressed by Joseph Pouabou,[2] the highly competent and well-educated president of the supreme court, who wanted the justice department to be Africanized, but not by sacrificing the quality of its personnel.

Africanization of the administrative cadres would have been desirable for every reason had serious, even if semitrained, Congolese replaced French officials, especially in the rural areas, but such was not often the case. The result was general retrogression throughout the hierarchy, notably in the regions where the population neither respected nor obeyed administrators who, in their eyes, were no more qualified than themselves to exercise authority. In a speech made to a meeting of prefects,[3] Minister of the Interior N'Zalakanda noted how much harm this had done to the functioning of the administration. He admonished his listeners to watch jealously over their authority, which, like their responsibilities, must be

> total, exclusive, and indivisible. I stress this because I have noticed that the important concept of hierarchy has become blurred. Many officials, including even subprefects, are trying to free themselves from its discipline.

What was happening in the provinces was also taking place in the central administration, perhaps to an even greater degree. In Brazzaville, nepotism and political pull rather than competence had become the sine qua non for acquiring and holding a job, with the result that subordinate officials now occupied the top posts with no qualifications other than the veneer given them by a rapid-training course. This situation was quite obvious to their envious colleages or subordinates, who vented their spleen by sitting at their desks with folded arms. Thus, throughout the whole administration, apathy was superimposed on incompetence. To be sure, some of the new African bureaucrats were frank enough to admit their shortcomings and to seek counsel from the French technical advisers. The latter, out of a sense of professional duty, let themselves be transformed into general work-horses. But they, too, yielded to discouragement in the face of manifold problems which, for one reason or another, could never seem to be solved. On top of all this, Opangault took it upon himself to remind the technical advisers that "the independent Congo Republic" had the right to expect satisfactory service from "its civil servants."[4]

Of itself, the Africanization of the administration might have led only to a temporary decline of its efficiency and standards of honesty, but it became positively detrimental to the nation when it assumed the form of "Larization." By filling the police, customs, and education services with Lari, Youlou was aggravating tribal discord and thus disrupting the national unity that he was trying to create. When he appointed his fellow tribesmen to ministerial posts, he was using the authority given him by the law of June 18, 1962 (which he supplemented by another law, adopted July 21, 1962) for the purpose of banning all ethnic propaganda and racial demonstrations. Only a few months before these laws were passed, his minister of the interior, in an official address, spoke of the Lari region as if it had existed as a nation in precolonial Africa. Youlou himself often addressed his Brazzaville constituents in the Lari language.

Such open favoritism toward the Lari had several adverse results. One of these was a further alienation of other Congolese tribes. As early as June 1960, the northern socialist deputy, Leyet-Gaboka, had complained in the assembly that all of the Congolese then studying in France had come from a single prefecture. Without going into details, he added: "We bitterly deplore this aberrant racism which our government has implanted in the administration." Of the Vili's traditional antipathy for the Lari, Youlou had personal proof when, during Tchichelle's absence at the U.N., he received a cool reception during a tour of the Pointe Noire region. His pro-Larism also influenced his attitude toward those of his political allies who belonged to other tribes, particularly if they dissented from his policy. Tchichelle had lost his posts as vice-president and minister of the interior because of his frankness and his refusal to give the unquestioning obedience that Youlou exacted from all his collaborators. Opangault was not so summarily treated, but he preferred to withdraw from politics rather than hold a purely honorary position. Youlou could not forgive Massamba-Débat for his stinging reprimand in the legislature's budgetary session, and compelled him to exchange the presidency of that body for the secondary portfolio of the Plan. By replacing Massamba-Débat with the superfaithful Ibalico, Youlou avoided an unprofitable clash with the legislature and at the same time strengthened his own authority. Nevertheless, neither such "semipurges" of dissenters, nor the naming of a troublesome politician as ambassador to a distant post enabled him to eliminate wholly a politically dangerous opposition.

In the domain of public relations, Youlou's pro-Lari policy evoked adverse reactions in France and in the resident French community. For internal political reasons, he encouraged the cult of Matsoua and of his early followers as Lari patriots. By picturing them as martyrs to French colonialism, however, he was not likely to induce France to increase its largesse to the Congo nor French capitalists to invest in the Kouilou dam. In any case, private investors could not afford to ignore the laws of economics, as did

Youlou, his ministers, and his deputies. They might have been more disposed to heed Youlou's pleas for additional investments had he been less spendthrift, less indifferent to the country's basic economic problems, and less prone to depend on foreign subsidies as an easy solution for his financial difficulties.

To be sure, the Congo government remained the most important client of the local French business community. The latter did well to the extent that Youlou's administration spent far more money than had its colonial predecessor, but the government was in no hurry to pay its bills. Such delays were due in part to the slower pace at which its inexperienced financial services operated, but more to the fast-growing budget deficits. To some degree, Youlou's temperament and background accounted for his easy-going attitude toward the deficiencies of his civil servants and the growth in public expenditures, but his real interests lay elsewhere. He preferred to devote most of his time and energies to strengthening his personal political authority at home and to trying to settle the problems of countries other than his own.

After independence, Congolese politicians and officials took full advantage of the facilities that became available to them for foreign travel. It was mainly to France that the personnel of the police, the bureaucracy, the army, and the gendarmerie went for advanced training that would give them access to the upper ranks of their profession. (Their preference for France derived more from their knowledge of the language and previous education than from sentimental attachment.) Some Congolese trainees also went to Israel, the United States, West Germany, and other countries. But the number of such travelers was as nothing compared with that of the deputies, ministers, and high-ranking civil servants who became inveterate junketers. It was understandable that the Congolese should want to use their new freedom to leave familiar surroundings and to live, if only for a few days, in a way that only a few years before had been reserved for white men.

Youlou was the first to set such an example. After visiting all the African capitals, he went to Israel, Italy, the United States, West Germany, and, especially, France, where he made innumerable private and official visits. His collaborators embarked on missions to the Far East, south Asia, northern Europe, the Western hemisphere, the Near East, the Soviet Union, Ethiopia, and Greenland. Their travels brought good business to the air lines, but were a drain on the Congo's meager revenues. Youlou justified such expenditures by likening them to "the investments made by the father of a family," and a few of them did bring some dividends to the country. Kikhounga-Ngot induced Israel to offer scholarships to Congolese students in the fields of agriculture and social service, and Youlou persuaded Washington to send an economic mission to study the Congo's needs at first hand.

In addition to soliciting funds for building the Kouilou dam, which remained central to his preoccupations, Youlou had other objectives in his many journeys. The aim of such expenditures of time and money was to gain prestige for himself and his country and to promote international reconciliation. Youlou returned from his trips brimming over with enthusiasm, for he immensely enjoyed his role as self-appointed spokesman for the legitimate aspirations of the Third World. On the African scene, he hoped to reconcile not only the leaders of Congo-Léopoldville but also those of the UAM and of the Casablanca bloc. His ambitions, however, did not stop there.

In 1960, when five Congolese deputies visited the U.S.S.R., Youlou used the opportunity to send Khrushchev a "personal message of peace." Although his delegates to the U.N. had consistently refused all invitations emanating from the Soviet bloc, Youlou felt no hesitation about proposing to Khrushchev that Brazzaville should be the site for a summit meeting on the Berlin question, which had not been solved at a conference of the powers held at Paris in 1959. In writing to Khrushchev, Youlou asserted that

> the UN is not a suitable place for the success of such negotiations. Brazzaville is the capital of the peaceful and hospitable Congo, where the black man rallied to the cause of the free world and fought against the forces of evil, and it is ready to welcome you...

This unexpected proposal caused considerable merriment among members of the diplomatic corps, but in Youlou's eyes it had the merit of drawing the world's attention to his little Congo, so often overshadowed by its notorious neighbor.

Youlou was not discouraged by his setbacks in defending Tshombe and in eliciting a favorable response from Khrushchev. Perhaps he could indirectly set the stage for a conference on Berlin by inviting certain heads of state to attend the republic's third anniversary celebrations, and to that end, he sent good will missions to London, Bonn, Rome, Paris, and even Tunis. All the nations he invited did send representatives, but they were only silent ambassadors or ministers and were not the heads of state. From this failure, Youlou learned that top-level foreign affairs were not a game that could be manipulated as he wished, but he did not learn to economize on unproductive expenditures.

Not only were public funds spent on foreign travel and independence celebrations but the national revenues were squandered on other projects. When Youlou took a large sum from the Fonds Routier to appease the unemployed of Brazzaville by giving them jobs for a few weeks, he might better have spent that money—as originally intended—on improving roads in the north or the rural economy in general. Another of his extravagant and grandiose schemes was his much-publicized plan for the urbanization of Greater Brazzaville, whose immediate aim was to provide work for the Congolese repatriated from Gabon. To carry it out would have required all the wealth of the Indies, and, in any case, it would have attracted more immigrants to that already overcrowded city. He would have done far better to allocate funds to the rural villages that were dying for lack of decent housing. In 1962, the Société Immobilière du Congo announced that it would help to finance the construction of 160 dwellings in Brazzaville, Pointe Noire, and Dolisie, only a few weeks after the government had deplored the loss of 500 peasant houses destroyed in a flood of the Congo River. Under such circumstances, officials could hardly have believed that the hearts of their Mbochi, Bondjo, and Kouyou inhabitants would be warmed by another of their plans—that of building air fields in the north.

All such expenditures, however, were as nothing compared with the allocation of half the national revenues to paying the elitist civil servants, while the agriculture and animal husbandry services were allotted, respectively, only 1.50 percent and 0.35 percent of the total. Consequently, the Congolese peasant could not fail to feel himself oppressed, despised, and forgotten in his native heath, especially on occasions when he was urged to welcome warmly to his village visiting officials covered with decorations. Today the people look upon such visitors with curiosity and astonishment, but tomorrow this may change to disillusionment and revolt. To be sure, the government offered free education to the peasant's son as an avenue for entering the privileged bureaucracy, but from this he could expect no improvement in his rural setting that would inspire him to produce more. The peasant of the Congolese basin would certainly not work any harder if he took as a model his brother, an agricultural monitor who had been trained in a French school or a subprefect who had graduated from the Ecole Nationale de la France d'Outre-Mer.

The declining rural production of the Congo clearly reflected the peasantry's alienation from the life of the nation. The Congolese farmer, primitive as he appears to be, certainly does not disdain the cultural opportunities that the government has opened to him, but above all he wants improvements that effect directly and immediately an improvement in his working and living conditions, and a better future for his children. It may have been true, as the minister of economic affairs told the Brazzaville Chamber of Commerce, that the Congo always had been exploited, rather than developed, according to a Europe-oriented mercantilist policy. "In a technically backward country, characterized by economically irresponsible natives," he said, "this system of exploitation has given birth to a veritable brotherhood of gatherers of wild produce, hunters, and jacks-of-all-trades, whom we must transform into genuine planters and herders." But Youlou's government was doing little to promote national interests in the place of the abscess created by colonialism.

Like many other African leaders, Youlou was so dazzled by impressive statistics that he misinterpreted them. This defect was obvious from his message to the nation on August 15, 1962, to the effect that the Congo's progress in all domains could be easily measured by the increase in its operating budget from 4,465 million CFA francs to 7,232 million between 1960 and 1962. He asserted that "this simple comparison proves, if proof is needed, the effort made and the progress achieved." He did not mention that the deficit in the latter year came to 750 million CFA francs.

An analysis of the total 1960 budget showed that the Congo's public expenditures amounted to some 16 billion CFA francs, of which only about 25 percent was derived from local revenues and the balance came from external sources—the Community budget, the French treasury, and the European Common Market Development Fund. As to the Congo's indigenous revenues, 67 percent of its income came from indirect taxes, of which some 42 percent was represented by duties and levies on imports and exports. Operating expenditures alone absorbed 70 percent of its revenues, and 40 percent of these were spent on the health and education services. As early as June 1960, Leyet-Gaboka had noted that between June 1959 and April 1960 the staffs of 11 ministries had grown from 60 to 120 and that all the newcomers were political appointees. Moreover, he added, those figures did not include the propaganda agents, euphemistically called chargés de mission, who were given public funds for distribution. By 1962, the civil service expenditures had risen by 40 percent within less than three years. In the budget for that year, the cost of personnel in the so-called "political services" alone accounted for 21 percent of the total expenditures, whereas those serving economic development came to only six percent, marking an increase in the former category and a decrease in the latter during that period. In all the government departments, the greater part of their budget allocations went to paying the salaries of their personnel.

It should be noted that revenues had also grown since 1961—those from customs duties and taxes by 9.6 percent, direct taxes by 29.1 percent, and business turnover by 56.9 percent—but an analysis of those figures confirmed the stagnation of the Congo's economy. Export duties were swelled by 22 million CFA francs from diamond shipments, which were merely reexports from South Kasai smuggled out by way of Brazzaville, where a diamond market had been opened at the suggestion of Israeli businessmen.

A comparison with the 15 other francophone Black African states is instructive, inasmuch as all their populations were small and most of their national revenues also depended very largely on indirect taxation derived from foreign trade. As regards population, the Congo occupied thirteenth place, and in terms of exports, eleventh. Of the Congo's exports, logs and sawn wood represented 60 percent of their value and 84 percent of their volume, and in the event of a fall in world market prices, this left a very small margin for its revenues. As a coffee and cocoa exporter, the Congo held the lowest rank among francophone Black Africa's seven nations producing those commodities. It was in fifth place among the exporters of oleaginous products and fourth among those exporting diamonds, and its position was much the same for all its other shipments. Certainly the Congo Republic could not be reproached for its natural poverty, but it was guilty of refusing to live within its means and of failing to narrow the gap dividing it from its peers by increasing its production.

With characteristic frankness, Youlou admitted that his country's trade balance was unfavorable and its finances in trouble, but to remedy these serious deficiencies, he had few constructive steps to offer other than his Kouilou "mirage," a nebulous development plan, and what he called austerity measures.[5] The last mentioned were repeatedly pledged in response to the noisy demands of an impatient youth angered by and envious of the swathe cut by the Congolese deputies and ministers. Among the so-called austerity measures was the official announcement of a return to the office hours that had prevailed during the colonial administration, but this was more in the nature of a move to restore order to a disorganized and demoralized bureaucracy than genuine austerity.

The next step was to restrict to official business the use of government-owned cars by civil servants. The government further required officials going abroad to travel in economy class, but it made no attempt to curtail the number of such trips. In one year alone, 100 official missions were sent abroad, involving 300 individual journeys. Aside from the millions paid to foreign air lines, this meant the loss of 2,000 working days, not to mention the hours wasted by officials and troops mobilized at the airport to salute arrivals and departures. Any invitation to attend conferences, expositions, and festivities was accepted regardless of its source. Youlou's excuse was that the Congo's policy of neutralism required it to avoid hurting the feelings of any country or of any members of the "great African family."

The imposition of "austerity" affected only the prerogatives of a few individuals. Because there were always cases of "exceptional priority," the abuses continued and draconian regulations were progressively forgotten or ignored. Superficially, such measures looked impressive, for they enabled the government to make some cuts in its expenditures, but these fell far short of bringing the budget into balance. Furthermore, they did not deceive the public, which was fully aware of the administrative bourgeoisie's sources of easy enrichment. This could be seen from a letter written to the government newspaper on September 30, 1962. Its anonymous author ironically complained of the "poverty of the Congolese vocabulary, because it does not contain even a word for 'austerity'." Genuine austerity would have meant a real reduction in the overnumerous, inactive, and incompetent personnel that filled all the government offices and was maintained exclusively for political purposes.

Another of Youlou's unfulfilled pledges made to appease the opposition was the promise to check speculation by a strict application of his price-control regulations. In making it, Youlou thought of himself as the defender of the poor and the consumer, but in reality he was pleasing no one. The chain of parasitic middlemen responsible for high prices was merely the symptom of the national malady of unproductivity, which the government after four years in power seemed incapable of curing. When Youlou spoke in strong terms of fighting against high prices, he was addressing a deaf audience, for the limits of taxation had been reached and trade was at a standstill for lack of investments. In 1962, agricultural exports showed a decline, and, so as to have on hand an adequate food supply, rice had to be imported. Wood exports were also falling below the 1961 level. At the same time, retail prices had risen appreciably, notably those for such basic foodstuffs as salted fish, palm oil, and manioc, which had been increased by 10 percent to 25 percent. The Congolese government had little time to lose if it were to stop drifting and get back on course.

Of the Kouilou dam, the Congo's great hope, there was less and less talk as the Congolese leaders traveled abroad in a vain search for funds to finance it. In November 1961 at Paris, General de Gaulle had pledged Youlou the money needed to begin its construction, but no more. Reporting to the nation on his trip, Youlou said that he had solemnly begged France not "to abandon the Congolese people like lost children." This was his indirect way of telling the French government that the promise made him in Paris was not enough.

In the avalanche of speeches delivered by Youlou throughout the Congo's third birthday celebrations, he never forgot to pay flowery tributes to the local European community, and to offer full protection for their persons, property, and investments in the country. He also again promised to apply austerity measures to all those about him, sparing no one, and he begged his listeners to help build the Kouilou dam, "on which the future of our youth depends." These frequent and sometimes anguished appeals reflected the government's fears of the growing social malaise. The Congolese youth had a legitimate grievance in that it was led to believe in an industrialization that never materialized. Unless the authorities could win the support and confidence of the population, any economic plan the government could devise was doomed to failure.

On May 8, 1961, a few weeks after Youlou was elected president of the republic, he outlined to the legislature his program for the "construction of the Congo and the reconstruction of Africa." Rather surprisingly, his plan stressed utilizing the Congo's "exceptionally favorable geographic situation as a crossroads for merchandise in transit." The authors of his plan

proposed to do this by creating a free-trade zone at Pointe Noire and by enlarging and modernizing its port. Unfortunately, there was nothing new in
this project, which was basically sound but which by itself could hardly
raise the country out of its economic morass. It also ignored the probable
decline of Brazzaville and Pointe Noire as entrepot ports, as well as
changes in trade routes that were likely to occur if plans for railroad construction in countries to the north were carried out.

The Plan's second objective—development of crafts and small enterprises in both urban and rural areas—was even more surprising. Only a few
weeks before Youlou announced his program, he had taken a step that in effect prevented the Congolese from sharing to any large extent in the country's trade. By raising the minimum cost of import licenses from 40,000 CFA
francs to 372,000, Youlou had inadvertently played into the hands of the big
foreign companies which had branches in the Congo. He seemed to believe
that by giving the country a government that looked stable and according the
import-export firms certain facilities he could persuade their directors to
invest their profits in the Congo and help him carry out his Plan.

All Youlou's eloquence could not disguise the fact that the Congo's
economic stagnation during the past few years had been due to the lack of
investments by private European capitalists.[6] He had failed to inspire confidence in them for many reasons. One was the wave of xenophobia that had
swept over the Congo since independence, as expressed in the demand by some
labor leaders for the dismissal of all the European cadres. The reason
given was that the latter behaved in as disdainful a manner to their African
clients and employees as they had done in the days of colonialism. Another
cause of the Europeans' lack of confidence was Youlou's insistence that the
private sector emulate his policy of "Congolization" of the government services by replacing their Dahomean and Togolese accountants and clerks by
Congolese employees. They were scarcely encouraged to do so by the thefts
of imported merchandise at the port of Pointe Noire, where, moreover, their
costs were rising because the longshoremen were deliberately dilatory about
unloading ships. This combination of pressure and inertia was beginning to
convince the European traders and industrialists, who formed the backbone of
the country's economy, that they had become the milch cows of the Congo.
Further contributing to their caution and pessimism were sporadic rumors to
the effect that their funds would be frozen or used to meet the growing
budget deficits.

The third goal of Youlou's Plan was the development of the Congo's
northern region, which France had done little to promote. It was a huge and
depressed area inhabited by several hundred thousand tribesmen, whose average annual per capita cash income came to barely 2,000 CFA francs. Because
the great majority of the northerners were members of the MSA opposition, it
was politically important to Youlou for them to be drawn into the Congolese
family and to support his government. To relieve their isolation, he proposed to expand the scanty means of communication, create a lumber industry
in the region, increase their medical facilities, and modernize the villages
that had been abandoned by their young people. In brief, he called for a
public-works program whose cost would far exceed the resources of the Congolese government.

Aside from the financial difficulties involved, there was the even
greater obstacle of the rural exodus. To be sure, a mechanized lumber

industry might not make heavy demands on local labor, but its output would encounter competition from that of the south, whose forests were also slated for intensive exploitation. Increasing the northern production of crops, fish, and livestock would certainly require a working force that simply was not available locally. In the Congo's current stage of evolution, the urge to emigrate seemed to be as strong and as irreversible as had been the drive to achieve independence. Rather than drawing up elaborate and costly programs of public works, the Congolese planners should have tried to improve village housing, extend credit for buying agricultural equipment, and promote the evolution of rural women, as the means of stabilizing the northern population. To check the flood of migrants to the overcrowded towns, rural settlements would have to be made more attractive, physically and culturally, for young people.

Some perceptive observers attributed the current malaise of the Congolese and the decline of their countryside to cultural causes. Such was the view of M. Foundou, the Congo's delegate to UNESCO and one of the most Gallicized and highly educated members of its elite, who asserted:

> The disintegration that results from the failure to protect and perpetuate a culture generates a social imbalance and the loss of individual personality...Of Congolese civilization there remain only some troubled and dishonored customs. Prostitution has spread rapidly from the towns to the countryside, where the tam-tams are now silent and there is nothing but endless boredom. The dead are no longer ceremoniously buried, and their tombs are covered with brush. Everyone hastens to divest himself of anything that might be denigrated as barbaric or pagan. We are no longer a one-eyed people but are now totally blind, for we are without an inheritance. The customs and traditions of a people cannot die without destroying the people with them....
>
> Certainly we are happier today than we were yesterday, but we are less our true selves than we were. If we are better off, it is due to a Western civilization, but it is a civilization to which we have not brought, and cannot bring, any contribution—that is, any part of ourselves.

For Youlou, such philosophical reflections had little meaning, and he never seemed to have time to consider cultural problems. His concern was with immediate results, and his feverish search for aid from every quarter to carry out his program was largely due to his fear of being outdistanced by neighboring countries. For more than three years, Youlou had been talking about his economic plan, for whose formulation he had all the data at hand, while his impatient people were waiting for him to carry it out. Youlou had failed to do so because he could not decide on basic guidelines. Had he promoted agricultural exports by encouraging the whole population to cultivate all the arable land, he would have lost the support of the civil servants and politicians. This he could not bring himself to do, although in the long run it would have won him the confidence of the masses and got the Congo off to a good start.

1. An analysis of Congolese legislators by Wagret in 1962 (op. cit., pp. 140 and 189) generally substantiates that of Gauze. Of the 122 candidates on the UDDIA slate for election to the legislature in June 1959, half were civil servants and of these 17 were teachers. This proportion was roughly the same as that prevailing among the territorial assemblymen elected in 1952 and in 1957. Furthermore, all but 11 candidates in 1959 ran in the localities where they were born because they could count only on their fellow tribesmen as loyal constituents. In discussing the disparity between the living standards of Congolese wage earners, Wagret noted that a chauffeur employed by the administration earned an average monthly wage of 21,000 CFA francs ($84), whereas his counterpart in the private sector was paid only 7,000 CFA francs a month.

2. See p. 160.

3. Reported in L'Homme Nouveau, April 1961.

4. Ibid.

5. Some political economists agree with this viewpoint to the extent of believing that Youlou's downfall resulted mainly from his lack of a positive economic development program. See Samir Amin and C. Coquery-Vidrovitch, Histoire Economique du Congo, 1880-1968.

6. In 1960-61, private investments in the Congo totaled 625 million CFA francs, representing the expenditures made to improve local gasoline service stations (Wagret, op. cit., p. 109). As of 1962, virtually the sole accomplishment by the government in the field of economic development was the drafting and promulgation of an investment code designed to attract more private capital. It should also be noted, however, that studies by the Société Française d'Etudes et de Développement, initiated by Youlou's government, had provided basic data on the country's economy. The experts who wrote this six-volume report, which was not completed until December 1962, advised the Congolese authorities not to rely on large internationally financed projects for their country's development. They urged, rather, concentration on various small enterprises embracing all phases of the economy to be developed through the initiative of the Congolese population. They further proposed that the government start its program with an interim two-year plan, in which some pilot experiments in processing industries should be financed by private capital.

7. Quoted in L'Homme Nouveau, November 1961.

SUPPLEMENT

THE DECADE 1962 TO 1972

by

Virginia Thompson and Richard Adloff

CHAPTER 18

YOULOU'S DOWNFALL AND THE SECOND CONGO REPUBLIC

In July 1962, Youlou used the powers granted to him a few months earlier by the assembly to ban all associations he deemed harmful to national unity. A month later, he dissolved the three existing parties, claiming that they had become superfluous inasmuch as their leaders were now members of his government. Then, on August 25, he announced that all the spokesmen for the UDDIA, MSA, and PPC had agreed to the establishment of a single party. Yet at the end of the year, Opangault resigned from the government, which suggested that he disagreed with Youlou's policies.

Superficially, the economic situation had been bettered by a reduction in the chronic trade deficit and by an expansion and diversification of the industrial sector,[1] but the public debt was large and growing. Furthermore, the increase in customs revenues was due to higher duties collected on bigger shipments of lumber, manganese from Gabon, and contraband diamonds in transit from Congo-Léopoldville. Together they represented more than 80 percent of total exports in terms of value; only one of the major revenue earners, lumber, was an indigenous product and all three were produced by foreign companies. At the same time, the local output of agricultural produce was declining, as were exports of crude oil.

The Kouilou dam, on whose construction Youlou had pinned his hopes for the Congo's large-scale industrialization, still hung fire, his development plan had not progressed beyond the stage of studies, and the extraction of potash from the vast Hollé deposits was a distant if promising prospect. Because the rural exodus continued unabated, the urban proletariat expanded in the south, and this problem was suddenly and greatly aggravated by the expulsion of thousands of Congolese from Gabon in the fall of 1962. Only foreign aid, notably that from France, and the imposition of what was euphemistically called a "tax of national solidarity" saved the Congo from bankruptcy.

By January 1963, the stagnation of the domestic economy had created so crucial a financial situation that Youlou announced a curtailment of the recruitment and promotions in the bureaucracy. Government employees then accounted for 0.9 percent of the total population and absorbed more than half the national revenues. In view of the rapid rise in living costs, the prospect of no pay increase for another year caused resentment among the civil servants, and the suspension of further recruitment disappointed the ever more numerous unemployed school graduates. Early in 1963, it was estimated that 31 percent of the adult male population of the country were without remunerative employment.[2] As before, no effective steps were taken to curb the corruption and nepotism that permeated the ranks of the bureaucracy and the government, and their ostentatious way of living in Brazzaville was a constant provocation to the unemployed urban masses. Also, as before, Youlou underestimated the population's discontent, for he could conceive of a dangerous opposition to his government only in strictly political terms. Apparently he believed that he had created national unity when he absorbed all the major political leaders into his government.

On April 13, 1963, those leaders and the legislature unanimously accepted Youlou's plan to set up a single party. He then went on to clear the next hurdle by rendering his individual political opponents harmless. In May, his most outspoken critic, Massamba-Débat, was demoted from the presidency of the legislature and given a minor portfolio in the cabinet. Germain Bicoumat was the next to be eliminated from the government, and he was exiled to Pointe Noire as head of the Office du Kouilou. Later that month, to appease what remained of his formal opposition, Youlou took back the now innocuous Opangault into his government. Opangault was even invited to accompany Youlou to the conference at Addis Ababa, where the Organization of African Unity (OAU) was born. There Youlou did little to improve his image among the revolutionary African leaders, who regarded him as a French stooge, an advocate of compromise with Lisbon, the apologist for Tshombe, and an only lukewarm Pan-Africanist. To be sure, Youlou endorsed at Addis the principle of African unity, but obviously he could see it in only the Gaullist terms of a loose grouping of sovereign states.

In other aspects of his foreign policy, however, Youlou seemed to be making some progress. During the first half of 1963, a reconciliation between the two Congos was sealed by the exchange of state visits by Kasavubu and Youlou, which also ended their advocacy of a Great Bakongo republic. A more surprising development—and one that ultimately backfired—was the apparent endorsement of Youlou's government by francophone Africa's leading revolutionary, Sékou Touré, who spent four days at Brazzaville as the official guest of the Congo Republic. Ostensibly Sékou Touré had been invited to propound the advantages of the single-party system, of which he was an ardent exponent. The Guinean president, however, used this opportunity to arouse the Congolese labor unions against the abbé's regime. While praising the principle of the single party, Sékou Touré clearly implied that its leadership by Youlou would constitute a threat to the survival of the local organized labor movement.

Thus encouraged by Sékou Touré, the Confédération Africaine des Travailleurs Croyants (CATC), the Confédération Générale Africaine du Travail (CGAT), and the Confédération des Syndicats Libres (CCSL, formerly the FO) formed a joint committee. It presented to Youlou their common demands for a drastic reform of the government, the election of a new legislature, and the dismissal of incompetent and corrupt ministers, notably N'Zalakanda, the minister of justice. For several days, Youlou had talks with labor leaders, politicians, and army officers, but suddenly, on August 6, he broke off negotiations and announced over the radio that his single party would be set up on August 15, the third anniversary of the Congo's independence. In the meantime, he banned all public meetings, including those of the labor unions. The joint committee reacted by calling a general strike on August 13, and Youlou promptly retaliated by arresting two outstanding union leaders, Gilbert Pongault and Julien Boukambou.

On the morning of August 13, some 3,000 men from Poto-Poto and Bacongo, dressed in rags, tried to hold a meeting at Brazzaville in defiance of Youlou's order. They refused to obey the gendarmes' order to disperse, and in the ensuing clash three persons died and 12 were wounded. The crowd then stormed the prison, released the labor leaders, and from there went to burn the houses of some unpopular ministers. That evening, Youlou proclaimed a state of emergency in the three southern regions of the Congo, forbade the assembling of more than five persons, and instituted a curfew in Brazzaville. He also announced the cancellation of the independence celebrations and appealed for calm, after claiming that the disorders were due to a foreign plot.

On August 14, the crowd gathered again, and became so threatening that Youlou called for French troops to be flown in to restore order. In the meantime, he promised to form a new government and to dismiss all his ministers except Opangault, Tchichelle, and N'Zalakanda. He also agreed to postpone setting up the single party until "national harmony" had been restored. Obviously such half measures were insufficient, and when the strike entered its third day on August 15, the mob, which had grown to some 7,000 persons, converged on the presidential palace and shouted demands for Youlou's resignation. At 11:00 a.m., the French troops withdrew, leaving the Congolese army in control. Two hours later, the top-ranking Congolese officers, Majors David Mountsaka and Félix Mouzabakany, convinced Youlou that he must resign. On hearing the news, the crowd dispersed, thus ending the three days of revolution that became known in local annals as "les trois glorieuses."

The army then proceeded to intern in a military camp Youlou and all his ministers except Ibalico, who escaped to Léopoldville, and they handed over authority to a Conseil National de la Révolution (CNR), headed by Massamba-Débat. The joint committee appealed to all wage earners to return to work, and then presented Massamba-Débat with a list of "potential cabinet ministers" who were said to enjoy the confidence of the working class. It was noteworthy that this list contained the name of no union official or army officer.

The ease and rapidity with which Youlou's government was overthrown proved that he had no strong segment of the population behind him and had, in fact, antagonized its most dynamic elements—the country's youth and labor leaders—as well as the Catholic hierarchy. Youlou left the Congo more divided than before, its resources depleted, its economic problems unsolved, and without friends among the other African governments. His main positive accomplishment was to have liquidated the Matsouanist resistance. Perhaps he also should be credited with having united—against himself—the Congolese elite for the first time. But their unity did not survive his resignation as head of state, for there was no basic agreement among his opponents as to which course the Congo should now follow. At this time, none of the labor or youth leaders, nor even the army officers, was prepared for or capable of taking over the government.

In many ways, the Congo revolution was strikingly similar to that of Dahomey, which occurred two months later. In both countries, regionalism-cum-tribalism had dominated the political scene since World War II, and economic problems had been neglected during the power struggles between their leaders. An unusually well-educated and enterprising southern tribe staffed a plethoric civil service, and national revenues were too meager to provide jobs for more than a small proportion of the school graduates, unskilled rural immigrants, or wage earners who had been forcibly repatriated from nearby countries. In the underdeveloped countryside, the peasants remained miserable, passive, and deaf to official appeals to increase agricultural production.

The urban proletariat and wage earners were concentrated in the main towns, where their conditions of life contrasted so sharply with those of the politicians that they were highly responsive to demagogic appeals. The labor and youth organizations showed unity and strength, however, only when it came to ousting the government in power, for thereafter they produced no leaders who had a constructive program for national development. In the Congo and Dahomey, the army was the only organized and partially disciplined force, but it was as divided as the rest of the population by ethnic animosities and leadership rivalries. In both countries, the result of their "revolutions" was chronic governmental instability and economic stagnation, which eventually brought to power a military regime.

Nevertheless, there were certain political and economic divergencies between the Congo and Dahomey that account for significant differences in their subsequent history. In the latter state, it has been the port and commercial town of Cotonou and not the administrative capital, Porto Novo, that has been and still is the center of political and social unrest. In the Congo, on the other hand, the center of political and social turmoil is Brazzaville, with the commercial port of Pointe Noire playing only a minor role in such action. Brazzaville owes its preeminence mainly to the fact that it is the hub of an interterritorial transport system and the headquarters of an overabundant bureaucracy inherited from the days when it was the federal capital of FEA. It is also the home of the Congo's outstanding tribe, the Lari, whose proximity to their fellow Bakongo in Léopoldville (renamed Kinshasa in June 1966) makes them highly sensitive to the political and religious influences emanating from that city, which is the capital of a far larger, richer, and more populous country. Dahomey, too, has had its messianic sects but none so cohesive and intransigent as Matsouanism, and though it has also feared being overpowered by a bigger and more powerful neighbor, Nigeria, it has never felt this to the same degree.

Another important difference in the postindependence history of the two countries lies in the caliber and ideological orientation of their respective leaders. Since the elimination of Youlou, Tchicaya, and Opangault, the Congo has produced no regional or tribal spokesmen who have as strong or as loyal a personal following as have those of Dahomey. On the other hand, neither Brazzaville's tribal massacres in the late 1950s nor the ideological excesses of some Congolese—the anticommunism of Youlou and the militant Marxism of some youth and labor leaders—have had their counterparts in Dahomey. In the latter nation, no deep-seated ideological differences have ever divided their competing elites, all of whom are basically conservative and almost wholly regional spokesmen or tribal symbols. Although both Dahomey and the Congo suffer from chronic financial deficits, the latter country has attracted far more foreign interest and investments. Not only has the Congo a much greater economic potential but its proximity to Zaïre as well as the instability of its own government have helped to make it the scene of conflicting international as well as local ambitions.

As of late 1963, the conflict in the former Belgian colony was far from settled, Congo-Brazzaville itself was undergoing a troubled period of transition and isolation, and it soon became apparent that Massamba-Débat was not in full control of his country's centrifugal forces. The elites which had engineered the coup were gradually forming into two ideological camps, in which ethnic and regional origins were also influential factors. One of these groups comprised the Catholic trade unions and moderate deputies and the other the hard-line Marxist labor and youth leaders; as for the army, its officers were divided among themselves in their political and tribal allegiances.

Initially, the provisional government formed on August 15, 1963, seemed to have the support of the labor unions, youth groups, and army. Massamba filled his cabinet with competent, generally honest, and well-trained young technicians chosen without regard to their tribal or regional affiliations. Conspicuous by their absence from it were all the oldtime politicians except Germain Bicoumat. He was a politically experienced left-wing member of the PPC and influential in the Pointe Noire region, and probably for those reasons, he was given the portfolios of interior and information. Massamba himself took over the defense ministry as well as the premiership; he gave the foreign affairs post to Charles Ganao; that of labor, health, and youth to Bernard Galiba; planning and public works to Paul Kaya; agriculture, forests, and livestock to Pascal Lissouba; finance and transport to Edouard Babackas; and justice and civil service to Gérard Nkoumkou. Majors Mountsaka and Mouzabakany were confirmed in their military commands, and Michel Bindi was made head of the security police. The great majority of these ministers were far better educated than their predecessors but they were also political unknowns, and almost without exception they have now disappeared from the governmental scene.

In his first policy statement, on August 16, Massamba promised an honest government free of tribal favoritism and nepotism, as well as financial austerity, greater productivity, and the maintenance of the Congo's traditional friendships and membership in international organizations. He also stressed his government's temporary character, pledging to draft a democratic constitution and to hold free elections as soon as possible. Despite Massamba's assurances and his reputation for integrity, foreign governments were slow to recognize a regime that had come to power through mob action, even though Youlou had been no more popular abroad than at home. This diplomatic isolation weakened the government and enabled forces opposing it to gather strength. So it is not surprising that within a month of his accession, Brazzaville was the scene of demonstrations that showed the Lari's hostility to Massamba who, albeit a Bakongo, was not a member of their subtribe. Propaganda tracts and a bulletin, Vérités sur le Congo, written by pro-Youlou partisans in Kinshasa and Cameroun, fanned the flames of Lari discontent.[3]

In reaction to the Lari demonstrators, many of whom were armed as a result of Youlou's generous distribution of hunting permits, the police, army, and youth groups set up roadblocks and conducted house searches, ostensibly to prevent more weapons from filtering into the Bacongo district. Most of these repressive activities were unauthorized by the authorities, and were simply a settling of tribal or personal accounts or acts of gratuitous violence by roving bands of armed youths. They aroused so many misgivings on the part of the European community that Massamba moved to exert more control over them. In particular, he decided to incorporate all the Congolese youth groups into the Jeunesse du MNR, or JMNR, as the youth branch of the Mouvement National de la Révolution (MNR) that he was forming.

That party was almost fully organized by December 8, the day on which the Congolese were to vote on their new constitution and for a 55-man legislature. Massamba described his constitution as a compromise between a presidential and a parliamentary regime. Like that of the Fifth French Republic, after which it was largely modeled, it provided for a high court of justice and a social and economic council. For the posts of deputy, the only candidates were those on the single slate drawn up by the MNR, and they included no member of any previous Congolese legislature. Deputies were to serve for a five-year term, as was the president of the republic. A few days later, Massamba was elected to that office by a restricted college composed of the recently elected deputies. After local-government institutions were created, that college was also to include popularly elected municipal and prefectoral councilors.

Under the constitution of the Second Congolese Republic, the president had the power to select and dismiss his premier and ministers and, under certain circumstances, to dissolve the unicameral assembly and rule by decree. His exceptional authority, however, could be terminated by a two-thirds vote of the legislature. The president of the republic was ex-officio also president of the CNR, which, during the period required to "consolidate the revolution," was to coexist with the government and guide its policy. The most significant innovations introduced by this constitution were the post of prime minister, the elimination of salaries for deputies, and the institution of an executive body parallel to the government.

The elections of December 1963 were notable for the small number of abstentions—less than 10 percent of the respective electorates for the two votes—and for the smaller percentage of affirmative votes for the constitution (84.5 percent) than of those cast for the legislature (90.7 percent). Ten days later, Massamba was overwhelmingly endorsed as president, and on December 24 he named Pascal Lissouba as his prime minister. Lissouba promptly formed his government, which differed little from the preceding one. Six of the former ministers were retained, though with some changes in their portfolios. Nkoumkou was dropped from the cabinet, and three new members were added—Pascal Okiemba (justice), Aimé Matsika (trade and industry), and Gabriel Betou (labor and civil service). Another newcomer to the political scene was Léon Angor, elected president of the legislature. The choice of Lissouba and, even more, of Angor tipped the scales of the government in favor of the radical wing of the MNR.

Notes

1. As of 1963, there were 62 companies of all kinds operating in Congo-Brazzaville, and their capital aggregated about 10 billion CFA francs. Of these, only the Société Industrielle et Agricole du Niari (SIAN) at Jacob was capitalized at more than one billion CFA francs. Next in order of their capital resources were the Kronenbourg Brewery and the Foncier de Brazzaville. The capital of the remaining companies ranged between 30 and 200 million CFA francs (Bulletin de l'Afrique Noire, June 23, 1964).

2. Europe-France-Outremer, no. 473, June 1969.

3. L'Observateur du Moyen-Orient et de l'Afrique, November 15, 1963.

CHAPTER 19

THE GOVERNMENT OF MASSAMBA-DEBAT

In August 1963, Massamba-Débat inherited an economic situation which he described as "catastrophic." His regime had to cope with an accumulated debt amounting to more than 1,300 million CFA francs,[1] a steadily declining agricultural production, and an unemployment problem of staggering dimensions. After a slow start, his provisional government actually practiced the financial austerity that Massamba had preached and promised, and within six months, it had reduced the public debt to between 300 and 400 million CFA francs.[2] Fortunately, his cabinet included such trained and experienced technicians as Babackas, Kaya, and Lissouba, and by the end of 1963, they had even begun to carry out the long-delayed development plan.

The operating budget for 1964 was smaller by 62 million CFA francs than that for 1963, and was balanced at 8,429 million CFA francs. Moreover, for the first time in the Congo's history, it included an investment budget, amounting to more than 1.2 billion CFA francs, for the execution of an interim plan covering the 1964-1968 period. The aims of this plan were much the same as those that had been frequently enunciated by Youlou—full employment, promotion of the Congo's transit trade, increased revenues from the rural economy, and industrial development.[3] A new feature, however, was to be a reorganization of the local administration into nine regions, mainly with a view to facilitating execution of the plan and checking the rural exodus. In Brazzaville and Pointe Noire, the two cities which were to become the eighth and ninth regions, "urbanization" was to be promoted "rationally" and prices and wages were to be controlled. Each of the seven rural regions was to specialize in a single project, and their infrastructure and commercial systems were to be developed accordingly.

In the overall distribution of the plan's funds, half was to go to industry and the economic services, 18 percent to the infrastructure, 17 percent to urbanization projects, six percent to agriculture, and two percent each to the health and education departments. This allocation of the funds, as well as their geographic distribution, showed that there had been little change in the thinking of Congolese planners. The Kouilou dam was still regarded as the key to industrial expansion, for the area surrounding it would receive 40 percent of the total, whereas the northern Likouala region was to get the smallest allotment of all. Execution of this plan was expected to increase the number of jobs in the private sector by some 16,000, while employment in the public sector was scheduled to grow by only half that amount. In 1964, the cost of the plan was estimated to total 50,347 million CFA francs, of which public and semipublic funds were to supply 60 percent, the balance to be provided by private investors.

Obviously, for the execution of the plan, foreign sources, both public and private, would have to make large contributions. As inducements for such investments, the Congo could offer abundant forests, huge potash deposits, petroleum resources of unknown extent, and a considerable hydroelectric potential. Also, there existed in the south a well-developed commercial network, a satisfactory transport system, and a plentiful supply of urban manpower. Offsetting these assets, however, were the inaccessibility and underdevelopment of the northern half of the country, inadequate food production, a very limited domestic market, and an unskilled and turbulent labor force averse to manual occupations and to jobs outside the main towns. In late 1963 and early 1964, the resident European community was given good cause to appreciate the seriousness of the last-mentioned drawback. The sporadic violence in the streets of Brazzaville reached a climax in February 1964 when, during the course of an antigovernment demonstration by the Lari, a member of the West German diplomatic mission was manhandled, and subsequently, all of the Western embassies were accused by the JMNR leaders of inciting the riots.

The feeling of insecurity engendered by such incidents was aggravated by Premier Lissouba's first policy statement after his investiture.[4] Insofar as he promised to practice financial austerity, reduce the rising cost of living and "creeping fiscality," and consult the private sector before making major economic decisions, he was reassuring to local businessmen. But at the same time, he also foreshadowed a "socialization" of the Congo's resources and its transport system, as well as a "selective nationalization" of trade, notably in the north. Although Lissouba was deliberately vague about the more socialistic aspects of his program, the legislature under Angor's presidency could hardly have been more explicit in its radical demands. In a series of resolutions voted by its members on March 17, they asked for nationalization of the three French companies which monopolized public utilities and transport in Brazzaville, the Congolization of all employment, a revision of the agreements with France, and the Congo's withdrawal from the UAM.

Although Lissouba ignored the more extreme resolutions passed by the deputies, his government moved in the spring of 1964 to implement a more radical economic and political program than before. Late in March, Lissouba gave his official blessing to a merger between the CGAT and the autonomous unions (CCSL) that deliberately encouraged organized labor to play a political role. That same month, the government nationalized Air-Congo, after expelling its two French directors, who held a majority of its stock. Then in June, two state enterprises—the Office National du Commerce (ONAC) and the Office National de Commercialisation des Produits Agricoles (ONCPA)—were created, the latter as an organization to monopolize trade in the agricultural output of the north. Since the ONCPA was to function in an area of only negligible interest to European firms,[5] their managers were far more concerned by the concurrent establishment of diplomatic relations with the governments of Peking, Moscow, Prague, and Belgrade.

Clearly, the government's trend was leftward, but to what degree did not become obvious until July 1964. That month, the MNR was made the Congo's single party, dedicated to achieving economic independence through the application of scientific socialism.[6] At the MNR's constituent congress, the delegates denounced the free enterprise system as ineffectual and demanded that the state take over control of foreign trade and of the forest industry from European companies. They also urged that the investment code be altered so as to reduce the fiscal advantages enjoyed by foreign capitalists, as well as their right to repatriate profits. As to the party's structure, it was to be organized along lines similar to those in other francophone Black African single-party states. Party cells would duplicate the pyramidal pattern of the administration, and all Congolese wage earners, youth, and women were to be mobilized in mass movements that would be placed under the supreme authority of a 51-member central committee of the MNR, or politburo.

Although Massamba was reelected general secretary of the MNR and was still president of the republic, it seemed increasingly doubtful that he would be able to assert his authority over the extremist elements nominally under his control. He tried to balance the Congo's closer ties with the communist countries and revolutionary African states by friendly gestures to the Western powers. But in midsummer 1964, the radicals' position was strengthened by two events, both involving Congo-Léopoldville. The first of these was the discovery of a traffic in firearms leading to an abortive raid and allegedly involving Major Mouzabakany, Captain Tsika, and Bernard Kolelas. The second was Tshombe's sudden expulsion from Congo-Léopoldville of alien Africans, including several thousand Brazzavillians. This drastic step was interpreted by the MNR left wing not merely as Tshombe's revenge for the overthrow of his friend Youlou but as evidence of his intention to undermine Brazzaville's economy by swelling the number of its unemployed nationals.

Lissouba's failure to react strongly to such "provocation" from Léopoldville now exposed the Brazzaville premier, as well as Massamba, to the charge of weakness. They were savagely attacked by Angor in the legislature, which refused to give the government the special powers it had requested to cope with the refugee problem. Angor criticized Lissouba for failing to "implement the revolution that had brought him to power," gave him 72 hours in which to purge his government of counterrevolutionaries, and initiated the proposal voted by the deputies to establish a people's court empowered to try traitors.[7]

Before yielding to this pressure, Lissouba let more than a month pass, partly because of dissension in the ranks of the MNR and partly to let Kaya complete his fund-seeking mission in Japan, the United States, France, and Israel. Thanks to his diplomacy, training, and experience, Kaya succeeded in gaining commitments from those countries to finance certain development projects in the Congo. On October 28, however, three weeks after his return to Brazzaville, Kaya was dropped from the cabinet at the same time as another moderate, Pascal Okiemba, minister of justice. Although Okiemba had played a leading role in Youlou's overthrow, he was an official of the CATC, whose leaders were increasingly opposed to the MNR's radical policies. Okiemba's replacement by Pierre Mafoua and Kaya's by Aimé Matsika confirmed a hardening of the party's left-wing position.

Throughout the last months of 1964, radical policies predominated, but European capitalists also had their innings. The predominantly French-financed Compagnie des Potasses du Congo was making progress at Hollé, and officials laid the cornerstone of the SIAN's industrial complex (called Sosuniari) in the Niari valley. On the latter occasion, Matsika told private investors that a large place would be left for them in such industries as those producing textiles, cement, and beer. Yet foreign businessmen were hardly reassured by concurrent developments related to the economy. For some time the radicals, particularly the JMNR, had been gunning for the Catholic mission in general and for its labor union in particular. At the annual CATC congress in September, the delegates—only the postal workers' union dissenting—voted against the politicization of its membership. Soon afterward, its president, Fulgence Biayoula, was arrested and the two French priests who tried to help him escape from the police were expelled from the country. Following the formation of the Confédération des Syndicats Congolais (CSC) on November 24 as the Congo's sole labor movement, the CATC was offically dissolved. A few days later, a motion censuring the government—proposed by the leading CATC deputy, J. A. Makosso—was disallowed for debate in the legislature by Lissouba. Three months later, the four CATC members of the MNR politburo were expelled from that body and, in June 1965, the CATC deputies were eliminated from the national assembly.

Early in February 1965, the dramatic discovery of the mutilated bodies of three high-ranking officials on the banks of the Congo River clearly revealed that the peaceful period of the Congolese revolution had been succeeded by a reign of terror. The victims were Joseph Pouabou,[8] president of the supreme court, Anselme Massoumé,[9] director of the state information service, and Lazare Matsecota,[10] the attorney general. Reportedly, the murdered men had been slated for ministerial posts in a government that was to be set up by some Lari who were plotting to free Youlou. Although those responsible for this triple crime were never brought to justice, the fact that all the victims were pro-Western, political moderates, and advocates of the independence of the judiciary convinced a large segment of public opinion of the guilt of some MNR hotheads.[11] Only a few days before, the latter had manifested anger after Lissouba's announcement of a conspiracy hatched in Léopoldville by "international financial circles."

The assassinations of February 1965 shocked and outraged both the Congolese and foreigners. Although this reaction did not put a stop to the arrest and expulsion of the so-called "enemies of the revolution," nor check the hysterical denunciation of foreign plotters against the MNR regime, never again did physical violence in Brazzaville take such an extreme form. The sobering effects of the episode were evidenced in the government's playing down potentially inflammatory events that occurred in the Congo during the following weeks. Even the escape of Youlou from Brazzaville to Léopoldville in March did no more than revive the usual accusations against Tshombe and denunciations of Lari tribalism. Massamba and other MNR leaders blandly dismissed Youlou's flight as an April Fools' Day joke, although it did prove beyond a doubt that the abbé had kept the loyalty of many of his fellow tribesmen. Probably the government realized that no important element in the country really wanted Youlou's return to power; and for different reasons of self-interest, many Lari, Massamba himself, the army, and the JMNR doubtless all connived at his escape. Each of them preferred to have him out of Congo-Brazzaville rather than be revived as a divisive issue, either by being murdered or being brought to trial. Furthermore, the welcome that Youlou received at Léopoldville gave the JMNR and other radicals fresh ammunition for their intransigence.

The cabinet reshuffle of April 5 reflected the government's refusal to compromise with any conservative opposition, above all with Youlou's Lari sympathizers. Of the five newcomers to the government, the replacement of the comparatively moderate Bicoumat by André Hombessa as minister of the interior, the appointment of Claude Ndalla as secretary of state for youth, and the promotion of Bernard Zoniaba to head the information ministry marked the triumph of the JMNR. Other straws in the same wind that blew across Congo-Brazzaville in the course of 1965 were the MNR's rejection of the OCAM's denunciation of Ghana's subversive activities (in April), four death sentences pronounced in absentia by the reactivated people's court (June), the failure of still another raid on Brazzaville by commandos based at Léopoldville (July), the diplomatic rupture with the United States and Portugal (August), and the sponsoring of Congolese volunteers to fight Ian Smith and his "club of Nazis" in Rhodesia (November). Moreover, the Congo was also cultivating ties with a new group of communist countries, namely, North Korea, North Vietnam, and, above all, Cuba. The Mouvement pour la Libération d'Angola, a more radical group than that of its rival headed by Holden Roberto in Kinshasa, was encouraged to establish its headquarters in Dolisie.

The year 1965 was also marked by the strengthening of the authority of Hombessa, Ndalla, Zoniaba, and Angor—all former militants of the JMNR or CGAT—none of whom had played any significant role in the overthrow of Youlou. With the purge of the older and more moderate technicians and labor officials from the government, Congo-Brazzaville to all appearances had irrevocably chosen the revolutionary path. Massamba obviously could no longer hold the line, notably in muting the young militants' verbal outbursts, and even Lissouba, who had been regarded as a firebrand at the time he became premier, was now viewed by them as a tepid revolutionary.

In domestic policy, these two men had to make significant concessions to the radical wing of the MNR, especially after the commando raid in July had revived its insistence on stronger measures, notably a more rapid application of scientific socialism. In August, the JMNR acquired de facto control over the army, the state was made the sole agency for the extraction of minerals, a monopoly for internal air service was granted to the new national company of LINA-Congo, and a Bureau pour la Création, le Contrôle, et l'Orientation des Entreprises de l'Etat (BCCO) was created to take over the state industrial sector. The culmination of this trend came in January 1966, when the MNR was institutionalized as the Congo's single party, and its ascendancy over the government was legally confirmed.

In the field of foreign relations, however, Massamba and Lissouba pursued a middle-of-the-road course despite their commitment to Marxist doctrines and an official policy of nonalignment. They were sufficiently realistic and experienced to know that neither the large loans that had been granted to the Congo by China and the U.S.S.R., nor the state's growing control over the economy, could of themselves solve the country's perennial problems of underdevelopment and unemployment in the visible future. They still wielded enough authority to resist the radicals' pressure for the Congo's withdrawal from the OCAM and the UDEAC,[12] a rupture with France, and the nationalization of the country's outstanding foreign firms. Not only did the government refuse to make a clear-cut choice between the eastern and western power blocs and between the revolutionary and reformist African nations but Lissouba and Massamba even avoided the danger of taking sides in the Sino-Soviet dispute. They managed to remain on good terms with both the major communist powers and also to neutralize their influence by cultivating the friendship of smaller communist states. The overthrow of Nkrumah in

161

February 1966, following that of Ben Bella in the preceding June, made the Congolese revolutionaries realize that neither Moscow nor Peking would come actively to the aid of even their favorite African protégés. Then the coups d'état that put military governments in control of Congo-Léopoldville (in November 1965), Dahomey (December 1965), and Upper Volta and the Central African Republic (January 1966) had a further sobering effect.

As a result of the foregoing developments in Africa, the pendulum of Congolese politics swung back to a more conservative position early in 1966. Two rapid cabinet reshuffles left most of the former ministers in the government, albeit with some shifts in their portfolios, but the removal of Ndalla from it seemed to portend a significant move to the right. More far-reaching were the resignation of Lissouba as premier and the elimination of Zoniaba in April, followed by the defeat of Angor when he ran for reelection as assembly president in May. Some observers interpreted these changes as a defeat for the pro-Peking faction and a victory for the pro-Moscow element, while others expressed a wholly contradictory view. The changes may or may not have been related to the arrest of a small but politically important group which was discovered distributing tracts against Massamba late in March.

It was Lissouba's resignation that aroused the most speculation but little surprise. It was variously attributed to his family problems, poor health, often-expressed desire to resume his agronomic studies, a power struggle between him and Massamba, and the dissatisfaction of the MNR radicals with his performance as premier or, conversely, that of the moderates at the government's subordination to the party. As for Lissouba's successor, Ambroise Noumazalaye, his views were not fully known because never before had he possessed political power, although his post as general secretary of the MNR suggested a strongly Marxist orientation. Furthermore, Angor's replacement by André-Georges Mouyabi could be interpreted either as a success for the moderates or as the penalizing of a highly placed member of the politburo who had flouted party discipline by running against the MNR's official candidate and was allegedly involved in the "affair of the anti-Massamba tracts." The retention of Babackas and Ganao in Noumazalaye's cabinet suggested the persistence of a moderate policy, yet Hombessa and Matsika, two militant radicals, were also confirmed in their key posts. In brief, there was no clear-cut trend, and the only certainty was that behind the scenes a tug of war was still going on between the MNR's two main factions.

Noumazalaye's public statements in late May stressed the ascendancy of the party as the Congo's supreme organ and of the state's role in controlling the economy. These pronouncements, as well as his denunciations of American policy in Vietnam and of Britain's "odious and disgusting complacency" in the Rhodesian situation, showed that the change in premiers had entailed no abatement of the MNR's revolutionary zeal.[13] This intransigence was confirmed in June when the legislature accepted Noumazalaye's proposal to place the army and civil defense corps under the control of the MNR's politburo and to transform both into a people's army commanded by a new corps of political commissars.

For some time, the army had resented the activities of the JMNR militia, the employment of Cuban instructors for the civil defense corps, and the dismissal or transfer of some officers, allegedly for complicity in the commando raid of July 1965. While Massamba was attending an OCAM conference at Tananarive in late June 1966, the army's exasperation reached the danger point after Captain Marien Ngouabi, the popular paratroop commander, was demoted. Ngouabi's fellow tribesmen in the army mutinied on June 27, sacked the JMNR headquarters, kidnapped the commander-in-chief, Major Mountsaka, and its head of the sûreté, Michel Bindi, and forced Noumazalaye and his ministers to take refuge in the sports stadium at Brazzaville.

After negotiating for two days, during which Noumazalaye promised to reconsider Ngouabi's demotion, the army returned to its barracks. Officially, Noumazalaye blamed the mutiny on resurgent tribalism, but he was careful to reinstate Ngouabi inconspicuously as commander of the paratroops in Brazzaville. He would not yield, however, to the mutineers' demand for the Cubans' dismissal and the dissolution of the JMNR militia and the civil defense corps, and he refused to relinquish the government's control over all the armed forces. Massamba, upon his return to Brazzaville, was more inclined to compromise than was Noumazalaye. He had talks with many officers and replaced Major Mountsaka as commander-in-chief by an obscure and apolitical captain, Ebadeit Damas, who immediately proclaimed his loyalty to the revolution and pledged that the army would never try to take over the government.[14]

By mid-July 1966, to all appearances the situation had returned to normal, and the radicals had won still another victory. The people's court had a new spurt of activity and handed down many severe prison sentences to those who had been arrested for involvement in the numerous "plots against the revolution." It had also condemned to death in absentia the Catholic labor leader, Gilbert Pongault,[15] who had long since fled from the Congo. Yet the army mutiny had injected a new factor of uncertain dimensions into an increasingly tense local political situation. As for the Congo's international position, relations with Congo-Kinshasa had markedly improved after Mobutu's coup d'état in November 1965, but those with France were deteriorating. In August 1966, two French residents were expelled, the French military mission at Brazzaville was dismissed, and the government issued treasury bonds rather than reduce its expenditures as its French technical experts had advised.

During the last half of 1966, Massamba's government seemed more self-confident and stable, but the financial situation was going from bad to worse. Noumazalaye's statement on May 10 concerning the economy had foreshadowed a continuation of Lissouba's policy of expanding governmental control through the establishment of more state organizations and companies of mixed economy[16] and encouraging wholly private investments only in specific industries.

On the credit side of the ledger, many new projects were being carried out with public funds, mainly of foreign origin. The U.S.S.R. was financing construction of a hotel and a maternity hospital in Brazzaville and irrigation works on the Batéké plateau; Peking, a textile plant at Kinsoundi; and North Korea, a match factory. France and other Common Market countries were providing considerable funds for various enterprises,[17] of which the most spectacular was the West German cement plant at Lutété. Israel continued to give technical aid, and American private capital was still committed to the Hollé potash company. Of greater immediate benefit was the prospect that the OCAM sugar agreement would soon provide a new market for the Niari valley's

surplus output. Mining and forestry remained the most flourishing industries in the Congo, and they were still under foreign control.

While the large, long-established, private enterprises[18] were doing
well, the economic picture as a whole had its dark side. Prices for essential commodities had increased by nearly 14 percent during 1966, and the
cost of living continued to rise rapidly. Many of the communist-financed
state enterprises were becoming heavily indebted and their eventual viability was far from assured. Even more dismal were the prospects of those
financed wholly from Congolese revenues. LINA-Congo, the internal air line,
was operating with a growing deficit, as was the Kinsoundi textile factory,
but it was the failure of the government's most ambitious state company, the
ONCPA, that caused it most concern. The monopoly granted to the ONCPA for
the purchase and sale of all the northern agricultural produce had not arrested the decline of such exports. Little progress had been made in cultivating more than half of the country's arable land, and the experiment of
creating cooperative villages and regrouping them had neither increased production nor notably improved farming techniques. Moreover, the ONCPA was
having difficulties with its personnel and with the transport and stocking
of its purchases, and even the domestic sale of most agricultural products
had decreased. By the end of 1966, the income earned that year by the ONCPA
amounted to only 10.9 percent of the value of the Congo's total exports.[19]

The cost of meeting the state companies' deficits weighed heavily on a
budget already in trouble because of the increasingly unfavorable balance of
foreign trade. (Lumber and uncut diamonds were still the Congo's major
revenue earners.) In 1966, total exports were valued at 9.6 billion CFA
francs, whereas imports cost 15.5 billion. The public debt stood at 3 billion CFA francs, of which the Congo owed France about half and its UDEAC
partners another 800 million in unpaid customs duties. In the period between 1960 and 1967, state expenditures grew fourfold, rising from 3.9 billion to 14.5 billion. As a means of balancing its budget, the government
rejected any drastic reduction in the number and pay of its civil servants
and preferred to issue short-term bonds.

Apparently the MNR judged an immediate reduction of the bureaucracy as
too risky politically, but its selection of industries for promotion by
state enterprises was economically shortsighted.[20] The eventual output of
Brazzaville's cement and match factories would have to compete with similar
production from Cameroun and Kinshasa, which had already established their
markets in Tchad, Gabon, and the Central African Republic. Even more dubious was the outlook for the Kinsoundi textile plant, for which the raw material had to be imported, whereas Tchad and the Central African Republic not
only themselves manufactured cloth but also grew their own cotton. In this
instance, however, the Congolese authorities could not be held wholly responsible for failing to give sufficient study to the limitations of the
equatorial market. The machinery for the Kinsoundi plant initially had
been destined for Ghana, but after Nkrumah's overthrow, its Chinese donors
offered it to the Congo.[21] Obviously the Kinsoundi case was exceptional,
but it was only an extreme example of a communist country's political motivation in providing "aid" to the Brazzaville government. Not surprisingly,
private capitalists preferred to put their money in the more financially
profitable enterprises of mining and forestry, but even in those areas, few
fresh large-scale investments were forthcoming.

In 1964-65, only 700 million CFA francs from private sources were invested in the Congo;[22] the flight of such capital during that same period was estimated at 13 billion CFA francs.[23]   In vain, the MNR leaders exhorted private investors to have confidence in the country and its resources, affirmed the Congo's membership in the franc zone, and stressed the fact that there had been no appreciable increase in industrial taxes or any major nationalizations. No doubt the government's profession of scientific socialism was more theoretical and verbal than actual, yet the MNR extremists' persistent demands for a national currency, the expropriation of all foreign trading and industrial companies, and the fostering of ties with the communist countries, combined with denunciations of Western neocolonialism and imperialists' plots—all contributed to an unsettling climate of insecurity.

Except for Massamba's growing concern about the country's economic stagnation, there was no perceptible change in the Congolese scene during the first half of 1967. The Brazzaville radio and press continued to lambaste the OCAM and American imperialism, new agreements were signed with various communist countries, and the two French public utilities companies in the capital were at long last effectively nationalized. In the last months of the year, however, there were signs of a change in the government's political orientation, though none in its economic policy. Relations with France were improved, diplomatic ties with Ghana were restored, and those with India and Nigeria were established. Moreover, the army remained quiescent, probably because Massamba had either quietly sent most of the Cubans home or dispersed them throughout rural camps. He even went so far as to denounce excessive nationalizations and corruption among office holders and civil servants and to insist that the JMNR concentrate on economic reconstruction and accept closer control by the government. Massamba's increasing self-confidence was perhaps best shown when, to celebrate the Congo's fourth independence anniversary, he dared to commute Mouzabakany's death sentence to 20 years in prison and to free Tchichelle and N'Zalakanda. Inevitably, the MNR extremists reacted strongly against these moves, and they succeeded in setting up a 25-man permanent committee in the politburo for the purpose of controlling Massamba's activities. Rumors began to circulate in December, after Massamba's dismissal of Paul Banthoud as head of the CSC, that the JMNR was planning to overthrow him. A trial of strength between Massamba's moderate supporters in the government and the radical party leaders was clearly shaping up.

To forestall such a move from the left, Massamba dismissed Noumazalaye from his government and himself took over the premiership on January 12, 1968. As usual, however, he temporized, for at the same time as he removed the moderate Mondjo as foreign minister, he gave Hombessa's interior portfolio to the authoritarian Bindi and forbade the Congolese to make unauthorized contacts with any foreign embassy in Brazzaville. The overall impression left by Massamba's zigzag course was that he felt the Congolese revolution should now mark a pause, albeit without renouncing its socialistic orientation, and that he must firmly assert his government's control over the MNR extremists. By March, he must have believed that he had won the first round in this battle, for he went on a long African journey that included the conservative as well as the revolutionary francophone nations.

The situation indeed seemed well in hand until mid-May, when another plot was uncovered, this time led by a European (Jacques Lebreton) described as a mercenary in the pay of international finance. This was all that was needed to spur the radicals on, and their attacks, combined with his own blunders, culminated in Massamba's downfall. It occurred almost exactly five years after Youlou had been overthrown, but the scenario and actors were not the same as in August 1963. This time no role was played by the labor unions or by a mob of unemployed youths; the coup was spearheaded by the students' association, not the JMNR, and the army was the prime element in it.[24]

On July 22, Massamba wearily announced over the radio his intention of handing over his authority to anyone who felt more qualified than he to head the government.[25] When no candidate presented himself, however, Massamba declared that he would remain in power. On July 24, the Union Générale des Elèves et Etudiants Congolais (UGEEC) held a congress at Brazzaville in the presence of Ndalla, Poungui, and Peking's chargé d'affaires. Its members, mainly university students on vacation from France, accused Massamba of having sold out to the imperialists. Massamba promptly retorted that the students were deceitful self-appointed spokesmen for the proletariat, and he also severely criticized the "sordid maneuvers of certain politicians and bureaucrats." He capped this on July 27 by suddenly arresting several dozen persons who were reportedly "Maoists." They included the paratroop captain, Marien Ngouabi, whose demotion two years earlier had touched off the army mutiny.

On the last day of July, there were mass demonstrations, some for and some against Massamba. Unduly encouraged by this qualified support, Massamba dissolved the legislature and the politburo on August 1, but retained some of their members to form an enlarged version of the old CNR. He called a meeting of MNR militants for the next day, entrusted the maintenance of public order to the army, and said that he would rule by decree until elections for a new legislature could be held. These drastic measures caused a strong reaction, and that same afternoon, the first barricades appeared in Brazzaville. Early on August 2, the paratroopers went into action, stormed the prison, and released Ngouabi and other prisoners, and began patrolling the streets of the capital. A few hours later, Massamba announced an amnesty for all political prisoners, including Mouzabakany and Tsika, and called a meeting of the CNR after making an appeal for national unity. However, the next day, the army moved decisively to place the militia under its control. Its spokesman at the same time publicly accused Massamba of having acted illegally in dissolving the legislature and in having imprisoned his political opponents so as to avoid holding elections as called for by the constitution. Clearly, Massamba had now forfeited the support of the army.

Communication between Brazzaville and the outside world was cut off at this dramatic juncture, so it became difficult to follow the course of events during the next few days.[26] It was soon learned, however, that Massamba had abruptly left Brazzaville on August 3 after naming Lieutenant Poignet acting head of state and that that officer had promptly appointed Ngouabi commander-in-chief of the army. Two days later, the mystery of Massamba's whereabouts was cleared up by the announcement that, after spending the weekend in his native village of Nkolo, he had returned to Brazzaville at the request of Ngouabi, who also guaranteed his personal safety. On August 5, Massamba formed a new government in which the post of premier was reestablished and from which the radical Hombessa and the moderate Ganao were both excluded.

166

Ngouabi was confirmed in his command and given control of the civil defense corps, Captain L. S. Goma was named army chief of staff, and Poignet was appointed head of the defense ministry with the rank of captain. Lissouba reappeared to take over the foreign affairs portfolio, and, most surprisingly of all, Mouzabakany emerged from prison to become minister of the interior. A general amnesty was declared for all political offenders at home and abroad, excluding Youlou but including Kolelas, who soon returned to Brazzaville after four years in exile.

For the next few days, it looked as if Massamba had weathered the strongest attempt that had yet been made to unseat him, but the first sign of a significant change occurred at the initial meeting of the 30-member CNR held on August 9 under Ngouabi's chairmanship. Four days later, a 12-man directorate was created inside the CNR, with Ngouabi at its head, Noumazalaye its general secretary, Ange Poungui and Lieutenant Aimé Portella as its first and second vice-presidents, and five secretaries—for defense (Captain Alfred Raoul), propaganda (Martin M'Berri), education (Pierre Nze), finance (François Makouzou), and administration (A. G. Mouyabi). Except for Mouyabi and M'Berri, these secretaries were newcomers to Congolese politics, and, aside from Makouzou, all the members of the CNR directorate occupied prominent positions under the next government.

On August 13, the same day the CNR directorate was formed, a Fundamental Act replaced the constitution of 1963. It made the CNR directorate the supreme organ of the MNR party and of the state, and as such it became a supergovernment placed over and above the government still headed by Massamba. Furthermore, under this act, the powers of the president of the republic were sharply curtailed, for the premier (Captain Raoul) was to be responsible no longer to him but to the CNR directorate, which also was required to countersign all presidential decrees.[27]

For three weeks after his sudden return to Brazzaville, Massamba managed to hold on to the presidency of what was now only a shadow government. On independence day, he made a conciliatory foreign-policy statement that included veiled overtures to Washington, London, and Taipeh. In the last days of August, however, he remained on the sidelines in the violent settling of accounts that took place between the army, on the one hand, and a strange mixture of its opponents, including Bindi, Hombessa, some supporters of Massamba, and above all, the JMNR irreconcilables. When the fighting broke out on August 29, Massamba decided he had had enough. In a broadcast to the nation that evening, he disclaimed any responsibility for the conflict, made a half-hearted appeal for unity and peace, and then handed his resignation as president of the republic and head of the government to Captain Poignet.

This time the army officers, judging Massamba no longer capable of governing the country under their aegis and annoyed at the procedure he had followed, did not ask him to reconsider his decision. On September 4, his resignation was accepted by the CNR directorate because he had "failed in his essential duty of ensuring respect for the nation's institutions, national unity, and peace."[28]

This harsh judgment on Massamba's government was justified neither by his personal behavior while in office nor by the policies he pursued. As an austere, disinterested, and thrifty Protestant schoolteacher, who sincerely believed in a socialistic form of democracy and who placed national unity and development above tribal loyalties, his character and style of government contrasted sharply with those of his flamboyant and extravagant predecessor. During his four and one-half years as president of the Second Congo Republic, Massamba gave his country a reasonably honest government and a democratic constitution, vastly improved and widened its foreign relations, and tried to hold the balance between conservatives and radicals and between the Lari and Mbochi. He also tried to develop the Congo's economy under state control on a more regionally equitable basis and by soliciting external aid from widely varying sources.

Massamba constantly stressed the nationalistic aspect of his foreign policy, drawing a distinction between an alignment with the communist countries and the Congo's indigenous brand of socialism, whose "application requires no help from Malians, Guineans, Chinese, or Cubans."[29] When asked which foreign country he most cherished for the aid it had given to the Congo, Massamba refused to commit himself. He compared his position to that of a polygamous husband who "fears to cause jealousy by showing favoritism to any of his wives."[30] His flexible approach was not always understood or appreciated abroad or at home. By pursuing an ideologically inconsistent foreign policy, Massamba succeeded in attracting large-scale investments from both the eastern and western blocs, while remaining on generally good diplomatic terms with both. When he applied the same pragmatism to domestic affairs, however, Massamba opened a Pandora's box of forces that he could not control. He lacked a personal power base, and his theoretically sound policy of governing through competent technocrats failed in practice because it had no firm tribal or regional support.

Massamba inherited problems that were even more difficult to resolve than those that had faced Youlou in 1960. These were a depleted treasury, rural stagnation and urban unemployment, poor-to-bad foreign relations, and, worst of all, a people divided against itself by deep-seated tribal and regional antagonisms that were only partly masked by conflicts ostensibly stemming from political ideologies. He came to power without any solid political organization or the charisma that might have given him a mass following, simply because of his record as a courageous and competent opponent of Youlou and because no one else at the time was prepared to take over the government. There was no unity in the country aside from the common determination among the elite to get rid of Youlou. As soon as this was accomplished, all the centrifugal tendencies among the Congolese reasserted themselves, and there was no cohesive force to hold them in check.

From the outset, Massamba had to contend with opposition from the right and from the left, which gradually eroded the authority he had assumed in August 1963 with the approval of most of the Congolese elites. Through a lack of foresight, Massamba allowed the radicals to destroy the Catholic labor unions and to oust from the cabinet the key technocrats who might have become his staunchest supporters. Through his overwillingness to compromise, he permitted their places to be taken by the young and inexperienced Marxist leaders of the CSC and JMNR—the very organizations that he had created for the purpose of controlling the anarchic youth and laborers. Not only did their aggressiveness and demands for a more radical policy alienate many foreign businessmen whose investments might have helped develop the economy but they also antagonized the army, the only organized force in the country capable of maintaining order.

Massamba's regime marked a far sharper break with the past than did that of Youlou with its predecessor, the colonial administration. Deliberately, Massamba set the Congo on a new course of close relations with communist countries, state control of ever larger sectors of the economy, and commitment to Marxist principles which gave the Congo an orientation it had theretofore lacked. Had he had more time to carry out his policy of socialism by stages, the transition might have been accomplished without the upheavals that have become a standard feature of Congo-Brazzaville's governments. He was able to make only a beginning in erasing the economic inequities that were a main cause of tribal and regional antagonisms, without appreciably attenuating the misery of the northern peasantry or that of the unemployed in the Congo's southern towns. Because the Congo had not yet developed the indigenous cadres, organization, and experience required to utilize effectively the foreign funds it received, those funds were dissipated in launching state enterprises that proved financially disastrous. By opening the Congo to competitive communist influences, Massamba strengthened the Marxist trends among the elite, thus adding more disruptive ideological differences. Furthermore, because he permitted the Congo to be used as a training center for guerrillas who aimed to overthrow the governments of Yaoundé and Kinshasa, the Congo's relations with neighboring countries were badly damaged.

By late 1967, Massamba finally became convinced that he was on a collision course and that the intransigent Marxists in the single party he had created were determined to take over the government, but in an effort to reassert his authority and redress the balance of forces, he moved too far and too fast to the right. His regime became oppressive and abusive, and he antagonized not only the extreme Marxists but also the army, which until then had backed him. Like Youlou, he had contributed to his country's disunity, but unlike Youlou, he was not overthrown by organized labor or by a threatening street mob. Massamba simply faded away for lack of support and to the regret of only those Western powers who saw in him a moderating influence and a bulwark against the rising tide of communism in the Congo.

Notes

1. Marchés Tropicaux, September 13, 1963.

2. Brazzaville radio broadcast, January 21, 1964.

3. "Le Plan Quinquennal," Europe-France-Outremer, November 1964.

4. Marchés Tropicaux, February 8, 1964.

5. The only important enterprise operating in the north was the Compagnie Française du Haut et du Bas Congo (CFHBC), which in 1899 had been granted a concession covering 70,000 square kilometers and a 30-year monopoly of its trade. With difficulty the CFHBC was able to survive until after World War II, when it was taken over by the Banque de l'Indochine. Another crisis occurred in 1961, at which time the CFHBC was operating most of the river boats in the north, producing nearly one-third of the Congo's total vegetable oil exports, and employing 660 persons. In response to its plea for aid, the government bought some

of its palm plantations in the Haute-Sangha. A recurrence of its financial difficulties in 1964 precipitated the government's decision to take over the CFHBC and to replace it by the ONCPA.

6. _Marchés Tropicaux_, July 18, 1964.

7. _Ibid._, September 12, 1964.

8. See p. 138.

9. Significantly, the Agence Congolaise d'Information, which Massouemé had headed, printed only a three-line obituary, in which it was noted that he had been born on November 22, 1920, was married, and was the father of four children.

10. See p. 208.

11. _Afrique Nouvelle_, March 3, 1965, November 5, 1968; _West Africa_, February 27, 1965.

12. See pp. 200-203.

13. Brazzaville radio broadcast, May 26, 1966.

14. _Le Mois en Afrique_, September 1966.

15. In January 1965, Pongault fled to Lagos, where three months later he was reelected president of the Pan-African Christian Union.

16. These were companies financed jointly by public and private capital, the most outstanding of them being the Savonnerie du Congo, Société Nationale des Transports Fluviaux, Complexe de Pêcheries Industrielles, Sosuniari, Sonel, and Compagnie des Potasses du Congo. The Congo state provided 38 percent of Sosuniari's capital and 15 percent of that of the Compagnie des Potasses.

17. Between 1964 and 1968, the Common Market Fund (FED) provided more than 5 billion CFA francs, mainly for infrastructure, and the French government (through FAC) nearly 3 billion, chiefly for social equipment and production. See _Dossier d'Information_, October 1970, p. 19.

18. The most important, long-established private enterprises were Socobois, Afribois, Shell Oil, Bata Shoes, Africaplast, Grands Moulins du Congo, and the Kronenbourg Brewery.

19. _Le Monde_, January 12, 1967; _Marchés Tropicaux_, January 7, June 24, 1967.

20. During Massamba's administration, the state companies operating in the primary sector were the Régie Nationale du Palmier Congo, Office National des Forêts, Société Nationale d'Elevage, and Bureau Minier du Congo; in the secondary sector, Bureau pour la Création, le Contrôle, et l'Orientation des Entreprises de l'Etat, Régie Nationale des Transports et Travaux Publics, Office Congolais de l'Habitat, Société Nationale de l'Energie, and Société Nationale de la Distribution d'Eau; and in the tertiary sector, Office National du Commerce, Office des Bois de l'Afrique Equatoriale, Office National des Postes et Telecommunications, Régie Nationale des Transports de Brazzaville, Liaisons Nationales Aériennes, and Office National pour la Commercialisation des Produits Agricoles.

21. Le Monde, January 12, 1967.

22. Investments from all sources during the interim plan period (1964-65) were: in agriculture and forestry, 11.9 percent; industry and mines, 19.8 percent; transport, telecommunications, and trade, 20 percent; education and health, 5.5 percent; urbanization and housing, 8.2 percent; and Comilog and the Compagnie des Potasses, 33 percent. In 1967, private investments, except for the two last-mentioned companies, began to taper off appreciably.

23. Marchés Tropicaux, September 25, 1965.

24. See Afrique Nouvelle, August 14, 21, 28, 1968; Marchés Tropicaux, August 31, September 7, 1968; Revue Française d'Etudes Politiques Africaines, September 1968; Le Monde, September 5, 1968.

25. According to La Semaine, July 28, 1968, Massamba said: "I would be overjoyed to find an especially talented and dynamic brother, civilian or military, who could bring happiness quickly to the Congolese people. If he will come forward, I shall have the pleasant duty of presenting him to the population at the next mass meeting and, after the independence celebrations, have him officially confirmed. This is a good procedure to follow, for it will forestall an attempt to seize power."

26. See West Africa, August 10, 1968.

27. Afrique Nouvelle, August 21, 1968; Marchés Tropicaux, August 24, 1968.

28. West Africa, September 14, 1968.

29. Speech reported by the Agence Congolaise d'Information, January 10, 1967.

30. L'Express, January 14, 1968.

CHAPTER 20

NGOUABI AND THE PEOPLE'S REPUBLIC

In the fighting that began at Brazzaville on August 29, 1968, the main protagonists were the army, commanded by Ngouabi, and the JMNR, led by Hombessa. The latter, together with other enemies of Ngouabi, barricaded themselves in a military camp which they called Biafra to show their determination to fight to the end. Nevertheless, they surrendered on September first, after about a hundred men had been killed. Within a few days, 45 persons were arrested, including Hombessa, Banthoud, Thaulay-Ganga, and Massamba's brother, but Bindi escaped, as well as an unknown number of armed men. No time was lost by the Brazzaville criminal court in trying 68 individuals charged with inciting to revolt, and the ringleaders were sentenced to two to five years in prison. At about the same time, the JMNR militia and members of the civil defense corps who had received military training were incorporated into the regular army, and the CSC's executive committee was dismissed. The MNR structure itself was retained even after its mass organizations were in effect dissolved, but alongside the party cells the army set up Committees for the Defense of the Revolution to control them.

Ngouabi, Raoul, Jacques Yhomby (now the paratroop commander), and Norbert Tsika (head of the gendarmerie) were all promoted in rank, and five officers were given the key posts in the provisional government formed after Massamba's resignation on September 4. The CNR itself underwent two successive shakeups in October and still another at the end of December, when almost all the members of former governments were dropped from its council and directorate or politburo. By January 1, 1969, Ngouabi had become head of state, replacing Raoul, who was named vice-president and premier. Inasmuch as Ngouabi was also chairman of the CNR, minister of defense, and commander-in-chief of the armed forces, virtually all the power was concentrated in his hands. Among the newcomers to the cabinet were Pierre Nze (education) and Prosper Matoumba-Mpolo (youth). Nicolas Mondjo (foreign relations), Jacques Bouiti (health), and Pierre-Félicien Nkoua (finance) were held over from the provisional government, as was Pascal Lissouba (whose portfolio was changed from planning to agriculture). Some of the ministers dropped at this time, including Aimé Portella, Ambroise Noumazalaye, Martin M'Berri, André-Georges Mouyabi, and Ange Diawara, were given compensatory appointments in the CNR council or politburo. The most significant changes were the elimination of the two Lari ministers, Félix Mouzabakany and Lévy Makany. In his New Year's message to the nation, Ngouabi promised that elections for a new legislature and for municipal and regional councils would be held after the next MNR congress, which he scheduled for the following fall. He also pledged to eliminate tribalism and reactionary elements from that party and to pursue a "policy of permanent revolution."

Immediately after he seized power, Ngouabi freed most of the politicians who had been imprisoned by Massamba, retained the services of some of his ministers, and even took into the government for a short time a leftover from Youlou's regime, Kikhounga-Ngot. The rupture of relations with Congo-Kinshasa in October 1968,[1] which was the most dramatic event of Ngouabi's first year in office, was for once unrelated to internal political developments. During the last months of 1968, the frequent changes in the personnel of the government and of the CNR organs indicated Ngouabi's uncertainty as to the course he should pursue. The dropping of the two Lari ministers at the end of December gave the first inkling of a marked change in Ngouabi's policy.

Opposition to Ngouabi's Government

Early in 1969, Lieutenant Pierre Kikanga, a Lari officer of the Brazzaville garrison, fled to Kinshasa, and Major Mouzabakany was caught while attempting to do likewise. Shortly afterward, Ngouabi announced the discovery of a "vast network of reactionaries organized by Youlist Laris" and what was called the Mpita Group.[2] Their aim was said to be a "restoration of the American capitalist system."[3] This was a curious combination of conspirators, considering the discrepancy between the aims of the Brazzaville Lari and those of the Vili Mpita Group, aside from their common opposition to a government headed by northerners. Obviously it was a catch-all accusation to serve Ngouabi's purpose of rounding up his most formidable adversaries, particularly the Lari. All those arrested for crimes against the security of the state were tried by an 18-member revolutionary court named by the CNR for that purpose.

Ngouabi told a meeting of army officers convened at Brazzaville on February 22 that the conservatives had taken advantage of his liberal policy to undermine the revolution[4] and that his attitude toward them had hardened. The evidence of Lari dissidence in the army was, in Ngouabi's eyes, by far the most serious aspect of the attempted uprising. Forthwith he divided the Congo into six operational or defense zones and made Brazzaville an autonomous military unit. This reorganization of the army was accompanied by changes in its command, including the appointment of Lieutenant Ange Diawara as political commissar of the army while he also remained secretary of state for defense.

No sooner had Ngouabi moved to stem subversion in his army than he had to cope with civilian unrest. Once again official news sources provided no details, but in June some civil servants were arrested, allegedly for preparing a coup d'état to restore Massamba-Débat. Whatever the truth in this affair may have been, it had the dual result of reviving accusations against Massamba and of causing drastic changes in the government and in the CNR. Although the CNR remained the supreme organ of the state, the number of its councilors was reduced from 35 to 32 and of its politburo from eight to five. Of the latter's former members, only Ngouabi, Raoul, and Nze remained, and to them were added Justin Lekounzou and Ange Poungui. In the government, the ministry of information was suppressed, and Mondjo, Lissouba, Nithoud, Bongo-Nouarra, and Matoumba-Mpolo were dropped. They were replaced by five new ministers—Moudileno-Massengo, Charles Assemekang, Auxence Ikonga, Charles Sianard, and Henri Lopez—and by four secretaries of state. Although those appointments followed no wholly consistent pattern, the dropping of moderates like Mondjo and Lissouba and the promotion of such hard-liners as Poungui and Lekounzou suggested a shift of power into radical hands.

The atmosphere of tension, which had been rising since announcement of the plot in February, was evident throughout the spring and summer of 1969. Although Banthoud and Bernard Matingou were released from prison in May, that same month the two Frenchmen—Lebreton and Laurent—who had been arrested under Massamba's government for attempting a coup d'état and for espionage, respectively, were brought to trial. Lebreton was sentenced to life imprisonment and Laurent to 10 years in prison and a fine of three million CFA francs. Two months later, the revolutionary court gave Lieutenant Kikanga a death sentence in absentia, Major Mouzabakany life imprisonment at hard labor, and Captain Poignet a suspended sentence of eight years in prison. The severity of these sentences created a malaise in the European community, but to some Congolese militants, they seemed too lenient. In response to the latter's demands, two more "revolutionary officers" were added as judges to the court.

In August, members of the former JMNR held a congress which was also attended by Ngouabi, Raoul, and some foreign diplomats. On the proposal of the JMNR's former president, Matoumba-Mpolo, the delegates voted to reconstitute that organization as the Union de la Jeunesse Socialiste Congolaise (UJSC) and to participate in the economic reconstruction of the Congo. For good measure, they also passed resolutions condemning American and Israeli aggression and supporting the admission of the People's Republic of China to the U.N.[5] Ngouabi gave the assembled youths a lecture on service to the masses, but he made no public response to the demands which they presented to him. These included a reform of the school curriculum and the admission of their officers to the CNR politburo.

Ngouabi celebrated the first anniversary of his accession by announcing the imminent transformation of the MNR into a people's party, with new regulations for membership and with the goal of carrying out a genuine socialist revolution. Already he had formed three preparatory committees inside the CNR council to draft plans for giving the country "dynamic revolutionary institutions," an educational program for training party cadres, and new projects for economic development. Before he could carry out his proposals, however, several events occurred that required immediate action on his part.

The first was a strike at the end of September by civil servants in the finance department, which Ngouabi forthrightly settled by arresting or dismissing their union officials and by removing Nkoua from his cabinet as the minister responsible for "this illegal action against a socialist government." This precipitated another game of musical chairs, in which ministers and CNR councilors judged to be ineffectual revolutionaries were transferred to high-ranking technical but politically insensitive posts. In this way, Ngouabi disposed of Nkoua, who was made head of the ONCPA; Ganao, who became the Congo's permanent delegate to international organizations based at Geneva; and Ngounimba, who was named director of the People's Colleges in Brazzaville. Bongo-Nouarra was returned to the agricultural service, and Martin M'Berri was named head of the National School of Administration.

Just what prompted Ngouabi in October to imprison Massamba, who had been under house arrest for more than a year, is not known. In any case, he was tried by the revolutionary court, along with those of his former supporters who had reportedly tried to restore him to power in the preceding June. Perhaps because charges of misgovernment against Massamba were considered too weak, the accusation of responsibility for the murder of the

three Lari civil servants in February 1965[6] was added. Even more surprising
was the inclusion, among the 20 or so Congolese similarly charged, of such
diverse former collaborators of Massamba as Lissouba, Ndalla, Lounda, and
Hombessa. In bringing all these men to trial, Ngouabi was perhaps trying to
bury the past and, in particular, to "clean the abscess" of the unsolved
murders that had been festering for nearly five years. That this may have
been his motivation was substantiated by Ngouabi's consultations, the last
day of October, with the former politicians Opangault, Kikhounga-Ngot, and
Tchichelle, whose general views on the situation in the Congo he solicited.

     Before the court could hand down its verdict on Massamba and his fellow
defendants, still another attempt was made to overthrow Ngouabi's government.
On the evening of November 8, Ngouabi announced with considerable fanfare
that he had just foiled a coup d'état led by Bernard Kolelas, at the head of
armed commandos. Unnamed foreign powers were accused of backing the raiders,
stocks of captured arms were put on public display, and about 40 arrests were
made. Brazzaville opinion automatically attributed this plot to Kinshasa,
although the official accusations were characteristically vague. Because
vigilance brigades were immediately formed throughout the country and still
another exceptional law court was set up, some qualified observers became
skeptical about the authenticity of the "plot." They believed that the current military authorities were either suffering from a conspiracy complex or
using this classical device to get rid of potentially dangerous opponents.
An article voicing such doubts that appeared in Le Monde[7] aroused Ngouabi's
ire, but perhaps also made him more circumspect. At all events, Massamba,
Lissouba, Noumazalaye, and Ndalla were all acquitted on November 21 of the
charges brought against them, and Laurent was released after a year in
prison. To be sure, Matsika and Gandzion at the same time were sentenced to
death, but they were never executed.

The Parti Congolais du Travail

     With the army once more at least nominally united and the trials out of
the way, Ngouabi could turn his full attention to party reorganization. To
all appearances, he went far beyond the transformation he had hinted at earlier. On the last day of 1969, he dissolved the CNR, renamed the country
the People's Republic of the Congo and the MNR the Parti Congolais du Travail
(PCT), replaced the national anthem ("Les Trois Glorieuses") by "La Congolaise," gave the Congo a new red flag with the hammer-and-sickle symbol, and
recommitted his government to the principles of Marxism-Leninism. By giving
the Congo all the visible trappings of a communist state, Ngouabi tried to
placate the extreme left wing and at the same time to consolidate his own
personal power.

     Although Ngouabi grandiloquently described these changes as "the bold-
est steps taken as yet in the history of the Congolese revolution, which give
our country a place in the world proletariat revolution," they produced almost no fundamental transformation in the preexisting setup. The party's
domination of the government was reaffirmed and the parallel structure of
the two executive organs was retained. To be sure, a state council replaced
the former cabinet, the legislature was abolished, and the people's will was
to be expressed through elected municipal, regional, and district councils,
but these changes were more nominal than substantive. The legislature had
long since ceased to exercise any real influence, such local government

bodies as still existed were already controlled by party militants, and the PCT politburo of eight members as well as the 30-member central committee, which replaced the legislature, included many of those who had belonged to the CNR organs.

Since, inevitably, Ngouabi was elected head of the party and of the state, while remaining commander-in-chief of the army, and since Raoul was named premier and vice-president of the state council, those two men were simply confirmed in the number one and number two positions they already held. Furthermore, all the former ministers were reappointed to the state council except Assemekang, for whom an honorable post was found as president of the supreme court. Perhaps the most significant innovation was the naming of Ndalla as first secretary of the PCT, for this in effect made him Ngouabi's principal rival and also strengthened the extremist trend in the Congo's leadership. After his acquittal late in 1969, Ndalla had been sidetracked only briefly by his duties as ambassador to Peking—within less than two months he had left that post to return to Brazzaville.

Kikanga's Raid

If Ngouabi was casting about for some further means of making his authority—at least over the army—unassailable, he seemed to have found it in another abortive plot, for which the evidence this time was incontrovertible. On the morning of March 23, 1970, Lieutenant Kikanga led a band of 30 armed men across the river from Kinshasa, captured the radio station at Brazzaville, announced prematurely that he had overthrown Ngouabi's government, and called on Gabon, Kinshasa, and the Central African Republic for help. None of those countries responded, the army remained loyal to Ngouabi, and Kikanga and all his men were killed after a few hours of fighting. As usual, the imperialists in general and the Kinshasa government in particular were held responsible for hatching this plot with a view to ridding the Congo of a socialist government. Its failure proved among other things that Ngouabi was still in control of the army and that his conservative opposition, including the gendarmerie, which was implicated because of its cooperation with Kikanga, was organizationally and militarily weak.

The absurdly small number of men involved in the raid just described showed how badly Kikanga and his sponsors had misjudged the situation in Brazzaville. They apparently expected to be received there with open arms, especially by the local garrison, because of widespread Lari disaffection from the government. Kikanga's recklessness not only exposed his own men to slaughter but also endangered his partisans throughout the country. On the eve of the raid, Kikanga's supporters had staged demonstrations in the capital and also at Pointe Noire, Dolisie, Jacob, and Mouyendzi. Consequently, the PCT militants knew just who they were and easily rounded them up.[8] The PCT formed its own special criminal committee to try all those arrested as enemies of the state, and its harsh verdicts virtually assured the authorities that there would be little such overt opposition in the future. It should not be concluded, however, that all those accused, then or later, of trying to undermine the PCT regime wanted to restore Youlou to power, or were ipso facto opposed to a socialist policy for the Congo. The trials of Martin M'Berri and certain army officers, among others, disclosed regional or personal grievances that did not derive from any right-wing ideology.

Divisions in the PCT and Army

The March 23 raid and the trials that followed had significant repercussions on the internal political situation, for they went far to nullify the reinforcement of the authority that Ngouabi had achieved through his reorganization of the party and government three months before. If he no longer had to fear that his enemies would try to overthrow him by force of arms, the elimination of a conservative opposition left him without any element in the country that could counterbalance the extreme left wing in his party, which demanded that the government immediately adopt a more radical policy. Ngouabi was compelled to reinstate Noumazalaye in the politburo, arm the people's militia, and absorb the gendarmerie into the army. Then in April, he was pressured into cutting off the salaries of village and tribal chiefs and even to replace them in the local administration by party militants. The net result was to strengthen the PCT's control over the government and that of the "Maoists" inside the party. These were Ndalla, Diawara, Poungui, Lekounzou, and now Noumazalaye. This left only the moderate Nze siding with Ngouabi, who was now clearly in a minority position in the politburo. Furthermore, by merging the gendarmerie with the army, whose unity was already weakened by the addition of the JMNR militia and civil defense corps, Ngouabi's hold on the armed forces was further diminished. A visible indication of this decline in Ngouabi's authority was the appointment, also in April, of a radical young officer, Captain Denis Sassou N'Guessou, to the politburo, where he was placed in charge of the PCT's relations with its mass organizations.

There could be no doubt but that the army and party were beset by internal divisions, but these were not due to basic divergencies among their leaders as to the goal of transforming the Congo into a Marxist state. They concerned very largely such matters as who would effect this transformation, by what methods, and at what pace. Ngouabi realized more than did his radical colleagues that the Congo's viability as an independent nation depended on tapping all sources of foreign aid, on not becoming too deeply committed to the communist bloc in general and involved in the Sino-Soviet dispute in particular, and on controlling regionalism and tribalism but not to the point of alienating irretrievably any one element of the population. (Ngouabi went so far as to court the conservative Catholics by paying a graceful tribute to the memory of Mgr. Théophile M'Bemba,[9] who in 1965 had opposed the nationalization of mission schools, and by refusing to let Ndalla transform the churches into people's assembly halls.) Actually, there was no clear-cut division between conservatives and radicals among either Ngouabi's supporters or his opponents. They came from all regions and all tribes, though in practice his policy tended to favor the northeners.

Since the spring of 1970, the nationalization of foreign-controlled enterprises has increased in number and in scope. Less than a year after Ngouabi had taken over the Agence Transéquatoriale des Communications (ATEC), he nationalized the French sugar company SIAN in September 1970, and the following spring saw the nationalization of the Office Equatorial des Bois.[10] Although he promised compensation, these moves risked alienating the UDEAC countries, with which the Congo had its only favorable trade balance, and France, its main source of aid. Two cabinet reshuffles in February and June 1971, albeit of a minor nature, reinforced the position of Poungui and Diawara. Ngouabi's announcement of further attempted coups d'état, in August 1970 and again a year later, were perhaps a desperate attempt to keep the radicals at bay by emphasizing the indispensability of his role as the armed forces' commander-in-chief. The supposed plots also gave Ngouabi the opportunity to make numerous arrests and thus rid himself of dissident regional leaders, such as Bongho-Nouarra. On the other hand, by frequently calling "wolf, wolf!" Ngouabi risked undermining his credibility and creating an atmosphere of such instability as to discourage potential foreign investors.

Economic Policy

Since independence, the Congo's unfavorable trade balance has steadily increased, as has its public debt and, with them, deficits in the budget. Two-thirds of its national revenues still depend on customs duties, mainly those on imports. Under the military regime, exports have risen less rapidly than imports, which now consist very largely of consumer goods, including foodstuffs. Exports of agricultural products and of crude oil continue to shrink, and the country's major revenues are still derived from shipments of timber, manganese, and diamonds, all of which are either of foreign origin or under alien control. Congolese merchants still handle only the distribution of some foods and local industrial produce to the big towns and up-country settlements, whereas almost all the lucrative foreign and domestic trade remains in European hands. Beginning in late 1971, however, steps were taken to reverse this situation.

To increase revenue from sources other than import duties, the Ngouabi administration introduced in October 1971 a sales tax on all merchandise sold in the Congo, and four months later raised the rate of taxation on local industrial, real estate, and trading companies. To check the fast-rising cost of living, the government first forbade the sale of certain goods unless specifically authorized by the ministry of trade, and then established price controls for 51 articles of prime necessity.[11] In May 1972, it moved even more drastically to strengthen the competitive position of Congolese traders. Thenceforth, alien merchants and businessmen had to pay 5,000 CFA francs for an identity card granting permission to trade, and such permits were to be granted only to those who had been domiciled in the Congo for the preceding five years and who agreed to maintain minimal stocks of the merchandise they were allowed to sell. Proceeds realized from trading permits would be added to a government guaranty fund to finance Congolese merchants unable to meet normal banking requirements for loans. Still another step toward state control of trade was taken on July 18, 1972, when the government set up the Office National du Commerce (OFNACOM) to monopolize the import of a wide range of foodstuffs, textiles, and enamelware.

At about the same time, a greater effort was made to earn more revenue from existing sources through higher tax rates and better methods of tax collection, but they were accompanied by no corresponding curtailment of government expenditures. The claim made by successive finance ministers that a policy of austerity was being practiced was belied by the Congo's expanding budgets, which rose from about 16 billion CFA francs to 21.8 billion between 1960 and 1972. The cost of government personnel has regularly absorbed nearly half the country's revenues—more than 10 billion CFA francs in 1972—and in that year, allocations to the health and education ministries (34 percent of total expenditures) were only two percent smaller than those for the more financially fruitful economic services. Each month, the Congolese treasury has been hardpressed to meet the wage bill for its civilian and military employees, and it has been able to do so only because of foreign loans and subsidies. Consequently, the public debt payments, which rose by 100 million CFA francs between 1971 and 1972, constitute a heavy burden on the budget.

To some extent, the government's policy can be justified by the prospect that appreciably higher revenues probably will be derived from mining and petroleum exports, notably those from recently discovered potash and oil deposits, by the ease with which the Congo continues to attract foreign capital, and by its own long-term investments. In 1972, the Congo's investment budget received 1,871 million CFA francs from national revenues, marking a 10 percent increase over the preceding year and larger allocations to the economic objectives of the revised development plan.

The orientation of Massamba-Débat's national plan, 1964-68, differed considerably from that of the investment policy pursued by Youlou, and its termination date generally coincided with the military government's advent. In the wood and transport industries, the goals set under Massamba's plan were reached, but in other domains they fell below expectations, in part because they failed to attract all the capital investment required. The output of cocoa and coffee increased only on the few occasions when their sales prices rose, that of fishing proved unsatisfactory, and palm oil production declined. These disappointing results were attributed to the peasantry's continued use of traditional farming techniques, the shortage of agricultural labor, the lack of adequate communications in the north, and mismanagement by the ONCPA. Although the GNP in the 1961-68 period attained an annual growth of 10 percent, the rural component (which constituted 85 percent of the active population) was responsible for only 1.4 percent, whereas the industrial sector accounted for 25 percent of the growth rate.

To remedy this imbalance, the authors of the military government's interim plan for 1970-72 gave priority to improving communications in the north. A road connecting Brazzaville with the Sangha region is under construction, as well as an air field at Souanké. In 1970, a river port was completed at Ouesso, and four others along the Oubangui and Congo rivers were improved the following year. Traffic on those rivers and their tributaries has been growing at an annual rate of about 15 percent and is expected to top 1 million tons by the end of 1972. A larger increase is anticipated from the construction of more boats at the new Brazzaville shipyard and from the nationalization in 1971 of the Compagnie Générale des Transports en Afrique Equatoriale (CGTAE), a private French company that had monopolized for 60 years the river traffic on the 5,000-odd kilometers of waterways common to the Congo and the Central African Republic.

Some of the foregoing projects should certainly diminish the northern Congo's isolation, open up a large forest and cocoa-growing region, and stimulate the transit trade with Bangui and southeastern Cameroun. At the same time, however, improved communications may encourage rather than curtail the northern population's exodus to the southern towns, which has been growing at the rate of seven percent annually, largely at the expense of the rural settlements, where about one-fourth of the inhabitants are over forty-five years of age.[12] Furthermore, it seems doubtful if such measures, of and by themselves, will arouse the northerners' enthusiasm for farming. The government has proclaimed that "the land belongs to the people," and has set as its agricultural goals self-sufficiency in foodstuffs and more raw materials for the Congo's processing industries, but has been vague as to the means to achieve them. The PCT congress of August 1972 simply noted the vital importance of agriculture for at least a quarter of the population, but as a solution to the difficulties in increasing agricultural production and exports, the congress could only suggest organizing interregional markets, increasing prices to farmers for their output, and reforming the "semi-feudal social structures." The northern agricultural population seems unlikely to benefit from the experiments in mixed farming being conducted at the Chinese-sponsored model farm in Kombé, 18 kilometers south of Brazzaville. For some years, there has been little change in the exportation of the north's main crops of cocoa, coffee, and palm kernels, each of which hovers around the 2,000-ton mark. In the Congo as a whole, moreover, modern farming and herding are highly developed only by Europeans in the fertile Niari valley.

As to forestry and fishing, the other principal sectors of the rural economy, official policy has similarly concentrated on improving transportation and on nationalizing the sale of their output rather than on directly increasing production. It has been an agency of the U.N. that has undertaken, at Mossendjo, the training of Congolese forest personnel and the expansion of the local wood industries for domestic use. The government's role in this domain has been largely confined to nationalizing the purchase and sale of the Congo's timber that was formerly monopolized by the Office des Bois de l'AEF for okoumé, and by French firms for its other precious woods. In late 1971, the Office Congolais de l'Okoumé and the Bureau Congolais du Bois were organized under the ministry of agriculture, and at about the same time, a new law was promulgated requiring all vessels fishing in Congolese waters to be locally registered and to fly the Congolese flag. New fishing and lumber ports are being built at Pointe Noire, financed less by national revenues than by funds offered by France and other European Common Market countries.

Innovations have not been notable in the planning policy of the Ngouabi administration, but it should be credited with concentrating on hitherto neglected sectors of the economy. By the allocation of far larger funds than before to enlarging and modernizing the Congo-Ocean railroad,[13] ports, and the road network, it is facilitating the flow of trade and thus indirectly encouraging production. (Neither Congolese nor international investments have been devoted to improving air services, although the operations and organization of the national air line, LINA-Congo, are notoriously deficient.) As of 1971, the traffic handled by the port of Pointe Noire reached 3.2 million tons and that of the railroad 3.8 million tons,[14] and for the past few years, Congolese trade has exceeded the capacity of those facilities. Currently about half the freight for both the railroad and port consists of Gabon's manganese shipments, but soon the proportion of the Congo's own mineral exports passing through Pointe Noire should be much larger. This will not help, however, to solve the Congo-Ocean's main problem, which is to find equivalent merchandise to carry on its eastbound runs. Nevertheless, the foregoing improvements in the means of communication should enhance the Congo's role as pivot for the transit trade of the UDEAC states.

The nationalization of the ATEC in 1969 (and that of the CGTAE two years later) gave birth to the Agence Transcongolaise des Communications (ATC), which has become the Congo's first truly profitable state enterprise, although the government's earlier expropriation of the public utilities system in Brazzaville has brought some minor benefits to the national treasury. Large-scale investments in industry and the creation of state industrial companies initiated by the Massamba government have been perpetuated by the military administration—with mixed results financially. For an underdeveloped tropical country with a population of less than one million, the Congolese have an exceptionally high per capita cash income, estimated by the World Bank in 1970 at about $200.[15] As an industrial nation, the Congo holds fourth rank among the former French Black African dependencies, largely because it has produced a remarkably wide range of consumer goods for the equatorial market. From local raw materials, the Congo makes sugar, cement, furniture, cigarettes, matches, soap and perfume, and smoked and dried fish. From mostly imported raw materials, it also produces shoes, beer, textiles, phonograph records, and metal and chemical items. To attain these results, the Congo disposed of some 100 billion CFA francs from foreign and private sources during the first postindependence decade. Of the total, some 40 percent were invested in transport, trade, and telecommunications, 36 percent in industry and electric power, five percent in agriculture and industry, and one percent in general administration.[16]

Offsetting these gains is their cost to Congolese revenues, notably in terms of a huge increase in the public debt and in operating deficits of the state enterprises. The ONCPA and BCCO, both set up by the Massamba regime, were so ineffective that the former has been repeatedly reorganized and the latter was simply suppressed in May 1972. Much the same could be said of the more recent state enterprises financed by the communist countries—specifically the Kinsoundi textile plant (China),[17] the Hotel Cosmos (U.S.S.R.), and the match factory (North Korea), whose operating costs have absorbed a large share of the national revenues and foreign investment funds. In 1970-71, the nationalization of the SIAN,[18] three forest concessions, and the CGTAE increased such expenditures. Moreover, the government must now cope with the same difficulties as plagued their former proprietors—rising labor costs and strikes and, in the case of sugar, the problem of marketing the surplus abroad. The PCT, at its congress in August 1972, publicly acknowledged these difficulties when it recommended that the government curtail industrial growth and concentrate on quality output.[19]

As a matter of fact, the only industries in the Congo that are making substantial profits, or are likely to do so in the near future, are still those owned or managed by Western capitalists. (In time, the Loutété cement plant may work to capacity, but it is not yet paying its own way.) Of the country's forest companies, only about one-fourth are owned and run by Congolese. There is only one African employers' association, the Syndicat Professionnel des Commerçants et Transporteurs Africains du Congo. No landed bourgeoisie exists because the soil is poor and land is collectively owned. In the towns, there exists an embryonic mercantile middle class made up of retail merchants, truckers, and owners of small enterprises, who have generally prospered despite numerous bankruptcies. The Congolese bourgeoisie, properly speaking, is that of the civil servants and other government employees.

The fact that the state enterprises, except possibly the ATC, are losing money, whereas the 7,000 French residents in the Congo—who still control the foreign trade, most of the profitable enterprises, and provide many of the jobs—live well and prosper, has naturally been irksome to the Congolese. They are unanimous in wanting the Congo to control its own economy and to have its nationals enjoy full employment, but they do not all agree on how to reach those goals. Until 1970, Ngouabi favored a cautious approach which gave him appreciable returns in the form of foreign investments, but he then realized that such a policy had become politically dangerous in that it was providing ammunition to his extreme left-wing opponents, particularly as regarded the labor situation.

The proliferation of new industries had increased the country's employment opportunities, but this was being largely offset by the annual 1.6 percent growth in the population. Moreover, the short-sightedness of some of the big foreign private firms operating in the Congo was justifying the pressure exerted by the "Maoist faction" of the PCT to hasten the nationalization process. European employers have inspired little confidence because of their practice of arbitrarily dismissing workers and then often rehiring them at a lower wage. The outstanding recent example of such arbitrary conduct was that of the Grands Moulins de Paris, which, by threatening to close down and to dismiss its employees, virtually forced Ngouabi to nationalize the SIAN. As a sequel to this, the delays in the production schedule of the Hollé potash company, caused by technical and financial difficulties, have been interpreted by Congolese radicals as the prelude to compelling the government to take over its operations.[20] Inevitably, the atmosphere of mutual distrust thus created is unpropitious for the Congo's economic development.

More than the vast majority of his compatriots, Ngouabi has accepted the profit motivation of European private capitalists operating in the Congo, and his recent moves to extend the state's control over the economy may have been primarily inspired by his fear of their being used by his opponents to outflank him from the left. In principle, he has long been committed to the eventual expropriation of all foreign local enterprises and the institution of a national currency, but until late in 1971, he repeatedly stated that such measures were premature and might actually prove harmful to the Congo's economy. In a broadcast on December 31, however, he made an exceptionally strong attack on Western economic imperialism, and clearly had that of France in mind when he spoke darkly of his country's "exaggerated confidence in certain external friendships." Since then, his denunciations of the French grip on the Congo's trade have become more specific, although he signed new cooperation agreements with France in June 1972 and has not taken his country out of the franc zone. At the PCT congress in August 1972, he added the threat to withdraw from the OCAM, whose economic value to the Congo has sharply declined with the breakup of its sugar market and with the recent reinforcement of economic ties among the UDEAC countries. Such threats could be the prelude to drastic action, but many thought that they were made simply for internal consumption.

To the dedicated Marxists of the PCT, Ngouabi has been too pragmatic and dilatory in applying to the economy the principles of scientific socialism, which he has sworn to support. For example, to them the difficulty of selling the output of the Kinsoundi factory—sheets with holes in them and textiles that cannot withstand two washings—is of minor consequence compared

with the employment that the plant provides for some 1,400 Congolese. Similarly, the creation of competitive state enterprises and the immediate benefits to the Congo from unilaterally nationalizing the ATEC, the CGTAE, and
the Office des Bois weigh more heavily in the radicals' scales than does remaining on good terms with the country's UDEAC neighbors.

The Congolese hardliners denigrate an economic policy chiefly directed
toward making profits through efficient management. In their eyes, the all-
important goals are economic independence and total employment at remunerative wages for the country's active population. If the Congo has difficulty
selling its products in the world market, then it should trade only with the
communist countries, which operate under government-to-government agreements
and not according to the laws of supply and demand. The advocacy of a policy
that so defies bourgeois concepts is predicated on the assumption that the
Congo can always count on some wealthier foreign country to cover the losses—
an assumption which thus far has proved correct.

Although the government's instability, the radicalism of official statements, and the successive nationalizations of foreign enterprises are hardly
reassuring to Western nations and capitalists, French residents in the Congo
seem to believe that they can still do business with Ngouabi. Furthermore,
the Congo has continued to receive substantial aid from France and other EEC
nations, as well as from various international agencies, not to mention
large loans and gifts in money and in kind from China and the U.S.S.R. In
fact, in 1971-72, the largest investments in the Congo have been those of
Western governments and individuals. The only notable loan from other
sources has come from the African Development Bank for a comparatively modest total ($1,210,000) and at a higher interest rate (six percent). Western
capitalists seem to recognize that Ngouabi's basic policy is nationalistic
rather than Marxist and that, if he can remain in power, he will continue to
welcome investments regardless of the ideology of their sources.

Ngouabi's greatest success perhaps has been his ability to walk the
tightrope between rival power blocs which, because they are mutually competitive, will not let the Congo go to the wall. (Thus there has been no real
curb on a spendthrift financial policy, gauged to gratifying national pride
and providing maximum employment.) To be sure, there is some economic base
for this assumption, since the Congo possesses certain raw materials that the
world wants. Aside from such considerations, however, Ngouabi believes—as
did Massamba before him—that neither China nor France can politically afford
to let their influence in the Congo go by default. In the end, it may be
Ngouabi's failure to increase production and thus alleviate the misery of the
peasantry and of the urban unemployed that will prove his undoing. In the
meantime, perhaps because there is no sign of a popular uprising against his
government, he is concentrating on "Congolizing" trade and the means of
transportation so as to placate those he considers his most dangerous enemies—the extreme left wing of the PCT.

The Purge and the Putsch

For a year and a half after the Kikanga raid, Ngouabi seemed to be in
steady retreat as the Maoist faction in the PCT scored one success after another. In September 1971, however, he moved to the offensive in the economic
domain, but not aggressively enough to steal all of the left wing's thunder.

Two months later, a strike by secondary school students, aggrieved by the shortage of teachers, textbooks, and equipment, became rapidly politicized. Initially, Ngouabi agreed to discuss their scholastic complaints with the strikers, whom he reminded that most of their wishes would be met by the establishment of his new "People's School" before the end of the year. Yet the students, far from being placated, began to attack his regime openly, holding it responsible for the high cost of living and a reactionary foreign policy, and denouncing the nepotism and "nonrevolutionary behavior" of certain leaders. Their main target was Yhomby, who they claimed "lives like a capitalist in his luxurious villa."[21] The strikers refused to heed Ngouabi's appeals, as well as those of the heads of the UJSC and CSC, to return to their classrooms. Ngouabi therefore closed all the schools above the primary level and ordered the army to occupy the school buildings and track down subversive elements.

Rightly or wrongly, Ngouabi had concluded that Ndalla and other hardliners in the PCT were inciting the students' agitation, and he used the strike as an excuse to purge his entourage of "reactionary, anarchic and degenerate" persons. At a party meeting he called on December 5, Ngouabi attacked them for their "incoherence and unrealistic idealism," in reply to their charges that he had failed to carry out the central committee's directives to arm the workers and peasant militias and cut the Congo's ties to France and its bourgeois school system. He then proceeded to expel 50 members from the PCT, eliminate some posts (premier and second party secretary), split up or suppress three ministries (education, development, and information), and reorganize the politburo into six working committees.

In this process, Ndalla was removed from the government and the party, Raoul and Diawara were demoted to minor posts, Noumazalaye became its first secretary, Lekounzou was named minister of industry, and moderates like Bouiti and Assemekang were dropped from the cabinet. Although the purge generally downgraded the most extreme left-wingers, it did not follow strictly ideological lines. Rather, Ngouabi seemed to be rewarding followers on whose personal loyalty he counted and eliminating those who he felt endangered his authority. Obviously, this political reshuffle marked only a lull in the storm, for Ngouabi's opponents now spoke openly of revenge and swore to "liquidate the opportunist clique."

Early in the morning of February 22, 1972, Congolese listeners heard martial music broadcast over their radios—the sure sign of a coup d'état. During the night, Diawara, Matoumpo-Mpolo, and their followers kidnapped three of Ngouabi's staunchest supporters (Nze, Moudileno-Massengo, and Lopez), and announced that "right-wing tribal officers" led by Yhomby had arrested members of the politburo preparatory to seizing power while Ngouabi was absent in Pointe Noire. By midafternoon, however, Yhomby had not only broadcast a denial but staged a successful countercoup, in the course of which Matoumpo-Mpolo was killed but Diawara had taken flight with some armed partisans. Ngouabi, returning hastily to Brazzaville, took charge of the situation and announced that there would be severe reprisals and no change in his government's "political option." It was reported that 1,500 persons were arrested and some tortured, but the official account stated that only three persons had been killed and 169 imprisoned. Among those apprehended, tried by court-martial, and given sentences ranging from the death penalty to long terms in prison were Raoul, Noumazalaye, and Atondi-Monmondjo.

In some ways, the putsch of February 22 resembled that of Kikanga two years earlier, in that both were led by lieutenants trying to create divisions in the armed forces as a means of overthrowing Ngouabi's government, but the differences between the abortive coups were more striking. In the 1972 conflict, there was virtually no violent fighting, the power struggle was essentially between two factions of the ruling party and not between members of the armed forces, and the rebels were said to have been in collusion with some radical French coopérants serving in the Congo.[22] The last-mentioned charge was seemingly substantiated by the unusually strong protests against the harshness of Ngouabi's repressive measures expressed in France by the left-wing press and such outstanding radical intellectuals as Sartre.[23] They repeated the rebels' claim that Ngouabi had laid a trap for his opponents by inciting them to stage a coup so that he could break it up at a time of his own choosing and arrest its ringleaders. To this the government issued a denial, adding that the rebels, for their part, had made false accusations against Yhomby.

Aside from the mutual charges of deceit, the revolt was certainly poorly planned, badly timed, and based on a grave miscalculation of local support. Apparently the rebels' timetable had been speeded up to coincide with Ngouabi's visit to Pointe Noire rather than his trip to Paris in March, and they failed to induce labor and student leaders to join them as they had expected. Although most of the outstanding dissidents were promptly put behind bars, Ngouabi could not rest easy as long as Diawara was at large and retained a sizeable following in the army among former members of the JMNR and civil defense corps. He therefore moved rapidly to win over what remained of the party leadership by carefully preparing for a PCT congress to be held in early August, two years ahead of schedule. In the meantime, he made unsuccessful and secret overtures to Diawara, which came to light when Diawara again miraculously escaped capture in a gun battle that took place on May 17 in Brazzaville. Still not despairing of winning over his elusive adversary, Ngouabi in June broadcast an appeal to Diawara to surrender, promising him and his followers safe conduct if they accepted. It went unanswered.

Ngouabi held some undeniable trump cards when he appeared before the 700 PCT delegates assembled at Brazzaville the last day of July 1972. In Paris, he had negotiated a new financial agreement for the UDEAC, of which he was the current president, and at the recent OAU summit meeting in Rabat, he had won applause by his stirring appeal for volunteers to join the liberation movements throughout Africa. At the congress itself, he confirmed the supremacy of the party over the government, announced that both would be thoroughly reorganized in six months, pledged a complete overhaul of the civil service, and outlined a more radical economic and foreign policy than ever before. As proof of his self-confidence, he could say that none of the death sentences on the rebels had been carried out, and as evidence of his magnanimity, he announced the release from prison of Raoul. Nevertheless, Ngouabi learned a few days later of the flight from the Congo of Moudileno-Massengo, the man whom he had raised to the vice-presidency of the republic only six months before. This created a still greater void among the leaders on whom Ngouabi could count, and over his head still hovered the "spectre" of Diawara.

1. See pp. 198-199.

2. See p. 209.

3. West Africa, March 8, 1969.

4. Jeune Afrique, March 23, 1969.

5. Marchés Tropicaux, August 16, 1969.

6. See p. 160.

7. November 11, 1969.

8. Comte, C., "L'Embarras Français," Revue Française d'Etudes Politiques Africaines, June 1970.

9. See p. 220.

10. This organization was created by Gabon and Moyen-Congo in 1944, and the agreement between them was renewed in June 1963. The OBAE held a monopoly for the purchase and sale of okoumé logs in the two states until October 1971, when it was unilaterally annulled by the Brazzaville government. Ngouabi replaced it by an Office Congolais de l'Okoumé, which was granted a monopoly in the national trade of that wood.

11. West Africa, November 5, 1971; Marchés Tropicaux, June 2, 1972.

12. Vennetier, P., "L'Urbanisation et ses Conséquences en Congo-Brazzaville," Cahiers d'Outre-Mer, volume 16, 1963.

13. Among the railroads of francophone Black Africa, the Congo-Ocean holds first place, and among the ports, that of Pointe Noire ranks fourth. The ATC plans to invest 32 billion CFA francs in railroad improvements between 1969 and 1972.

14. Marchés Tropicaux, February 25 and April 28, 1972.

15. Europe-France-Outremer, no. 509, June 1972.

16. Marchés Tropicaux, September 12, 1970.

17. For an optimistic appraisal of the Kinsoundi enterprise, see "A Novel Experiment in Africa: the Kinsoundi Textile Mill," Africa Today, July 1971.

18. After a checkered career, the Société Industrielle et Agricole du Niari, founded in 1929, became the largest single private enterprise in the Congo. On its initial grant of 20,000 hectares, which straddles the railroad line, were cultivated successively manioc, peanuts, sisal, bananas, and above all sugarcane. By 1956, it grew mostly cane, and its labor requirements for permanent and seasonal workers ranged between 3,000 and 10,000. Its development gave birth to the town of Jacob, which has become the third largest in the country. Beginning in 1960, the SIAN expanded into the industrial field by processing its agricultural output. Its cane production is restricted by a limited market and low world prices for its sugar. The Congo's quota in the protected OCAM

market was 52,700 tons in 1970, leaving a surplus production of 100,000 tons for sale elsewhere.

19. Marchés Tropicaux, August 18, 1972.

20. Agence Congolaise d'Information bulletin, quoted in Marchés Tropicaux, October 23, 1971.

21. Afrique Nouvelle, December 8, 1971; Jeune Afrique, March 11, 1972.

22. AfricAsia, February 27, 1972.

23. Le Monde, February 29, 1972.

CHAPTER 21

THE CONGO'S FOREIGN RELATIONS

France and Other Countries of the Western Bloc

That close ties between France and the Congo have persisted since independence shows a rare continuity in policy on the part of both countries, despite significant changes in their respective governments. As is the rule in international relations, their common determination to cooperate springs from national self-interest. France's motivation has been almost wholly political and cultural, inasmuch as maintaining a base of operations and of influence in central Africa is still considered important by Paris. For the Congo, on the other hand, its far greater need to preserve France's financial and technical aid and local French business enterprises is reinforced by the retention of a common official language and similar institutions. In both countries, such considerations have transcended the frequent and often sharp dissensions between them. Each time that relations seemingly have reached the breaking point, realism has prevailed and one or the other government has drawn back from the brink.

At first, Youlou leaned heavily on his conservative French advisers, but as time went on, he dispensed with their services and also eased local French residents out of the political offices to which some of them had been elected. Yet at the end of his political career, Youlou cultivated France's friendship more assiduously than before, in what proved to be the vain hope that it would be a bulwark against communism's inroads in the Congo and that France would agree to finance construction of the Kouilou dam. In the crisis of mid-August 1963, General de Gaulle refused to come to his aid and, two years later, denied him asylum in France after he had left Léopoldville.[1] Immediately after Massamba-Débat came to power, he expressed his gratitude for France's "sympathy and comprehension," but he was profoundly hurt by General de Gaulle's long delay in formally recognizing his government. To show his displeasure, Massamba asked the French military mission to leave the country. By mid-October, however, friendly relations were restored after France had promised to resume its aid and new financial agreements were negotiated.

When Lissouba became premier at the end of 1963, relations rapidly cooled again. In his first policy statement, Lissouba said that the Congo would respect its agreements with France only for as long as they were based on reciprocity, and at the same time, he endorsed the principle of nationalizing all foreign firms in the Congo.[2] Then a commentator of the Voice of the Revolution, as Radio Brazzaville had been renamed, accused France in general and Jacques Foccart in particular of responsibility for the Lari uprising of February 7, 1964. After some prodding by the French ambassador, Lissouba issued a public denial of these charges, and Massamba went out of

188

his way to praise the local French community for its contributions to the Congo's development.[3]

Far more serious in French eyes than the foregoing verbal exchanges was the legislature's unanimous vote on March 14 in favor of negotiating new agreements with France and of removing the "inexplicable presence of French troops on Congolese soil."[4] Foreign minister Ganao hastily stated that there was no question of unilaterally denouncing the existing agreements, but Lissouba did not improve matters by asking France to send to the Congo no more former administrators as advisers but only young technicians.[5] As for the departure of French troops stationed in the Congo, this never became an issue. In October 1964, General de Gaulle on his own initiative announced that French garrisons throughout the Franco-African Community would be drastically reduced. By the end of 1965, 1,200 French troops had left the Congo, and about an equal number of Congolese soldiers had been demobilized from the French army. Congolese national pride was gratified by this measure, although it had adverse effects on local trade and increased the number of Brazzaville's unemployed.[6]

Beginning in 1964, the growth in the Congo's diplomatic and economic ties with communist countries caused concern to the French government and French resident nationals. In June, Massamba made a quick trip to Paris, where he publicly scotched "malicious rumors to the effect that the Congo wants to drive France out of the country." Later, he added the obvious truth that "we have never refused the help offered by France; we only want to widen our sources, for we need all possible aid."[7] Since Massamba made no move to revise the Congo's agreements with France or to nationalize important local French firms, the Paris government began to view him as a moderating influence on the Congolese radicals and increased its grants-in-aid.

Reference to France as "l'amie de toujours" became a standard phrase in official Congolese speeches, and for the next few years, the periods of tension between the two countries tended to decrease. On one occasion, Massamba aptly described their relations as "those between a long-married couple who love each other, not perhaps with the first romantic glow but with that strong and deep affection which makes their reactions, attitudes, and even tastes strangely similar."[8] Massamba was once received by General de Gaulle, whom he later praised for his anti-American attitude and as "the statesman of this century whose advice is exceptionally wise and beneficial to all the African states."[9] The growing prosperity of the major French enterprises in the Congo throughout 1965 also contributed to this era of good feeling.

In early 1966, Massamba took further steps to promote the détente. He dispatched Ganao to Paris to "explain" Noumazalaye's replacement of Lissouba as premier, appointed the moderate Nicolas Mondjo as ambassador to Paris, and refused to yield to the radicals' pressure to withdraw from the franc zone and the OCAM. Later in the year, to be sure, there were flareups of ill feeling when some French residents were expelled from Brazzaville without explanation, France's military instructors were asked to leave the Congo, and the government adopted a financial policy that was contrary to certain terms of the Franco-Congolese cooperation agreements. In most cases, however, Massamba was able to smooth matters over, and relations took a decided turn for the better in the fall of 1967 when Yvon Bourges made the first visit to Brazzaville by any French minister since Youlou's overthrow.

France's minister of cooperation then promised to increase French aid for execution of the Congo's development plan, laid the cornerstone for a new university, and worked out a schedule for repayment of the Congo's substantial debt to France over a 15-year period. At the time of Massamba's downfall, relations between the two countries were more cordial than they had been at any time since the coup of August 1963.

Under the military administration, France's political and cultural influence has declined proportionately to the rise of that of the communist countries, but its economic stake remains preeminent in the Congo. France is still that country's main trading partner, and French residents form by far the largest foreign community in the Congo and control the biggest industrial and trading firms. As of March 1972, French technicians (coopérants) numbered 513, of whom 345 were in the education service and the rest in technical posts.[10] French public and private investments still form the backbone of the Congo's modern economy, and the potash and petroleum companies are controlled by French shareholders.

Until mid-1972, Ngouabi's policy toward the French government was basically the same as was Massamba's, although for some time he had been making stronger verbal attacks on French neocolonialism and had embarked on a more nationalistic economic course. After three times postponing his visit to France, he went there briefly in March 1972, albeit as president of the UDEAC and not as head of the Congo People's Republic. In Paris, French officials showed their desire for a rapprochement with Ngouabi by receiving him with the honors accorded a chief of state, despite the private character of his visit. However, they refused to do more than to agree "in principle" to revise the Franco-Congolese cooperation treaties as he requested. This failure, combined with the French left wing's support for the rebels in the February 22 putsch, probably accounted for another deterioration in relations between the two countries during the summer of 1972. Several French residents in Brazzaville and Pointe Noire were expelled, the denunciations of French imperialism by Congolese radio commentators and delegates to the PCT congress became sharper, and Ngouabi indirectly attacked France by threatening to leave the OCAM. He waited prudently to carry out this threat until a few months after he had signed new economic and cultural agreements with France.

French aid to the Congo has taken so many different forms and has fluctuated so widely with the Congo's political evolution that it is hard to estimate in money terms. It has been authoritatively stated that during the 1960s French grants-in-aid averaged 600 million CFA francs a year, supplemented by an annual subsidy of 425 million for Brazzaville's Center of Higher Education.[11] In 1971, French public funds allotted to the Congo amounted to 1,385 million CFA francs, and a larger sum was promised for the year 1972. Money on such a scale is the price France has been willing to pay to safeguard its nationals' considerable stake in the Congo and its own foothold in this strategic area of central Africa.

The price that Ngouabi was willing to pay in soliciting and accepting such aid had to be calculated in domestic political as well as economic terms. For four years, he was careful—by deed if not by word—to avoid jeopardizing France's substantial support. Then on September 22, 1972, he announced the Congo's withdrawal from the OCAM, the takeover of the French radio station at Brazzaville, and restrictions on the transfer of funds to

190

France. Ngouabi must have decided that fiery verbal denunciations of French imperialism and affirmations of his Marxist-Leninist principles would no longer conjure away the danger to his authority arising from the Congolese radicals' growing resentment of their country's continued dependence on France. He therefore took the calculated risk of directly and indirectly jeopardizing French aid and, at least for the time being, seems to have won his gamble. The Paris government did not take up the challenge, and by mid-October, it had quietly renegotiated the debt-payments agreement, whose terms had given rise to the disagreement that was the ostensible cause for Ngouabi's drastic action. The showdown may well come when the question of basically revising the cooperation agreements is seriously posed, especially if, at long last, Ngouabi actually decides to leave the franc zone and create a national currency.

As for the countries of the Western bloc other than France, Youlou had established diplomatic relations with the major industrial nations as well as with the governments of Israel, Taiwan, South Korea, and South Vietnam. Nevertheless, his overthrow was generally approved by the European and American press, which saw it as a popular uprising against a dictatorship. The Western countries were reassured by Massamba's prompt declaration that he would respect his predecessor's international commitments, guarantee the security and property of all foreign nationals living in the country, and restore civil liberties.[12] They were further pleased by his government's practicing financial austerity—at least for the first six months of its existence.

The first signs of trouble occurred after the February 1964 riots, when the four main Western embassies in Brazzaville were accused of encouraging the "Youlists." This was followed by Massamba's saying that "bad Europeans" would be expelled from the country, Angor's warning that "alien trouble-makers" would be severely punished, and Lissouba's statement that thenceforth the Congo's foreign policy would be one of strict nonalignment.[13] Already the last-mentioned policy had been substantiated by the Congo's formal recognition of the Chinese People's Republic, and by Ganao's comment that "for us Taiwan no longer exists."[14]

Considering the transformation in the political climate at Brazzaville, it is surprising that the aid-seeking visits made by Babackas and Kaya to Western Europe, Japan, the United States, and Israel were so successful in eliciting pledges of economic cooperation from those countries and that their aid continued throughout Massamba's tenure of office. The generosity and forbearance of the Western-bloc nations was the more remarkable in view of the repeated and violent attacks on their "imperialism" in the Brazzaville press and over the radio. Outstanding in this respect was the continuance of Bonn's aid despite the molesting of its press attaché in 1964 and a clash between its technical assistants and the JMNR in 1965. In 1966, the West Germans loaned the Congo 620 million CFA francs to build a cement plant at Lutété. Later, even after Ngouabi had formally recognized East Germany, Bonn continued to provide the Congo with funds and technicians, as well as to buy 80 percent of its timber exports.

To be sure, not all the Western-bloc countries took at their face value Brazzaville's repeated assurances that the Congo was not dropping its old friends just because it was making new ones. By the end of 1964, South Vietnam, South Korea, and Taiwan had closed their embassies in Brazzaville,

191

the United States withdrew its diplomats from that post in August 1965, and the following December, the Congo broke off relations with Great Britain over the Rhodesian issue. The rupture with London was almost wholly symbolic, for British aid to the Congo had been negligible. The American gesture, on the other hand, was of more importance, although Washington's aid, amounting to almost $1 million a year, already had been suspended in December 1964 because of the systematic Congolese harassment of its embassy's personnel. The root causes of Brazzaville's hostility were the war in Vietnam and, even more, American support for Tshombe at Léopoldville. Massamba refused to give the assurances required by Washington for a restoration of full diplomatic relations and, consequently, forfeited the American public funds that had been pledged to Kaya for the construction of a pineapple cannery, a glass factory, and other projects. Nevertheless, American capitalists did not withdraw the funds they had invested in the Hollé potash company, and in 1967, the World Bank loaned that firm $30 million.

After the Congo had broken off relations with Great Britain and Washington, the only countries of the Western bloc to actively aid and trade with the Congo were France, West Germany, and Israel. Under the military government, the United States, by its ever closer ties with Kinshasa, has even reinforced its position as the "number-one enemy of the Congolese revolution," although Ngouabi's rapprochement with Mobutu in 1972 may be modifying the Congo's hostility. In April 1971, Ngouabi received with fanfare a delegation of Black Panthers led by Eldridge Cleaver. In this unpopularity contest, Great Britain lags behind, although the Conservative government's decision in 1970 to sell arms to South Africa revived the opprobrium that London had earlier elicited because of its refusal to use force against white Rhodesia.

Brazzaville's denunciation of Israeli aggression became stronger and more frequent as its government drew closer to the Arab states; yet, as of early 1972, there were 110 Congolese studying in Israel, and Israeli technicians were running a model poultry farm near the capital. In December, however, the Tel Aviv government decided to downgrade its embassy at Brazzaville, leaving as its representative there only a nonresident chargé d'affaires. According to the December 26 issue of The Jerusalem Post, this action was due to the "inimical, even hostile, attitude of the Congo's radical regime." Soon after, Ngouabi retaliated by breaking off diplomatic relations on the ground that it disapproved of Israel's Middle Eastern policy. Since both alleged grievances were of long standing, the explanation for both moves has to be sought elsewhere. The new element which had entered the picture was the rivalry between two oil-rich Arab nations for leadership of the Black Africans. In the course of visits in November to Uganda and four francophone Saharan borderland states, King Faisal of Saudi Arabia had outbid Colonel Khadafi of Libya in persuading the presidents of Tchad and Niger to sever their ties with Tel Aviv so as to demonstrate their solidarity with the Arab and Islamic cause.

Although Congo-Brazzaville has no comparable Muslim populations to propitiate or proximity to the Arab states to consider, Ngouabi believed that at small cost to his country he could tap a new source of investment funds, and one, moreover, that would not increase his indebtedness to either the Western or the communist bloc. Israel, seeing the handwriting on the wall, had apparently decided that the expenditure of any further effort in those three countries was useless and so took the initiative in cutting its losses. Ngouabi, for his part, by officially denouncing Israel and breaking off diplomatic relations, must have believed that he was sacrificing only a small-scale technical aid program, in return for the likelihood of winning substantial financial rewards and of appeasing his domestic radical opponents. Yet, at the same time, he has taken no steps to end the anomaly of increasing the Congo's exports of tropical woods to South Africa while criticizing harshly those Black African leaders who advocate a "dialogue" with Pretoria.

Portugal is the only country of the Western bloc with which Brazzaville's relations have been consistently bad under both Massamba and Ngouabi. Youlou's attitude toward Lisbon was equivocal, but that of his successors was definitely hostile. Under Massamba, diplomatic relations were broken off, thousands of refugees from Cabinda and Angola were harbored in the Congo, and—despite denials—hundreds of them were given military training at Dolisie. Ngouabi has found a bellicose stance toward the Portuguese highly useful, for by periodically claiming that they were about to invade the Congo, he has won widespread African expressions of support and has fanned revolutionary fervor at home on behalf of his own government. Offsetting these advantages, however, have been the adverse effects on his relations with Mobutu, which resulted from the violent rivalry between the Angolese rebel movements established, respectively, in Brazzaville and Kinshasa.[15] Should the reconciliation that took place between them at Brazzaville in June 1972 endure, it may mark a turning point in the history of Angola and also in the relations between its two French-speaking neighbors.

The Communist Nations

During Massamba's regime, the most significant transformation in the Congo's foreign relations—and one that modified those with the Western world—was the rapid development of its ties with all the communist countries of Europe and East Asia. Youlou's obsession with the communist menace had isolated the Congo from contacts with those nations, but after Lissouba became premier, they were initiated and multiplied in short order.[16] In January 1964, the Congo became the first UAM member state to recognize the Peking government, hard on the heels of a similar move by General de Gaulle.

The Congolese foreign minister was promptly sent on a tour of Iron Curtain countries, during which he negotiated an exchange of diplomatic missions as well as economic and cultural agreements with Moscow, Prague, and Belgrade. The first Soviet envoys and technicians reached Brazzaville the following August, and by the end of 1964, Moscow had pledged to the Congo an eight-million-ruble loan for the construction of a hydroelectric dam on the Batéké plateau, a hotel and a maternity hospital at Brazzaville, and geological prospecting. A Soviet-Congolese cultural agreement followed in January 1965, and arrangements were made the next month to begin air service between Moscow and Brazzaville. Two days after Hombessa became minister of the interior in April 1965, he flew to Moscow, and in August, Massamba made the first of two state visits to the U.S.S.R. The Soviet government reciprocated by frequently sending delegations to Brazzaville and by signing a long-term trade agreement in March 1967. Within a year, trade between the two countries had nearly doubled, and by the end of 1966, the U.S.S.R. was supplying $2 million worth of the Congo's imports (machinery, trucks, and building materials), and was taking nearly $1 million of its exports (chiefly palm oil products and cocoa).[17] By the time Massamba fell from power, Moscow had loaned the Congo the equivalent of 3,059 million CFA francs, 60 Soviet professors were teaching in the country, and some 300 Congolese were studying in the U.S.S.R.[18]

If ties with Moscow developed quickly and fruitfully, those with the Peking government were even more rapid and spectacular. Less than two months after Massamba had formally recognized the Chinese People's Republic, Peking's ambassador reached Brazzaville, and by July 1964, the Congo had accepted an interest-free Chinese loan amounting to 1,235 million CFA francs ($5 million). The caliber of China's first envoys to Congo-Brazzaville indicated the great interest that Peking was taking in that country. They were Colonel Kam Mai, an expert in guerrilla warfare, who had been a counselor in the Chinese embassy at New Delhi in 1962, and Colonel Kao Liang, who had headed the New China News Agency at Dar-es-Salaam and who quickly made the JMNR organ, Dipanda, largely a medium for that agency's propaganda. Relations with China included official visits by Massamba and his ministers to Peking, the exchange of labor, press, and military missions, and agreements for financing a textile mill at Kinsoundi, model farms for rice and cotton, a palm oil mill, and a more powerful broadcasting station.

By August 1968, China had loaned the Congo in cash and in goods more than twice as much as had the U.S.S.R. and on terms more advantageous to Brazzaville, and its embassy there was larger and more fully staffed than was Moscow's. For as poor a nation as China to make such a disproportionately large contribution to so insignificant a country as the Congo astonished Western observers. It could only be explained in terms of Sino-Soviet rivalry and of the strategic advantages the Congo offered as a base for Chinese revolutionary activity in central Africa. As of 1966, reportedly some 200 Chinese military and political advisers were training and equipping guerrillas for action in Congo-Kinshasa and, to a lesser extent, in Cameroun, Angola, and Cabinda.[19]

From the Congolese viewpoint, the massive financial and technical aid given by China and the Soviet Union was a windfall for its stagnant economy, and it more than offset the concurrent decline in overall aid from the Western nations. National pride was also gratified by receiving so much attention from the world's two most powerful communist nations. Ideologically, too, close communist ties harmonized and reinforced the Brazzaville government's option for a policy of scientific socialism. To only a limited degree did dissension develop between the pro-Soviet and pro-Peking factions among the Congolese radicals, for many of them had a foot in both camps. Before Lissouba and Noumazalaye came to power, both were tagged as belonging to one or the other faction, but as premiers, they proved to be equally receptive to overtures from either communist power. With extraordinary skill, the Congolese leaders avoided taking sides in the Sino-Soviet dispute, being careful to show no favoritism but great cordiality toward both Peking and Moscow.

As time went on, however, Massamba became worried by China's growing influence, especially as the Chinese-trained guerrillas were damaging the Congo's relations with Cameroun and Gabon, not to mention Congo-Kinshasa. He therefore turned down a Chinese offer to finance the party's press organ, Etumba, but balanced this by expelling Izvestia's Brazzaville correspondent in May 1968 because he had maintained contacts with Noumazalaye against Massamba's expressed request.

Early in 1965, Massamba began cultivating relations with the smaller communist nations, particularly Cuba, and by the end of that year, there were said to be more than 300 Cubans in the Congo.[20] Socially, the Cubans—many of whom had mixed blood—were more popular in Brazzaville than were either the more aloof Russians or Chinese, and soon they took charge of training the Congolese paramilitary units as well as most foreign guerrillas. However, because of the key role played by the Cubans in the army mutiny of June 1966,[21] Massamba realized that he must drastically reduce their number or, at least, make their presence in the capital less obvious.

This decision narrowed down his choice among the small communist nations to North Korea, North Vietnam, Yugoslavia, and Rumania, whose aid he believed would not have such dangerous political implications. Although those countries obviously had less to offer materially than China or the U.S.S.R., they did provide the Congo with some matériel and, above all, with doctors and technicians for its economic and social development. Perhaps more skillfully than any other African Marxist head of state, Massamba managed to stay on good terms with all the communist countries and, at the same time, maintain financially rewarding relations with Paris, Bonn, and, to a much lesser degree, the United Nations specialized agencies.

Since Ngouabi came to power, China has become France's leading competitor among the foreign nations active in the Congo, except in the educational sphere. Peking's large loans antedated the advent of the military government, but since then, it has financed additional projects such as construction of a fish processing plant, an oil mill, a shipyard, and a hydroelectric dam on the Bouenza River.[22] Of more political significance has been the spread of its influence among the young PCT radicals, who are exercising increasingly effective pressure on the government. Estimates of the number of Chinese currently in the Congo range widely from several hundred to several thousand, partly because they always appear there in groups and partly because they are extremely mobile. Ngouabi told a French journalist that

> the Chinese are far less numerous than the French, and they do not come here to settle. They leave the country as soon as they have finished their work, and that is one reason why we call on them to meet our needs. The Chinese never give orders, make demands on the Congolese government, or give us advice on foreign policy. Their technicians are deeply appreciated by our people, and technicians form the largest category among them. The majority of the Chinese are in the Fort Rousset region, where they average only 12 for every 100,000 Congolese....We employ no Chinese teachers at all.[23]

The Congolese leaders, individually and in delegations, make many visits to Peking and almost as many to North Korea and Hanoi. They are also careful to balance this by travels to European communist countries, notably the U.S.S.R., with stopovers in Albania, Hungary, Yugoslavia, and Rumania. Many and varied missions are exchanged between Moscow and Brazzaville, and Soviet technicians work in the Congo. However, the latter are outnumbered by Chinese technicians, for the U.S.S.R. has concentrated on completing projects initiated during Massamba's regime and has not undertaken any important new ones.[24] Yet on those occasions when the Congolese consider China too aggressive, they tend to draw closer to Moscow.

Both major communist states are about equally active and competitive in the field of propaganda, but it is only in the cultural domain that the U.S.S.R. has a definite edge on China. As of 1972, it was reported that some 400 Congolese scholarship holders were studying in the Soviet Union and 83 Soviet professors were teaching in the Congo—about the same number as in Massamba's day. Diplomas awarded by Brazzaville's Centre d'Enseignement Supérieur (Center of Higher Instruction) have been recognized by the U.S.S.R. as the equivalent of those granted by Soviet universities, and the Congo government has reciprocated.[25] It remains to be seen whether the communists' ideological imperialism will awaken the same Congolese nationalist reflex as has the "cultural neocolonialism" of the West.

North Africa and the Revolutionary Black African States

Upon coming to power, Massamba reinforced the Congo's few existing contacts with the revolutionary states of west and north Africa, and established diplomatic relations with those that Youlou had ignored. Needless to say, such governments approved of his regime's Marxist orientation. However, whereas Algeria, Egypt, Mali, and Ghana promptly sent Massamba their congratulations in mid-August 1963, Guinea failed to do so.

Although Sékou Touré had encouraged the Congolese trade unions to overthrow Youlou, he misjudged the nature of Massamba's government when it was first installed. On August 19, he attacked it in a broadcast over Radio Conakry on the ground that it had been dictated from abroad. To this surprising assault, Massamba retorted that "if there has been any external intervention, it came from Sékou Touré himself, for it was during his state visit to Brazzaville that he opened the door to Congolese revolution."[26] Quickly Sékou Touré made amends by acknowledging his mistake, and soon relations between the two leaders became cordial if not notably productive for the Congo. When Noumazalaye attended Guinea's independence anniversary celebrations in October 1965, he paid a graceful tribute to "our brother Sékou Touré, who was the real spark of our revolution."[27] In March 1966, the MNR politburo wired its approval of Guinea's hospitality to Nkrumah, and at the OAU's next meeting at Addis Ababa opposed seating the delegation sent by Ghana's new military government. Despite their approval of Guinea's overall policy, the Congolese leaders were fully aware of its economic plight, and this doubtless influenced their decision to remain on good terms with France and the other European Common Market countries.

Among the Arab states, only Egypt provided Massamba with aid that proved useful to the Congo. In 1964 and 1965, various missions between the two states were exchanged, and Nasser sent a few military instructors to Brazzaville, most of whom trained guerrillas for subversive operations in neighboring countries. Egypt also invested 1,175 million CFA francs ($4.8 million) for the construction of a technical college, a public health center, and a hotel in the Congo.[28] Despite the grant of such a substantial sum, Massamba refused to burn his bridges with Israel, and he unobtrusively continued to solicit aid from Tel Aviv.

Ngouabi's first travels abroad were to the Arab states of north Africa. In the spring of 1969, he went to Cairo, Tripoli, and Khartoum, but his longest and most cordial visit was in Algiers. Since then, his government has often voiced its support for the Palestinian guerrillas, as well as for the Arabs' struggle against Israel in general,[29] but again this did not entail any rupture of diplomatic and economic relations with Tel Aviv until late 1972. Ideologically speaking, Algeria has displaced the UAR as the north African country with which the Congo feels the strongest affinity, and Houari Boumediène has reciprocated by supplying the Congolese army with radios, trucks, and even uniforms. Both governments have promoted commercial exchanges, in which Algerian wine is traded for Congolese sugar.[30]

Among the Black African revolutionary regimes, Ngouabi finds Guinea the most congenial, "for we share its stand against imperialism."[31] When Ngouabi succeeded Massamba in August 1968, Sékou Touré was not caught short as he had been five years before. He promptly sent the president of the Guinea legislature to reassure Ngouabi of his solidarity with the Congo's new government.[32] The Congolese leaders have also found much in common with Mauritania, which like their own country has turned increasingly to the Arab north African states and away from its former associates in francophone Black Africa. Nevertheless, both Ngouabi and Raoul, in their west African journeys, included visits to such conservative capitals as Abidjan and Yaoundé.

Congo-Kinshasa (Zaïre)

Of all the nations in Africa, the Democratic Republic of the Congo—renamed Zaïre in October 1971—has played the most important role in the history of Congo-Brazzaville but not vice versa. Brazzaville has always been jealous and resentful of its powerful neighbor because of the disparity in the size of their areas, populations, and natural resources, and has harbored and encouraged the enemies of anyone who rules at Kinshasa. Zaïre, on the other hand, cannot regard the People's Republic of the Congo as a rival in any sense of the term, but mainly as a nuisance. And if Kinshasa, too, has sheltered and given support to Brazzaville's dissident expatriates, it has been simply in the hope of replacing one troublesome set of leaders by others beholden to it.

By its great potential, Zaïre has aroused the covetousness of the world's rival power blocs, and because Brazzaville offers easy access to Kinshasa, it has also become the scene for international competition, albeit on a minor scale. It was only in part fortuitous that when the radical Patrice Lumumba was in the ascendant at Léopoldville, the ultraconservative Youlou reigned in Brazzaville. Conversely, when Mobutu seized power in Kinshasa and accepted large-scale American aid, a left-wing government under Massamba-Débat was ruling in Brazzaville with increasing support from the communist nations. Inevitably, relations between the two Congos have been chronically turbulent and tense, with only infrequent periods of mutual tolerance and peaceable coexistence. Yet, because of the proximity of their capital cities and the ethnic ties that unite their Bakongo peoples, the two countries are bound indissolubly together, and they must eventually work out some modus vivendi.

After Youlou's overthrow, Lumumba's widow was among the first to send congratulations to Massamba. This set the tone for a very rapid deterioration in the relations between the two Congos that was precipitated by the welcome given in Brazzaville to the opponents of Premier Adoula and his right-wing supporters. Later in 1963, the breakup of Adoula's coalition government sent into exile three outstanding Marxist leaders—Pierre Mulele, André Loubaya, and Christophe Gbenye. At Brazzaville, those expatriates set up a Comité

National de Libération (CNL), which some called a government-in-exile, and a training camp for guerrillas at nearby Gamboma. The presence of those pro-Peking leaders—although Gbenye at first leaned more toward Moscow—and the facilities offered them by Massamba's government (including the columns of Dipanda for its propaganda), made Brazzaville especially attractive to the Chinese communists as a base for revolutionary action against Léopoldville. Consequently, Brazzaville became Mulele's headquarters throughout 1964-65, as well as a transit center for smuggling arms and funds across the Congo River.

Late in August 1963, Ibalico received a similarly cordial welcome in Léopoldville, where he also set up an organization called the Front de Libération Nationale du Congo-Brazzaville, which carried on propaganda against Massamba's regime. Although this gave Massamba ammunition in replying to Adoula's accusations, there was in fact no comparison between the strength of the two "governments-in-exile." The CNL effectively promoted the revolts that broke out in 1964, first in Kwilu province and then in northern Katanga, whereas Ibalico's Front simply faded away after he was killed that same year in an auto accident; Bernard Kolelas, finding that he could not revive it when he fled to Kinshasa a year later, moved on to Paris.

Charges and countercharges were exchanged between the governments of the two Congos during the first half of 1964, culminating in Léopoldville's closing their common frontier in May. After the U.N. troops left the country at the end of June and Adoula resigned, there was a brief interval of friendlier relations, although the head of the new Léopoldville government was none other than Youlou's old friend Moïse Tshombe. Within two months, however, Tshombe's expulsion of thousands of alien Africans, in great majority Brazza-villians, on charges of subversion revived and intensified all the hatred he had inspired in Youlou's day. When Massamba accused Tshombe of using such indirect means to overthrow a left-wing government, the latter retorted that he had the military means to capture Brazzaville within two hours if he were so minded.[33] The frontier was again closed, and the propaganda warfare carried on between the two Congos reached a record pitch of intensity during the last months of 1964 and most of 1965. Léopoldville's share of responsibility for Youlou's escape in March and for the commando raid in July could not be denied, and this provided fresh ammunition for Brazzaville's radio and press attacks on Tshombe.

After Mobutu ousted both Tshombe and Kasavubu in November 1965, overtures were made from both sides of the river. Neither government could approve of the other's political orientation, but to both a normalization of their relations now seemed advisable, especially as it was to their mutual interest to curtail the persistent transfrontier contraband trade. Official contacts were resumed with decorum if not with enthusiasm, and for nearly three years the two Congos enjoyed their longest period of relative amicability. Feathers were ruffled in Kinshasa when Brazzaville refused to join the Union des Etats de l'Afrique Centrale (UEAC), which Mobutu sponsored early in 1968,[34] but there was no new rupture until the following October after the Kinshasa authorities summarily executed Pierre Mulele.

Mulele had long enjoyed Brazzaville's hospitality, and the recently installed Ngouabi government had permitted his repatriation to Kinshasa only after Mobutu's foreign minister had personally pledged a safe conduct for Mulele. When he was shot 48 hours after his return to Kinshasa, Brazzaville broke off diplomatic relations and closed the Congo River to traffic. Ngouabi accused Mobutu of breaking his word and betraying African hospitality, while Mobutu justified his action by claiming that Mulele was a criminal and had been legally tried and executed. The old propaganda war between the capitals was renewed with vigor, each side accusing the other of encouraging subversive activities.

Late in 1969 and early in 1970, two abortive raids led, respectively, by Kolelas and Kikanga, both based on Kinshasa, added more fuel to the old flame of discord. The spectacular prosperity of capitalistic, pro-Western Kinshasa just across the river was the more galling to the Brazzaville radicals, who were beset by growing unemployment and budget deficits. Mobutu hardly poured oil on troubled waters by repeating Tshombe's boast that, if he gave the command, his troops could capture Brazzaville in short order.[35] Brazzaville's official news agency retorted by saying that Mobutu could never conquer the Congo in 10 years of fighting, and by calling him an African Hitler.[36]

In his feud with Mobutu, Ngouabi tried to enlist the support of other African leaders, and the latter in turn managed to cool off the main protagonists and eventually to bring them together. Despite the arrogance and impatience of Mobutu and the opposition of the Brazzaville Maoists—notably Ndalla and Combo-Matsiona—Presidents Albert-Bernard Bongo (Gabon), Jean-Bedel Bokassa (Central African Republic), and Ahmadou Ahidjo (Cameroun) succeeded in effecting a reconciliation. Mobutu and Ngouabi met in midstream on the Congo River and signed what became known as the Manifesto of June 16, 1970. This reopened communications, but it was not until the following December that diplomatic relations were reestablished.

No more than six months were to pass before there was more trouble between the two Congos. A demonstration by Brazzaville students in favor of their counterparts at Lovanium University in June[37] was followed two months later by the recall of both countries' diplomatic representatives, the arrest and trial of some Kinshasa refugees in Brazzaville, and a revival of the mutual charges of aggression.

In the autumn of 1971, similar accusations were prompted by minor clashes on the Congo River, Zaïre's unilateral decision to rename that waterway, and the expulsion of 12 Congolese from Kinshasa along with a far larger number of west Africans. Early in 1972, however, Mobutu strove to calm the indignation expressed by Brazzaville's Catholic community over his campaign against the Kinshasa cardinal, Malulua, and he hastened to congratulate Ngouabi for his defeat of the February "putschists." When Mobutu crossed the river in June to join with Ngouabi in reconciling Neto and Roberto,[38] he received a warm welcome from the Brazzavillians, and a few months later, the two Congolese leaders jointly and successfully mediated a dispute between Gabon and Equatorial Guinea. Nevertheless, Mobutu has recently spoken with bitterness of the black market in Zaïre currency that reportedly flourishes in Brazzaville. Although both heads of state seem determined to ease the tension between their two populations and, in August 1972, reestablished diplomatic relations, so profound is their mutual distrust that probably even a small incident could reawaken the hostility between these <u>frères-ennemis</u>.

The OCAM and the UDEAC

Congo-Brazzaville's continued membership in two organizations of moderate francophone Black African states has been one of the paradoxes of its foreign policy. Both were formed in 1960 with Youlou's active participation, and despite appreciable changes in both groups, especially in Congo-Brazzaville's government, the OCAM and the UDEAC survived for a decade as entities with their original membership largely intact. In 1965, the predominantly west African states that created the UAM, which was the OCAM's nucleus, were deserted by Mauritania but soon acquired four new adherents—Togo, Congo-Kinshasa, Rwanda, and Mauritius—while the French Equatorial African countries that organized the Union Douanière Equatoriale (UDE) on the eve of their independence were joined by Cameroun and later lost Tchad. The increasingly economic orientation of the OCAM and the preservation of the UDEAC's basic economic framework, as well as France's sponsorship of both, furthered Congo-Brazzaville's interests and impelled its leaders to overlook the political conservatism of its partners.

Although Youlou was host to the first meeting of the Brazzaville Bloc in December 1960, his ardent championship of Tshombe, then and later, made him odd-man-out in the group. When Massamba-Débat came to power in August 1963, President Philibert Tsiranana of Madagascar was the first head of any state to recognize his government, but the other leaders of the UAM—the name taken by the Bloc in March 1961—were more cautious. The coup at Brazzaville, so soon after the assassination of President Olympio of Togo, made most of them reluctant to condone a regime that had been born of violence.

They did not follow Madagascar's example until the UAM's general secretary had visited Brazzaville in September and submitted a favorable report. Six months later, however, their suspicions were reawakened by the vote of the Congo's legislature to withdraw from the UAM. Subsequently, since Massamba ignored that resolution—in part because the UAM was transformed in 1964 into a wholly economic organization—its heads of state followed France's lead and overlooked the Congo's increasingly radical coloration. Above all, they wanted to avoid weakening their united front and their ties with France, and to prevent the Congo's leaving the franc zone. Perhaps they also hoped to convert Massamba to their way of thinking, or to prove to the revolutionary African states that their organization was flexible enough to contain a left-wing government. In any case, they came to look upon Brazzaville as an acceptable if somewhat dubious member of their francophone club until the spring of 1965, when Massamba's government expressed strong disapproval of the organization's second transformation, this time into a quasipolitical Organisation Commune Africaine et Malgache (OCAM), and of Tshombe's admittance to its fold. Yet Congo-Brazzaville did not leave the OCAM, as was frequently predicted, although some Congolese ministers often attacked it as "an instrument of neocolonialism and African disunity."[39] To be sure, Massamba refused to sign the OCAM charter in January 1966 because of its political implications, but he agreed to cooperate with the organization in the economic, technical, and cultural spheres.

Ngouabi made no change in that policy for four years after he seized power in 1968. Congo-Brazzaville's long-standing equivocal attitude toward a group of whose principles it disapproved was explicable only on economic and psychological grounds. Its responsible leaders feared that withdrawal might cost the Congo the support of France and also access to the common market for sugar that the OCAM had created. The psychological factor was their growing realization of the disadvantages of the Congo's isolation from its francophone neighbors, all of which were members of the OCAM. By mid-1972, however, this situation had been appreciably modified by the evolution of that organization. The sugar agreement had largely broken down, the OCAM's air line enterprise (Air-Afrique) had lost several members, ideological rifts had been caused by Ivory Coast's proposal of a "dialogue" with South Africa, and, finally, Zaïre had formally withdrawn from the OCAM in March. The subsequent efforts by the OCAM's hard-core members to tighten their remaining links alarmed Ngouabi into fearing lest the Congo be forced to pursue joint policies of which it disapproved and which would strengthen the hand of his left-wing opponents.

Another factor that led to Ngouabi's cancellation on September 22, 1972, of the Congo's membership in all but the OCAM's technical committees was the development of alternatives more congenial and perhaps more rewarding than had been the support given by France and its OCAM satellites. Ngouabi was now the leader as well as president of the UDEAC, a central African group that shared the same colonial administrative heritage, was geographically compact, and had developed more economic interests in common than had the OCAM.

Youlou's legacy of membership in the UDE had more personal and political overtones than had that in the UAM.[40] After being a prime mover in promoting unity among the FEA territories, he became diverted from that objective by his ambition to head a Great Bakongo republic. In large part, this accounted for Youlou's relegating to the background his initial project for a political equatorial union, in favor of a loose economic federation of sovereign states. Thus he shared with Léon Mba responsibility for transforming the Conference of Equatorial Heads of State, founded in 1960, into a purely advisory body concerned with the management of existing economic and cultural agencies such as the Agence Transéquatoriale des Communications (ATEC), the Export Standardization Service, and the Fédération de l'Enseignement Supérieur en Afrique Centrale (FESAC). More important was the Conference's decision to form a customs union (Union Douanière Equatoriale, or UDE) as the first move toward creating a central African common market. In June 1961, an even bigger step forward was taken when Cameroun was admitted to the UDE as an observer, and the Conference decided to establish a permanent secretariat and to harmonize their fiscal and industrial regulations. A treaty embodying its decisions to establish a common tariff, tax structure, investment code, and industrial program was signed in December 1964 between the four FEA states and Cameroun, which brought the Union Douanière des Etats de l'Afrique Centrale (UDEAC) into being on January 1, 1966.

The equatorial states' union had to surmount the obstacles that derived from the long-standing resentment of its three partners against Congo-Brazzaville's privileged position in the FEA, notably by its control of the port and railroad facilities used by all four territories. This was most acutely felt by Gabon, which also suspected Youlou of irredentism at its expense, and with which Brazzaville's relations were worsened by the expulsion of its Congolese residents in 1962.[41] Not surprisingly, Léon Mba was among the first to congratulate Massamba on his accession in 1963, and the Central African Republic and Tchad quickly followed suit.

Quietly Massamba fitted into the place in the UDE vacated by Youlou, and throughout his tenure of office, many good will missions were exchanged among the four states. Even the Congolese radicals never questioned their country's continued partnership with the four conservative UDEAC governments, as they had done in the case of the OCAM. They accepted the necessity for living on good terms with their northern neighbors, if for no other reason than that the Congo was financially the main beneficiary of the UDEAC through the revenues earned by its transport installations and favorable balance of trade. Consequently, Massamba had little hesitation in turning down Mobutu's proposal to join the Union des Etats de l'Afrique Centrale (UEAC). This was a central African grouping that Mobutu formed in February 1968 with Tchad and the Central African Republic, to which he gave a structure and objectives similar to those of the UDEAC but with a better financial deal for the hinterland states.

The rupture between the two Congos that occurred two months after Ngouabi had succeeded Massamba would have led in any case to Congo-Brazzaville's withdrawal from an organization dominated by Mobutu, and the Central African Republic's return to the UDEAC fold the following December left the UEAC restricted to Congo-Kinshasa and Tchad, which, moreover, lacked a common boundary. Ngouabi, however, was not satisfied with this setback for the UEAC and reinforcement of the UDEAC's strength, and he moved to improve Congo-Brazzaville's already favored position in the latter organization. In October 1969, unilaterally and without prior consultation of his partners, Ngouabi expropriated the ports and railroad which had been their common property and replaced the ATEC by a national Agence Transcongolaise des Communications. In so doing, he claimed that he was not nationalizing the ATEC but "normalizing" a de facto situation, because the ATEC's installations were all located in Congolese territory. Only Cameroun, which had its independent transport system, was not adversely affected by Ngouabi's high-handed action, but its relations with Congo-Brazzaville were already tense as the result of operations against the Yaoundé government by guerrillas using a Congolese base.

By precipitating this breach of the union that had been formed a decade before, Ngouabi revived his partners' old grievances against the Congo's egocentricity. Yet because almost all the foreign trade of Gabon, the Central African Republic, and Tchad perforce passed through the port of Pointe Noire, and because the Congo-Ocean railroad carried 60 percent, 95 percent, and 30 percent, respectively, of their imports and exports, those countries could do nothing but acquiesce. Grudgingly each of them negotiated with Ngouabi's government bilateral agreements which practically, if not legally, restored the status quo. Concurrently, Ngouabi's promotion of Congolese industries competitive with those of his UDEAC partners hardly improved his standing with them. They could also justly criticize the special tariff privileges granted by the Congo to Soviet and Chinese imports—privileges that violated the union's charter. Congo-Brazzaville's relations with all its neighbors deteriorated to a degree equalled only in Youlou's time, and they were not placated or reassured when Ngouabi told them that they need not fear the contagion of communism from his regime.[42] Ngouabi's policy reinforced his partners' determination to free themselves from their dependence on the Congo's ports and railroad by developing alternative means of transport for their trade. The UDEAC's erosion seemed to gain momentum during

1970 with the dissolution of the Conference of the Equatorial Heads of State and of the FESAC, following a unanimous decision to that effect by its members. The circumstances that had induced the FEA territories to band together on the eve of their independence no longer prevailed, and each state was pursuing an ever more nationalistic course.

Perhaps because of a growing awareness of their increasing isolation, dissatisfaction with the OCAM,[43] or a greater recognition of the OAU's inefficacy, or all three phenomena, the former FEA states drew closer together in 1971. Although Tchad did not rejoin the UDEAC, its government cooperated more closely with its southern and western neighbors, the Central African Republic ironed out a frontier dispute with the Congo, and Bongo reinforced his personal ties with Ngouabi. The culmination of this new trend came at the UDEAC summit meeting held at Bangui in mid-December 1971. There Ngouabi was elected its president for 1972, and under his leadership, the central African states made progress in closing their ranks.[44] Although the UDEAC's formal aim was still to achieve economic integration by means of a customs union, a single tax on industrial output, and a balanced development of the region as a whole, its heads of state for the first time showed a willingness to accept all the implications of such a policy. Specifically, they agreed on a draft plan to integrate their industries, harmonize their political objectives, and exert greater pressure on France to review the structure of their monetary union.

The success of Ngouabi's mission to Paris in March 1972, with the object of increasing the central African states' representation on the managing board of their common equatorial bank and eliciting French private investments in the hinterland countries, augured well for the UDEAC's future. Of all its member nations, the Congo has the greatest interest in reinforcing the UDEAC, for that organization curtails to some degree economic competition between them, provides an indispensable market for the Congolese processing industries, and strengthens Brazzaville's position vis-à-vis Zaïre. All of them, however, feel mutually interdependent, want to affirm Central Africa's identity as distinct from that of West Africa, and need some joint organization which can represent them as a whole in negotiations with international economic groups, notably the European Common Market.

Notes

1. After being denied admittance to France, on the basis of the legal technicality that he was no longer a French citizen since the Congo had become independent, Youlou took up residence in Madrid. He was accompanied during his exile by four persons, including Madame Jeannette Bounzakala, who was believed to have paved the way for his escape from Brazzaville. From 1966 on, Youlou devoted himself to arousing Western public opinion to the dangers of Chinese communism. In his book, J'accuse la Chine, published at Paris in February 1966, Youlou argued that Marxism in general and Maoism in particular were responsible for all of Africa's present troubles. He believed Lumumba to have been Mao's first African victim, and Nasser and Nkrumah the Chinese leader's African accomplices. Youlou died at Madrid on May 6, 1972.

2. Brazzaville radio broadcast, January 21, 1964.

3. <u>Ibid</u>., February 11, 24, 1964.

4. France kept garrisons in all the former French equatorial states under the terms of a collective agreement negotiated with them on the eve of their independence.

5. Interview with Lissouba published in <u>Jeune Afrique</u>, May 16, 1964.

6. <u>Marchés Tropicaux</u>, November 28, 1964; Cooley, J. K., <u>East Wind Over Africa</u>, pp. 114-118.

7. <u>Marchés Tropicaux</u>, July 18, August 1, 1964.

8. <u>Ibid</u>., September 25, 1965.

9. <u>Ibid</u>., January 1, 1966; <u>Le Monde</u>, October 19, 1965.

10. <u>Europe-France-Outremer</u>, no. 509, June 1972.

11. <u>Revue Française d'Etudes Africaines Politiques</u>, June 1970.

12. Brazzaville radio broadcast, August 15, 1963.

13. <u>Ibid</u>., February 12, 1964; <u>Le Monde</u>, February 11, 1964; <u>Marchés Tropicaux</u>, February 15, 1964.

14. Brazzaville radio broadcast, January 21, 1964.

15. The People's Movement for the Liberation of Angola (MPLA), founded in 1956, was the first to take up arms against the Portuguese administration in 1961. Under the leadership of a self-styled Marxist revolutionary, Agostinho Neto, it was a widely representative coalition of three existing rebel organizations, with headquarters in Léopoldville. The MPLA's rival, the Angolese revolutionary government in exile (GRAE), was similarly a regrouping of existing rebel associations, which also established itself in the former Belgian Congo. Both demanded immediate and total independence for Angola, but differed in their tribal composition and ideology. Because its members were mainly Bakongo and its leader, Holden Roberto, was a moderate liberal, the GRAE was favored by the successive governments of Adoula, Tshombe, and Mobutu, and their recognition of Roberto as the sole valid spokesman for the Angolese rebels was followed by the OAU.

    In 1964, Massamba not only allowed the MPLA to open an office in Brazzaville but persuaded the OAU to allocate some of its funds to Neto. Thanks to these facilities, the MPLA was able to coordinate its activities with analogous rebel movements in Mozambique, Portuguese Guinea, and São Tome, and to conduct effective guerrilla action in eastern Angola and Cabinda. Holden Roberto, on the other hand, seemed more zealous to destroy the MPLA than to attack the Portuguese administration, and this caused dissension in his own ranks. In 1966, one of his lieutenants, Jonas Savimbi, broke away to form a third resistance movement, the Unita. Roberto was able to get his staunch supporter Mobutu to close Zaïre's frontier to both the MPLA and Unita and, in March 1972, to quell a mutiny among the GRAE troops stationed near Kinshasa. By this time, the OAU, Mobutu, and Ngouabi had come to realize that the rivalry between the Angolese rebel groups was harming not only the anti-Portuguese struggle but also relations between the two Congos. Therefore, joint efforts were made to unite the MPLA and GRAE, and, on June 8, 1972, Mobutu and Ngouabi brought about a formal reconciliation between Roberto and Neto. (See Le Monde, January 5, 1972; West Africa, April 7, 1972; Jeune Afrique, June 24, 1972.)

16. Lissouba's wife, Annette, was reportedly an influential member of the French communist party. See Le Figaro, May 6, 1965.

17. West Africa, April 9, 1969; Europe-France-Outremer, no. 473, June 1969.

18. Afrique Nouvelle, November 12, 1969.

19. Christian Science Monitor, May 21, 1966.

20. The stipends of the Cubans serving in the Congo were paid by the Havana government. By late 1965, also, 210 Congolese had been sent to study in Cuba at the latter's expense. After the fall of Ben Bella in June 1965, Cuba shifted the headquarters of its African activities from Algiers to Brazzaville.

21. See p. 225.

22. Christian Science Monitor, June 7, 1970.

23. Le Monde, March 27, 1970.

24. In 1971-72, the Congo signed supplementary cooperation agreements with the U.S.S.R., China, Hungary, East Germany, and Rumania, and decided to establish diplomatic relations with Chile.

25. Mizan, January-February 1970; Marchés Tropicaux, June 20, 1970.

26. Brazzaville radio broadcast, August 20, 1963.

27. Conakry radio broadcast, October 3, 1965.

28. Europe-France-Outremer, no. 473, June 1969.

29. Jeune Afrique, March 10, 1970.

30. Le Monde, September 23, 1969. On July 8, 1972, a new cultural agreement was signed at Algiers.

31. Marchés Tropicaux, February 27, 1971.

32. In February 1972, Sékou Touré wired his congratulations to Ngouabi on quelling the putsch, likening his victory to Guinea's repelling of the Portuguese invasion in November 1970.

33. Marchés Tropicaux, September 12, 1964.

34. See p. 202.

35. The New York Times, November 25, 1969.

36. West Africa, November 29, 1969.

37. See p. 223.

38. See note 15.

39. Le Monde, November 29, 1969.

40. See chapter 14.

41. See pp. 111-114.

42. West Africa, April 9, 1971.

43. Their grievances against the OCAM included the operations of Air-Afrique, Houphouët-Boigny's proposal of a dialogue with South Africa, and the breakup of the organization's sugar market.

44. See Jeune Afrique, April 1, 1972.

Tribalism and Regionalism

Inevitably, the Lari have been the chief tribal opponents of both
Massamba-Débat and Ngouabi because, after having enjoyed exceptional privileges under Youlou's regime, they were quickly relegated to the political
background by his successors. Numerically, they still predominate in the
civil service, and they are the best paid among the Congo's wage earners,
but in Lari eyes, these advantages do not compensate for their demotion
politically. Frustrated time and again in their attempts to reassert themselves by force, they have now been reduced to covert opposition, and their
present position resembles that of the Mbochi in Youlou's day. Much of the
Mbochi and Vili opposition to Youlou's proposal to form a single party
stemmed from their fear lest it institutionalize Lari predominance—a fear
that played a large role in the abbé's downfall. To mark the reversal of
Youlou's policy, Massamba immediately released all prisoners "whose only
crime was to have belonged to a tribe other than that of Youlou,"[1] and in
forming the government, he by-passed the old tribal leaders, Opangault and
Tchichelle. Massamba's impartiality, however, was to prove a source of
weakness, for it deprived his government of any strong tribal and regional
support and alienated the traditional chiefs.

Under the French and Youlou, the chiefs had acted as agents of the administration in both rural and urban areas, and Massamba moved rapidly to
undermine their influence. In most cases, the urban districts, or quartiers,
were inhabited by a single tribe, whose oldest male member served as "mayor."[2]
The coup of August 1963 eliminated such mayors, but the reelection of many
former municipal councilors on February 2, 1964, which perpetuated the tribal
character of the towns' administration, impelled the government to cancel
those elections. To replace the councilors, MNR militants were appointed to
the special municipal delegations which thenceforth ran the urban settlements, and in the rural areas, party cells elected some of their members to
control the activities of the civil servants. It was only when he tried to
undermine the authority of the great chiefs that Massamba encountered formidable obstacles. Rumors to the effect that he planned to destitute the Makoko,
paramount chief of the Batéké tribe, of his powers were reinforced by false
reports of the assassination in April 1965 of the Batéké politician, Prosper
Gandzion.[3] A strong protest from the Organisation des Chefs Traditionnels
soon forced Massamba to deny that he was trying to undermine the customary
chieftaincy.

On the part of the Vili and of their paramount chief, the Ma Loango,
tribal reactions to the MNR's policy were less apparent. Perhaps this was
because they were tempered by the more regionally representative character

of Massamba's government, social divisions among the Vili, and, above all, by the eclipse of the Lari. Pointe Noire did experience periodic agitation, but mainly in the form of labor crises. (When Kaya was dismissed from the government in October 1964, he fled to Pointe Noire, but the fact that he soon sought refuge abroad suggested that no prominent Lari could ever feel wholly secure in that Vili stronghold.) In his first government, Massamba took the precaution of giving a ministerial post to a Vili, Germain Bicoumat, but when he was dropped from the cabinet in 1965, no protests were registered at Pointe Noire. Nor did Tchichelle, after being amnestied in August 1967, try to reconstitute a Vili party, and he simply resumed his former post as stationmaster at Pointe Noire. Nevertheless, during his frequent tours of the countryside, Massamba became aware of the depth of regional feeling, and knew that he must come to terms with tribalism throughout the south so as to eliminate the opposition there to his plan for developing the disfavored north.

From the outset, Massamba realized the danger of antagonizing the south's most dynamic, populous, and westernized tribe, the Lari of Brazzaville and the Pool region. He therefore offered a cabinet post in his first government to Lazare Matsecoto,[4] a relative of Youlou and a left-wing lawyer trained in France. Allegedly because he was not offered the premiership, Matsecoto refused, but later he agreed to become the Congo's attorney general.[5] Two other Lari Christians, Paul Kaya and Lévy Makany, did accept posts in Massamba's government, and a third, Félix Mouzabakany, was named commander-in-chief of the armed forces. Not only did these appointments not appease their fellow tribesmen's sense of grievance but they also antagonized leaders of the non-Lari tribes.

Marcel Ibalico, the only one of Youlou's ministers who escaped arrest after the coup of August 15, 1963, organized a Front de Libération Nationale du Congo-Brazzaville at Léopoldville,[6] which liberally distributed anti-Massamba tracts in the Bacongo quarter of the capital. These fanned the flames of Lari opposition, as was shown, successively, by their street demonstrations in September, a partial boycott of the elections in December, and the riots of February 1964. Clearly the Lari were not reconciled to Youlou's overthrow, but also they obviously were not strong enough either to free him or to unseat Massamba's government. Their continued resistance may well have motivated the murders of the three high-ranking Lari officials in February 1965,[7] and it certainly played a large part in Youlou's escape from Brazzaville the following month. The abbé could hardly have "traveled for three days and nights through forests and across rivers," without the active connivance of his fellow tribesmen, who now had good reason to fear for his life.[8] It was also likely, however, that the government may have facilitated his escape, for had he been murdered in Brazzaville, or even brought to trial there, the Lari might have erupted en masse.

So long as the Lari expatriates enjoyed the hospitality of Léopoldville, they were a source of agitation and armed raids against the Massamba government, as well as a cause of the bad relations between the two Congos. Whether or not the Lari or Tshombe actually wanted to reinstate Youlou is open to doubt, for after those two men had gone into exile at Madrid, the Lari continued actively to oppose the government at Brazzaville. Although the abbé still had some strong supporters at home and abroad, he was increasingly regarded as a forlorn hope, and gradually his reinstatement ceased to be even nominally a motive for the Lari's resentment of their ever more insignificant political status.

Massamba must be credited with eliminating tribalism as an organized political force, but it was far from moribund. On many occasions, he and Lissouba denounced tribalism as the greatest obstacle to national unity, and they aimed to neutralize it by a more equitable regional development. This process, however, was too slow to be effective, for each time they penalized or demoted an outstanding tribal leader, his fellow tribesmen staged protests and street demonstrations that proved irresistible. Tribalism per se had neither the organization or the cohesion required to overthrow the government, but it served as a catalyst for the forces that coalesced to effect the coups d'état of 1963 and 1968. In Massamba's case, his downfall was due to the vigorous and sudden flare-up of tribal emotions in the army, whose Kouyou troops he had twice angered by injudiciously penalizing their popular captain, Marien Ngouabi.

After both coups d'état, tribal and regional groups quickly took advantage of the ensuing period of political uncertainty to form organizations to defend their particular interests. At Pointe Noire, some former members of the PPC and UDDIA organized what was called the Mpita Group, which held meetings and distributed tracts hostile to the CNR in general and to its northern leaders in particular. In the party organ, Etumba,[9] the Mpita Group was said to be made up of "the straw-men of Pointe Noire's reactionary European residents...who want the Congo to become the private property of the Vatican." Some of its leaders were arrested on charges of trying to harm the security of the state, but their trial in the fall of 1969 brought to light a far more complex situation than one based solely on any ideological or religious opposition to the government. Obviously, the Mpita Group was united in its resentment of the military regime's appointment of non-Vili to the committee for national defense of the Pointe Noire region, but less apparent was the class struggle that divided its Vili members. As the trial progressed, it became clear that the aristocratic families of the Dosso region (residence of the Ma Loango) were bitterly opposed to sharing administrative posts with the low-born Vili of Madingo, Kayes, and Mvouti. Indeed, the trial stirred up such a hornets' nest that the government abruptly halted the proceedings and dropped charges against the principal defendants, reportedly as the result of compromise reached behind the scenes.[10]

Basically, the Vili's attitude has been one of refusal to cooperate with the Brazzaville government rather than of overt hostility to its political ideology. Pointe Noire in the economic domain, like Brazzaville in the administrative sphere, had been provided with an infrastructure geared to the whole FEA federation. The Vili had been restive but not in active opposition to Youlou's government, thanks to his vigorous promotion of the Kouilou dam project and of the creation of a free port for the Pointe Noire area. Indeed, the hopes aroused by those prospects led to a phenomenal growth in Pointe Noire's population, which increased by 25,000 between 1958 and 1962, and even after such hopes failed to materialize, the newcomers simply stayed on.[11] Since the public works program there had come to a halt and the only new enterprise of the mid-1960s were a brewery and a plywood factory, there was considerable unemployment and an increasing resentment against the Brazzaville authorities because of their failure to promote the region's development and their earlier removal of the capital from Pointe Noire.[12]

Ngouabi, more than Massamba, has recognized the danger to national
unity of this regional reflex, and he is actively working to improve the
Congo-Ocean railroad and enlarge the port of Pointe Noire. At the same time,
due to a marked increase in its European population (3,200 in 1971), the
mining and exportation of Hollé's potash, expansion of the local fishing industry, and the recent discovery of offshore petroleum deposits made the
economic future of the region look promising but also foreshadow greater unrest. It was noteworthy that the only clashes between students and the army,
in November 1971, occurred at Pointe Noire and that its mayor was arrested
three months later for supporting the putschists.

While Pointe Noire's hopeful economic outlook might help to calm antigovernment sentiments in the southwestern region, Brazzaville's unemployment
problem is likely to persist. No analogous industrial expansion that could
greatly enlarge job opportunities is contemplated there, although the work
being done to modernize its river port should improve its trading potential.
Furthermore, the Bacongo district has continued to expand through the influx
of Lari from the Pool region, whereas the number of its immigrants from
other rural areas remains fairly constant.

Even more swiftly than did Massamba, Ngouabi felt the backlash of Lari
hostility. Not only was Ngouabi a northerner and his running-mate, Raoul,
was from the southwest but the government they formed largely ignored Lari
aspirations. Seeing the handwriting on the wall even before Massamba had
resigned as head of state, the Lari offered armed resistance to the military
government late in August 1968. In so doing, the cooperation between such
ideological adversaries as Hombessa and Bindi at the Biafra camp can be explained only in terms of their common fear, as Lari, of a government headed
by the traditional opponents of their tribe.

It is noteworthy that neither the government's spokesmen nor its opponents have ever forthrightly acknowledged that tribal loyalties motivated
their political activities, for there is a general consensus in the newly independent African states that tribalism is a retrogressive force and that
only ideological divergencies are a "respectable" cause for opposition to a
national government. When Ngouabi began to purge his administration of its
Lari members, this step was always attributed to reasons other than their
tribal affiliation. In February 1969, the dismissal of the Lari director of
the Agence Congolaise d'Information[13] was explained in its bulletin on the
ground that he was a "political illiterate, a reactionary who has sold out,
body and soul, to American imperialism." Hombessa was accused of having done
no constructive work for the Congolese people, and Bindi was charged with
having "defrocked our security services, and having failed to pay sufficient
attention to the operations of the CIA."[14] It was only when the Lari tried
by overt agitation or armed force to reassert their political power that the
tribal issues became too obvious to be denied. Most unusual and refreshingly
frank was the admission by Martin M'Berri, after his arrest in March 1971,
that he had written subversive tracts "because the government has been doing
everything for the north and nothing for the south."[15]

Lari opposition to the military regime surfaced conspicuously after the
two Lari ministers in Ngouabi's government were dropped at the end of 1968.
Lari dissidents may have dared to come out into the open then because they
believed that the dismissal and arrest of Major Mouzabakany had created discontent in the armed forces. Moreover, Lieutenant Kikanga's escape to
Kinshasa soon afterward provided them with professional military leadership.

But time was to prove that Kikanga was no more successful than was Bernard
Kolelas, the leading Lari civilian conspirator, in the armed raids against
Brazzaville which they led, respectively, in March 1970 and November 1969.
Both men had overestimated the support they would receive in Brazzaville and
had underestimated that given to Ngouabi by the army. Their failures effectively ended all the Lari's hopes of overthrowing the regime by force,[16] as
well as Ngouabi's few attempts to strike a better-balanced tribal representation in his government. Moreover, his replacing of all the village chiefs
by PCT militants—decreed in April 1971—was a blow directly aimed at destroying tribalism at the local government level. Ngouabi, however, like
Massamba before him, stopped short of tampering with the Lari's dominant
position in the civil service, although he was more rigorous than his predecessor about disciplining the bureaucracy and keeping it in line.

Despite his stern measures, Ngouabi finally learned that tribalism and
regionalism were not a spent force but had simply shifted ground and become
protean. Naturally, the older, rural Congolese clung to their tribal traditions, both social and religious, and their ethnic solidarity came to the
fore only when other tribesmen infiltrated into their region. The younger,
urban Lari, Mbochi, and Vili, on the other hand, had little knowledge of, or
interest in, tribal customs.[17] Indeed, they tended to reject those traditions that conflicted with their newly acquired Western scale of values, but
in different ways they displayed just as deep-seated ethnic animosities in
their competition with other tribes for power, wealth, and prestige. The
Lari, in particular, manifested their sense of frustration either in petulant
outbursts, such as tearing to bits the Congo's new red flag, or in organizing
dissidence in the army, PCT, and UJSC. When arrested, the ringleaders usually claimed that they were motivated by ideological disagreements with the
authorities, but their trials often brought to light irrefutable evidence of
the tribal basis of their grievances.

Organized Labor and the Civil Service

Massamba's first year in office was marked by only one minor labor conflict. It involved the railroad management and its employees, and was
quickly settled. His main problem in the labor field was the perennial one
of urban unemployment, and to cope with it, Massamba created a Comité de
l'Emploi in February 1964. In June, he reinforced the labor code of 1952 by
regulations increasing the protection of workers against "abusive dismissals"
and of woman and child labor, and improving collective agreements and the
conditions for pay and promotion. He also altered the procedure for handling
labor disputes, and entrusted their enforcement to a Conseil Supérieur du
Travail, composed of an equal number of employers, employees, and members of
the Economic and Social Council.

Late in 1964, Massamba's efforts to ameliorate the legal status of wage
earners in the Congo were largely nullified by the expulsion to Brazzaville
of thousands of its nationals who had been working in Léopoldville. Their
presence, in conjunction with that of the thousands of Congolese who had
been repatriated from Gabon in 1962, caused the number of unemployed in the
capital to increase vastly, and the country's financial burden to grow correspondingly. Moreover, both their expulsion and their presence gave more
political leverage to the radical wing of the MNR, and the labor movement was

soon to feel its impact. Under pressure from the radical politicians and labor leaders, the social security charges for employers were raised by four percent late in 1964, and the minimum wage for the two wage zones[18] was increased in January 1965 when an office to promote technical education was created. In 1966, the labor service was reorganized and enlarged, and two years later, a law was passed requiring that all employment in the private sector be progressively Congolized so that by 1974 only native workers could be hired.

The increasingly radical policy of the Massamba government inevitably affected the Congo's civil servants, who had always formed the strongest group of organized wage earners. By early 1964, the MNR had honeycombed the country with party cells and brigades of youthful vigilantes, and JMNR youths trained in a camp at Malaka were dispatched to the hinterland "to strengthen the revolutionary structure." The subsequent replacement of elected municipal and regional councilors by MNR appointees not only precipitated the decline of elective local-government institutions but also enhanced the party's power over the bureaucracy. This was further increased in 1967 by the constitution of a corps of agents supérieurs de l'état to head the administrative units that were to be created in the new nine regions and five full communes. They were chosen from among the most trusted MNR members and given almost unlimited powers, including the authority to replace prefects under certain conditons.

The steady sapping of the civil servants' authority naturally aroused their resentment, the more so as the majority were Lari already aggrieved by their tribe's loss of political power. Because of their numerical preponderance, intelligence, and educational attainments, the Lari were indispensable to the administration, and Massamba wanted to avoid goading them into open revolt. His efforts to propitiate them by increases in the bureaucrats' number and salaries were only partially successful. The deterioration in the civil servants' ethical standards, as evidenced by the growth in their corruption,[19] was perhaps at least in part a covert expression of the Lari's deep-seated discontent. Although the Lari bureaucrats had become so financially privileged a caste that their pay absorbed more than half the state's revenues,[20] they were frequently and energetically chided by Massamba and Lissouba for their lack of civic spirit.

The technocrats who headed Massamba's first government gave preference in promotions to bureaucrats with university degrees over the less educated, older civil servants.[21] Despite this and other changes made in their recruitment and in their assignments, the bureaucracy's ingrained habits of indiscipline, corruption, and apathy were not modified. It proved to be as impossible for the new leaders as it had been for Youlou to enforce austerity measures and to apply the draconian laws voted by the legislature against civil servants who abused their authority. By late 1965, their resistance to control by the MNR government was largely due to its ruthless treatment of the Catholic labor unions, of which the civil servants had been the backbone.

The cooperation between the Catholic, radical, and autonomous unions, which had spearheaded the attack on Youlou, lasted only for the duration of Massamba's provisional government. During that six-month period, no union offical accepted a cabinet post, and the minister of labor was an apolitical physician, Bernard Galiba. This situation was not appreciably modified when, in December 1963, Galiba was replaced by the innocuous Gabriel Betou, another newcomer to the political scene. It was the choice of Pascal Lissouba as premier and, even more, the election of Léon Angor as president of the legislature early in 1964 that brought the radicals in the labor movement to the political forefront. Under Angor's aegis, the CGAT and CCSL merged in March to form the Confédération Syndicale Congolaise (CSC). At that time, it was estimated that 52,000 of the 57,000 or so wage earners in the Congo had been organized into unions and that 41 percent of the union members belonged to the CATC, 32 percent to the CCSL, and 27 percent to the CGAT.[22] The formation of the CSC not only altered the balance of union power but also heralded the incorporation of the organized labor movement into the MNR.

At its fourth annual congress held the following September, the CATC refused to join the CSC and also confirmed its traditional stand against any politicization of the Congolese unions. The next month, its president, Fulgence Biayoula, was molested by a group of JMNR members and then arrested on the charge of distributing antigovernment tracts. In vain the CATC protested against his imprisonment to the ILO in Geneva and to the OAU, and, on December 17, the legislature voted to dissolve the CATC as an organization. This move followed the designation on November 24 of the CSC as the Congo's sole labor federation and its integration into the MNR, and it was accompanied by attacks on all the CATC leaders. In 1965, the CATC officials were expelled from the MNR politburo and the legislature, and some of them were arrested on trumped-up charges.

At the CSC's constituent congress, its policy was set by Idrissa Diallo, who emerged at this time as the Congo's most radical labor spokesman. He denounced in strong terms those labor leaders who "refused to promote the revolution simply to gratify their personal ambitions and religious preferences." He further asserted that peasants and workers must join together in conducting an "implacable struggle against imperialism and feudalism."[23] Much the same brand of Marxist nationalism was voiced by Abel Thaulay-Ganga, who added that scientific socialism was the only remedy for the Congo's economic plight. Modeling the structure of the newborn labor federation on that of the MNR party, these leaders organized CSC unions in all the main enterprises. So completely was the CSC integrated into the MNR that its leaders were given high posts in the government as well as in the party. The elimination of the CATC followed by the absorption of experienced CSC officials into the government and party left its member unions in the hands of young and often irresponsible leaders. The overall result of this merger was a remarkable absence of labor disputes during Massamba's five-year tenure of office.

Two other characteristics of the CSC throughout that period merit attention. One was its leadership by men who earlier had been prominent in the UJC[24] as well as in the CGAT, and the other was their rapid eclipse after a brief period in power. In December 1965, Betou was replaced as minister of labor by the militant youth leader, Bernard Zoniaba, but he was dropped from the cabinet four months later. Men like Matsika, Thaulay-Ganga, and Bamboukou, who had been officials of the UJC or CGAT at the time of Youlou's downfall and had risen to eminence in Massamba's first years in power, were rapidly transferred to relatively unimportant posts or simply replaced. Furthermore, Diallo, Zoniaba, Ndalla, and Banthoud—who were the CSC's radical standard bearers in 1966 and 1967—were forced out of the government one after the other. Some of them were even accused of embezzlement and brought to trial after Massamba moved to the right early in 1968. A few of them, notably Ndalla, staged a comeback under the military government, but the majority sank into political oblivion.

The first signs of dissension between Massamba and the radical labor leaders occurred after the CSC held its second congress in April 1967. At that meeting, Paul Banthoud, then its general secretary, asserted that the CSC would not be "domesticated" by the government, and called for the nationalization of all banks and industries then operating in the Congo. Massamba immediately retorted that such a policy would be "nonsense, because there is nothing to nationalize in this country."[25] He also took issue with other resolutions passed by that congress condemning American policy in Vietnam and asking for recognition of East Germany and for support for the WFTU and liberation movements everywhere. He advised Congolese wage earners to leave politics to the government and to concentrate on their essential task of promoting the country's productivity.

In trying to damp down the CSC's militancy, Massamba showed his awareness of its disturbing effect on the local private employers who were responsible for 16,000 to 18,000 of the nongovernmental jobs in the Congo. Not only had his government been unable to diminish appreciably the number of unemployed but the rapid rise in living costs, especially food prices, was contributing to urban unrest in the last months of 1967. There is no doubt but that that situation, compounded by Massamba's "opening to the right" early in 1968, helped to erode his support. However, because organized labor had now lost its separate identity, it did not play the same role in the coup d'état of August 1968 as it had five years earlier. Indeed, labor's passivity at this time caused the rank and file of the CSC to lash out against its "indolent" officials because of their failure to participate in setting up the new regime.[26] Their insistence that the CSC be represented in the CNR directorate derived in part from their long-standing suspicion that the military leaders were less than ardent about applying the principles of scientific socialism to the economy.

For many of the same reasons, the history of labor policy under Ngouabi was in fact largely a rerun of that under Massamba, with the differences between them those of degree rather than of kind. Faced with the same problem of the Congo's chronic and growing budget deficits, urban unemployment and rural underemployment, both men reacted pragmatically and sacrificed ideological consistency. This brought them into conflict with the extreme radicals in their party, many of whom were also influential leaders of the single labor federation. Ngouabi personally is more of a Marxist and an even stronger advocate of state control over the economy than was Massamba, and, consequently, he is more vulnerable to the radical pressures. On the other hand, he seems more determined than was Massamba to control organized labor, and in thus asserting his authority and in keeping order, he has the general support of the army, which at the end was denied to his predecessor.

Although farming is the occupation of more than half a million Congolese dispersed in some 4,200 villages, agricultural labor per se has been ignored by Ngouabi as well as by Massamba. However, the military government has drawn a distinction in this domain that was lacking in Massamba's time. Currently, rural wage earners employed in the forest and sugar industries elicit more official attention because they have become unionized by the CSC and are employed by foreign firms. In consequence, when they have gone on strike in recent years, their unions have enjoyed the government's support for their demands. Thus, in 1970, the cane cutters employed by the SIAN and the lumberjacks at the Fouet forest company were encouraged by the state-controlled CSC to hold out for higher wages and for improvements in their "inhuman working conditions." In the former case, this led to the nationalization of the SIAN, and in the latter, to paying the wages of Congolese strikers, although they were working for a firm located in Gabon,[27] both of which policies have cost the government funds it could ill afford.

Under both regimes, the government's main concern has been to create more jobs for the urban unemployed and to acquire a better control over its own employees in the bureaucracy and in the state enterprises. In its dealings with those two categories of workers, the political aspect of official policy has been notably more influential than its economic substance.

The number of "unemployed" in Congolese towns has never been accurately known, partly because the urban population is mobile and is swelled by a growing number of rural youths who have no skills and have never been wage earners previously. In 1962, it was estimated that 31 percent of the adult male population of the Congo was without regular paid employment, and there is no evidence that this proportion has appreciably declined. Although the number of jobs in industry rose between 1960 and 1966 from 9,300 to 19,900[28] and has certainly increased since then, there has been concurrently a rapid growth in the total population and especially of its urban component.

The most marked expansion in wages occurred in the public sector, thanks to the steady growth of the bureaucracy and of the state industries. By 1968, the number of employees in government (21,000) was rapidly overtaking that of private enterprises (33,000).[29] The following year, 25,000 persons were on the government payroll, and in 1970, nearly 10,000 more were added when the sugar company and three forest concessions were nationalized. To reach the official goal of full employment, increasing pressure is being exerted on private employers to hire only Congolese nationals, and in principle this will become mandatory by 1974. What the government cannot control, however, is the pay scale in the private sector. There Europeans, who form less than 10 percent of all wage earners, receive salaries which total eight times more than the aggregate for the far more numerous African labor force.[30] Upon coming to power, the military government appreciably raised the minimum wage for workers in both zones.[31] Since then, however, their wage increase has been cancelled out by the very rapid rise in living costs. Taxes are high on imported foodstuffs, which have become necessities because of declining domestic production, and the agents charged with enforcing the official price controls reportedly accept bribes offered them by unscrupulous merchants.[32] And it is the consumer who ultimately pays for both bribes and high prices.

The military government's solicitude for the employees of private foreign firms contrasts with its treatment of the bureaucracy and, more recently, of its own employees in the state enterprises. Ngouabi has been financially indulgent to the civil servants for the same political reasons that motivated Massamba. Despite the treasury's dire straits, their ranks have not been reduced, and in January 1969, their pay was even increased from 15 percent to 40 percent, depending on their category. However, it should also be noted that the military government has been more effective in trimming the bureaucracy's political influence and its prerogatives than was Massamba. Furthermore, it has at the same time brought the CSC under so much closer control that that organization refused to join the student strikers in 1971 and the putschists in 1972.

Late in 1968, all the mass organizations of the MNR, including the CSC, were reorganized and placed under officials handpicked by the government. Concurrently, CNR-appointed Committees for the Defense of the Revolution were formed throughout the country and were given authority over local administrators. During the winter of 1968-69, Ngouabi and his ministers took turns in publicly castigating the bureaucracy for the same faults as had been the target of Massamba's indictments. When the finance ministry personnel went on strike in September 1969 because their pay was three months in arrears, Ngouabi reacted more swiftly and harshly than his predecessor had ever done. The strike was "settled" by the dismissal or arrest of union officials while the CSC president, J. B. Missamou, was attending a WFTU congress in Budapest.[33] This was followed not only by a turnover in the CSC's top leadership but also by the transfer of high-ranking bureaucrats to unimportant posts. In 1970, 80 civil servants were dismissed for their alleged involvement in the raid of March 23, government employees were no longer allowed to live in state-owned lodgings, and all persons on the public payroll were required to take a course in Marxist-Leninist ideology. The disciplining of the bureaucracy was carried even further in February 1971, when civil servants charged with embezzlement were tried by the revolutionary court which, theretofore, had handled only cases of political crimes against the state. Finally, four months later, all civil servants were required to hold "certificates of militancy"[34] to be issued by their local Committee for the Defense of the Revolution.

As the number of wage earners in the state industries has grown by leaps and bounds, the government has tried unsuccessfully to treat them in much the same way as its civil servants. A strike by workers at the Kinsoundi factory in July 1969 was followed six months later by a much more serious one on the part of the cheminots of the Congo-Ocean railroad. In the latter case, the strikers' demands included the prompt payment of their wages as well as an increase in them, better medical care, more perquisites, and greater security of tenure. More significantly, the cheminots demanded a new collective labor agreement and the right to choose the union officials who would represent them in their negotiations with the government. In vain, the PCT leaders scolded the cheminots for being poor patriots and Marxists and especially for using such a bourgeois weapon as the strike against a socialist government. The strikers held out for three months, and so paralyzed the operations of the railroad and the port of Pointe Noire that the government finally gave in and met most of their demands. Ngouabi was careful to give no publicity to this capitulation or to the strikes in early 1972 by the SIAN workers and postal carriers; yet he dared to propose as an economy measure that the pay of all wage earners in government services be reduced.

More confrontations with labor can be expected should the military regime actually carry out that proposal, as well as its declared intention of retiring those high-ranking officials who had been trained under the French administration. Any reduction in their number and privileged financial status would surely be resisted by the Lari bureaucrats, who have not been wholly cowed into political docility. Probably the reaction of the unskilled workers on the government payroll would be even more violent, as the progressive nationalization of the economy is rapidly swelling their number. Even assuming that the regime could readily replace the strikers in that category from the huge reservoir of urban unemployed, it could not be assured of controlling labor leadership.

No strict controls over union organization and no amount of ideological indoctrination or patriotic exhortations can satisfy, in the long run, poorly and belatedly paid workers faced with inflation. Labor's present malaise may reach the point of explosion if the PCT radicals succeed in breaking all ties with the Western capitalist system or, conversely, if, by giving in to the workers' demands, the government is pushed so far over the financial brink that no foreign country will be willing to come to its rescue.

Youth Organizations

In Congo-Brazzaville, as in other francophone Black African countries, the proportion of its nationals under fifteen years of age has soared to over 42 percent. Moreover, in its southern towns, educated young people are especially numerous, and their goal there, as elsewhere, is admission into the highly privileged civil service. Alongside them exists a much larger element of the youthful urban population, which consists of rural immigrants with little schooling and no skills to offer and whose ties to their milieu have been weakened. For both categories of young town dwellers, job opportunities are very limited. However, Brazzaville's educated indigenous youth can count on their family connections, if not their diplomas, for support, and tradition still has some influence on their activities. The young rural immigrants, on the other hand, must fend for themselves and they feel no such constraints upon their behavior. Nevertheless, both groups share a sense of frustration and of resentment against whatever government is in power for failing to provide them with the means of livelihood, if not with the means of upward mobility.

These interrelated problems of unemployment and potential violence existed to a minor degree under the French administration, but have become far more acute since independence. (This was the view of G. Althabe and R. Devauges when they published in 1963 the results of a sociopsychological study of Brazzaville's unemployed youth three years before the Congo's independence.) The uneducated rural immigrants and the indigenous school graduates both knew that they could not realize their ambitions for material success in traditional society, whose power was in the hands of the older generation. Nor could they find the employment they needed if they were to win access to the Western social system and its rewards. To mitigate their feelings of isolation and frustration, the young people of Brazzaville formed many small clubs of a tribal or regional character for social gatherings and for sport; but, psychologically, they could not accept permanent unemployment as their status and lived in a state of latent revolt.

Youlou had hoped to satisfy the school graduates by expanding the bureaucracy, but soon its ranks were filled to overflowing. For financial reasons, he had to call a halt long before he had absorbed into the civil service even an appreciable minority of the qualified candidates. For those youths who had no skills or schooling, he created a compulsory civic service

217

and also vocational training centers. But the former proved to be a costly and temporary expedient, and there were almost no jobs available for the several thousand Congolese trained at the new centers. Like all his fellow politicians, Youlou was fully aware of the dangers as well as the opportunity for his leadership represented by the mass of restless and idle urban youths and sought to bring them under his control.

During the last years of the colonial administration, all of the major political parties formed their own youth branches, as had the Catholic mission many years before.[35] Theoretically, all the youth organizations belonged to a Conseil de la Jeunesse, affiliated with the World Assembly of Youth, but in reality there was little coordination between them, and the UJC wholly escaped official controls. Only the Jeunesse Catholique was strongly structured, with branches in the main southern towns, but it attracted urban youths less than did the more dynamic and revolutionary UJC. Initially, the UJC had been an offshoot of the Union des Jeunesses in France, but it came increasingly under the influence of the local CGAT. The UJC was most active in Brazzaville, where briefly it had its own mimeographed bulletin, L'Eveil, but in the late 1950s, it began spreading to the smaller settlements along the railroad. When it succeeded in infiltrating the Jeunesse de l'UDDIA, Youlou became alarmed and forbade the youth of his party to belong to both organizations. In May 1960, some UJC leaders were arrested along with those of the CGAT.

More for material than for ideological reasons, a majority of the youth groups opposed Youlou's regime. But because their membership was small and there was little coordination between them, the youth organizations, as such, played an unimportant part in his overthrow. Nor did they exert any influence in the formation of Massamba's government comparable to that of the labor unions or the army. Actually, it was a mob of teen-agers, called mwanas, who could be described as the principal activists during the first two days of the "Trois Glorieuses." They stoned the police and soldiers loyal to the government with impunity, for the troops did not dare to open fire on them.[36] And again, during the fall of 1963, it was the same trigger-happy adolescents who in roving armed bands harassed European residents and allegedly pro-Youlou Lari in the streets of Brazzaville.

Gradually these bands were formed into a multitude of small groups, of which some were organized by radicals such as Claude Ndalla, and they passed fiery political resolutions. To quell their aggressive agitation and to bring them under his wing, Massamba tried to absorb them into the party he was forming as its youth branch, or Jeunesse du Mouvement National de la Revolution (JMNR). To the Europeans who complained about the youths' free-wheeling behavior, Massamba replied soothingly that they were no different from young people in other parts of the world and that their "exuberance" could easily be contained if foreign employers would only give them jobs.[37]

Massamba began to take a more serious view of the lawlessness of Brazzaville's youth after their violent reaction to the Lari uprising of February 1964 threatened to worsen the Congo's already poor relations with the Western countries.[38] Premier Lissouba also felt impelled to remind the JMNR members that it was not they but the government that determined the Congo's policy. Nevertheless, it was at the JMNR's insistence that the MNR was institutionalized as the Congo's single party, its representatives were included in the politburo, the moderate ministers, Kaya and Okiemba, were dropped from the cabinet, and the CATC was dissolved and its leaders arrested or removed from all public bodies. Although the JMNR's responsibility was never proven, public opinion attributed the murders of February 1965 to its members, because such attacks conformed with the established pattern of their conduct. As the self-appointed watchdogs of the revolution, the JMNR and especially its militia made the law and imposed it on the streets of Brazzaville and, to an increasing extent, on the government.

As early as April 1964, the growing influence of the JMNR was confirmed by a cabinet reshuffle in which Hombessa, then minister for youth, was given the interior portfolio and Ndalla succeeded him in the youth ministry. Furthermore, a majority of the newcomers in the cabinet at that time were JMNR officials. As could be expected, Ndalla proved to be the most ardent advocate of arming the JMNR militia and of replacing the civic service by a more radical organization, the Action de Rénovation Rurale. Despite its innocuous name, the "seminars" which the new organization launched at Makala[39] in May were actually training camps for young men between the ages of fifteen and thirty. By the end of 1964, the JMNR had sent 3,000 or so Makala vigilantes to the hinterland, where they were to replace the gendarmerie and to control the political activities of local officials. Then the commando raid of July 1965 impelled the legislature to vote full powers to the JMNR shock troops so that they could "liquidate all enemies of the revolution."[40]

At the same time that the MNR was institutionalized as the Congo's single party, the JMNR was officially confirmed as its youth branch. The JMNR thus gained both an organization and a legitimacy that it had theretofore lacked. However, this accretion in the JMNR's powers gave pause to the moderates in the government, and they moved to promote the civil defense corps, which had been somnolent since its creation in 1963, as a more disciplined youth group and to place it under their direct control. During the army mutiny of June 1966, the government was to find that corps a very weak reed on which to lean.

Up to that point, students in the Congo had played a politically negligible role compared with that of the JMNR, for their only organization was an Association des Etudiants Congolais in France (of which Lissouba at one time had been president), which was more formally than actively affiliated with the FEANF. This association had confined its activities to passing resolutions supporting the MNR's Marxist policies during its congresses at Brazzaville, where its 85 or so members spent their vacations. In July 1965, the JMNR decided that it was high time to bring Congolese secondary and university students together in an organization that would become an integral part of its movement. So the Union Générale des Elèves et Etudiants Congolais (UGEEC) was duly formed, and its members promptly passed a resolution urging nationalization of the school system. On August 12, the legislature voted this measure, and two weeks later, all the mission schools in the Congo were placed under state control.[41]

In sponsoring the UGEEC and its proposal, the JMNR's obvious target was the Catholic church, whose hierarchy would no longer accept the doctrines and methods of the MNR leaders, whom the mission organizations had initially helped to overthrow Youlou. In the fall of 1965, the JMNR opened its attack on the Catholic labor unions by a virulent anticlerical press campaign in its organ, Dipanda. This was followed by the expulsion of three European missionaries and the imprisonment of Abbé Louis Badila, the outspoken

Congolese editor of the influential Catholic weekly, <u>La Semaine de l'AEF</u>.[42]
The arrest and alleged torture of Abbé Badila aroused the ire of the Catholic
community against the JMNR, and Archbishop M'Bemba, heading a delegation of
priests, lodged a formal protest with the government. To supplement its attack on the CATC, the JMNR sought to bring under its control members of the
Catholic youth association and scout troops. To this end, it formed two new
branches of the MNR—the Jeunesse Ouvrière for young wage earners and the
Pioneers for boys and girls between the ages of five and seventeen. Members
of these fledgling groups were told that they must no longer restrict themselves to "idealistic good works," but should actively promote the "social
and economic adaptation" of the Congo to the new order.[43]

The mobilization and radicalization of Christian youth by the JMNR gave
concern to the party moderates, for it threatened to alienate permanently
the Catholic community, which constituted 38 percent of the total population.[44] Furthermore, the education service was hard pressed to staff the
nationalized schools, because the mission's primary and secondary institutions had been instructing nearly 80,000 students.[45] The mission schools'
nationalization had led to the immediate departure of nearly all the 150
priests and monks who had been their teaching personnel. It dramatically
marked the culmination of a series of futile protests to the MNR by the
church authorities, including Mgr. M'Bemba, the recently consecrated Congolese archbishop of Brazzaville. The mission's action surprised and dismayed
Massamba, who told journalists in Paris that "we never intended to drive them
away, since our revolution does not attack personal religious beliefs."[46]
Eventually, a compromise was reached whereby the mission continued to control
its theological seminaries, and schoolchildren were permitted to receive religious instruction for a half-day every week.

In December 1965, the removal of Ndalla from the cabinet suggested a
setback for the JMNR, but the replacement of Premier Lissouba by Noumazalaye
the following April marked a new victory for that organization. Not only
was Noumazalaye a strong believer in arming the JMNR militia and hiring
Cuban instructors to give military training to the civil defense corps but
he promoted the JMNR's control of the people's army. Here, however, Ndalla
overreached himself, for his policy led to the army mutiny of June 1966 and
the subsequent eclipse of the JMNR for more than a year. Although the JMNR
gradually regained some of its strength under new leaders, it was not able
to bring off the coup d'état against Massamba that it allegedly planned to
carry out in December 1967. After Noumazalaye was dismissed as premier and
Hombessa lost his interior portfolio in January 1968, the JMNR's power was
broken.

Ironically enough, it was not the JMNR but its offshoot, the UGEEC,
whose activities first prompted Massamba to stage his minicoup of January
1968, and then touched off the series of events that culminated in the army's
takeover of the government the following August. In February 1967, a manifesto issued in the name of the UGEEC was published in France by <u>L'Humanité
Nouvelle</u>, the organ of the pro-Mao French communists. In it Massamba was
strongly attacked as the agent of French neocolonialism, and the pamphlet
bore the legend "printed in China." (When it was circulated through the
mails in Brazzaville the following July, the Chinese Embassy there denied
any responsibility for its distribution.[47]) Almost exactly a year later,
Peking's chargé d'affaires attended a congress at Brazzaville called by some

members of the UGEEC who had participated in the May 1968 student riots at Paris. Its delegates passed the violently worded resolution drafted by Ndalla and Poungui (who was president of the UGEEC) which triggered Massamba's sharp reaction and his arrest of the so-called Maoists, including Ngouabi. As soon as the meeting was over, the Chinese diplomat took Ndalla and Poungui away in his car to a safe hiding place.[48]

There was no doubt but that the student activists heartily disliked Massamba, but this did not mean that they were enthusiastic about the military leaders whom they had inadvertently helped to replace him. Their lukewarm attitude toward Ngouabi became apparent in April 1970 when, at the UJSC congress convened after the abortive raid of Kikanga, the UGEEC delegate refused to support the strong resolution voted at that meeting condemning the "imperialist authors of the plot."[49] It was then surmised that the UGEEC militants might be following a directive of the FEANF and that they concurred with that organization in believing that the Congo's military government was not truly revolutionary but was in the hands of the country's administrative bourgeoisie. From its inception, the UGEEC has been a far-left association, and since 1967, it has relayed the Maoist element in the JMNR and its organ, Dipanda, when they began to lose ground.

The history of the youth movement during the 1963-68 period strongly resembles that of the labor unions. Indeed, the leaders of both were often the same, or interchangeable, and the identity of their interests was for some years implicitly recognized by Massamba's entrusting to the same minister in his cabinet responsibility for both labor and youth. After formation of the single labor federation, the CSC, and of the sole youth organization, the JMNR, both were integrated into the government party. But whereas organized labor remained relatively quiescent throughout Massamba's regime, the youth branch of the MNR increased its strength at the government's expense to the point where it became for a time the dominant force in the Congo. In fairness to the JMNR, however, it should be noted that not all of its activities were disruptive and directed toward gaining political power. Some of its members set an example to their compatriots by cultivating the soil, repairing roads, and promoting the indigenous arts of painting, writing, and the dance.[50] The JMNR's fatal error was to have tried to wrest control of the army from its officer corps, and as a result, the paramilitary youth organizations were crushed in the trial of armed strength between them that just preceded Massamba's resignation. Ngouabi used his troops to quell the JMNR and civil defense corps, not because he disagreed with their ideological orientation but because he would not tolerate their disputing his authority.

After the army had cleared out the rebels from the Biafra camp early in September 1968, Ngouabi arrested their ringleaders. He then deprived the JMNR of its military arm and the means to challenge his rule by incorporating its militia (as well as the civil defense corps) into the regular army. Yet Ngouabi courted the Congolese youth, for he knew that, as the most dynamic segment of the population, they could either give him precious support or become his most dangerous adversaries. Far more than Massamba had been, Ngouabi was sensitive to the aspirations of Congolese students, who, as early as October 1968, had strongly criticized his regime for its moderation.[51] Their demands for a reform of the educational system and for the admission of representatives to the CNR directorate were spelled out in a cahier de doléances, which they presented to him on the fifth anniversary of the founding of the revolutionary youth movement in February 1969. Ngouabi concurred with the UGEEC's insistence that the party control the government, but he took issue with other resolutions it had passed, such as the students' denunciation of American and Israeli aggression, of France's "neocolonialist pillage of the Congo's economy," and of any reconciliation with the Kinshasa leadership. Then and later, in much the same terms as Massamba had used a few years before, Ngouabi criticized their intemperate language, indiscipline, and lack of realism.

In August 1969, Ngouabi called a congress of former JMNR members, renamed the youth movement the Union de la Jeunesse Socialiste Congolaise (UJSC), and assigned it the task of helping to reconstruct the economy. He also reorganized the Pioneers, who were now to conduct Marxist propaganda courses in the Congo's primary schools. Later, he disbanded the Action de la Rénovation Rurale as a paramilitary and political avant-garde movement, and incorporated its members into the new groups he was forming to teach farmers modern agricultural techniques.

Albeit shorn of their military potential and forcibly committed to economic development, the youth of Brazzaville soon proved that they still had the spirit to defy army control. At the youth movement's sixth anniversary celebrations in February 1970, the UJSC organized a tumultuous demonstration at Poto-Poto. From 2,000 to 3,000 youths, clothed in Chinese-style uniforms, paraded before Ngouabi, who was seated in a grandstand draped with red flags and adorned with portraits of Lenin and Mao.[52] Combo-Matsiona, the UJSC president, denounced French imperialism in fiery terms and demanded that the Congo break all its ties with Western countries. A few days later, a humorous story giving an unflattering portrayal of Ngouabi, presumably written by Combo-Matsiona, appeared in the party weekly, Etumba. It brought down Ngouabi's wrath on its editor-in-chief, Atondi-Monmondjo, and on Combo-Matsiona, but his reprimand to them amounted to no more than a slap on the wrist.[53]

Ngouabi was also surprisingly indulgent toward the Congolese students. A strike called by the UGEEC in May 1969 succeeded in impelling him to make minor changes in the school curriculum. A year later, Ngouabi increased the stipend for Congolese university students in Europe, and permitted them to return home at government expense during their summer vacations.[54] That association's more intransigent members, however, were not to be deflected from their insistence on a complete break with the French educational system, the use of a local dialect as the language of school instruction, greater stress on technical subjects in the curriculum, and the transformation of Brazzaville's Centre d'Enseignement Supérieur into a national university.[55] Strong backing for this program was given to the UGEEC by the UJSC, Ndalla, and Henri Lopez, then minister of education. For those organizations and individuals, "cultural alienation" had become the main target of their opprobrium, particularly centered on students who "had their heads in Paris and their feet in Brazzaville." This anti-Western intellectual trend was reinforced by a puritanical reflex against dancing, prostitution, alcoholic beverages, and foreign films—all of which were said to be "incompatible with the spirit of socialist youth."[56]

If Ngouabi hoped that he had successfully channeled the political militancy of Congolese youth toward cultural nationalism and turned its energies to performing economic tasks, he was disillusioned early in 1971. The irrepressible Combo-Matsiona, in a speech in February, asserted that the state was "reactionary and riddled with corruption, hypocrisy, and disdain for the masses...If we don't snuff out the bourgeoisie, it will stifle the revolution," he added.[57] Then in June, the UJSC and UGEEC organized a mass meeting of several thousand Congolese youths to express solidarity with the rebels at Lovanium University and denounce Mobutu's bourgeois government for its "ferocious repression."[58] Finally, in November, it was the politicization of the strike by Congolese secondary-school students that precipitated Ngouabi's purge of the party the following month, which, in turn, led to the putsch of February 1972.

Although Ngouabi was able to prevent the UJSC and the CSC leadership from supporting the student strike and to use the army to quell dissidents in both organizations, his government's relations with militant youth and labor have been no more harmonious than were those of Massamba's regime. At the outset, both governments received at least the nominal support of the two most vital forces in the Congo, but soon were the target of their attacks. Neither Massamba nor Ngouabi was unseated by the youth or labor organizations, but they could not keep the JMNR-UJSC and the CSC from contributing to their governments' instability and undermining the Congo's relations with nonrevolutionary states.

In his struggle with the same forces and particularly with Congolese youth, Ngouabi has more assets than had his predecessor. Unlike Massamba, he belongs to the same generation as his strongest opponents and to a greater extent shares their views, especially in regard to reforming the inherited French school system. Yet his most intransigent critics are the Congolese students abroad, who numbered 1,027 in 1971, were geographically beyond his control, and for the most part were affiliated with the notably anti-Ngouabi FEANF.[59] As for the dissident students in the Congo, Ngouabi can keep them from getting out of hand as long as he retains the loyalty of the armed forces, which alone have the organization and the weapons to back up his authority effectively.

The Armed Forces

Under the collective defense agreement negotiated between France and the equatorial states on the eve of their independence, small French garrisons were stationed throughout the former Federation, and French military missions were sent to train and equip their national armies. In 1961, the Congo formed a national army and gendarmerie of about 2,000 men, and 51 Congolese NCOs went to France for special training.

Just what role the Congolese army played in the events of mid-August 1963 is still far from clear. Le Figaro's usually well-informed Brazzaville correspondent saw in Youlou's overthrow the culmination of a plot long prepared by the Iron Curtain countries, using Sékou Touré's visit to Brazzaville as the opening wedge and the CGAT unions as its chief executors.[60] According to that source, the coup was to have been carried out in two stages, of which the first would be the eviction of all of Youlou's cabinet and the establishment of a committee of public safety, and the second the application of a program of revolutionary reforms that were eventually to spread to Congo-Léopoldville. Allegedly, the tracts spelling out this program that emanated from the Czech embassy at Léopoldville were distributed in the African districts of Brazzaville. This plot miscarried because Youlou submitted his resignation to Majors Mouzabakany and Mountsaka and not to the union leaders as expected, and those two officers chose to support a government under Massamba-Débat. Still another version of the story behind the coup[61] assigned the primary role to the Congolese army, which supposedly used the labor leaders to carry out its designs. Aggrieved at being commanded by French officers and at receiving less pay than the Community's armed forces, so this argument runs, the Congolese army was inspired to take action by the Togolese mutineers who had assassinated Sylvanus Olympio six months before.

Neither of these stories seems to fit all the known facts. Youlou, well aware of the army's material grievances, had increased the defense allocation in the 1963 budget by 35 percent over that of the preceding year. Furthermore, the army defended the government against the street demonstrators until the third day of the general strike, and then intervened only after the French troops had withdrawn and left to it the task of maintaining order. Moreover, after Mountsaka and Mouzabakany had persuaded Youlou to resign, they immediately handed over to a civilian government the power that they could easily have retained. In recompense for their self-abnegation and to meet their aspirations for greater authority, Massamba replaced a French colonel by Mountsaka as commander-in-chief of the Congolese army, and raised most of its officers in rank. Later, he wholly Congolized the police and the gendarmerie.

Nevertheless, the armed forces soon showed signs of unrest, not all of which were politically inspired. As early as September 1963, some officers began to act independently of the government's orders by conducting house searches for hidden arms and ammunition and by arresting "suspects," including the CATC leader, Gilbert Pongault. Since the JMNR was also then engaged in such unauthorized activities, it was inevitable that antagonism should develop between those two forces, each of which regarded itself as vested with responsibility for maintaining order. In November, there occurred a minimutiny on the part of soldiers whose pay was several months in arrears. These mutineers actually arrested Major Mountsaka, and refused to release him until Massamba had promised them prompt payment. Such evidences of indiscipline probably determined Massamba, after his election as president of the republic, to take over the defense portfolio in Lissouba's first cabinet.

The increasing radicalization of the regime, accompanied by a downgrading of the officer corps, brought to the fore as many tribal and ideological divisions in the armed forces as were evident in the government and in the party. Generally speaking, there was no adverse reaction in January 1965 when the armed forces were renamed the "people's army." Yet even those officers who concurred in the Marxist-Leninist policy of placing the army under collegial political control and subject to the party's directives were increasingly hostile to the JMNR militia's usurpation of the army's legitimate functions. This was most acutely felt by the Lari officers, who began to look nostalgically back to the days when their fellow tribesman, Youlou, headed the government, as well as by those officers who disapproved of the Congo's growing relations with the communist countries. The dismissal or transfer to distant posts of many officers accused of complicity in the abortive commando raid of July 1965 further contributed to the army's demoralization and loss of prestige. Toward the end of 1965, when France withdrew its garrison from the Congo and demobilized 1,000 or more Congolese soldiers, the number of malcontents who had had military training was appreciably enlarged. Probably it was no coincidence that the government announced in December that it had nipped an army plot in the bud and arrested many officers. One captain was murdered and his body dumped on the grounds of the municipal hospital.[62]

Early in the new year, the injury done to the morale of the armed forces by the successive purges of its officers was compounded by still another humiliation. This was the employment of Cuban military instructors for the civil defense corps commanded by Ange Diawara and the creation of a 300-man Cuban presidential guard. In 1963, the government had created the civil defense corps as a paramilitary body whose task was to defend the revolution against a possible Lari attempt to restore Youlou.[63] In contrast to the regular army, composed of professional soldiers charged with defending the country's frontiers, the civil defense corps was recruited from among MNR civilians on a rotating basis. The corpsmen were given political indoctrination along with military training, and after a few months, they were returned to civilian life and their places taken by other volunteers. Massamba's motive in upgrading the civil defense corps in the spring of 1966 may have been to neutralize the mounting influence of the JMNR militia, but the army saw it as still another competitive military force whose numerical strength now approximated its own.

The army's cumulative resentment came to a head when Noumazalaye, a few weeks after he became premier in April 1966, appointed political commissars to take charge of all the armed forces. He could hardly have done this without Massamba's consent, but it is not known whether the latter initiated it or allowed himself to be influenced by his new premier. One interesting if rather implausible theory[64] is that Massamba had concocted a clever compromise whereby he hoped to offset the power of both the JMNR militia and the civil defense corps by indirectly giving more authority to the army by way of the government's appointees. To win the consent of the MNR hardliners to his plan, he had to agree to the removal of some "dubiously revolutionary officers." But he failed to explain his strategy to the paratroop commander, Captain Ngouabi, who protested so strongly that he was transferred from Brazzaville to Pointe Noire. Since this was, in effect, a demotion of their popular fellow tribesman, 150 Kouyou soldiers mutinied in June 1966 when Massamba was out of the country. The mutineers imprisoned Major Mountsaka, whom they held responsible for Ngouabi's transfer, sacked the JMNR headquarters, and held Noumazalaye and his cabinet virtually prisoners in the sports stadium, where they were protected by the Cuban guard. A few days later, the mutineers returned to their barracks after scoring only minimal gains.

Noumazalaye, judging correctly that the uprising had no widespread support among the armed forces and was strictly limited in its objectives, made only minor concessions. Obviously the army, as in August 1963, neither was prepared to seize power nor intended to do so. Ngouabi was quietly reinstated in his former post and Mountsaka was not, but the government stood firm against meeting the mutineers' demands that the Cubans be dismissed[65] and the civil defense corps be disbanded.[66] Later, Massamba reassigned some of the Cuban instructors and repatriated others, but to him and even more to Noumazalaye, the main lesson taught by the mutiny was that the armed forces must be brought under closer control. This decision was reflected in the severe sentences imposed in July 1966 by the people's court on Major Mouzabakany and on Bernard Kolelas, accused of smuggling arms in from Kinshasa, and in August by the dismissal of the French military mission in Brazzaville. There was to be no relaxation in the MNR's determination to "democratize" the army, and, indeed, all its officers and troops were ordered to take a more active part in economic reconstruction and to undergo intensive political indoctrination. To all appearances these measures were effective, for the army remained submissive to the party's control for another year.

Among the most significant changes made in his government in January 1968 was Massamba's appointment of Lieutenant Augustin Poignet as secretary for defense. This was the first time that a moderate and a professional officer trained in France had occupied that post. Three months later, however, Massamba felt that he must appease the radicals, so he named Thaulay-Ganga, long a leader of the UJC and the CGAT, as the first political commissar for the Congo's armed forces. To what extent these two men neutralized each other in their influence on policy can only be surmised. In any case, the failure of the so-called "mercenaries' coup" in May,[67] whose aim was allegedly to revive dissension in the army, indicated that Massamba had the backing of its officers. Yet two months later, he lost that support when he belatedly tried strong-arm methods that included the arrest of Ngouabi.

This time the army went into action and by force of arms liberated Ngouabi, who, after a brief hesitation, decided to retain the power that he had almost inadvertently acquired. After further temporizing, Massamba accepted the inevitable and resigned, for he had no means of putting up further resistance. In the Congo, his departure caused barely a ripple, for frequent turnovers in leadership had become a standard feature of its political evolution. In any case, his peaceable withdrawal left face to face the only organizations that possessed arms. It took but three days of fighting to prove that the JMNR militia and the civil defense corps were no match for the regular army's might.

After their victory in early September 1968, the armed forces under Ngouabi's command seemed to be firmly in the saddle. As their commander-in-chief, Ngouabi promoted the three ranking officers—Raoul, Tsika, and Yhomby. Others, notably Mouzabakany, were appointed to important posts in the CNR or the government, or both, and three of them had formerly served in the French army. Within a month, however, there was clear evidence that all was not harmonious in the ranks of the military. Mouzabakany's demotion at the end of the year was followed by his arrest and by the flight to Kinshasa of Lieutenant Kikanga, both being charged with trying to restore Youlou to power.

Ngouabi's fear lest such dissension further contaminate the officer corps led to a big shakeup in military commands and to a reorganization of the whole country into six defense zones. Captain Sylvain Goma was named chief of staff and Ange Diawara, now a lieutenant in the reserve force, was appointed political commissar of the army as well as the CNR secretary for defense. Late in February 1969, Ngouabi announced that thenceforth he would commission as officers only "proven revolutionaries," and that the entire male population would be given military training. Six months later, the gendarmes were placed under the command of the army officer in whose defense zone their company was stationed.

The mystery surrounding Kolelas' attempted coup of November 9, 1969, has never been cleared up, but undoubtedly it involved some high-ranking officers, particularly in the gendarmerie, which strongly resented its recent subordination to the army. Four months later, this came to the surface when the gendarmes showed their sympathy for Kikanga's attempt to overthrow the government. At the same time, the decisive failure of Kikanga's raid also proved that there was no substantial support in the army for a "Youlist" restoration, for the great majority of its officers remained loyal to Ngouabi. Because no civilians were actively involved in this episode, it threw more light than before on the current temper and dissensions in the different branches of the armed forces.

Divisions along tribal lines certainly existed among the military, but other divisive influences were due to differences in age, training, ideology, and personality of the officers. The most tangible evidence of tribalism was the collaboration of the predominantly Lari gendarmerie with Kikanga. This fresh proof of the gendarmerie's disaffection for the government,[68] which also betrayed its ineffectuality as an armed force, led to its suppression as a separate unit and its replacement by a new people's militia. The disbanding of the gendarmerie as such and the arming of the militia, undertaken reluctantly by Ngouabi, were outstanding victories for the Maoist leaders, Diawara and Ndalla. Then another Marxist officer, Captain Sassou N'Guessou, who had warned Ngouabi about Kikanga's raid, was rewarded by being taken into the politburo, where he handled the PCT's relations with its mass organizations.

Among other military repercussions of the Kikanga raid was the temporary eclipse of Major Joachim Yhomby, unpopular with the Maoists allegedly because he was considered pro-Soviet. His removal at the time as head of the general staff was officially attributed to "corruption in the army," but on several previous occasions, he had been suspected of actively sympathizing with his fellow Lari. He was reinstated in that post, however, after heading a successful mission to Peking in October 1970. Six months later, the police were incorporated into the army, and Captain Kimbouala Nkaya was removed from the PCT politburo and relieved of his command of the tank division. Although the captain's involvement in Martin M'Berri's "plot" was never proved, it was implied by the charge against him of "yielding to subjectivism and tribal pressures."[69]

Of all the divisive factors in the armed forces, tribalism and conflicting personal loyalties were undoubtedly the strongest and ideological differences the weakest, but the rivalry between the branches of the professional army and between career officers and former leaders of the paramilitary corps also played a part. To some extent, the ascendancy of the political extremists in the armed forces and in the PCT was offset by the competition between Diawara and Ndalla for predominance in both. Moreover, neither man was popular with the more conservative—or, rather, the less radical—professional officers, who could be counted upon in an open confrontation to give their support to Ngouabi because he was one of them. Yet it was Ngouabi himself who had sapped their loyalty and contributed to their dissensions by successively integrating the JMNR militia, civil defense corps, gendarmerie, and police into the regular army, with the aim of subjecting the hot-headed leaders of the latter forces to the soothing influences of a single command and a more rigorous discipline.

When it came to competition between the different branches of the regular army, the working agreement that long subsisted between Ngouabi and Raoul seemed to obviate the traditional rivalry between the elite paratroops and the infantry, whose respective commanders they were. For some years, Raoul effaced himself before the more dynamic Ngouabi, whom he served without any apparent personal ambition. Then, in December 1971, Raoul was suddenly demoted from his high posts in the party and cabinet, for in the stormy PCT meeting that month, he spoke in favor of Ngouabi's opponents. Although Raoul played no conspicuous part in the February 1972 putsch, he was immediately arrested and sentenced to 10 years at hard labor. The following August, however, Raoul was the only prominent prisoner among the putsch détenus to be freed, probably because Ngouabi considered him to have been used by Diawara as a puppet to sow discord in the armed forces.

In the trial of strength between the PCT radicals and Ngouabi that culminated in the putsch of February 1972, the regular army as a whole and the tank corps in particular sided with Yhomby and Ngouabi, and it was mainly the militiamen who took up arms on behalf of their former leaders, Diawara and Matoumba-Mpolo. Subsequently, 22 officers—none of them above the rank of captain—were demoted, the militia was given a new commander, and the security services were placed directly under Ngouabi's orders. The putsch and its aftermath created a void in the military cadres and also indicated to Ngouabi what elements among them were the weakest links in his chain of command over the armed forces. Since then, the most puzzling and—for the present regime—inauspicious development was Yhomby's threat in mid-May 1972 to resign as head of the general staff and military governor of Brazzaville, for it is mainly upon his loyalty and that of the northern tribesmen that Ngouabi's tenure of power depends.

Notes

1. Brazzaville radio broadcast, August 16, 1963.

2. Bigemi, F., "La Commune au Congo-Brazzaville," *Revue Juridique et Politique*, April-May-June 1968.

3. Agence France Presse dispatch, April 30, 1965.

4. See p. 160.

5. *Croissance des Jeunes Nations*, October 1963.

6. See p. 198.

7. See p. 160.

8. Youlou's press conference, April 1, 1965, as reported by Léopoldville radio.

9. Issue of March 1, 1969.

10. *Courrier d'Afrique*, October 14, 1969.

11. *Lettre Africaine*, no. 220, January 5, 1969.

13. *Bulletin de l'A.C.I.*, February 11, 1969.

14. <u>Bulletin</u> <u>de</u> <u>l'Afrique</u> <u>Noire</u>, October 29, 1969.

15. Agence France Presse dispatch, March 24, 1971.

16. In May 1972, Youlou's death had so few apparent repercussions in the Lari community that the government permitted his body to be brought from Spain to the Congo for burial.

17. Gérard Althabe, who made a study of the Lari and Mbochi residents of Brazzaville, found that they had only the vaguest knowledge of even the principal traditions of their respective tribes. See his <u>Etude</u> <u>du</u> <u>Chomage</u> <u>à</u> <u>Brazzaville</u> <u>en</u> <u>1957</u>, ORSTOM, <u>Cahiers</u> <u>de</u> <u>Sciences</u> <u>Humaines</u>, vol. 1, no. 2, 1963.

18. The first wage zone comprised workers in the towns of Brazzaville, Pointe Noire, and Dolisie, and the second those in the rest of the country.

19. In September 1966, the minister of justice reported that officials in the customs service had embezzled 18.3 million CFA francs, possibly in retaliation for the imposition that year of a withholding tax on their salaries. See also <u>Afrique</u> <u>Nouvelle</u>, July 6, 1966; <u>Marchés</u> <u>Tropicaux</u>, September 24, 1966.

20. <u>Marchés</u> <u>Tropicaux</u>, January 7, 1967.

21. <u>Afrique</u> <u>Nouvelle</u>, January 6, 1965.

22. <u>Marchés</u> <u>Tropicaux</u>, September 19, 1964.

23. <u>Ibid</u>., November 26, 1964.

24. See pp. 52-53, 83-85, 218.

25. <u>Afrique</u> <u>Nouvelle</u>, April 26, 1967.

26. Agence France Presse dispatch, August 8, 1968.

27. <u>West</u> <u>Africa</u>, November 14, 1970.

28. <u>Marchés</u> <u>Tropicaux</u>, April 19, 1969.

29. <u>Dossier</u> <u>d'Information</u>, <u>op</u>. <u>cit</u>., p. 18.

30. <u>Marchés</u> <u>Tropicaux</u>, August 8, 1970.

31. As of August 16, 1968, the hourly guaranteed wage for workers in the agricultural sector ranged between 31.7 and 39.7 CFA francs, and that for workers in the other sectors between 36.7 and 45.8 CFA francs.

32. <u>West</u> <u>Africa</u>, April 5, 1969.

33. <u>Marchés</u> <u>Tropicaux</u>, November 1, 1969.

34. <u>West</u> <u>Africa</u>, June 11, 1971.

35. Wagret, J.-D., <u>Histoire</u> <u>et</u> <u>Sociologie</u> <u>Politiques</u> <u>de</u> <u>la</u> <u>République</u> <u>du</u> <u>Congo-Brazzaville</u>, Paris, 1963, p. 215. See also G. Althabe, <u>op</u>. <u>cit</u>.

36. <u>L'Observateur</u> <u>du</u> <u>Moyen-Orient</u> <u>et</u> <u>de</u> <u>l'Afrique</u>, September 9, 1963.

37. <u>Marchés</u> <u>Tropicaux</u>, November 16, 1963.

38. See pp. 158, 191-192.

39. The Makala camp, located in the former CATC headquarters at Djoué, near Brazzaville, was both a school and a prison. In the former capacity, it gave JMNR trainees political indoctrination in the mornings and military instruction in the afternoons. As a prison, it served to discipline recalcitrant JMNR members. In an interview printed in Le Figaro, May 6, 1965, Ndalla admitted that some abuses had been committed by the JMNR, for which about 30 youths were interned at Makala, but he claimed that these were "exceptional cases which have been blown up by our enemies so as to discredit our movement." He also stated that arms had been given only to members over fifteen years of age, while younger trainees were permitted simply to carry stones as weapons (mitraillette populaire) as a reward for their services in helping to overthrow Youlou.

40. Le Monde, July 31, 1965.

41. The Collège des Pères at Brazzaville was renamed Collège Patrice Lumumba and placed under a Congolese principal. At this time, there were so few Congolese qualified to teach in the secondary schools that some French military conscripts were employed to staff them and a number of the colleges were suppressed.

42. This publication was later renamed La Semaine Africaine, and then La Semaine.

43. Afrique Nouvelle, October 6, 1965.

44. Marchés Tropicaux, December 3, 1966.

45. Ibid., September 25, 1965.

46. Afrique Nouvelle, July 13, 1966.

47. Le Figaro, September 6, 1968.

48. Afrique Express, September 8, 1968.

49. Etumba, April 18, 1970.

50. House, A. H., "Brazzaville, Revolution or Rhetoric?" Africa Report, April 1971.

51. Marchés Tropicaux, October 26, 1968.

52. Revue Française d'Etudes Politiques Africaines, April 1970.

53. Jeune Afrique, March 10, 1970.

54. Marchés Tropicaux, May 2, 1970.

55. Created in 1961, this center was an institution of higher learning for all the former territories of FEA. It was staffed by French professors, modeled after a French university, and almost wholly financed by the French treasury. As of 1970, it had a student body of 650, of whom the majority were Congolese.

56. West Africa, September 5, 1970.

57. Marchés Tropicaux, February 13, 1971.

58. <u>Ibid</u>., June 19, 1971. Because of the publicity given to this rally, which Ngouabi tried to cover up, the local office of the Agence France Presse was closed down.

59. In 1966, the Association of Congolese Students in France had given office space to the FEANF, which had refused to recognize the new military regime in Ghana and, consequently, was forced to evacuate the villa in Paris which had been given to the FEANF by Nkrumah.

60. Issue of August 22, 1963.

61. <u>France-Eurafrique</u>, November 1963.

62. <u>The New York Times</u>, June 29, 1966.

63. <u>Le Figaro</u>, August 10-11, 1968.

64. <u>France-Eurafrique</u>, October 1968.

65. Though the Cubans were gradually phased out, there were still enough left in Brazzaville for the Congolese officers to decide to stay in their barracks rather than participate in the August 1966 independence celebrations, lest in their absence the Cubans try to take over. See <u>Révolution Africaine</u>, August 1966.

66. The civil defense corps was unpopular not only with the army and gendarmerie but also the general public because of its members' indiscipline and violence. In November 1966, when a very popular soccer player was killed by corpsmen in the Brazzaville stadium, 200 of the spectators marched to Massamba's residence to protest. Even the corps commander, Diawara, admitted that they were a "disorganized horde" and urged that cadres be assigned to train them. See Agence France Presse dispatches, November 15, 1966; June 20, 1967.

67. See pp. 165-166.

68. In July 1966, Captain Norbert Tsika was arrested and charged with embezzling more than one million CFA francs. He was replaced as head of the gendarmerie by Captain Alphonse Mabiala, who was himself soon dismissed.

69. <u>Marchés Tropicaux</u>, April 17, 1971.

CHAPTER 23

CONCLUSION

It is difficult for Western observers and especially for Americans, who
are personae non gratae in Congo-Brazzaville, to understand what has been
happening in that country since 1963. Events there have followed a complex
and confusing course, and their interpretation has not been facilitated by
the frequent announcements of plots and coups d'état, by changes in the republic's name, institutions, and leadership at all levels, and by the army's
entry into the political arena. In the economic domain, reliable statistics,
especially concerning trade, are lacking or incomplete, and in any case, they
are difficult to extricate from those of the UDEAC as a whole. So the foreign student of contemporary Congolese history is reduced to depending on
official communiqués, radio broadcasts, press reports, and occasional personal contacts to discern the trends underlying the apparent contradictions
and inconsistencies in the Congo's foreign and domestic policies.

Nevertheless, beyond this bewildering kaleidoscope, there appear to be
certain dominant tendencies and "constants." These have persisted or developed since the Congo became independent, despite the obvious changes in the
government's orientation, style, and personnel. The outstanding trend is
that of increasing radicalism, while the principal "constants" are to be
found in the Congo's tribal pattern, geographical location, and economic situation. The interaction of an amorphous radical ideology with such permanent
phenomena accounts for many of the apparent or real contradictions in the
country's foreign relations and internal evolution.

Congo-Brazzaville is widely regarded as the most radicalized country in
francophone Black Africa. Certainly it is the only nation in the whole continent to call itself a people's republic, adopt a red flag, and order its
workers to wear Mao-style uniforms. However, knowledgeable Western observers
concur in considering these to be more the trappings than the reality of a
Marxist state. Even to those personally unable to delve below the surface,
there is an obvious disparity between the government's words and its deeds
and between the semiofficial expressions of hostility toward the capitalist
world and the friendly attitude of the Congolese toward the Westerners in
their midst.[1] Similarly, as regards the economy in a self-styled people's
republic, there is cause for surprise in the existence of a prosperous private sector side by side with stagnant or deficitary state enterprises. In
the judicial domain, the revolutionary court has frequently handed down death
sentences for enemies of the regime, but so far as is known, none has ever
been carried out. Finally, it is noteworthy that none of the French names
given to the country's main cities has ever been Congolized, despite repeated
verbal attacks on France's cultural imperialism.

The Congo's radical leaders are fully conscious of, and regretful about,
these inconsistencies, but they differ as to their cause and cure. The

232

editorialist of Etumba,[2] writing in the form of an autocritique, bewailed the Congo's budgetary expenditures on the bureaucracy and the army, which he blamed for the country's failure to achieve the socioeconomic structure of a socialist state. Both Massamba and Ngouabi, on the other hand, have taken a long-term view. To some Togolese visitors to Brazzaville who expressed astonishment at finding that the application of scientific socialism had wrought no visible changes in that city, Ngouabi admitted that the Congo had made little progress and that much more time was needed to bring about the desired transformation.[3] Yet all the Congo's present leaders insist that their country will eventually work out its own course, and they are highly sensitive to the implication that their government's policy is modeled on that of any foreign state. Even so dedicated a communist as Ndalla told a Western journalist that "the MNR is not of Marxist origin but is a nationalist movement that is simply seeking an African solution for its problems."[4]

The much-publicized influence of the Chinese People's Republic on Congo-Brazzaville and of the Congolese Maoists on the present regime may well be exaggerated. Nevertheless, there is no doubt that a very large segment of the indigenous military and civilian elites have been won over to Marxism, even if they do not fully understand its doctrines and differ sharply as to how and when to apply to their country the principles of Marxism-Leninism.

The question naturally arises as to why the Congolese in general and the youth of Brazzaville in particular should be so susceptible to the articulation of revolutionary doctrines. Poverty is not the explanation, for on the whole, the Congolese are relatively prosperous among the peoples of Black Africa, and the most miserable component of the population are the peasants, who seem untouched by Marxist concepts. Nor can the lack of educational facilities be held accountable, since the Congo has one of the most-developed school systems of the whole continent. Certainly the country's underdevelopment and its long subjection to a Western capitalistic power have played a part in impelling the Congolese to seek a radical solution for their emancipation. Yet some other newly independent African nations, such as Gabon, which share their colonial past, now have conservative governments, whereas others, like Guinea, which also follows the Marxist path, have not gone along it as far and as fast as the Congo. Obviously there is no single answer to the Congolese phenomenon, and the explanation seems to lie in an unusual concatenation of circumstances.

In chronological order, one might first consider the repercussions of the Congo Basin Treaty of 1885, which opened all the Moyen-Congo to disruptive external influences that affected the other FEA territories to nothing like the same degree. The division of the dynamic Bakongo tribe among three European colonial powers was paralleled by that of the enterprising Fang in Gabon, Cameroun, and Equatorial Guinea; but, subsequently, the Fang were not subjected to religiopolitical penetration to such an extent as were the Bakongo. From the Belgian Congo emanated messianic cults that were disguised movements of popular protest. They took deeper root among the Lari, the Bakongo subtribe that lived on the French side of the Congo River, because they were nearer their source of inspiration than were the Fang and even the Vili of southwestern Congo. Furthermore, the Lari found in André Matsoua a folk-hero who had no counterpart in the other two tribes. The cult which the Lari devoted to Matsoua had xenophobic and anarchistic characteristics that took the form of passive resistance to the French administration. The astute Fulbert Youlou utilized this cult among his fellow tribesmen to promote his own political career, but when he came to power, he had to use physical force to quell the minority of Matsouanists who refused to cooperate with his government, just as they had with the French administration.

In Youlou's struggle with the hard-core Matsouanists, he was aided at the outset by the UJC, which, along with the CGAT, had been promoted by the French communist party in the Moyen-Congo after World War II. The great majority of the members of those two organizations were Lari, who regarded the intransigent Matsouanists as reactionaries and therefore expendable. The UJC's cooperation with Youlou in his confrontation with the dissident Matsouanists was as violent as the Matsouanists' resistance was fanatical, and this encounter highlighted a Lari trait that was to influence profoundly the Congo's evolution after independence—the tribe's messianic compulsion. This trait showed itself in Youlou's self-imposed mission to conciliate all the Belgian Congolese leaders and to establish himself as leader of a republic composed of all the Bakongo peoples. It was also manifest in the Marxist crusade preached by young UJC leaders to indoctrinate their youthful relatives in Léopoldville.

Obviously these two "missions" were incompatible, and the open conflict that soon developed between Youlou and the UJC rapidly accentuated and broadened their points of difference. As Youlou's government became more conservative, pro-French, and pro-Tshombe, his young Marxist fellow Lari became correspondingly anti-Western, anticapitalist, and zealous in their support of Lumumba. The transfer of the territorial capital from Pointe Noire to Brazzaville in 1958 had brought the seat of government to the town that was the stronghold of the UJC and the CGAT and which had the largest concentration of unemployed men. Inevitably it was the UJC, the trade unions, and the jobless youths of Brazzaville that banded together to oust Youlou and to replace him with Massamba.

Massamba was a schoolteacher with limited government experience and without any personal following, and despite his socialist convictions, he fared no better at the hands of the radicals than did Youlou. Yet if any developments in Congo-Brazzaville during the postindependence decade could be properly termed revolutionary, they were due to the policy pursued by Massamba during his five years in power. Paradoxically enough, it was his establishing diplomatic relations with the communist countries and initiating the state's control over the economy that whetted the appetites of the young Marxists, who demanded a faster and more uncompromising application of scientific socialism. In exerting such pressure, they were inadvertently aided by the vain efforts made to overthrow Massamba by the tradition-bound Lari, because the Lari were no longer the tribe favored by the government. Step by step, Massamba forfeited or lost the support of the Catholic unions and the army—in brief, of all those who might have helped him withstand the rising tide of radicalism. When he tried to reverse the trend, it was too late, for he did not have the time to carry out his development plan, which might have improved the economy and thus endeared him to the peasantry and the unemployed. The remaining vestiges of his power were destroyed by his last-minute recourse to forceful methods and his alienation of the armed forces.

For most of the same reasons, the erosion of Ngouabi's authority has been strikingly similar to that of Massamba, although he started from a stronger power base and ideologically had more in common with the extreme Marxists. Actually, Ngouabi's stronger predilection for Marxism has made him more vulnerable than Massamba to pressure from the radicals, whose determination to dominate the government has been reinforced by the ease with which they overturned the two previous regimes. In policy-making, Ngouabi has been no innovator; he has followed the lines laid down by his predecessor in foreign as well as domestic affairs, albeit more effectively. Like Massamba, Ngouabi came to believe that his conservative adversaries were taking advantage of his early liberalism to undermine his authority, but he moved sooner and more forcefully against them.

Even more adroitly than Massamba, Ngouabi has achieved in his foreign policy a balance of competing influences between the great and small communist nations, the eastern and western blocs, and the revolutionary and moderate African states. China, North Korea, and North Vietnam, as well as the Iron Curtain countries, continue to invest funds and send technicians and advisers, and to flood the Congo with Marxist propaganda. The net effect of their efforts on domestic policy has been to strengthen the hand of the extremist faction among the Congolese radicals. This accentuation of the leftist orientation of the Congo's last two governments has led to a rapid and inefficient burgeoning of the state's control over the economy, a growth in the budgetary deficits, and an ever greater dependence on foreign aid. There is no likelihood, however, that a further worsening in its financial plight will cause the Congo to pursue a more conservative economic policy.

The Congo's relations with France, West Germany, and the UDEAC remain sufficiently good for it to continue receiving substantial benefits from them despite the Congolese radicals' persistent and harsh criticism of their conservative governments. These benefits take the form of investments and technical aid and also of markets for the Congo's exports. With regard to Zaïre (the former Congo-Kinshasa), there have been the same alternations as before in their love-hate relationship, the periods of tension predominating because of Mobutu's growing reliance on American support and his continuing sponsorship of dissident activities against the Brazzaville regime. Perhaps his most heinous sins in the latter's eyes are to have so brilliantly promoted his country's economic development and to have succeeded to some extent in disrupting the UDEAC, which Congo-Brazzaville had long dominated and on whose markets its processing industries depend.

In Ngouabi's overall policy, there has been a larger admixture of ideology than in that of Massamba, but the salient features of both have been their basic similarity and continuity. This constancy derives from the Congo's geographic location, natural resources, and urban concentration. Taken together, these factors have made the Congo not only exceptionally permeable to alien influences but also dependent on foreign aid, industry, and the transit trade. (To the Congo's geographical location was due its stellar role in the former FEA, notably the development of its southern transport facilities. In turn, it is those very assets which have been the main cause of the Congo's consistently poor relations with its resentful northern neighbors.) Had Congo-Brazzaville not been so strategically located in central Africa, its resources would never have attracted such massive foreign investments as they have, nor could it have served as a base for revolutionary activities in Kinshasa, Cameroun, Angola, and Cabinda. It has been a source of some bitterness—as well as benefit—for the Congolese to realize that they have been courted by foreign powers for reasons other than their <u>beaux</u> <u>yeux</u> and their own merits.

The concentration of the Congo's population in its southern towns, which has favored the country's industrialization, can also be largely attributed to natural phenomena. Dense vegetation and prolonged inundations have hampered the development of agriculture and trade in the northern half of the country. Such unpropitious physical conditions, combined with the location of the Congo's major mineral deposits and accessible forests in the south, have impelled the Mbochi to desert their countryside and migrate to the towns along the southern railroad. In the Congo's present stage of underdevelopment, this influx has been more than its economy could absorb, and has created an unemployment problem of huge dimensions. Brazzaville's overpopulation has made competition for the few available jobs especially acute, and this has aggravated the traditional antagonism between the Mbochi and Lari, who live there side by side without intermingling. To a lesser degree, Pointe Noire is subject to similar tribal tensions.

Ngouabi has certainly made a greater effort than his predecessors to redress the country's economic imbalance, curtail the rural exodus, and end the north's isolation by improving the means of communication. But largely because he is a northerner, this has laid him open to the charge of tribal and regional favoritism by the Lari. They feel that their superior education and abilities entitle them to political preeminence, and they are not reconciled to its loss, though they have maintained their privileged position in the bureaucracy and no longer dare to offer overt resistance to the government. As yet, the Congo has produced no truly national leader who could inspire in his compatriots a unifying sense of nationhood. Indeed, each of its three postindependence governments has inadvertently introduced or, in effect, reinforced the divisive influences of tribalism and regionalism.

Since Youlou's downfall, tribal and regional forces have no longer paraded as political parties but have assumed varied and sometimes strange forms. Generally speaking, ideological labels provide no clue to the ethnic and geographical divisions in the population because all politically conscious Congolese call themselves socialists or Marxists. Nevertheless, the recent trials of M'Berri and Captain N'Kaya showed that some of those accused of plotting against the government have been motivated, or have hoped to profit, by tribal and regional loyalties. One of the most bizarre evidences of the strength of contemporary tribalism has been the resurgence of animism, sometimes called the "watchdog of African traditions." This has occurred not only in the backward north but also in the more sophisticated south. In his study of Brazzaville's educated youth in 1957,[5] Althabe found that only 18 percent of those he polled said they did not believe in fetishism, whereas the balance were more or less convinced of its efficacy and consulted <u>féticheurs</u> as often as their means permitted to help them solve problems ranging from jobs to love affairs. More recently, in January 1971, six aged Mbochi <u>féticheurs</u> were given long prison sentences for causing the "disappearance" of more than 300 persons within the span of three years. That same month a government spokesman sharply reprimanded Brazzaville's soccer team for burying fetishes under the stadium just before a match.

These quasireligious manifestations may be a consequence of the government's liquidation of the conservative Catholic organizations, just as the concurrent upsurge of tribalism in the armed forces has been one result of their incorporation of the youth militias, gendarmerie, and police. Each time Massamba and Ngouabi thought that they were bringing such dissident groups under their control, they have found themselves dealing with a hydra-headed monster. Covert struggles for tribal influence or personal power are a greater threat to the stability of the present government and the maintenance of order than is open armed aggression. They are particularly insidious for Ngouabi, who probably can count on the army's loyalty in the event of an uprising or a commando raid but not when the opposition to him as a northerner saps his authority among its officers. Already the political significance of the military takeover in August 1968 has been largely dissipated by rifts in the ranks of the armed forces, which have paralyzed their capacity for joint action and have undermined their morale and prestige.

No Congolese government can hope to be even relatively secure unless it wins the support of a majority of the population, and this depends on its ability to improve their well-being and thus mitigate tribal and regional inequities. Any marked improvement of the condition of the peasantry and of the urban proletariat requires a better utilization of foreign investments than yet has been made for the promotion of agriculture and industry. Although China continues to pour funds into the Congo, as does France, and such investments have been politically and not economically motivated, this flow may not continue indefinitely. Conditions in central Africa may change to such a degree that Congo-Brazzaville will lose its present value in the eyes of its current benefactors. The fact that the U.S.S.R. is no longer providing as much aid as before to the Congo's government may be due in part to the Soviets' disillusionment with the unsatisfactory returns on their past largesse.

Given the Congo government's chronic instability and its determination to nationalize the economy, it is highly improbable that any Western industrial state will care to assume the burden of making such long-term massive and dubiously effective investments as would be needed to revive the Congolese peasants' zeal for farming and provide enough jobs to absorb even a majority of the urban unemployed. If present trends are maintained, private foreign capitalists will probably continue to put their money into large-scale, remunerative enterprises such as the Hollé potash and the petroleum companies. Ironically enough, this would strengthen the capitalist sector of the Congo's economy and, in reaction, intensify the radicalism of the party leaders. Furthermore, since this would promote development of the Pointe Noire region and might even revive the moribund Kouilou dam project, it could give the Vili tribe for the first time an ascendancy that would diminish the role that has been played in the Congo's evolution by Brazzaville and its Lari inhabitants.

Such prospects might conceivably impel the left-wing opponents of Ngouabi's pragmatic policy to make still another move to take over the government. In such a contingency, there is no certainty as to how the army would react. Even though the Congo is likely to undergo one or more coups d'état, whatever leaders come to power must face the same disruptive forces as have Massamba and Ngouabi. And they will also have to make many of the same compromises between their principles and these immediate realities which are determined by phenomena beyond their control.

Notes

1. A white Rhodesian visitor to Brazzaville in 1964 was astonished by the cordial welcome he received there from the Congolese nationals. See *Rhodesian Herald*, November 27, 1964.

2. Issue of December 7, 1967.

3. *Togo-Presse*, June 10, 1969.

4. *Le Figaro*, May 6, 1965.

5. Althabe, G., *Etude du Chomage à Brazzaville en 1957*, op. cit. The practice of fetishism and the occult sciences was the basis of the charges made against Bouiti and Assemekang when they were dropped from the cabinet in December 1971.

6. *Marchés Tropicaux*, January 30, February 6, 1971.

BIOGRAPHICAL APPENDIX

ANGOR, Léon: Born July 13, 1928, at Brazzaville, an accountant and labor
organizer. In January 1964, he was elected president of the legislature and
in March 1965, was reelected to that post. He headed a parliamentary mission
to Moscow and North Korea in October 1964. Defeated by A. G. Mouyabi when
he ran for the third time for the presidency of the legislature in April
1966, he was briefly held prisoner the following August by the JMNR, whose
spokesman he had been earlier in his career. Appointed by Ngouabi to the CNR
in August 1968, he was removed from that body two months later. In November
1969, he was named ambassador to the UAR.

d'ARBOUSSIER, Gabriel: A Franco-African mulatto born January 14, 1908, in
Soudan. Legally adopted by his father, who was governor of the territory, he
was a French citizen and educated in New Caledonia and France as a lawyer.
He entered the overseas service, and his administrative and political career
extended through both African Federations. He was elected from Moyen-Congo
and Gabon to the French constituent assemblies, and at various times represented Niger, Upper Volta, and Senegal in elected bodies in France and Africa.
Leader of the left-wing faction of the RDA since 1946, he broke with
Houphouët-Boigny in 1950 but was reconciled with him five years later. He
joined the Union des Populations Sénégalaises and rose rapidly in the Senegal
government, serving as minister of justice, 1960-62; ambassador to France,
1962-64; and ambassador to Bonn, Vienna, and Berne since 1968. For some
years, he has combined these duties with various assignments from the United
Nations, and has attended important international meetings.

ASSEMEKANG, Charles: Graduate of the Institut des Hautes Etudes d'Outre-Mer
and a doctor of laws. He was a magistrate in the Congo before becoming
Ngouabi's minister of foreign affairs in June 1969. He held that post until
appointed president of the supreme court in January 1970. In December 1971,
he was dismissed from the PCT on the charge of practicing occult sciences.

ATONDI-MONMONDJO, Lécas: Editor-in-chief of the MNR party weekly, Etumba,
when, in April 1970, he became a member of the PCT central committee. Five
months later, he was named head of the newly created political commissariat
for rural activities. In early 1972, he was arrested and imprisoned for
alleged participation in the putsch of February 22. His death sentence was
commuted to life imprisonment the following month.

AUBAME, Jean-Hilaire: A Gabonese Fang, born at Libreville, November 10, 1912.
A devout Catholic and a relatively high-ranking administrator, he was among
the few Gabonese officials who joined the Free French in 1940. Three years
later, he became an aide to Governor-general Eboué, and in 1944, president
of the municipal council of Poto-Poto. Returning to Gabon after World War II,
he founded the Union Démocratique et Sociale Gabonaise, and was elected to the

239

French National Assembly from 1946 to 1958. In interterritorial politics, he was first a member of the IOM and later of the PRA, and in 1958 he advocated forming a "state of equatorial Africa." In local politics, he regularly represented the Woleu N'Tem area in the territorial assembly, and devised a scheme for regrouping Fang villages. After Gabon became independent, he was reconciled with his perennial adversary, Léon Mba, joining his government as foreign minister in 1960. Named president of the supreme court in 1963, he was imprisoned on charges of participating in the abortive military plot against Mba in February 1964, and remained a prisoner until freed in August 1972.

BABACKAS, Edouard Ebouka: Born July 13, 1933, at Mossaka, he received his primary schooling from the Catholic mission at Dolisie and Brazzaville, and his law degree from the University of Nancy in 1960. From there he went to Paris to study at the Ecole des Douanes. In 1962, he returned to Brazzaville as chief inspector of the customs service. He had held no political office before becoming minister of transport and mines in Massamba's provisional government of August 1963. Four months later, Lissouba awarded him the finance portfolio, a post he held for five years. In September 1968, the military government named him minister-delegate to the presidency, but the next month, he became ambassador to France. He remained there until June 1970, when he was made head of the Agence Transcongolaise des Communications.

BANTHOUD, Paul: In April 1966, he succeeded Idrissa Diallo as president of the CSC. A year later, he accepted an invitation to study labor organization in the U.S.S.R., and upon his return, urged that foreign banks and enterprises in the Congo be nationalized. On December 20, 1967, he was dismissed as head of the CSC, having been charged with mismanagement of its funds; four months later, he played an active part in the strikes at Brazzaville. He participated in the revolt against the military authorities at the Biafra camp and on August 31, 1968, was arrested for incitement to revolt. Although sentenced to two years in prison, he was amnestied in May 1969.

BARBE, Raymond: As chairman of the communist group in the French Union Assembly, he was a principal organizer of the RDA and of the CGT unions in French Black Africa after World War II.

BAYROU, Maurice: Born March 2, 1905, in France. In 1932, he went to FEA as a veterinary surgeon, and became head of that federation's animal husbandry service. During World War II, he fought with distinction at Bir Hakeim as an officer in General Leclerc's army. He joined the RPF and was elected by the first college to the French Union Assembly for three successive terms, and was secretary of state for Overseas France in 1955. A strong conservative, he opposed the municipal reform bill of that year and also the institution of the single-college system in 1956.

BAZINGA, Apollinaire: Born January 2, 1924, at Impfondo. After attending a Catholic mission primary school, he entered the public health service as a pharmacist in 1952. From that year until 1959, he represented Likouala in the territorial assembly, and became vice-president of the FEA Grand Council from 1957 to 1959. In the latter year, Youlou named him minister without portfolio, and in 1960, made him head of the information service, and he took an active part in the negotiations for construction of the Kouilou dam. In 1965, Massamba appointed him ambassador to Peking, and he held that post briefly under Ngouabi. In January 1970, he succeeded Babackas as ambassador to France.

BIAYOULA, Fulgence: A Bassoundi, born at Poto-Poto October 30, 1936. He was trained as a carpenter at the Brazzaville Ecole de Formation Profession-nelle Rapide, and became involved in CATC trade unionism. In 1958, he was a founder of an interprofessional school for manual workers, whose bulletin, Le Travailleur Africain, he edited. Persuaded by Pongault to resume his CATC activities, he took an outstanding part in the overthrow of Youlou. As president of the CATC, he increasingly opposed the MNR's politicization of the labor movement, and in 1965, he was imprisoned after vainly trying to escape with the aid of French missionaries.

BICOUMAT, Germain: A Vili, born in the Pointe Noire region April 20, 1906. After primary school, he became an accountant for the Congo-Ocean railroad in 1940, and rose to be head of the public works service at Brazzaville, where he became a municipal councilor in 1958. He was a charter member of the PPC and leader of its left-wing faction. From 1960 to 1962, he was a minister in Youlou's government, in charge of the Office du Kouilou and the Congo's operations in the ATEC. In Massamba's first government, he was min-ister of the interior and information, and was reappointed very briefly to those posts when the military leaders took over. In April 1966, he was named ambassador to East Germany.

BINDI, Michel: A Lari, he was head of the security police throughout most of Massamba's administration. In the fall of 1963, he actively aided the enemies of Premier Adoula when they fled from Kinshasa to Brazzaville. Highly unpopular because of his harsh measures, he was kidnapped by the army mutineers in June 1966, but in January 1968, Massamba appointed him minister of the interior. He joined the armed opposition to Ngouabi's regime late in August 1968, but succeeded in escaping arrest when the Biafra camp surren-dered. Captured in November 1968, he was sentenced to 10 years in prison on charges of smuggling firearms into the Congo.

BIYOUDI, Jean: Born September 3, 1925, in Boko district, where he became a teacher in the Catholic mission school. A member of the PPC until he joined the UDDIA in 1956, when he became a deputy mayor of Brazzaville. The next year, he was elected to represent that city in the assembly. As an official of the CATC teachers union, he was sent to Orléans for training in labor or-ganization. Youlou named him secretary of state for youth in December 1958.

BOGANDA, Barthélemy: Born April 4, 1910, at Bobangui, Oubangui-Chari. He was trained at the theological seminary at Yaoundé, Cameroun, and ordained a priest in 1935. Initially encouraged by the church to enter politics, he was later defrocked for marrying his French secretary, but eventually he made his peace with the local Catholic hierarchy. From 1946 to 1958, he was Oubangui-Chari's deputy in the French National Assembly, where he joined first the MRP and then the Indépendants Paysans, but his main energies were devoted to founding and building up his territorial party, the MESAN. Elected to the Oubangui assembly from Lobaye, beginning in 1952, he also served two terms as president of the FEA Grand Council. On March 30, 1959, he died in an accident.

BOMBOKO, Justin-Marie: Born in 1928 in Equateur province, Belgian Congo. He received a master's degree in political science from the Université Libre of Brussels, and entered the Congolese administration as a clerk. He attended the congress of the Union Congolaise in October 1959 as an observer. After independence, he served as foreign minister in successive governments until he was dismissed by Mobutu in 1970 and imprisoned the following year.

BONGHO-NOUARRA, Stéphane: Born in 1937 at Ouesso. He was employed as an engineer in the public works service at Brazzaville. In 1966, when he was chairman of the Chambre Economique du Congo-Brazzaville and also of the Union des Jeunes Chambres d'Expression Française, Massamba appointed him president of the Economic and Social Council. A close friend of Ngouabi, he was named secretary of state, then minister of public works, but in September 1969, he returned to his engineering post in the administration. Arrested in August 1970, on charges of antigovernment plotting, he was sentenced to 10 years in prison for "promoting a movement harmful to the security of the state." On being freed in 1971, he went to live in Paris.

BOUITI, Dr. Jacques: Born December 14, 1922. He was a surgeon practicing in Brazzaville when named minister of health in January 1968. He retained that post until March 1970, when he was removed from the CNR's central committee. Ngouabi sent him, in September 1968, to explain the military take-over to the presidents of Tchad and the Central African Republic, and in November 1969, he accompanied Raoul on a mission to Peking. He was dismissed from the PCT in December 1971 on the charge of practicing occult sciences.

BOUKAMBOU, Julien: A Bassoundi, born April 17, 1917, at Mindouli. After attending a Catholic mission primary school, he became a monitor in that system at Brazzaville (1935-50). A former left-wing militant in the PPC, he was defeated in the Brazzaville municipal elections of 1956. After being dismissed from his job with Air France in 1952 for disseminating communist propaganda, he was unemployed until he became general secretary for the CGAT unions. In that capacity, he was sent by the French communist party to France and the Iron Curtain countries for training. On his return to the Congo, his passport was taken away, and in 1960, he was arrested by Youlou's police. In 1964, when he went to Peking, he held the posts of first vice-president of the Congolese legislature and administrative secretary of the MNR politburo. Ngouabi named him a member of the CNR in August 1968. From March 1970 to August 1971, he served as his ambassador to the U.S.S.R.

BRU, Henri: A Metropolitan Frenchman, he was a member of the UMC and president of the Syndicat Agricole du Congo when named minister for economic affairs in Youlou's government council in December 1958. Soon he added to this post the duties of technical adviser to the ministry of agriculture, but was dropped from the cabinet in June 1959. He was killed in an airplane accident in June 1967.

COMBO-MATSIONA, Bernard: An agronomic engineer, who became president of the UJSC in 1970. In the purge of the PCT in December 1971, he was eliminated from its central committee, and two months later, he was sentenced to death for alleged participation in the putsch of February 22. The next month his sentence was commuted to life imprisonment.

COMPIGNY, Dr. Jean-Marie: A Metropolitan Frenchman, he was practicing medicine in the Kouilou region when elected to represent that area in the territorial assembly in 1952. In the decade preceding independence, he served two terms in the Conseil de la République, where he joined the Republican Socialist Party. He was author of an article on the economic potential of the Kouilou published in Marchés Tropicaux, on April 16, 1952.

COULIBALY, Daniel Ouezzin: A Bobo, born in 1909 in Dédougou cercle, Upper Volta. After graduating from the Ponty Normal School, he became a teacher at Ougadougou and later at Gorée in Senegal. It was in Ivory Coast that his political career began in 1947, when he was elected to its assembly from Banfora on the RDA ticket. Twice elected to the French National Assembly, from 1946 to 1951 and from 1956 until his death in September 1958, he was Houphouët-Boigny's chief trouble-shooter and roving ambassador. Houphouët-Boigny sent him in 1956 to revive the RDA branch in Upper Volta, and he became vice-president of that territory's first government council. His death on the eve of the September 1958 referendum was a blow to the RDA and to the political unity of Upper Volta.

DACKO, David: Born March 24, 1930, in the Lobaye region of Oubangui-Chari, he was the son of a Baya night watchman. He attended secondary schools in Bambéri and Brazzaville, taught school in Moyen-Congo, and was appointed principal of a primary school in Bangui. There he became active in the socialist teachers' union, but he did not enter politics until he joined the MESAN and was elected to the territorial assembly from Ombella M'Poko in 1957. Soon he became a close collaborator of his uncle, Boganda, who named him, successively, minister of agriculture, of civil service, and of the interior. Against considerable opposition, he succeeded Boganda in 1959 as premier and as president of the MESAN. In January 1966, he was overthrown by Colonel Jean Bokassa, who imprisoned him in a fort near Bangui.

DADET, Emmanuel: Born in Impfondo. He became a French citizen, rose to being a prefect in the administration, and wrote a novel set in FEA, entitled Congolila, which was published in 1950. He resigned from the PPC in 1949, and was badly defeated when he sought reelection to the French Union Assembly in 1953. Two years later, he founded the short-lived Front Démocratique Congolais, and then in 1956, joined the UDDIA. He was rewarded by being named to its executive committee and to various ministerial posts, 1958-60, and ambassador to the United States in 1961.

DARLAN, Antoine: Born June 6, 1915, at Kouanga, Oubangui-Chari, where he received a primary education. He was a clerk in the administration when first elected to the territorial assembly in 1947, and with his brother, Georges, headed the local branch of the RDA, the Union Oubanguienne. Antoine was elected to the French Union Assembly (1947-58), to the FEA Grand Council (1957-59), and to Bangui's municipal council in 1956. He traveled widely in Africa, and an alleged visit to Moscow was the basis for his reputation of being a communist. By his political aggressiveness in the territorial assembly, he incurred the displeasure of French officials, and his contentious personality made him unpopular with his African colleagues. In 1957, he was expelled from the MESAN by Boganda, but remained a member of the assembly until 1965, when he retired from politics and entered the ministry of foreign affairs. In 1964, he went on a good will mission to Taipeh and was also a delegate to the U.N. General Assembly. As of July 1970, he was director of cooperation in the ministry of finance at Bangui.

DECORADE, Prosper: A clerk in the customs service at Brazzaville when he was elected to the territorial assembly from Poto-Poto on the socialist ticket in 1952. Three years later he became president of the assembly.

DIALLO, Idrissa: Born August 25, 1932, at Brazzaville, the son of a Sene-galese father and a Congolese mother. He entered the postal service in 1952 and became secretary of its CGAT union. In December 1964, he was elected first general secretary of the CSC. He held that post until April 1966, when he was dismissed and charged with embezzlement.

DIAWARA, Ange: Born in 1941, the son of a Malian father and a Congolese mother. He earned a master's degree in political economy, and also report-edly studied in the U.S.S.R. and Cuba. Returning to the Congo, he became commander of the civil defense corps, and in July 1967 was elected to the five-man executive committee of the JMNR. Ngouabi sent him on a good will mission to Mali and Guinea in September 1968, and named him a vice-president of the CNR directorate. One month later, he was appointed secretary of state for defense, and was given the rank of a second lieutenant. He still held his cabinet post when he became political commissar of the reorganized people's army in February 1969, and was credited with the spectacular defeat of Kikanga's raiders in March 1970. Because of his influence with the JMNR militia, he held high posts in the PCT politburo, and was one of the party's leading Maoists. Deprived of his portfolio as minister of development in December 1971, he remained commissar for the armed forces until he led the abortive putsch against Ngouabi on February 22, 1972. Twice he escaped ar-rest and was still at large as of August 1972.

EBOUE, Félix: Born December 26, 1884, in French Guiana of Antilles parents, he was educated in France and entered the colonial administration in FEA. Named governor of Tchad, he opted for Free France in 1940, and the next year was rewarded by General de Gaulle with the governorship-general of the FEA Federation. His role in the resistance and the reforms in colonial policy that he carried out made him a symbolic figure of Black liberalism after his death on May 17, 1944.

FOCCART, Jacques: Born August 31, 1913, in France, the son of a French Jew-ish planter and merchant of Martinique. In 1935, he was in the export busi-ness at Dakar. During World War II, he joined the Free French and met De Gaulle in London, where reportedly he earned the general's confidence. Twice elected to the French Union Assembly as a member of the RPF, he became that party's specialist in African affairs. In June 1958, De Gaulle named him his technical adviser, and two years later, he became general secretary of the Franco-African Community. As De Gaulle's envoy, he made many trips to francophone Africa, where he cultivated close relations with the conserva-tive African leaders. Because he disposed of ample funds and held the key to audiences with the French president, he was regarded as an éminence grise—a target for the opprobrium of African revolutionaries and French lib-erals. He has weathered harsh criticism, several lawsuits, and General de Gaulle's resignation, and plays an analogous role in the Pompidou government.

GALIBA, Dr. Bernard: A medical doctor, who was named minister of health and labor in Massamba's first two governments. In the reshuffle of October 1964, he retained the health portfolio but lost that of labor. He was released after being imprisoned briefly in connection with the murders of three high officials in February 1965, and retired from politics. In October 1971, he became head of the National Laboratory of Public Health in Brazzaville.

GANAO, Charles-David: Born July 20, 1928, at Djambala, he attended normal school at Mouyendzi from 1947 to 1950. He became a teacher and then inspector of primary schools at Brazzaville. After further training in France, he entered the foreign ministry of the Congo and became head of its political division. He was Massamba's foreign minister until January 1968, when he was assigned the portfolio of planning. In September 1969, Ngouabi named him permanent representative of the Congo government with the U.N. agencies based at Geneva.

GANDZION, Prosper: Born in 1927 at Ombina, a nephew of "King" Makoko of the Batéké tribe. He received a secondary education, and became a teacher in 1949 and an inspector of primary schools in 1958. After joining the UDDIA, he was elected to the territorial assembly from Djoué in 1957, and became its first vice-president in May 1958. A few months later, Youlou named him minster of education. Arrested after Youlou's overthrow, he was sentenced to 10 years' imprisonment in June 1965.

GBENYE, Christophe: Born in 1927, he became a Belgian Congolese leader in the MNC and minister of the interior in Lumumba's first government. After Lumumba's murder in 1961, he joined Gizenga's regime at Stanleyville, then sided with the central government after Gizenga's arrest. Late in 1963, he revolted against Adoula and fled to Brazzaville, where he became a leader of the CNL and its liaison officer with foreign governments. His followers captured Stanleyville in August 1964, whereupon he proclaimed himself Lumumba's heir and president of the Congo People's Republic. Three months later, he escaped from Stanleyville when it was captured by troops of the central government. Thereafter, he traveled in east and west Africa, seeking fresh support from revolutionary governments.

GIZENGA, Antoine: Born October 5, 1925, in Léopoldville province. After studying theology, he taught at the Catholic mission school at Léopoldville, where he founded the PSA in April 1958 and joined the coalition headed by Kasavubu. In January 1960, he attended the Brussels round-table conference, visiting Iron Curtain countries and Guinea on his way home. He was named vice-president in Lumumba's first government, but fled to Stanleyville late in 1960. There he announced that he was Lumumba's successor in February 1961, describing himself as a nationalist and socialist but not a communist. In August 1961, he briefly joined Adoula's government as deputy premier, representing it at the Belgrade conference of nonaligned nations. In January 1962, however, he was arrested on charges of incitement to revolt. After being released by Tshombe in July 1964, he was again interned the following year.

GOMA, Capt. Louis Sylvain: Named army chief of staff in August 1968 by Ngouabi for his role in effecting Massamba's downfall. The following November, he headed a delegation visiting the U.S.S.R., and a year later, was made secretary of state for defense after being appointed commander-in-chief of the people's army in February 1969. He held the defense portfolio until April 1970, when he was assigned that of public works and transport. In December 1971, he also became minister of civil aviation, and supported Ngouabi during the putsch of February 1972.

GONDJOUT, Paul: A Miéné, born June 4, 1912, at Zilé, Gabon. After attending secondary school, he entered the administration as a clerk. In 1954, he helped Léon Mba to organize the Bloc Démocratique Gabonais, of which he became secretary and editor of its press organ. From 1947 to 1960, he represented the Basse-Ogooué in the territorial assembly, of which he was elected president in 1958. Successively, he was a grand councilor of FEA (1952-57), municipal councilor of Libreville (1956), member of the French Conseil de la République (1956-59), and senator of the Community (1959-60). After imprisonment on charges of harming the state's security in 1960, he was named president of the Economic and Social Council in 1962. He held that post until after the abortive military putsch of February 1964, when he was tried and acquitted. In September 1968, he was appointed president of Gabon's supreme court.

GOUMBA, Abel: Born September 18, 1927, at Grimari, Oubangui-Chari. He attended the Ponty normal school and then graduated as an African doctor from the Dakar medical school. After joining the MESAN, he was elected to represent Ouaka in the territorial assembly. In May 1957, he became the vice-president of Oubangui's first government council, and the next year an active member of the PRA. In December 1958, he was succeeded as premier by Boganda, and accepted the portfolios of finance and planning in his government. After Boganda's death, he was elected a senator of the Community in July 1959. He was a minister in Dacko's first two cabinets, but was eliminated from the government in October 1959. Seven months later, he founded a party in opposition to the MESAN, which Dacko then headed. His party was banned, and he was arrested in December 1960; after being briefly amnestied, he was rearrested in 1962. Then he was sent to France, ostensibly to continue his medical studies. Despite his long exile abroad, he was said in 1969 to have retained a sizeable following in his own country.

GOURA, Pierre: A Bayaka, born January 2, 1917, in Sibiti district. After attending a Catholic primary school, he worked briefly as a forester. After becoming a PPC militant, he represented Niari in the territorial assembly from 1946 to 1957, when he was defeated for reelection by Kikhounga-Ngot. In 1957, he joined the UDDIA while he was serving as senator from the Congo (1955-59). In 1959, he was elected mayor of Dolisie and president of the UDE, and from 1959 to 1963, he was Youlou's minister of finance. Arrested after Youlou's overthrow, he was given a suspended sentence of two years in prison on June 8, 1965.

GUEYE, Doudou: A Ouolof Muslim Senegalese, his varied career as a doctor, journalist, and left-wing politician has been divided between his native land and Guinea and Mali. Despite his radical views, he remained loyal to Houphouët-Boigny in 1950 and headed the orthodox territorial branch of the RDA—the Mouvement Populaire Sénégalais. He then went to Guinea, where he joined Sékou Touré's party and was elected to represent Macenta in the Guinean assembly and that country in the French West African Grand Council. In 1958, he became an ardent federalist and was an active promoter of the Mali Federation and its general secretary. After that Federation's breakup in 1960, he became Modibo Keita's adviser on Senegalese affairs. For this defection, he was sentenced in absentia by a Senegalese court in 1963 to 20 years at forced labor. Amnestied the next year, he returned to Dakar and became editor of the UPS party organ, L'Unité Sénégalaise, and in 1970, he was named a member of the Economic and Social Council of Senegal.

HAZOUME, M.: A Dahomeyan immigrant, he served as general secretary for the PPC until he joined the UDDIA in June 1956. From 1957 to his downfall in 1963, Youlou used Hazoumé as his negotiator with Houphouët-Boigny and Tshombe.

HOMBESSA, André: A Lari, born at Brazzaville in 1935. There he received his B.A. degree from a Protestant lycée and was sent by Canadian missionaries in 1956 to study at an evangelical institute in Cameroun. After his return to Brazzaville in 1959, he was elected president of the Congolese youth council and to the executive committee of the World Assembly of Youth. As a JMNR militant leader, he was named secretary of state for youth by Massamba in October 1964, and six months later he replaced Bicoumat as minister of the interior. His strongly anti-Western and anti-Catholic views were reflected in the articles he regularly contributed to the JMNR organ, Dipanda, and they earned for him the name of "wild man of the Congolese revolution." In January 1968, Massamba took away his interior portfolio but left him with that of information. He was a leader of the resistance to Ngouabi at Camp Biafra in September 1968, and for this he was sentenced to five years in prison.

HOUPHOUET-BOIGNY, Félix: Born October 18, 1905, at Yamoussoukro, Ivory Coast. A coffee planter, canton chief, and graduate of the Dakar medical school, he organized the Syndicat Agricole Africain in 1944 to defend the interests of Ivorian farmers against European planters and trading firms. Two years later, he became president of the RDA, of which he was a founder and for which he accepted aid from the French communist party. Dramatically reversing the RDA's policy in 1950 to one of cooperation with the French authorities and businessmen, he became a bulwark of conservatism and the free enterprise system. Throughout the postwar years, he was Ivory Coast's deputy to the French National Assembly, and in 1956, he became the first African minister in a French government. In that capacity, he helped to draft the loi-cadre of 1956 in collaboration with the French overseas minister. After being a staunch foe of federalism and independence for francophone Africa, he founded the Council of the Entente in 1959 and led its member states to independence. Despite frequent drastic changes of policy, he remained francophone Africa's most influential political leader and, since independence, has been president of Ivory Coast, its most prosperous state.

IBALICO, Marcel: A Batéké, born near Brazzaville, September 30, 1924. He studied for the priesthood but, in 1953, entered the education service as a teacher. In 1956, he became a contributor to the literary periodical, Liaison, and entered politics. He joined the UDDIA and was elected, in 1957, to represent Djoué in the territorial assembly; in the same year, he became a vice-president of the FEA Grand Council. In July 1959, he was elected a senator of the Community and, subsequently, traveled widely in Europe. He was placed in charge of Radio Brazzaville in 1961, succeeded Massamba as president of the legislature in 1962, and after the coup of August 1963, fled to Léopoldville. There he organized the anti-Massamba movement, and was killed in an automobile accident in March 1964.

IBOUANGA, Isaac: A Babangui, born December 4, 1936, at Dolisie, where he took up teaching. Elected to the assembly from Nyanga-Louesse in 1959, he became a member of Youlou's government council the same year. He was arrested after the coup of August 1963, and sentenced in June 1965 to three years in prison.

IKONGA, Auxence: After serving as a provincial prefect and later in the foreign ministry, he was named ambassador to the UAR by Massamba in November 1966. He was allotted the portfolio of agriculture in June 1969 by Ngouabi and, six months later, also that of foreign affairs. At the OAU summit meetings, he spoke eloquently against American policy in Vietnam and the proposal of a dialogue with South Africa. Dropped from the cabinet and the PCT central committee in December 1971, he was named Ngouabi's directeur de cabinet the following month.

ITOUA, Dieudonné: An administrator under the French regime, he became commissar for the Likouala region in 1960. Ngouabi named him secretary of state in August 1968, member of the PCT central committee and minister of territorial administration in January 1970. He held both posts until December 1971, when he was given the portfolio of health and social affairs.

JAYLE, Christian: Born August 6, 1905, in Paris, where he received his legal training and became a lawyer for the Conseil d'Etat. In FEA, he embarked on a journalistic career, editing and publishing L'A.E.F. at Brazzaville and Le Cameroun Illustré at Douala, and also entered politics in the Congo. He joined the UDDIA and was elected to the municipal council of Brazzaville, the territorial assembly from the Pool, and to the presidency of the assembly from 1957 to 1959. Regarded as one of Youlou's most influential advisers, he probably originated the project to hold a referendum on secession in the north in 1959, as well as that of an economic union of the FEA states in 1960. Named secretary of state for information in July 1959, he was dropped from Youlou's cabinet in February 1960.

KALONDJI, Albert: Born June 8, 1919, in Kasai, Belgian Congo. He joined the MNC, but left it after Lumumba became its leader to form a splinter group called MNC-Kalondji. In August 1960, he proclaimed South Kasai an independent state and crowned himself Emperor Albert I of the Kasai Balubas. His state did not survive his arrest late in 1962, when he went to Léopoldville to attend a session of the national assembly, of which he was a member. Released from prison in 1963, he went briefly into exile, but returned to the Congo in 1964, when Tshombe named him minister of agriculture and later vice-president of the republic. His eminence during Tshombe's regime derived from his strong tribal support among the Balubas.

KASAVUBU, Joseph: Born in 1917 at Kumidizi in the Belgian Congo, he studied at the Grand Séminaire and became a monitor in the Catholic mission schools. After briefly working in the private sector, he entered the administrative service in 1942. Eight years later he joined the Abako and became its president in 1955. In December 1957, he was elected mayor of the Dindale suburb of Léopoldville, and president of the newly independent republic of Congo-Léopoldville on June 28, 1960. He held that office until he was ousted by Mobutu in 1965, and he died five years later.

KAYA, Paul: A Lari, born October 17, 1933, at Madingou. In 1959, he graduated as an engineer from the University of Paris, and the next year joined the staff of the Congolese embassy there as economic counselor. Upon his return to the Congo, he was named director of economic and social affairs, and in 1962, he was appointed to the analogous post in the UAMCE—the year in which he joined the UDDIA. After Youlou was overthrown, Massamba invited Kaya to join his government of technocrats, and he was named minister of economic affairs. He successfully completed an aid-seeking world tour but was eliminated from the cabinet in October 1964. Fearing arrest because of his moderate political views, he fled to Abidjan, where he became administrative secretary of the Council of the Entente's Guaranty Fund.

KERHERVE, André: Born in Brittany on August 14, 1911, he went to Africa soon after finishing secondary school. He became a merchant and small-scale entrepreneur in the Moyen-Congo, and after World War II, entered local politics. He represented Likouala-Mossaka in the territorial assembly from 1957 to 1959, and for most of that period, he also served as Youlou's minister of industry and mines.

KIBAHT, Charles: Born September 17, 1910, at Boundji. While holding a clerical position in the forestry service, he was a founder of the Front Démocratique Congolais in 1955. Two years later, he joined the UDDIA and was elected to the assembly from Djoué. He was a subprefect of Gamboma in 1959, and represented the Congo at a meeting in Bangui of the equatorial states in 1962.

KIKANGA, Lieut. Pierre (alias Sirocco): As a pro-Youlist Lari and officer stationed at Brazzaville, he served as Jacques Lebreton's contact man in preparation for the "mercenaries' coup" of May 1968. Again implicated in a plot, allegedly directed by Mouzabakany, he fled to Kinshasa in December 1968, and was sentenced to death in absentia by the Brazzaville revolutionary court in July 1960. At the head of a band of commandos, he was killed in a raid on Brazzaville in March 1970.

KIKHOUNGA-NGOT, Simon-Pierre: A Bakongo, born in 1920 near Dolisie. He attended primary school in that region and may have studied medicine briefly in the Belgian Congo. He was variously described as a merchant, stenographer, and labor leader, and is believed to have established contacts with left-wing groups during a trip to France and the Iron Curtain countries in 1954. Elected to represent the Niari region in the assembly in 1952, he had become vice-president of the socialist party and regional secretary for the CGAT unions when reelected to that body in 1957. Throughout Youlou's administration, he held various ministerial portfolios until May 1960, when he was briefly arrested for antigovernment activities. Released four months later, he resumed his former post as minister of economic affairs in January 1961, and in May 1963 became minister of labor. After Youlou's downfall, he was arrested, but was acquitted by the people's court in June 1965. After Ngouabi came to power, he was briefly a member of the CNR but was dropped from that body in February 1969.

KIMBOUALA N'KAYA, Capt.: In January 1970, he was named a member of the PCT central committee, commissar of the army in charge of economic activities, and commander of the Pointe Noire military zone. He still held those posts when arrested for alleged participation in the February 1972 revolt. His death sentence was commuted to life imprisonment the following month.

KOLELAS, Bernard: A Lari of Brazzaville, he became general secretary of the UDDIA and took refuge in Léopoldville after Youlou's overthrow. Following the death there of Ibalico in 1964, he took over leadership of the Front de Libération Nationale du Congo-Brazzaville, for which he was sentenced to death in absentia by a Brazzaville court in June 1965. Ngouabi invited him to return from his exile in August 1968, and he resumed his former post in the foreign ministry in June 1969. As the alleged mastermind behind the November 1969 plot against Ngouabi, he was, for the second time, sentenced to death but was freed on January 1, 1972.

LEKOUNZOU, Justin: A northern Congolese, he was director-general of the BCCO and chairman of the CNR committee for organization when named to the PCT politburo in January 1970. Three months later, he was appointed head of the state industrial enterprises. In December 1971, he was named minister of industry but dropped from the politburo.

LEYET-GABOKA, Maurice: A Kouyou, born November 5, 1925, at Fort Rousset. He was a teacher when elected from Djoué on the socialist ticket to the assembly in 1957, and he was reelected in 1959. After the Congo became independent, he represented Likouala-Mossaka in the legislature. Leaving politics after the coup of August 1963, he returned to the education service, where he became an assistant inspector of schools.

LISETTE, Gabriel: Born April 2, 1919, in Panama, of Guadeloupan parents. He was educated in France and married to a Frenchwoman. After graduating from the Colonial School, he was mobilized in 1939. Two years later, he was assigned to the administration in Tchad and rose rapidly in the hierarchy. He became a charter member of the RDA, founded its local branch, and was elected to the French National Assembly in 1946. Defeated in 1951 when he ran for reelection, he was elected to the territorial assembly in 1952, and became mayor of Fort Lamy as well as deputy again in 1956. In May 1957, he was elected vice-president of Tchad's first government council, but he left that country before it became independent. From the outset, he was prominent in the RDA, and in Paris made important political contacts which stood him in good stead when he reentered the French civil service there in 1958. He specialized in France's relations with the Antilles, and headed the French delegation to the Tangier meeting of the Economic Commission in Africa in 1960. Two years later, he was named representative of France on the U.N. Economic Commission for Latin America, and at the same time was elected president of the Gaullist party in Guadeloupe.

LISSOUBA, Pascal: Born November 29, 1931, at Mossendjo, he attended school at Dolisie and Brazzaville. From 1947 to 1952, he studied at the <u>lycée</u> of Nice and then at the higher school of agriculture in Tunis. From the Sorbonne he received his degree as an agronomic engineer, after which he returned to the Congo to head its agricultural service and also do research there for the ORSTOM. Named minister of agriculture in Massamba's provisional government, he retained that portfolio after becoming premier in December 1963. In April 1966, he was succeeded by Noumazalaye as premier, returning to the political scene from August 1968 to June 1969 as a minister in Ngouabi's government. Thereafter, he lectured on economics at the Ecole Supérieure des Sciences at Brazzaville.

LOPEZ, Henri: After receiving his master's degree in France, he taught history in the Paris region. On his return to the Congo, he became principal

of a school, and was named minister of education in June 1969. The next
month he attended the Pan-African Cultural Festival at Algiers, where he
distinguished himself by his strong speech against négritude. Late·in 1969,
he briefly held the portfolio of information; in January 1970, he was named
minister of justice at the same time as he was appointed to the PCT central
committee. In December 1971, he succeeded Ickonga as foreign minister.
That same year his book of short stories, entitled Tribaliques, was published at Yaoundé.

LOUNDA, Albert: A Lari, born May 15, 1905, at Boko, where he became a
planter and trucker. In 1946, he joined the PPC and, subsequently, was
twice elected to the French Union Assembly. He was concurrently a member of
the territorial assembly, of whose finance committee he became chairman.
Defeated when he ran for reelection in 1959, he disappeared from the political scene until 1969, when he chaired the PPC's first meeting in 12 years at
Pointe Noire.

LUMUMBA, Patrice: Born July 2, 1925, at Kasai, he entered the postal service of the Belgian Congo as a clerk. He was dismissed from that post and
sentenced to two years' penal servitude for forgery and embezzlement. A
member of the Amicale Libérale of Stanleyville, he participated in forming
the MNC, and became president of the Fédération des Batétéla in October 1958.
Although arrested in November 1959 for incitement to revolt, he was freed in
January 1960 so that he could attend the Brussels round-table conference.
After the Congo's independence, he became premier of the central government
as well as provincial deputy for Stanleyville in the Parliament. Late in
1960, he was arrested by Mobutu, who handed him over to Tshombe, and in February 1961, he was assassinated in Katanga.

MAHE, René: Born June 24, 1926, at Marseille, he grew up on Réunion Island
where his father served as an administrator. In the 1940s, he went to Brazzaville where, after several unsuccessful business ventures, he took up
journalism and became editor of Le Progrès. He was an early member of the
UDDIA and represented Youlou at a few international conferences. In November
1956, he was elected to the Brazzaville municipal council and to the assembly
from the Pool region. Youlou named him minister of economic affairs in
December 1958.

MAHOUATA, Raymond: A Lari, born October 25, 1920, in Oubangui-Chari. He became a doctor and practiced medicine there before being named head of the
Polyclinic at Pointe Noire. Youlou named him minister of health (August
1959—March 1962).

MAKANY, Lévy: A Lari who received his doctorate in science from a French
university. In 1957, he became director of the education service and president of the Alliance Française at Brazzaville, and in April 1966, he accepted
an invitation to visit Peking. He joined the JMNR in 1964, and two years
later was named minister of education by Noumazalaye. He retained that portfolio under Ngouabi until January 1969, when he became permanent secretary of
the National Council of Scientific Research.

MAKOSSO, François-Luc: Born October 19, 1938, at Madingo-Kayes. He was
manager of the Pointe Noire branch of the National Deveopment Bank when
elected to the legislature in December 1963. He was named minister of

justice and civil service in April 1965 and was also given the portfolio of labor in 1966. Ngouabi appointed him to succeed Bindi in August 1968 as head of the security police.

MAKOSSO, Jean-Aimé: Son of a tribal chief of the Mayombé region, he was employed in the postal service, and became an active member of the CATC. Defeated when he ran on the PPC ticket for the assembly in 1957, he joined the UDDIA the next year and was elected to the legislature in 1963. As a Catholic trade-union leader and outspoken critic of the Massamba government, he was expelled from the legislature in 1965.

MAMBEKE-BOUCHER, Auguste: Born February 2, 1919, at Brazzaville, where he became a teacher and was naturalized as a French citizen. After serving as a sociologist in the local office of the World Health Organization, he joined the MSA and became Opangault's minister of education as well as a member of the territorial assembly.

MASSAMBA-DEBAT, Alphonse: A Bakongo, born in 1921 in the Boko region. After graduating from a Protestant secondary school, he became a teacher in Tchad and in Moyen-Congo, and then a school principal in Brazzaville (1957-59). In the latter year, he was elected on the UDDIA ticket to the territorial assembly and became chef de cabinet to the minister of education. He was president of the assembly from June 1959 to May 1961, when he became Youlou's minister of planning; he was dropped from the cabinet two years later. After Youlou's downfall, he headed a provisional government from August to December 1963, at which time he was elected president of the republic. After the army seized power in August 1968, he resigned. Tried and acquitted in the fall of 1969, he did not return to public life.

MATOUMBA-MPOLO, Lieut. Prosper: Born in 1940, he was first a teacher and then an administrator in the education service. President of the JMNR in August 1968, when he was named minister of youth and information. Two months later he became a member of the CNR, and in January 1970 of the PCT central committee, when he was also appointed commissar of the Office du Kouilou. A ringleader of the putsch of February 22, 1972, he was killed five days later near Pointe Noire by government troops.

MATSECOTO, Lazare: A Lari, born August 12, 1931, at Brazzaville. After graduating from primary school in 1945, he entered the M'Bamou Seminary but was expelled from it two years later for indiscipline. He then joined the army, but in 1948 was awarded a scholarship to the Ecole des Cadres through family influence. After receiving his B.A., he studied law in Paris and joined the anticolonial student movement there. On his return to Brazzaville in 1957, he joined the UDDIA, headed by his cousin, Fulbert Youlou. Another scholarship enabled him to resume his studies in Paris, where he acquired his doctorate of laws in 1959. Back again in the Congo, he was named attorney general, a post he held when he was murdered in February 1965.

MATSIKA, Aimé: A Lari, born in Kinkala district. He was a student at the Vocational School in Brazzaville until expelled for indiscipline in 1951. He then worked as an industrial designer in the public works department but was dismissed again for his failure to respect regulations. He moved to Dolisie, where he worked as a shipping clerk, but after a year, returned to Brazzaville where he remained unemployed except for a brief job with a local architect. Then he joined the CGAT secretariat and became a popular orator for

Congolese independence at trade union meetings. He led the CGAT campaign for a negative vote in the September 1958 referendum, earning a reputation with the police as being the most active agent of communism in Brazzaville. After traveling extensively in Iron Curtain countries, he was briefly arrested upon his return in April 1960 for smuggling in communist propaganda. After his release, he became secretary of the UJC, editor of its organ, L'Eveil, and active in cultivating contacts with students. Massamba named him minister for trade and industry in December 1963, and eight months later he was assigned the portfolio for civil aviation. Charged with plotting against the military government in November 1969, he was sentenced to death but not executed.

MBA, Léon: A Fang, born at Libreville, Gabon, on February 9, 1902, he entered the customs service and was later appointed a canton chief. Specializing in Fang tribal law, he became an active member of the Bwiti cult, which aimed at reconstituting Fang society. Dismissed from the administration for his antigovernment activities, he lived in exile from 1933 to 1946 in Oubangui-Chari. Upon his return to Libreville, he found employment in a trading firm, dabbled in journalism, and belatedly became involved in politics. He soon became prominent in the Bloc Démocratique Gabonais, but was twice defeated by Aubame in elections to the French National Assembly in 1951 and 1956. In 1952, however, he was elected to the territorial assembly, and in 1956 became mayor of Libreville. In the process, he was transformed from being anticolonialist into an advocate of close ties with France, an admirer of General de Gaulle, and a warm friend of Houphouët-Boigny. Elected vice-president of Gabon's first government council in 1957 and president of the republic in 1961, he survived an abortive putsch by young army officers in February 1964, thanks to the intervention of French paratroops. After being restored to power, he punished severely all promoters of the coup, including Aubame. Taken seriously ill in 1966, he went to Paris for treatment. Before dying in November 1967, he named Albert Bongo as his political heir.

M'BEMBA, Mgr. Théophile: Born in 1917 at Brazzaville, he studied theology and was ordained a priest in 1951. Fourteen years later, he was consecrated archbishop of Brazzaville. That year he strongly opposed nationalization of the mission schools and led the Catholic opposition to Massamba's government. With the military regime, however, he came to terms, and when he died in June 1971, he was praised by Ngouabi for having rid the Congolese Catholic church of all colonial vestiges.

M'BERRI, Martin: A Lari teacher in the National School of Administration and a deputy in the legislature when he was elected president of the JMNR in February 1965. After Ngouabi succeeded Massamba, he was named secretary of state for propaganda and a member of the CNR directorate. He was dismissed from the CNR in December 1968, but was named director of the National School of Adminstration in September 1969. Charged with writing subversive tracts against the military government, he was tried and sentenced to five years in prison in May 1971.

MISSAMOU, Jean-Baptiste: A Lari labor leader who was a member of the CNR when elected president of the CSC in May 1969. Four months later, he was dismissed from that post for failing to prevent a strike by civil servants and for "unauthorized contacts" with French technicians.

MOBUTU, Gen. Sésé Séko (Joseph-Désiré): Born at Lisala, Belgian Congo, on October 14, 1930, he attended Catholic mission schools. In 1950, he joined the Force Publique and three months later was promoted to the rank of sergeant. He became interested in journalism, writing articles for L'Avenir and editing Actualités Africaines, and was sent to Brussels for higher training. After a tour of duty with the Congo Information Service in Belgium, he returned to the Congo prior to the mutiny of the Force Publique in July 1960. The newly independent Congolese government assigned him the task of reconciling it with the mutineers. He became a member of the MNC, was commissioned head of the army general staff with the rank of colonel, and was named by Premier Lumumba a secretary of state in October 1960. Soon he turned against Lumumba, whom he arrested and turned over to Tshombe, and expelled the Soviet nationals from the Congo. On November 24, 1965, he ousted Kasavubu from the presidency of the republic and named himself commander-in-chief of the army as well as head of state. Under his government, the mercenaries were eliminated, the administration centralized and a single party instituted, and the economy prospered.

MONDJO, Nicolas: Born June 24, 1933, at Fort Rousset. He entered the colonial administration, and after attending the Colonial School in Paris, he was named a provincial prefect and later served as director of the ministry of the interior in 1963-64. In September of the latter year, Massamba named him ambassador to France, and in January 1968, foreign minister. He retained that portfolio under the military government until June 1970, when he became the Congo's permanent representative to the United Nations.

MOUDILENO-MASSENGO, Maître Aloyse: Born March 11, 1933, at Vinza, he earned his law degree in France. He was named minister of justice and labor in August 1968 and also acquired the information portfolio in February 1971. As a result of the PCT purge in December 1971, he succeeded Raoul as vice-president of the republic while remaining minister of justice. In August 1972, he was expelled from the PCT because he refused to return to the Congo following an official trip abroad.

MOUNTSAKA, Major David: A Bakongo and a professional army officer, he was credited, along with Major Mouzabakany, with persuading Youlou to resign on August 15, 1963. Named by his cousin, Massamba, commander-in-chief of the armed forces, he was sent to Peking in September 1964 on a good will mission. He was unpopular with his troops, and was twice kidnapped by mutineers, in 1963 and 1966. After the second episode, he was not reinstated in his command, but in August 1967 was named ambassador to Algeria.

MOUYABI, André-Georges: Born in 1935 at Madingou. After attending school in Gabon, he became a teacher and school principal in the Congo. In 1960, he went to France for further training, and upon his return, Youlou placed him in charge of the Centre National de Documentation Pédagogique. Elected to the legislature in December 1963, he defeated Angor for the presidency of that body in May 1966. In September of the latter year, he led a parliamentary mission to Peking. The military government sent him on a good will mission to Gabon in September 1968, when he was appointed secretary of the CNR directorate. After three months he was dropped from the CNR, but a year later he was sent to Cuba as ambassador. In May 1970 he was appointed director of the Brazzaville general hospital.

MOUZABAKANY, Major Félix: Born at Brazzaville in 1932 into an influential Lari family. A professional army officer, he was named deputy chief of staff after Youlou's eclipse. The next year he was arrested for plotting to restore Youlou and, in June 1965, was sentenced to death by the people's court. In August 1967, this sentence was commuted to 20 years' imprisonment at hard labor, but after Massamba's overthrow, he was released and named minister of the interior. At the end of 1968, he was dismissed from the government because he "lacked socialist convictions." Brooding over his demotion, he allegedly conspired to restore Youlou to power, was arrested in February 1969, and nine months later was transferred to a prison in Fort Rousset.

MULELE, Pierre: Educated in a mission school in the Belgian Congo, he left the Catholic church at the age of fifteen, and was believed to have come under communist influence after World War II. After spending some time in Cairo and Conakry, he went to Peking for five months of training in guerrilla warfare. By 1960, he had returned to the Congo, where he served in Lumumba's first cabinet. Late that year, he fled to Stanleyville, and was appointed by Gizenga to be his liaison officer in Cairo and in charge of anti-Adoula propaganda. By 1964, he had set up his headquarters in Brazzaville, using the Chinese embassy there as a channel for money and arms to rebels in Congo-Kinshasa. He was still at Brazzaville in October 1968, when Mobutu's foreign minister came there and promised him safe conduct back to Kinshasa. Within 48 hours of his return, he was tried and executed in Kinshasa.

NARDON, Jean-Georges: Born October 4, 1917, at Bordeaux, where he received his secondary schooling. In Moyen-Congo, he was employed by the Congo-Ocean railroad until he was elected mayor of Pointe Noire in 1956. The following March, he was elected to the legislature on the MSA ticket. Opangault appointed him minister of civil service in 1957. He held that post until December 1958, when he was sent to Paris on a mission connected with the Kouilou dam project. He then withdrew from political life.

NDALLA, Claude: Born in 1937 at Brazzaville, where he attended secondary school. He then studied mathematics at the University of Toulouse, where he earned the nickname of "Graille" (crow) because of his voracious appetite. Without receiving a degree, he went to study chemistry in Moscow and also visited Peking. Returning to Brazzaville after Youlou's overthrow, he was elected to the JMNR executive committee and became editor of its organ, Dipanda, from 1964 to 1968. Named secretary of state for youth in April 1965, he was charged with embezzlement early in 1966 and dropped from the cabinet. He soon returned to public life, however, as director of the Brazzaville radio, and held that post until he was named ambassador to Peking in February 1969. On his return to Brazzaville late that same year, he became secretary of the PCT politburo in charge of propaganda. Regarded as a leading Maoist and the number two man in the military government, he was dropped, nevertheless, from the party in the purge of December 1971. Arrested as a leader of the February 1972 revolt, he was first given a death sentence, but later this was commuted to life imprisonment.

NGOUABI, Major Marien: A Kouyou, born at Ombele in 1938. He was admitted in 1960 to a military school in Strasbourg, and from there went to St. Cyr, graduating in 1962 with the rank of second lieutenant. On his return to the

Congo, he was assigned to the Pointe Noire garrison as second in command. In 1963, he was given charge of the newly created paratroop corps at Brazzaville, with the rank of captain. During this period, he was said to have become an avid reader of Marxist literature. His demotion in June 1966 and his arrest in July 1968 led, respectively, to an army mutiny and the military takeover of the government. Successively, he became commander-in-chief of the armed forces, founder and chairman of the PCT, and president of the republic.

NGOUOTO, Charles: An administrator during the French regime, he served as director of the National School of Administration from 1969 to 1970, when he became a member of the PCT central committee and its commissar for the Kouilou region. In March 1970, he was named minister of health, but in December 1971, he was dropped from the cabinet and made head of the new commission for information.

NGOUNIMBA, Henri Pierre: In July 1969, when he was director of the People's College at Brazzaville, he was appointed president of the revolutionary court. From January to April 1970, he was a member of the PCT central committee but was dropped from that body when named secretary of state in charge of development. In August 1971, he succeeded Boukambou as ambassador to the U.S.S.R.

NITHOUD, Jean-de-Dieu: A newcomer to politics when he became minister of trade and industry in September 1968. Six months later, he accompanied Nze to renegotiate cooperation agreements with the U.S.S.R. in Moscow. He lost his cabinet post in June 1969, and a year later was appointed to head the accountancy department of the UDEAC.

NOUMAZALAYE, Ambroise: Born September 23, 1933, at Brazzaville, where he attended the Salvation Army's primary school. He received his secondary education at Dolisie and Brazzaville and an M.A. in mathematics at the University of Toulouse. While in France, he married a Frenchwoman and joined the communist party and the FEANF. Interrupting his advanced studies at the Institut National de Statistiques, he returned to Brazzaville to become general secretary of the MNR in July 1964, and also its director of economic affairs. In April 1966, he succeeded Lissouba as premier after returning from Moscow, where he attended the Soviet communist party congress. He headed a delegation to Peking in September 1967, but in January 1968, Massamba dismissed him from the government. After Ngouabi took over the power, he served for two months as secretary of state for information. In November 1969, he was assigned a comparatively minor post in the planning ministry, and did not again become politically prominent until after the abortive Kikanga raid in March 1970, when he was taken back into the PCT politburo as head of the its planning committee. Soon after replacing Raoul as second secretary of the PCT, he was arrested and condemned to death—later commuted to life imprisonment—for his alleged participation in the February 22, 1972, putsch.

NZALAKANDA, Dominique: A Lari, born in 1917 in the Pool region. He received secondary schooling, and became a teacher in 1939 and an inspector of primary schools in 1958. From 1961 to August 1963, he was minister of the interior in the government of his cousin, Youlou, and became so unpopular with the labor unions that they demanded his dismissal. Arrested after Youlou's overthrow, he was sentenced to 15 years in prison at hard labor in June 1965, but was amnestied in August 1967.

NZE, Pierre: A professor at the Lycée Savorgnan de Brazza when named secretary for foreign relations and education in the CNR directorate in August 1968. Six months later, his rank was raised to that of minister. As of January 1969, he, Ngouabi, and Raoul were the only members of the government who were also members of the CNR executive committee. In June 1969, he lost his cabinet post only two months after having gone to Moscow to renegotiate the cooperation agreements. Returning to active politics in January 1970, he was named minister of justice and, three months later, placed in charge of organizing the PCT. Although he attended a meeting of the French communist party in October 1970, he has been regarded as a moderate and an ally of Ngouabi in the PCT politburo.

OKIEMBA, Pascal: As a leader of the CATC, he played a prominent part in the overthrow of Youlou, and was appointed minister of justice by Massamba in December 1963. Along with other CATC leaders, he was dismissed from his post in October 1964.

OKOMBA, Faustin: A Mbochi, born at Kellé on June 5, 1929. After attending primary school, he entered the administration as a clerk. He joined the MSA, and from March 1957 to mid-1959, represented Likouala-Mossaka in the assembly. Arrested and held briefly for alleged participation in the Brazzaville riots of February 1959, he was appointed minister of labor five months later. In December 1962, his portfolio was shifted to that of public works and transport. Arrested again after Youlou's overthrow, he was acquitted by the people's court in June 1965.

OPANGAULT, Jacques: Born December 13, 1907, at Ikagna, and educated in a Catholic mission school. In 1938 he became a clerk in the judicial service, and after World War I, entered politics and founded the Moyen-Congo branch of the SFIO. Beginning in 1946, he was elected regularly to the territorial assembly and was as regularly defeated when he ran as candidate for the French National Assembly, his political career being marked by extremes. An undisputed leader of the northern population and of the MSA, he was consistently loyal to France and the SFIO, and remained politically prominent until August 1963. Vice-president and then premier of the Congo's first government council, he was arrested after the Brazzaville riots of February 1959. He was released after six months in prison, and a year later, became a minister of state in Youlou's government. In 1961, he was named vice-president of the republic, only to be demoted to the post of minister of public works the next year. After Youlou's overthrow, he was again arrested, and upon his release, he returned to private life.

POIGNET, Capt. Augustin: A Franco-Congolese mulatto, born April 28, 1928, at Sibiti. He joined the aviation service of the French army and returned to the Congo after independence with the rank of lieutenant. Massamba sent him on a mission to Peking in 1964, and in January 1968, named him secretary of state for defense. During the crisis of August 1968, he was acting head of state for a short time after Massamba's resignation. Within a few weeks, he was eliminated from the military government and, in compensation, promoted to the rank of captain. Arrested in February 1969 on charges of trafficking in firearms, he was given a suspended sentence of eight years in jail. He was implicated in the abortive Kikanga raid of March 1970, but fled from the country before being condemned to death by a court martial.

PONGAULT, Gilbert: A Mbochi, born at Mossaka in 1925, he attended a Catholic mission primary school. After World War II, he was an employee of Radio Brazzaville and then wrote for Le Semaine de l'AEF. By the mid-1950s, he had become head of all the CATC unions throughout FEA, frequently attended labor congresses in Europe, and was a member of the French Economic and Social Council. In January 1959, the Christian labor unions of many African countries met at Brazzaville under his aegis and formed the Union Pan-Africaine des Travailleurs Chrétiens. The next year he was elected secretary of the ICFTU for FEA-Cameroun and, in 1961, vice-president of that organization. After Youlou's fall, in which he played an active part, he joined the MNR but was excluded from that party after the CATC was dissolved in November 1964. Accused of plotting to restore Youlou, he fled first to Lagos and then to Geneva, where he became prominent in international labor movements.

PORTELLA, Capt. Aimé: He first came to public notice in May 1968 when he was wounded in the skirmish known as the "mercenaries' plot." After Massamba's downfall, he was named second vice-president of the CNR directorate. Promoted to the rank of captain by the military government, he was for a brief period the third most important army leader in the CNR. In December 1968 he was dropped from the CNR but, at the same time, was placed in command of the Pointe Noire garrison. In April 1970, he was named director of civil aeronautics.

POUNGUI, Ange-Edouard: President of the UGEEC when it held its crucial congress at Brazzaville in July 1968 that harshly criticized Massamba. A year earlier, he had been elected to the five-man executive committee of the JMNR, in which he was regarded as an outstanding Marxist. In mid-August 1968, Ngouabi made him a member of the CNR and, in the next year, secretary of state for foreign affairs. In October 1969, he accompanied Raoul on an official mission to Peking, at which time he was president of the economic and social committee of the CNR. When the PCT was formed in December 1969, he became a member of its politburo and, a few days later, was placed in charge of its finances. In June 1971, Ngouabi named him minister of finance, and in August 1972, vice-president of the republic, succeeding Moudileno-Massengo.

RAOUL, Major Alfred: Born December 13, 1938, in the Pointe Noire region. He received his secondary education in Brazzaville and France. In 1960, he was admitted to the St. Cyr military academy, from which he graduated as an army engineer, and then he continued his studies in Angers. On his return to the Congo, he was awarded a captain's commission and named adjutant to the commander-in-chief of the armed forces, a post that he held when Ngouabi came to power in August 1968. Named secretary for defense in the CNR, he was chosen by Ngouabi to be prime minister and, briefly, acting head of state. In the latter capacity, he attended the OAU meeting at Algiers in September 1968, at which time he held the rank of major. After 1969, he held important posts in the cabinet and PCT but spent most of his time abroad as Ngouabi's roving ambassador. For siding with Ngouabi's opponents in the PCT confrontation of December 1971, he lost the vice-presidency and his portfolio of trade. Arrested and sentenced to 10 years in prison for alleged participation in the February 1972 putsch, he was freed six months later.

SAMBA, Germain: A Kouyou, born in 1922 at Souanké. After attending secondary school, he became a veterinary assistant. He was a militant of the MSA youth

organization until he joined the UDDIA in 1957. Named secretary of state
for health in December 1958 and minister of agriculture in January 1960, he
was briefly arrested along with Youlou after the latter's overthrow in
August 1963.

SATHOUD, Victor-Justin: A Baboussi, born January 27, 1927, in Nyanga-Louesse
prefecture. He attended primary school in Dolisie, and eventually became a
secretary in the administration and later a clerk in the Société Agricole et
Forestière. He represented Dolisie in the territorial assembly (1952-59),
served as municipal councilor for that town in 1956, and was secretary of
state for civil service from June 1959 to September 1960, when he was raised
to the rank of minister. In May 1963 he was appointed minister of planning.
Arrested after the 1963 coup d'état, he was sentenced in June 1965 to 10
years in prison.

SIANARD, Charles: Born November 12, 1927, at Bobo-Sangha. After graduating
from the Ecole des Cadres at Brazzaville, he entered the administration.
From 1961 to 1963, he served as Youlou's directeur de cabinet, and under
Massamba was director of economic affairs. Ngouabi appointed him minister
of finance, then minister of trade, which post he held from June 1969 to
April 1970. In the latter month, he was dropped from the state council but
named head of the territorial administration.

SYLLA, Dr. Youssoufa: Born at Dakar on October 26, 1923, he became a medical
doctor. He was Houphouët-Boigny's directeur de cabinet in Paris from 1956
to 1958, after which he was appointed technical adviser to Lisette, and was
his specialist in Common Market affairs. Upon returning to Africa in October
1963, he was named Senegal's ambassador to Liberia and Sierra Leone, and held
that post until May 1965. After a three-year interval, he again served as
ambassador, this time to Ethiopia and Tanzania. In September 1971, he became
director of foreign affairs in the Senegalese foreign ministry.

TCHICAYA, Félix: A leader of the Vili tribe in the Pointe Noire region; born
at Libreville, Gabon, on November 9, 1903. After graduating from the Ponty
Normal School at Dakar, he became an accountant and journalist in Moyen-Congo.
During World War II he fought with the Free French, and in 1945 he was
elected to the French Constituent Assembly. The next year he founded the PPC,
was elected deputy for Moyen-Congo to the French National Assembly, and attended the congress at Bamako, Soudan, which gave birth to the RDA. He became a Grand Councilor of FEA in 1952; in that year, and again in 1956, he
was reelected to the French National Assembly, where he was affiliated with
the UDSR. In 1958, he left the RDA, in which he had been a vice-president,
and joined Senghor's PRA. Although in political eclipse since Youlou's rise
to power in 1956, Tchicaya retained a following in the region of Pointe Noire
until his death there on January 15, 1961.

TCHICHELLE, Stéphane: Born January 12, 1915, in the Kouilou region, he was
educated in Catholic mission schools. In 1930, he was employed by the Congo-
Ocean railroad, and six years later became a stationmaster. He represented
Kouilou in the territorial assembly from 1946 to 1959, was a Grand Councilor
of FEA, 1958-59, and was elected mayor of Pointe Noire in 1956. The next
year, he left the PPC to enter Youlou's government, where he was, successively, minister of labor and health (1957) and of the interior (1958),

deputy premier and minister of foreign affairs (1959), and vice-president of the republic (in July 1962). After Youlou's overthrow, he was arrested and sentenced to 15 years in prison at hard labor, but was amnestied in August 1967, at which time he returned to private life.

THAULAY-GANGA, Abel: A Lari, born September 20, 1920, at Kinkala. He became a monitor in the Brazzaville Catholic mission school which he had attended. Leaving the teaching profession in 1939, he held successive jobs as accountant in the private sector, and became treasurer of the CGAT in 1953. Several years later, he took the labor training course offered by the CGT in France, after which he attended labor conferences in Peking, Prague, and Sofia. He returned to Brazzaville in December 1957 and became an active member of the UJC. Massamba named him secretary of the CNR in August 1963, and Congo-Brazzaville's first ambassador to the U.S.S.R. in April 1965. He was a member of the MNR politburo when he was appointed, in March 1968, the first political commissar for the people's army. Arrested at the Biafra camp on August 31, 1968, and freed September 5 by the criminal court, he was rearrested soon afterward, when a cache of arms was discovered in his native village. In November 1968, he was sentenced to five years in prison.

TOMBALBAYE, François: Son of a Protestant merchant of the Sara tribe, born June 15, 1918, at Bedaya in southern Tchad. After graduating from the Ecole des Cadres in Brazzaville, he returned to Tchad as a teacher in 1942. Soon he turned to trade and politics, organizing the local branch of the RDA at Fort Archambault in 1946. He became president of the federation of autonomous trade unions of Tchad, was elected in 1952 to represent Moyen-Chari in the territorial assembly, and five years later became a vice-president of the FEA Grand Council. At Fort Lamy, he quarreled not only with the territorial governor, Rogué, but also with Lisette and, in 1955, was dismissed from his post on the Cotton Price Stabilization Fund. In June 1959, he succeeded Lisette as premier of Tchad. After banishing Lisette from the country, he became head of state in August 1960, was elected president of the republic in April 1962, and was reelected in June 1969. Since the mid-1960s, his authority has been seriously threatened by a revolt in northern and central Tchad.

TOURE, Sékou: A Muslim Malinké, born January 9, 1922, at Faranah, Guinea. Without finishing secondary school, he entered the postal service as a clerk in 1941. Five years later, he helped to found the RDA and became head of its territorial branch. He rose to political prominence chiefly through his leadership of Conakry's trade unions, and in 1953, he was elected to the territorial assembly. Elected mayor of Conakry and to the French National Assembly in 1956, he became vice-president of Guinea's first government council in 1957. In the latter year, he organized the UGTAN, of which he became general secretary. Breaking away from Houphouët-Boigny, he advocated a negative vote in the referendum of September 1958 and led his country to independence, becoming Guinea's first president. For many years he has been regarded as francophone Africa's leading Marxist nationalist and Pan-Africanist.

TSHOMBE, Moïse Kapenda: Born November 18, 1919, in Katanga, Belgian Congo, son of a wealthy merchant related to the royal family of the Lunda tribe. After attending an American Methodist mission school, where he took the name of Moïse, he launched several unsuccessful business ventures. Entering politics in 1947 as a member of the Katanga advisory council, he founded a Lunda tribal group which in 1959 became the Confédération des Associations du Katanga (CONAKAT). This party favored a federal form of government for an independent Congo, closely associated with Belgium. In the summer of 1960, Tshombe's opposition to U.N. intervention in Congolese affairs brought him into conflict with Lumumba, and on July 10, Tshombe declared himself president of an independent Katanga. Implicated in Lumumba's murder in February 1961, Tshombe was arrested by Kasavubu in April and charged with high treason. After promising to support the central government at Léopoldville, he was freed two months later, but he persisted in his secessionism with the backing of Belgian mining interests. Finally, in January 1963, U.N. troops forcibly took possession of Katanga, and Tshombe exiled himself to Europe. In June 1964, after the U.N. troops left the Congo, Kasavubu invited Tshombe to return to the Congo and succeed Adoula as head of the central government. He held that office until dismissed by Kasavubu in October 1965. Tshombe then went back to Europe and was living in Spain when he was sentenced to death in absentia by a Kinshasa court in March 1967. Two months later, he was kidnapped under mysterious circumstances and taken to Algiers. He remained a prisoner in Algeria until he died of a heart attack on June 30, 1969.

TSIKA, Capt. Norbert: Head of the Congolese gendarmerie in August 1963, he was arrested by Massamba but, five years later, was freed by the military government as well as given back his command. For failing to warn Ngouabi about the plot of November 8, 1969, he was demoted to the rank of a private soldier and prosecuted for criminal negligence before the revolutionary court.

UM NYOBE, Reuben: A Bassa, born about 1921 in southwestern Cameroun, he was educated by Presbyterian missionaries, and entered the administration as a clerk. Active first as a trade union leader and later as a politician, he founded—in collaboration with Félix Moumié—the UPC in April 1948, and two months later it joined the RDA. The UPC's main goals were reunification of the British and French Camerouns and their independence. His alleged communist views have been attributed to his extensive travels in eastern Europe and close contacts with Prague and Moscow. He defended the UPC cause on several occasions before the U.N. Trusteeship Committee. When the UPC was banned in Cameroun following its revolt in May 1955, he headed the group that conducted guerrilla warfare in the southwest, where he was killed in an ambush in September 1958.

VIAL, Joseph: Born in southern France on January 5, 1908. After completing his university studies, he went to Moyen-Congo, where he became manager of several companies and, after World War II, was active in local politics. From 1947 to 1960, he represented Djoué in the territorial assembly; in November 1956, became an assistant mayor of Brazzaville; and from May 1957 to February 1960, a minister in Youlou's government. In early 1958, the MSA reportedly insisted on Vial's dismissal as finance minister as a condition of its reconciliation with the UDDIA, but he was not dropped from the cabinet until February 1960. Allegedly he was important to Youlou because of his contacts with French capitalists and contributions to the UDDIA.

VOUAMA, Pierre: Born May 24, 1934, into a prominent family of tribal chiefs in the Kinkala district. He received his early schooling at Brazzaville and his higher education at the universities of Grenoble, Bordeaux, and Paris. In the French capital, he acquired a doctorate in engineering and was elected president of the Congolese students association. On returning to Brazzaville in July 1965, he was employed in the telecommunications service, of which he was minister, 1966-69.

YHOMBY, Major Joachim Opango: A Lari professional army officer, who was military attaché at the Congolese embassy in Moscow before succeeding Ngouabi as commander of the paratroop corps in September 1968. After Tsika was implicated in the abortive coup of November 1969, Yhomby replaced him as head of the gendarmerie. Briefly in eclipse because of his conservative political views and close contacts with Lari dissidents, Yhomby was named head, nevertheless, of the armed forces general staff and led a military mission to Peking in October 1970 and one to Moscow in May 1971. Regarded by the left wing of the PCT as Ngouabi's strongest supporter in the army, Yhomby was the initial target of the abortive putsch of February 1972, against which he organized the successful countercoup that enabled Ngouabi to retain his power.

YOULOU, Fulbert: Son of a minor Lari merchant, born June 9, 1917, in the region of Brazzaville. Baptized a Catholic in 1926, he entered the seminary three years later, and completed his secondary education in mission schools in Cameroun and Gabon. Probably it was during this period that he met Aubame and Boganda. He became a teacher in mission schools in Moyen-Congo, and was ordained a priest in 1946. Reproached by his superiors for his lack of zeal and of discipline, he was forbidden to exercise his priestly vocation when, despite their disapproval, he decided to campaign for public office. He was elected mayor of Brazzaville in November 1956 and vice-president of Moyen-Congo's first government council in May 1957 as head and founder of the UDDIA party. President of the Congo Republic after it became independent in 1960, he held that post until the coup of August 1963, when he was arrested. In April 1965, he escaped to Léopoldville, and from there he went to live in exile at Madrid until his death on May 6, 1972.

ZONIABA, Bernard: A civil servant in the education service when named to the newly created post of secretary of state for information and civic education in December 1965. Although considered to be a leading Maoist member of the MNR, he was dropped from the government when Noumazalaye became premier in April 1966. He was appointed ambassador to the U.S.S.R. in February 1968 but has been in political eclipse under the military government.

ABBREVIATIONS

ABAKO	Association des Bakongo
AEF	Afrique Equatoriale Française
ATC	Agence Transcongolaise des Communications
ATEC	Agence Transéquatoriale des Communications
BCCO	Bureau pour la Création, le Contrôle, et l'Orientation des Entreprises de l'Etat
BUMCO	Bureau Minier du Congo
CATC	Confédération Africaine des Travailleurs Croyants
CCSL	Confédération Congolaise des Syndicats Libres
CFHBC	Compagnie Française du Haut et du Bas Congo
CFTC	Confédération Française des Travailleurs Chrétiens
CGAT	Confédération Générale Africaine du Travail
CGT	Confédération Générale du Travail
CGTAE	Compagnie Générale des Transports en Afrique Equatoriale
CNL	Comité National de Libération
CNR	Conseil National de la Révolution
CSC	Confédération des Syndicats Congolais
FAC	Fonds d'Aide et de Coopération
FEA	French Equatorial Africa
FEANF	Fédération des Etudiants de l'Afrique Noire Française
FED	Fonds Européen de Développement
FESAC	Fédération de l'Enseignement Supérieur en Afrique Centrale
FO	Force Ouvrière
GPS	Groupement pour le Progrès Social du Moyen-Congo
ICFTU	International Confederation of Free Trade Unions
ILO	International Labor Organization (Geneva)
ILO	Intergroupe Libéral Oubanguien
IOM	Indépendants d'Outre-Mer
JMNR	Jeunesse du Mouvement National de la Révolution

```
LINA-Congo Liaisons Nationales Aériennes du Congo
MESAN        Mouvement d'Evolution Sociale en Afrique Noire
MNC          Mouvement National Congolais
MNR          Mouvement National de la Révolution
MRP          Mouvement Républican Populaire
MSA          Mouvement Socialiste Africain
OAU          Organization of African Unity
OBAE         Office des Bois de l'Afrique Equatoriale
OCAM         Organisation Commune Africaine et Malgache
OCH          Office Congolais de l'Habitat
OFNACOM      Office National du Commerce
ONAP         Office National des Forêts
ONCPA        Office National de Commercialisation des Produits Agricoles
ONPT         Office National des Postes et Télécommunications
ORSTOM       Office de Recherche Scientifique et Technique d'Outre-Mer
PAI          Parti Africain de l'Indépendance
PCT          Parti Congolais du Travail
PPC          Parti Progressiste Congolais
PRA          Parti du Regroupement Africain
PSA          Parti Solidaire Africain
RDA          Rassemblement Démocratique Africain
RNPC         Régie Nationale du Palmier Congolais
RNTB         Régie Nationale des Transports de Brazzaville
RNTP         Régie Nationale des Transports et Travaux Publics
RPF          Rassemblement du Peuple Français
SFIO         Section Française de l'Internationale Ouvrière
SIAN         Société Industrielle et Agricole du Niari
SNDE         Société Nationale de la Distribution d'Eau
SNE          Société Nationale de l'Energie
SONEL        Société Nationale d'Elevage
UAM          Union Africaine et Malgache
UAMCE        Union Africaine et Malgache pour la Coopération Economique
UDDIA        Union Démocratique pour la Défense des Interêts Africains
UDE          Union Douanière Equatoriale
```

UDEAC	Union Douanière et Economique de l'Afrique Centrale
UDSR	Union Démocratique et Sociale de la Résistance
UEAC	Union des Etats de l'Afrique Centrale
UGEEC	Union Générale des Elèves et Etudiants Congolais
UGTAN	Union Générale des Travailleurs de l'Afrique Noire
UJC	Union de la Jeunesse Congolaise
UJSC	Union de la Jeunesse Socialiste Congolaise
UMC	Union du Moyen-Congo
UPC	Union des Populations du Cameroun
UPS	Union Progressiste Sénégalaise
URAC	Union des Républiques d'Afrique Centrale
WFTU	World Federation of Trade Unions

U.S. DOLLAR EQUIVALENTS OF THE CFA FRANC

Before the devaluation of December 29, 1958: $1.00 = 210.80 CFA francs

Between December 29, 1958, and the
        devaluation of August 8, 1969: $1.00 = 245.25 CFA francs

After August 8, 1969: $1.00 = 256.60 CFA francs

BIBLIOGRAPHY

"A la Recherche d'une Harmonisation des Activités," Marchés Tropicaux, February 4, 1967.

"A Novel Experiment in Africa: The Kinsoundi Textile Mill," Africa Today, July 1971.

Althabe, G., Etude du Chomage à Brazzaville en 1957, ORSTOM Cahiers de Sciences Humaines, vol. 1, no. 2, 1963.

Amin, S., and C. Coquery-Vidrovitch, Histoire Economique du Congo, 1880-1968, Dakar, 1969.

Andersson, E., Churches at the Grass-roots: A Study in Congo-Brazzaville, London, 1968.

_____, Messianic Popular Movements in the Lower Congo, Uppsala, 1958.

Arnault, J., "L'Afrique Noire au Tournant de son Destin," L'Humanité, January 25, 29, 1964.

Baba Miske, A., "Brazzaville: Il Faut Armer le Peuple," AfricAsia, May 3, 10, 1970.

Badila, L., "Mythes et Réalites au Congo-Brazzaville," La Semaine Africaine, December 15, 1963.

_____, "La Révolution Violée," La Semaine Africaine, November 12, 1964.

Balandier, G., "Messianisme des Bas-Kongo," Encyclopédie Mensuelle d'Outre-Mer, August 1951.

_____, Sociologie Actuelle de l'Afrique Noire, Paris, 1955.

Ballard, J., "Four Equatorial States," in Carter, G. M. [ed.], National Unity and Regionalism in Eight African States, Cornell University Press, 1966.

Bemba, S., "Ou en est le Congo?" Bingo, January 1965.

Bigemi, F., "La Commune au Congo-Brazzaville," Revue Juridique et Politique, April-May-June 1968.

Bonnafé, P., "Une Classe d'Age Politique, la JMNR du Congo-Brazzaville," Cahiers d'Etudes Africaines, vol. 8, 1968.

"Brazzaville—Nouvelle Base Cubaine?" Revue Africaine, August 1966.

Chauvel, J.-F., "Révolution au Congo-Brazzaville," Le Figaro, May 6, 7, 1965.

Chauvet, P., "Le Réalisme de la Politique Economique," Europe-France-Outremer, December 1967.

Choupaut, Y.-M., "Un Saint-Cyrien au Pouvoir," France-Eurafrique, December 1969.

Comte, G., "Echec aux 'Conservateurs'," Revue Française d'Etudes Politiques Africaines, April 1970.

_____, "L'Embarras Français," Revue Française d'Etudes Politiques Africaines, June 1970.

_____, "Le Congo-Brazzaville en Proie à la Révolution," Le Monde, March 25, 26, 27, 1970.

_____, "Une République Populaire sous les Tropiques," Le Monde Diplomatique, May 1970.

"Congo: Echec à la Contre-Revolution," AfricAsia, April 12, 1970.

"Congo-Brazza: An V de la Révolution," Jeune Afrique, July 28, 1968.

"Congo-Brazzaville," Bingo, August 1968.

"Congo-Brazzaville: 15 Mois de Révolution," Europe-France-Outremer, November 1964.

"Congo-Brazzaville: De Réelles Possibilités d'Avenir qui Cachent trop les Difficultés Actuelles," Le Moniteur Africain, October 30, 1969.

"Congo-Brazzaville Finds its Path," The African Communist, 3rd quarter, 1970.

Conseil Economique et Social, Brazzaville, Rapports Annuels, 1964 to date.

Cooley, J. K., East Wind over Africa, New York, 1965.

Croce Spinelli, M., Les Enfants de Poto-Poto, Paris, 1967.

Decraene, P., "Congo-Brazzaville: Deux Capitaines au Pouvoir?" Revue Française d'Etudes Politiques Africaines, September 1968.

_____, "Confusion et Désarroi," Le Monde, November 11, 1969.

Devauges, R., Les Conditions Sociologiques d'une Politique d'Urbanisme à Brazzaville, 2 vols., Paris, 1959.

Diallo, S., "Congo: Entre Révolutionnaires," Jeune Afrique, March 11, 1972.

Dreux-Brézé, J. de, Le Problème du Regroupement en Afrique Equatoriale, Paris, 1968.

Ekani-Onambele, M., "Le Congo-Brazzaville Face à son Evolution Sociale," Communauté France-Eurafrique, January 1963.

Etude Economique de la Cuvette Congolaise, pamphlet published by the Agence
    Congolaise d'Information, July 11, 1964.

"Fluctuations Politiques au Congo-Brazzaville," Revue Africaine, August 1968.

France, Ministère de la Coopération, Economie et Plan de Développement:
    République du Congo-Brazzaville, 1965.

_____, Enquête Démographique, 1960-1961, République du Congo-Brazzaville,
    1965.

Frey, R., "Brazzaville," Encyclopédie Mensuelle d'Outre-Mer, August-September
    1954.

Friedland, W. H., "Paradoxes of African Trade Unionism, Organizational Chaos,
    and Political Potential," Africa Report, June 1965.

Garric, D., "Le 'Coup d'Etat pour Rien' de Brazzaville," Le Figaro,
    August 10-11, 1968.

Gonidec, P. F., "Le Droit et la Pratique des Conventions Collectives du
    Travail au Congo-Brazzaville," Penant, July-September 1969.

Gross, Rev. Père, "Comment Vivent nos Futurs Prêtres au Congo-Brazzaville,"
    Afrique Nouvelle, March 2, 29, April 5, 12, 1967.

House, A. H., "Brazzaville: Revolution or Rhetoric?" Africa Report, April 1971.

"Institut de Recherches Scientifiques au Congo," Journal of Modern African
    Studies, November 1964.

Kiba, S., "Le Congo-Brazzaville est Toujours en Proie à ses Difficultés
    Politiques," Afrique Nouvelle, November 5, 1969.

"La Conjoncture Economique Nécessite des Actions Immédiates, en Prélude au
    Prochain Plan 1970-1975," Marchés Tropicaux, April 19, 1969.

"La Mise en Valeur des Pays du Niari," Industries et Travaux d'Outre-Mer,
    August 1968.

La République du Congo, La Documentation Française, Notes et Etudes
    Documentaires, no. 2732, December 17, 1960.

Latour, H., "L'Avenir du Congo-Brazzaville," Afrique Nouvelle, December 23,
    1970.

"Le Congo en Rouge, Jaune et Noir," La Libre Belgique, March 10, 11, 12, 1970.

"Le Congo-Brazzaville à l'Avant-Garde de la Révolution," Marchés Tropicaux,
    January 17, 1970.

"Le Congo-Brazzaville Accentue Encore d'Avantage l'Orientation Socialiste de son Economie," Marchés Tropicaux, September 12, 1970.

"Le Congo-Brazzaville Poursuit sa Politique dans un Climat de Coopération avec la France," Marchés Tropicaux, June 24, 1967.

"Le Kouilou," Industries et Travaux d'Outre-Mer, September 1958.

"Le Mystère s'Epaissait," Le Mois en Afrique, September 1966.

"L'Equilibre des Finances Publiques, ou l'Etat et la Révolution," Etumba, December 7, 1967.

"Le Régime de l'Abbé Fulbert Youlou," Révolution Africaine, August 24, 1963.

"Le Régime de la République Populaire du Congo se Radicalise," Marchés Tropicaux, April 24, 1971.

Les Structures Economiques de la République du Congo, Brazzaville, May 1963.

"Les Successeurs de Youlou," Revue Africaine, May 1964.

Lucas, G., Formal Education in the Congo-Brazzaville, Washington, D.C., 1964.

Maisonneuve, A., "Réflexions sur la Crise de Brazzaville," L'Observateur du Moyen-Orient et de l'Afrique, September 6, 1963.

Makosso, J. A., "Une Révolution qui Tourne Mal," Afrique Nouvelle, January 6, 1965.

Marchat, P., "D'une Révolution à l'Autre au Congo-Brazzaville," Revue Militaire Générale, September 1969.

"M. Massamba-Débat Clarifie une Situation Ambiquë," Marchés Tropicaux, January 20, 1968.

Menza, G., "La Révolution Congolaise à Deux Ans," L'Afrique Actuelle, Sommaire no. 1, 1965.

Nere, J., "Promesses et Faiblesses du Congo-Brazzaville," Le Monde, December 31, 1966; January 12, 1967.

P. B., "Congo-Brazzaville: Un Coup de Barre à Droite," Le Mois en Afrique, February 1968.

Pargoire, J., "La Vallée du Niari," Encyclopédie Mensuelle d'Outre-Mer, January 1955.

Perrot, C., and H. Sauvahé, République du Congo-Brazzaville, Répertoire Bibliographique (mimeographed), B.D.P.A., n.d.

"Perspectives Economiques Favorables à Moyen Terme," Europe-France-Outremer, December 1971.

Plan Intérimaire de Développement Economique et Social, Brazzaville, 1964.

Prévost, P.-L., "L'Union Douanière et Economique de l'Afrique Centrale (UDEAC)," Revue Française d'Etudes Politiques Africaines, October 1968.

"Quel Socialisme à Brazzaville?" Jeune Afrique, March 10, 1970.

"Redressement Sûr mais Difficile du Congo," Marchés Tropicaux, August 1, 1964.

"Remous au Congo-Brazzaville," Marchés Tropicaux, October 26, 1968.

Renaud, D., "Difficultés Economiques et Tensions Politiques," Revue Française d'Etudes Politiques Africaines, February 1970.

République Populaire du Congo, Dossier d'Information Economique, Paris, 1970.

Soret, M., Démographie et Problèmes Urbains en AEF: Poto-Poto—Bacongo—Dolisie, Montpellier, 1964.

_____, Les Kongo Nord-Occidentaux, Paris, 1959.

Terray, E., "Les Révolutions Congolaise et Dahoméenne," Revue Française de Science Politique, October 1964.

"The Coup that Wasn't," West Africa, August 10, 1965.

Thomas, L. V., "Le Socialisme Congolais," Le Mois en Afrique, November 1966.

"Une Révolution Inquiète et Permanente," Revue Française d'Etudes Politiques Africaines, December 1969.

Vennetier, P., "L'Urbanisation et ses Conséquences au Congo-Brazzaville," Cahiers d'Outre-Mer, vol. 16, 1963.

_____, "La Société Industrielle et Agricole du Niari (SIAN)," Cahiers d'Outre-Mer, January-February-March 1963.

Viellard, J.-L., "Mythes et Réalités Congolaises," France-Eurafrique, June 1966.

Vincent, J. F., Femmes Africaines en Milieu Urbain, Paris, 1966.

Wade, G., "L'Armée contre le Pouvoir," L'Afrique Actuelle, October 1966.

Wagret, J.-D., Histoire et Sociologie Politiques de la République du Congo-Brazzaville, Paris, 1963.

Youlou, F., J'accuse la Chine, Paris, 1966.

_____, Le Matsouanisme (pamphlet), Brazzaville, n.d.

INDEX

Belgian Congo (Zaïre), xv, xviii, 3, 8, 23, 28, 31, 45, 54, 60, 61, 67, 79, 82, 84, 89, 94, 103, 110, 115-123 passim, 125-134 passim, 151, 152, 154, 159, 163, 169, 173, 176, 194, 197-199, 200, 201, 203, 204, 208, 211, 222, 223, 226, 233-235
Biayoula, F., 160, 213, 241
Bicoumat, G., 11, 25, 81, 97, 152, 155, 161, 208, 241
Bindi, M., 163, 165, 167, 172, 210, 241
Biyoudi, J., 58, 66, 94, 241
Boganda, B., 14, 24, 26-29, 32, 33, 34, 36, 47, 49, 50, 56, 59-62 passim, 68, 73, 79, 84, 99, 106, 109, 116, 119, 127, 130, 241
Bomboko, J., 127, 129, 241-242
Bongo, A.-B., 199, 203
Bongo-Nouarra, S., 173, 174, 178, 242
Bouiti, J., 172, 184, 242
Boukambou, J., 52, 53, 55, 89, 96, 152, 213, 242
Brazzaville bloc (see also OCAM; UAM), 103, 106, 200
Budgets, xviii, xxi, 67, 97, 98, 103, 140, 142-143, 144, 157, 164, 178-179, 214, 224, 233, 235
Business, small. See Trade, internal

Cabinda, xv, xxvii, 23, 67, 120, 131, 193, 194, 204, 235
Cameroun, 28, 61, 122, 155, 164, 169, 194, 199-202 passim, 233, 235
Casablanca bloc, 130, 134, 140
CATC (Confédération Africaine des Travailleurs Croyants), 54, 55, 58, 76, 83, 87, 152, 159, 160, 168, 212, 213, 219, 220, 224, 230
CGSL (Confédération Congolaise des Syndicats Libres), 58, 152, 158, 213
Censorship, 92
Central African Republic (Oubangui-Chari), xv, xxi, xxii, xxiii, xxiv, xxv, 8, 10, 11, 14, 24, 26-29, 33, 46, 50, 57, 58, 61, 62, 67, 68, 95, 99, 106-111, 162, 164, 176, 199, 201-203
CFHBC (Compagnie Française du Haut et du Bas Congo), 169-170
CFTC (Confédération Française des Travailleurs Chrétiens), 52, 54
CGAT (Confédération Générale Africaine du Travail), 45, 46, 50-55 passim, 57, 58, 62, 76, 82, 83, 84, 87, 92, 93, 95, 96, 152, 158, 161, 213, 218, 223, 226, 234
CGT (Confédération Générale du Travail), 52, 53, 54, 57, 83
CGTAE (Compagnie Générale des Transports en Afrique Equatoriale), 179, 181, 183
Chiefs, customary, xv, xvi, xxvi, xxvii, 3, 4, 19, 25, 38, 39, 46, 55, 103, 177, 207, 211
Chinese People's Republic (see also Relations with Far Eastern countries), 158, 161-164 passim, 166, 174, 176, 180, 181, 183, 191, 194, 195, 196, 198, 202, 203, 205, 220-221, 233, 235, 237
"Civic service," compulsory, 86, 101, 217, 219
Civil-defense corps, 162, 163, 167, 172, 177, 185, 219, 220, 221, 225, 226, 227, 231
Civil servants, xxiv, 2, 3, 54, 81, 101, 136-144 passim, 147, 151, 153, 154, 164, 165, 173, 174, 178, 179, 181, 185, 207, 212, 215, 216, 217
CNR (Conseil National de la Révolution), 166, 167, 172-176 passim, 209, 214
Combo-Matsiona, B., 199, 222, 223, 242
Comilog (Compagnie Minière de l'Ogooué), 91, 95
Common Market. See European Economic Community
Communist party, French, 10, 11, 12, 15, 52, 55, 84, 85

Congo-Kinshasa. See Belgian Congo (Zaïre)
Congo-Léopoldville. See Belgian Congo (Zaïre)
Congo-Ocean railroad, xvi, xviii, 3, 19, 81, 95, 111, 113, 180, 186, 201, 202,
    210, 211, 216
"Congolization." See Africanization
Constituent assemblies, French, xx-xxi, 3, 9, 10
Constitution, revision of, 100, 103, 155-156, 167, 168
Cornut-Gentille, B., 42, 44, 45
Corruption, 151-152, 155, 165, 212, 215, 216, 229, 231
Cost of living, xix, 144, 151, 158, 164, 178, 184, 214, 215
Council of the Entente, 115, 123
Coups d'état (see also Plots, alleged), 172-173, 184-185, 190, 209, 211, 214,
    220, 221, 223, 232, 237
Courts, xx, xxiv, 5, 26, 86, 156, 159, 160, 163, 172-175 passim, 216, 232
Crops: export, xviii-xix, 5, 143, 144, 146, 151, 169, 180, 186-187, 197; sub-
    sistence, xviii, xix, 180, 186
CSC (Confédération des Syndicats Congolais), 160, 165, 168, 172, 184, 213-216
    passim, 221, 223
Cuban military instructors. See Relations with Cuba
Currency, 104-105, 165, 182, 189, 191, 199, 200
Customs-union project (see also UDE; UDEAC), 106, 110, 114

Dacko, D., 59, 99, 106, 107, 108, 111, 243
Dadet, E., 10, 12, 13, 16, 17, 20, 23, 26, 37, 89, 130, 243
Darlan, A., 10-14 passim, 52, 56, 243
Decorade, P., 20, 24, 243
Diawara, A., 172, 173, 177, 178, 184, 185, 225-228 passim, 231, 244
Duties, customs, xxi, 142, 143, 151, 164, 178

Eboué, F., xv, xvi, 2, 244
Education: expenditures, 142, 157, 171, 179; higher, 190, 196, 201, 203, 222,
    230; mission, xvi, 2, 81, 177, 219-220; primary and secondary, xvi, 184,
    196, 220, 230, 233
Elections, 6, 9, 10, 13, 14, 16, 17, 20, 21, 22, 24, 26, 28, 30, 32, 33, 37-38,
    39, 43, 68, 70, 72-75 passim, 81, 104, 155, 156, 172, 207, 208
Electorate, xx, xxi, xxiv, xxv, 2, 3, 9, 13-17 passim, 21, 25, 28, 30, 32, 55,
    56, 58, 74, 92, 104
Equatorial states, relations between, xxi, xxiv, 28, 59-63, 68, 89, 106-114,
    164, 198, 200-203, 235
European Economic Community, 142, 163, 180, 196, 203

FDC (Front Démocratique Congolais), 26, 31
FEANF (Fédération des Etudiants d'Afrique Noire Française), 84, 221, 223, 231
Federalism issue, 33, 34, 42, 44, 45, 59-63, 88, 106-111 passim, 113, 201
Fetishism (see also Animism), 4, 18, 19, 236, 238
Fishing, xix, 146, 170, 179, 180, 195, 210
FO (Force Ouvrière), 16, 52, 54, 55, 58, 83, 87, 152
Forestry, xviii, xix, 143, 145-146, 151, 158, 164, 171, 178-181 passim, 191,
    215, 236
France, postindependence relations with (see also Aid, French and other foreign;
    Relations with Western countries), 95, 101, 104-106, 108, 109, 111, 115,
    139-140, 142, 144, 158, 163, 165, 182-185 passim, 188-191, 203, 204, 224,
    230, 237

277

Franco-African Community, xx, xxiv, 29, 33, 34, 43, 46, 54, 60, 61, 64, 88, 90, 91, 106, 108, 109, 115
French Union, xx, 2

Gabon, xv, xviii, xxi, xxii, xxiii, xxv, xxvii, 3, 10, 23, 33, 34, 46, 57, 58, 61-63, 90, 95, 99, 106-115, 151, 164, 176, 180, 186, 194, 199, 201, 211, 215, 233
Galiba, B., 155, 212, 213, 244
Ganao, C.-D., 155, 162, 166, 174, 189, 191, 245
Gandzion, P., 31, 39, 89, 175, 207, 245
Gaulle, C. de, xxiv, 9, 15, 42, 44, 45, 46, 49, 50, 61, 62, 67, 68, 73, 80, 88, 89, 91, 95, 115, 116, 144, 188, 193
Gbenye, C., 197, 198, 245
Gendarmerie, 41, 64, 101, 121, 152, 172, 176, 177, 219, 223, 224, 226, 227, 231, 237
Gizenga, A., 117, 123, 128, 131, 133, 245
Goma, L. S., 226, 245
Gondjout, P., 99, 108, 246
Goumba, A., 46, 47, 99, 246
Goura, P., 10, 16, 17, 20, 36, 38, 41, 75, 89, 246
GPS (Groupement pour le Progrès Social en Moyen-Congo), 25, 26
Guerillot, R., 24, 28
Gueye, L., 31, 33, 34

Hazoumé, M., 41, 128, 247
Health, 142, 157, 163, 171, 179, 193, 196, 216
Hombessa, A., 161, 162, 165, 166, 167, 172, 175, 193, 210, 219, 220, 247
Houphouët-Boigny, H., 4, 10-15 passim, 32, 33, 34, 41, 43, 50, 60, 61, 63, 88, 115, 123, 206, 247
Housing, 141, 146, 171

Ibalico, M., 30, 39, 70, 98, 99, 118, 119, 120, 137, 139, 153, 198, 208, 247
ICFTU (International Confederation of Free Trade Unions), 54, 58
Ileo, J., 121, 123, 131, 132
ILO (Inter-groupe Libéral Oubanguien), 24, 26, 28, 33, 36
Independence issue, 45-50 passim, 56, 83, 84, 88-95 passim, 107-110 passim
Indigénat, xx, 6, 8
Industry, xix, xxvi, 73, 74, 79, 90, 102, 144, 147, 151, 157, 161, 163, 164, 170, 171, 179-183 passim, 186, 190, 191, 192, 195, 203, 209, 210, 214-217 passim, 232, 235
Investments, private, 73, 74, 92, 139-140, 145, 147, 154, 156-161 passim, 163, 164-165, 168, 170, 171, 177, 179, 181, 182, 183, 188, 189, 190, 203, 235, 237
IOM (Indépendants d'Outre-Mer), 12, 15, 17, 31

Jayle, C., 21, 44, 59, 64, 73, 75, 89, 105, 248
JMNR (Jeunesse du MNR), 155, 158-163 passim, 166, 167, 168, 172, 174, 177, 185, 191, 194, 212, 213, 218-222 passim, 224-227 passim, 230
JUDDIA (Jeunesse de l'UDDIA), 58, 218

Kalondji, A., 117, 118, 123, 125-132 passim, 248
Kasai secession, 125, 127, 129, 131

Matoumba-Mpolo, P., 172, 173, 174, 184, 252
Matsecoto, L., 53, 160, 208, 253
Matsika, A., 46, 52, 53, 55, 89, 156, 159, 162, 175, 213, 252-253
Matsoua, A., 4-5, 6, 9, 13, 14, 16, 19, 21, 22, 31, 233
Matsouanism, 2, 4, 6, 7, 19, 20, 21, 24, 25, 31, 38, 39, 55, 76-78 passim, 83, 84, 85, 100-101, 139, 153, 154, 233-234
Mba, L., 3, 10, 12, 33, 59, 62, 90, 99, 106-109 passim, 111-114 passim, 123, 201, 253
M'Bemba, T., 177, 220, 253
M'Berri, M., 167, 172, 174, 176, 210, 227, 236, 252
M'bochi tribe, xxvii, 1, 2, 7, 20, 31, 39, 64, 66, 67, 69, 70, 76, 81, 82, 168, 207, 211, 229, 236
MESAN (Mouvement d'Evolution Sociale en Afrique Noire), 24, 28, 33, 34, 39, 50, 99
Messianic cults (see also Kimbangism; Matsouanism; N'Gounzism; N'Zambie Bougie sect), xxvi, 23, 101, 233
Minerals, xix, 79, 82, 90, 95, 111, 113, 151, 158, 159, 161, 164, 170, 171, 178, 179, 180, 190, 192, 210, 236, 237
Missions, Catholic and Protestant (see also Education: mission), 1, 2, 3, 8, 26, 29, 54, 134, 160, 218, 236
MNC (Mouvement National Congolais), 116, 118, 123, 130
MNR (Mouvement National de la Révolution), 155, 156, 158-162 passim, 164-167 passim, 172, 174, 175, 196, 207, 211, 212, 213, 216, 218, 219
Mobutu, J., 101, 121, 122, 123, 126-131 passim, 163, 193, 197, 198, 199, 202, 204, 223, 235, 254
Mondjo, N., 165, 172, 173, 189, 254
Moudileno-Massengo, A., 173, 184, 185, 254
Mountsaka, D., 153, 155, 163, 224, 225, 254
Mouyabi, A.-G., 162, 167, 172, 254
Mouzabakany, F., 153, 155, 159, 165, 166, 167, 172, 173, 174, 208, 210, 224, 226, 255
Mpita Group, 173, 209
MSA (Mouvement Socialiste Africain), 10, 15, 31, 33, 35-43 passim, 47, 50, 55, 59, 60, 62-77 passim, 80, 81, 82, 85, 92, 93, 94, 97, 110, 145, 151
Mulele, P., 197, 198, 199, 255

Nardon, J.-G., 35, 36, 59, 255
Nationalization, 161, 177, 179-183 passim, 188, 189, 214, 215, 217, 237
Ndalla, C., 161, 162, 166, 175, 176, 177, 184, 199, 213, 214, 218-222 passim, 227, 230, 233, 239, 255
Ngouabi, M., 163, 166, 167, 172-178 passim, 182-185 passim, 190-193 passim, 196-205 passim, 207, 209, 210, 211, 214, 215, 216, 221, 222, 223, 225-228 passim, 233, 234, 235, 237, 255-256
N'Gounzism, 4, 8, 31
Nkrumah, K., 60, 61, 161, 164, 203, 231
Notables, xvi, xxiv, xxvii, 4, 25, 38, 103
Noumazalaye, A., 162, 163, 165, 167, 172, 175, 177, 184, 189, 194, 196, 220, 225, 256
Nuclear tests, French, issue of, 84
Nzalakanda, D., 20, 138, 152, 153, 165, 256
N'Zambie Bougie sect (Lassyism), 18, 23, 38
Nze, P., 167, 172, 173, 177, 184, 257

OAU (Organization of African Unity), 152, 185, 196, 203, 204, 213
OBAE (Office des Bois de l'Afrique Equatoriale), 170, 177, 180, 183, 186
OCAM (Organisation Commune Africaine et Malgache), 161, 163, 165, 182, 189, 190,
    200-203 passim, 206, 235
Okiemba, P., 156, 159, 218, 257
ONCPA (Office National de Commercialisation des Produits Agricolas), 158, 164,
    170, 174, 179, 181
Opangault, J., 1, 2, 3, 7, 9, 10, 13, 14, 16, 18, 20, 21, 22, 25, 31, 35, 36,
    37, 39, 41, 42, 45, 47-50 passim, 55, 59, 61, 62, 64-70 passim, 72, 78, 81,
    86, 89, 93, 94, 95, 97, 98, 103, 110, 120, 126, 133, 135, 139, 151-155
    passim , 175, 207, 257
Oubangui-Chari. See Central African Republic
Overseas Labor Code of 1952, 51, 82, 87, 211

PAI (Parti Africain de l'Indépendance), 45, 46, 57
Pan-Africanism, 61, 84, 123, 152
PCT (Parti Congolais du Travail), 175, 176, 177, 180-185 passim, 190, 195, 211,
    217, 227, 228
Peasantry, xvi, 136, 141, 142, 153, 169, 179, 183, 233, 234, 237
Planning, economic, xix, xx, 91, 110, 143-147 passim, 151, 157, 171, 174, 179,
    180, 190, 203, 234
Plots, alleged (see also Coups d'état), 95-96, 153, 165-166, 173-176 passim,
    178, 183, 216, 223-228 passim, 232
Poignet, A., 167, 174, 226, 257
Pongault, G., 54, 58, 152, 163, 170, 224, 258
Population, xvi-xviii, xix, 1
Portella, A., 167, 172, 258
Ports, xvi, xviii, xix, 66, 79, 90, 111, 145, 154, 179, 180, 186, 201, 202, 209,
    210
Poungui, A.-E., 166, 167, 173, 177, 178, 221, 258
PPC (Parti Progressiste Congolais), 3, 4, 9-13 passim, 15, 16, 17, 18, 20, 21,
    24, 30, 33, 37, 38, 39, 43, 55, 74, 81, 85, 97, 151, 155, 209
PRA (Parti du Regroupement Africain), 41, 43-47 passim, 88
Press, 10, 11, 12, 13, 22, 43, 44, 61, 62, 68, 71, 113, 144, 165, 198, 209, 218-
    222 passim, 231, 233
Price controls, xix, 144, 157, 178, 215

Radiobroadcasting, xvi, 165, 188, 190, 191, 194, 198
Railroads (see also Congo-Ocean railroad), 90, 91
Raoul, A., 167, 172, 173, 174, 176, 184, 185, 197, 210, 226, 228, 258
RDA (Rassemblement Démocratique Africain), 4, 10-15 passim, 32, 33, 34, 41, 43,
    44, 45, 49, 50, 52, 62, 88
Referendum of Sept. 28, 1958, xxiv, 41, 48-52 passim, 55, 56, 57, 83, 88, 90,
    109
Regionalism, xxvi, 2, 20, 21, 22, 25, 34, 39, 67, 68, 69, 72, 94, 120, 145, 153,
    154, 177, 207, 209-210, 211, 217, 236
Relations with: Arab countries, including North Africa, 55, 115, 123, 192-193,
    196-197; Cuba, 161, 163, 168, 195, 205, 220, 225, 231; Eastern European
    countries, 158, 159, 161, 193-196 passim, 205, 223-225, 235, 237; Far East-
    ern countries (see also Chinese People's Republic), 161, 164, 166, 168,
    180, 183, 191, 193-196 passim, 235; Israel, 137, 140, 159, 163, 174, 191,
    192-193, 196-197, 222; revolutionary African countries, 159, 161, 168, 196,
    235; Western countries, 158, 161, 191, 192, 193, 195, 210, 222, 235

281

Rhodesia issue, 116, 161, 162, 192, 238
Riots and disorders, 5, 22, 26, 40, 41, 64, 65, 66, 69-70, 74, 76, 77-78, 82, 112-113, 135, 152-155 passim, 158, 191, 198, 208, 210, 218
Rivers. See Waterways
Roads, xviii, 6, 98, 141, 179, 180, 221
Roberto, H., 120, 161, 199, 204, 205
RPF (Rassemblement du Peuple Français), 9, 11, 14, 15, 16, 17, 20, 30

Sambat-Dalhot, Dr., 14, 16, 22
Sathoud, V.-J., 36, 38, 41, 89, 259
Senghor, L., 15, 17, 31, 33, 44, 61, 88
SFIO (Section Française de l'Internationale Ouvrière), 2, 9-17 passim, 24, 26, 30, 31, 68, 80, 94
SIAN (Société Industrielle et Agricola du Niari), 159, 177, 181, 182, 186, 215, 216
Sianard, G., 173, 259
Single-party system (see also MNR, UDDIA), 73, 100, 135, 151, 152, 153, 207
Slave trade, xv, 3
Socialists. See MSA; SFIO
South Africa issue, 192, 193, 201, 206
Soviet Union (see also Relations with Eastern European countries), 52, 93, 119, 130, 131, 141, 158, 161, 162, 163, 181, 183, 193-196 passim, 202, 205, 237
Strikes, 51, 78, 87, 152, 153, 174, 181, 214-217 passim, 224
Students in Europe, 55, 84, 85, 87, 101, 139, 166, 196, 219, 222, 223, 231
Sylla, Y., 33, 67, 259

Taxation, 36, 76, 77, 142, 143, 151, 178, 201, 203, 215, 229
Tchad, xv, xxi, xxii, xxiii, xxv, 5, 10, 14, 28, 33, 57, 58, 60, 63, 95, 99, 106-111, 164, 201-203
Tchicaya, J.-F., xxi, 3, 4, 7, 9-18 passim, 20, 21, 22, 24, 25, 30, 33, 38, 39, 41, 42, 43, 46, 47, 49, 50, 52, 59, 62, 63, 64, 75, 86, 97, 154, 259
Tchichelle, S., 4, 10, 16, 17, 18, 20, 21, 24, 25, 26, 30, 35, 36, 38, 59, 60, 65, 66, 67, 72, 75, 77, 80, 81, 89, 94, 102, 103, 104, 110, 112, 120, 121, 130, 131, 133, 134, 139, 153, 165, 175, 207, 208, 259-260
Technicians (coopérants), French, 185, 189, 190
Thaulay-Ganga, A., 52, 53, 172, 213, 260
Tombalbaye, F., 99, 106, 108, 110, 260
Touré, S., 50, 55, 57, 84, 89, 90, 152, 196, 197, 205, 223, 260
Trade: foreign, xviii, xix, xxi, xxvi, 142, 143, 145, 151, 158, 164, 169, 178, 179, 182, 190, 191, 193-194, 197, 202, 235; internal, 111, 145, 147, 158, 178, 180, 232; transit, xviii, xxvi, 144-145, 151, 157, 178, 179, 180, 202, 235
Transport. See Air services; Congo-Ocean railroad; Railroads; Roads; Waterways
Tribalism, xxvi, 6, 12, 17, 22, 24, 25, 26, 35, 36, 37, 40, 65, 66, 69-70, 81-82, 97, 100, 119-120, 139, 153, 154, 155, 163, 168, 169, 172, 177, 207-211, 217, 224, 227, 236, 237
Tshombé, M., 104, 113, 117, 119, 123, 125-134 passim, 141, 152, 159, 160, 192, 198, 200, 204, 208, 260-261
Tsika, N., 159, 166, 172, 226, 231, 261

UAM (Union Africaine et Malgache), 113, 114, 122, 132, 134, 140, 158, 193, 200, 201

UDDIA (Union Démocratique pour la Défense des Interêts Africains), 4, 7, 24-26 passim , 30, 31, 33, 35-47 passim, 50, 52, 56, 60-77 passim, 81, 82, 83, 86, 89, 93, 97, 98, 100, 104, 105, 110, 113, 147, 151, 209
UDE (Union Douanière Equatoriale), 201, 202
UDEAC (Union Douanière et Economique de l'Afrique Centrale), 161, 164, 177, 180, 182, 183, 185, 190, 200-203 passim, 232, 235
UDSR (Union Démocratique et Sociale de la Résistance), 14, 15, 17
UEAC (Union des Etats de l'Afrique Centrale), 198, 202
UGEEC (Union Générale des Elèves et Etudiants Congolais), 219-223 passim
UGTAN (Union Générale des Travailleurs de l'Afrique Noire), 57, 84
UJC (Union de la Jeunesse Congolaise), 46, 52, 53, 55, 57, 58, 66, 83-86 passim, 89, 92, 93, 95, 96, 106, 116, 213, 218, 234
UJSC (Union de la Jeunesse Socialiste Congolaise), 174, 184, 211, 222, 223
UMC (Union du Moyen-Congo), 26, 30, 33
Unemployment, 51, 65, 67, 68, 73, 76, 88, 89, 92, 93, 98, 102, 113, 114, 137, 141, 151, 153, 157, 161, 168, 169, 183, 189, 209, 210, 211, 214, 215, 217, 234, 236, 237
United Nations, 95, 103, 110, 115, 119-123 passim, 128-133 passim, 174, 195, 198
United States (see also Relations with Western countries), 140, 163, 174, 192, 210, 222
URAC (Union des Républiques d'Afrique Centrale), 109, 110, 111
Urbanization, xviii, xix, xxvi, 1, 65, 141, 151, 154, 157, 179, 209, 217, 236

Vial, J., 35, 37, 44, 80, 89, 91, 105, 261
Vili tribe (see also Ma Loango), xxvi, xxvii, 1, 2, 3, 4, 7, 17, 21, 25, 38, 41, 66, 75, 81, 82, 86, 120, 131, 139, 173, 207, 208, 209, 211, 233, 237
Vouama, P., 11, 21, 262

Wages, 105, 138, 147, 157, 212, 215, 216, 229
Waterways, xvi, xviii, 1, 79, 199
WFTU (World Federation of Trade Unions), 52, 53, 57, 83, 84, 96, 214, 216
Women, status of, 31, 146, 159

"Yambot affair," 37, 64
Yhomby, J., 172, 184, 185, 226, 227, 262
Youlou, F., xxiv, xxvi, 2, 4, 5, 6, 7, 10, 13, 17, 20, 21, 22, 24, 26, 30, 31, 35, 36, 37, 39, 41, 43, 45, 47, 49, 50, 57, 59-62 passim, 65, 66, 67, 68, 72-78 passim, 85, 86, 89, 90, 92-123 passim, 125-147 passim, 151-155 passim, 160, 161, 166, 167, 168, 176, 179, 188, 189, 191, 193, 197, 198, 200-203 passim, 207, 208, 212, 217, 218, 223, 224, 226, 229, 230, 234, 236, 262
Youth organizations (see also JMNR; UJC; UJSC), 47, 51, 55, 57, 76, 82, 89, 98, 100, 153, 154, 155, 159, 185, 216, 217-223

Zaïre. See Belgian Congo (Zaïre)
Zoniaba, B., 161, 162, 213, 262